D0369440

THE FUTURE OF TRANSATLANTIC RELATIONS

Perceptions, Policy and Practice

Edited by Andrew M. Dorman
and Joyce P. Kaufman

Stanford Security Series,
An Imprint of Stanford University Press
Stanford, California

Stanford University Press
Stanford, California

Special discounts for bulk quantities of Stanford Security Series are available to corporations, professional associations, and other organizations. For details and discount information, contact the special sales department of Stanford University Press. Tel: (650) 736–1782, Fax: (650) 736–1784

Printed in the United States of America on acid-free, archival-quality paper

Library of Congress Cataloging-in-Publication Data

    The future of transatlantic relations : perceptions, policy and practice / edited by Andrew M. Dorman and Joyce P. Kaufman.
      p.   cm.
    Includes bibliographical references and index.
    ISBN 978-0-8047-7196-2 (cloth : alk. paper)
    ISBN 978-0-8047-7197-9 (pbk : alk. paper)
    1. Europe—Foreign relations—United States.   2. United States—Foreign relations—Europe.   I. Dorman, Andrew M., 1966–   II. Kaufman, Joyce P.
D2025.5.U64F88   2010
327.4073—dc22

                                                              2010010787

Contents

Preface   vii

Notes on Contributors   ix

Introduction   1
Andrew M. Dorman and Joyce P. Kaufman

1   Transatlantic Relations: A Theoretical Framework   16
    Serena Simoni

2   The Future of Trans-Atlantic Relations: 33
    A View from Canada
    David Rudd

3   The United States and the Transatlantic Relationship: 56
    A Test for U.S. Foreign and National Security Policy
    Joyce P. Kaufman

4   Transatlantic Relations: The United Kingdom   78
    Andrew M. Dorman

5   France and Transatlantic Relations   95
    Adrian Treacher

6   Germany: From Civilian Power to International Actor   113
    Gale A. Mattox

7   Turkey and the US: A Transatlantic Future?   137
       Bill Park

8   The Transatlantic Relationship: Poland and the   155
       United States
       Anna Zielińska

9   Russian Views on the Future of Transatlantic Relations   174
       Alex Marshall

10   Transatlantic Relations: A View from Ukraine   191
       Deborah Sanders

11   Georgia and the Transatlantic Relationship: 211
       The New Kid on the Block
       Tracey C. German

       Conclusions: Reflections on the Future of   232
       Transatlantic Relations
       Andrew M. Dorman and Joyce P. Kaufman

       Glossary   239

       Notes   243

       Selected Bibliography   299

       Index   313

Preface

THIS VOLUME HAS BEEN A FEW YEARS IN THE MAKING AND grew from a paper that the editors presented at the meeting of the Inter-University Consortium for Armed Forces and Society in Fall 2007. The paper focused on the challenges that were then facing the Transatlantic alliance. One of the audience members was Geoffrey Burn, editor at Stanford University Press, who approached us about the possibility of expanding some of those ideas as the basis for an edited volume. The concept he presented to us, and that we wholeheartedly supported, was to enlist scholars and country specialists on both sides of the Atlantic to write chapters that focused on a number of themes, but from the perspective of the specific country. The themes would be introduced at the beginning of the volume, with conclusions drawn at the end based on what each of the chapters stressed. We thought that this would be a very realistic approach for an edited volume, especially when there seemed to be so much turmoil among the partners on both sides of the Atlantic.

We worked closely with Geoffrey to outline a time line, and then used the annual meetings of both the International Studies Association (ISA) and American Political Science Association (APSA) as benchmarks to have chapters drafted and as the basis for discussion. Both organizations were helpful in giving us panel time; Jeanne White of ISA also provided space for the group to meet so that we had a quiet place to develop our ideas and review our thoughts after our panel. As we discovered, this approach of presenting papers for professional conferences, and then using feedback to revise, worked extremely well.

We were also fortunate in recruiting a superb group of colleagues to draft each of the chapters. Although we do not see each other often, the ongoing e-mail contact punctuated by the face-to-face discussions at the professional meetings helped us develop into a coherent group, a point that is reflected in this volume. The themes developed in each chapter and the approach taken were the result of discussion and collaboration among all the contributors. The ongoing dialogue among us also helped ensure a more cohesive volume.

The editors would like to thank all those contributors for their willingness to work together, meet deadlines, attend the various meetings, and provide input and suggestions that, we think, make this an unusually strong edited work. We have nothing but the highest praise for Geoffrey Burn, who met with us regularly to toss around ideas and provide feedback. His suggestions, as well as insistence that we remain true to the time line, ensured the production of this volume in a timely fashion. He has been nothing but helpful throughout.

Also at Stanford, editorial assistant Jessica Walsh helped us track all the nitty-gritty (contracts, maps, etc.) without which this volume would not have been possible. She was available to answer questions and to further guide us through the process.

Finally, both of us want to say what an honor it has been to work together and with such a wonderful group of scholars. Many people complain about the difficulties associated with doing an edited volume. We did not see any of that and, in fact, found this volume to be a wonderful and exciting project to be part of.

Andrew M. Dorman, Oxford
Joyce P. Kaufman, Whittier, CA

Notes on Contributors

ANDREW M. DORMAN IS A SENIOR LECTURER IN THE Defence Studies, King's College London based at the United Kingdom's Joint Services Command and Staff College and an Associate Research Fellow at the Royal Institute of International Affairs (Chatham House). He is a member of the Governing Councils for the International Security Studies Section of ISA and the International Security and Arms Control Section of APSA as well as founding chair of the Kenneth N. Waltz Dissertation Prize and the British Representative on NATO's Human and Societal Dynamics Panel. His primary research interests relate to policy and decision-making focusing on British defense and security policy, European security, defense transformation and civil-military relations. His most recent books are *Blair's Successful War* (Ashgate, 2009) and *War and Diplomacy* (Potomac Books, 2008). A former chartered accountant with KPMG, Dr. Dorman has previously taught at the University of Birmingham, where he completed his master's and doctoral degrees, and the Royal Naval College Greenwich.

JOYCE P. KAUFMAN is Professor of Political Science and Director of the Whittier Scholars Program at Whittier College. Since joining the academic world, Dr. Kaufman has taught primarily in the areas of International Relations and American Foreign Policy. Her primary research interests deal with national and international security. Her recent books on the topic are *Women and War: Gender Identity and Activism in Times of Conflict* (with Kristen P. Williams) (Kumarian Press, 2010) and *Women, the State and War: A Comparative Per-*

Journal of Slavic Military Studies vol. 21, no. 4 (2008); and "Can Ukraine Create an Effective Navy to Protect Its Interests in the Black Sea?," *European Security* vol. 16, no. 2 (2007).

SERENA SIMONI is a Lecturer in International Relations in the Department of Political Science at California State University Long Beach (CSULB), where she teaches mainly in the areas of international politics and international law. Her primary research interests deal with transatlantic relations and international security. She works on issues of traditional security and human security within the contextual dynamics of "Europe" and the United States. She is currently working on a book titled *The Evolving West: Traditional and Non-traditional Security Issues in Europe and the United States (1991–2008)*. Her most recent articles include "Split or Cooperation? Contending Arguments on the Future of the Transatlantic Relations (1991–2001)." Before joining the academic world, Dr. Simoni worked for the Organization for Security and Cooperation in Europe (OSCE) in Albania, and Bosnia-Herzegovina, and she has been a consultant for the Italian Ministry of Foreign Affairs in the Bureau for Political Affairs. Dr. Simoni received her Ph.D. in 2008 from the University of Southern California, her M.A. from CSULB and her B.A. from the Universitá degli Studi di Roma, La Sapienza.

ADRIAN TREACHER is a Lecturer in the Department of Politics and Contemporary European Studies, University of Sussex. Following six and a half years of postgraduate, doctoral and post-doctoral study at the University of Birmingham, Dr. Treacher has spent the last eleven years at the University of Sussex's prestigious Sussex European Institute. In addition to researching European security and EU external relations, he has also focused on French foreign policy, publishing articles in *International Peacekeeping* and *European Security* among others. He is also the author of *French Interventionism: Europe's Last Global Player?* (Ashgate, 2003).

ANNA ZIELINSKA is a teaching assistant at the Department of International Relations at Collegium Civitas (Poland) and Junior Research Fellow at the Centre for Security Studies at Collegium Civitas. She is currently researching the EU's Eastern Partnership. She received a Master's degree in international relations, and her thesis title was *Together and Apart: EU-US Relations at the Beginning of the Twenty First Century*. She has participated in the European Union Institute for Security Studies (EUISS) 2009 Cambridge Summer School (UK) analyzing national security cultures. Project coordinator for Collegium

Civitas in the EU's Seventh Framework Programme *INEX: Converging and Conflicting Ethical Values in the Internal/External Security Continuum in Europe*, and coordinator of a joint EEA project between Collegium Civitas and the International Peace Research Institute in Oslo (PRIO) *The European Neighbourhood Policy-Background, Status, Outlook.*

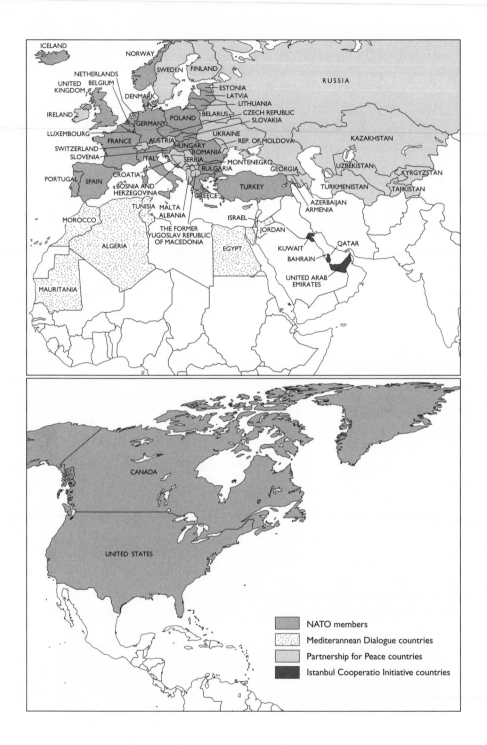

NATO members

Mediterannean Dialogue countries

Partnership for Peace countries

Istanbul Cooperatio Initiative countries

Introduction

Andrew M. Dorman and Joyce P. Kaufman

R OBERT KAGAN BEGAN HIS 2003 VOLUME *OF PARADISE and Power: American and Europe in the New World Order* with an appropriately controversial thesis. His argument centered on the thesis that

> [Europe] is turning away from power into a self-contained world of laws and rules and transnational negotiation and cooperation. It is entering a post-historical paradise of peace and relative prosperity, the realization of Immanuel Kant's "perpetual peace." Meanwhile, the United States remains mired in history, exercising power in an anarchic Hobbesian world where international laws and rules are unreliable, and where true security and the defense and promotion of a liberal order still depend on the possession and use of military might.

This linked directly to Edward Luttwak's thesis of "post-heroic warfare,"[1] and the consequence of all this is that "on major strategic and international questions today, Americans are from Mars and Europeans are from Venus: They agree on little and understand one another less and less. And this state of affairs is not transitory—the product of one American election or catastrophic event."[2]

Donald Rumsfeld, the then US Defense Secretary, echoed a similar view in a January 2003 Department of Defense press briefing. He saw Europe as more divided, making reference to an old and a new Europe, with its center of gravity moving eastwards as the North Atlantic Treaty Organization (NATO) admitted former members of the Warsaw Treaty Organization.[3] Four years later the British Prime Minister, Tony Blair, also echoed this belief of a divided transatlantic partnership. In his "Our Nation's Future" speech on defense policy, he stated: "There are two types of nations similar to ours today. Those who do war fighting and peacekeeping and those who have, effectively, except in the most exceptional circumstances, retreated to the peacekeeping alone."[4] A few months later, President Barack Obama may well have elicited some sympathy with this view after his initial call for a troop surge by NATO to Afghanistan was largely ignored.[5] Playing on the words of his campaign catchphrase, the British newspaper *The Times* led with the headline, "Europe: No We Can't."

What all were wrestling with were changes to the definitions of security, matched to questions about the role of the armed forces and the future development of transatlantic relations. Taken together, these elements raise the question of whether we really are at a "turning point" in the transatlantic consensus that has underpinned thinking for over half a century and whether the thesis of realist thinkers, such as John Mearsheimer, is finally proving to be correct (see next chapter).

This volume seeks to address this question. To undertake this task it is first worth remembering that, despite the strains that have emerged and appear to threaten the relationship, the importance of the relationship to all countries is generally still accepted as a given. Illustrative of this is NATO.[6] NATO has been one of the most enduring and effective alliances in modern history, and it has brought together the countries on the two sides of the Atlantic in ways that go far beyond the collective defense purposes embodied in Article 5 of the Atlantic Charter.[7]

A decade ago, few would have imagined running military operations in Afghanistan with a number of countries, notably the Canadians, the Dutch and the Danes, having sustained casualty levels over a number of years that were significant in relation to the size of their populations.[8] The strains that exist within NATO are symptomatic of the tensions that exist among countries on both sides of the Atlantic. Since the end of the Cold War, they have largely worked together to help frame a new type of relationship. Many of these countries, including former adversaries in NATO and the Warsaw Treaty Organization (also known as the Warsaw Pact), fought alongside one another in the first Persian Gulf War in 1991 and worked together through the "Contact Group"[9] as negotiators and mediators to try to address ethnic strife in the former Yugoslavia. These efforts gave the illusion that the relationship was being transformed from one that was defined by the tensions of the Cold War to one more appropriate to meeting the needs of a changing international order, with the challenges that accompany it.

In that sense, the case of NATO is illustrative. In effect, since the end of the Cold War, the purposes stated in Article 2 of the Atlantic Treaty have become even more important, perhaps even eclipsing the goals of Article 5. Article 2 notes that the parties "will contribute toward the further development of peaceful and friendly international relations by strengthening their free institutions" and seek "to eliminate conflict in their international economic policies and . . . encourage economic collaboration between any or all of them."[10] Clearly, Article 2 provides the foundation for post-Cold War collaboration among countries with democratic political institutions and a capitalist economy that the original members dreamed about but saw as far from reality in 1949, when the North Atlantic Treaty was drafted. It was in recognition of the attractions of liberal democracy that the countries of the former Eastern Bloc clamored to get into NATO; it was an acknowledgment that they had thrown off their past, and were now part of "the West." However, much has changed since the alliance was founded in 1949, and especially since its post-Cold War enlargement. Whilst acknowledgment of democracy has proven an important driver for membership, the Article 5 guarantee remains important and helps explain the desire of both Georgia and Ukraine to join the organization. Moreover, Russia too has remained central to transatlantic relations, and much of the discussion has revolved around the triangular relationship of individual states to both NATO and Russia.

The terrorist attacks on mainland America of September 11, 2001, represented the first and only case in which the collective security statute (Article 5) has been invoked.[11] However, the United States chose not to work within the NATO framework for its response but rather to move forward with a "coalition of the willing"; this had worked well in the first Persian Gulf War in 1991 but, as history has shown, proved not nearly so effective in the response to the attacks of 9/11. But, more importantly, in choosing to go outside the NATO framework, the Bush administration set a course that led to division and factionalism within an alliance whose fault lines were already not far below the surface. At the same time, the prospect of membership of countries such as Georgia and Ukraine has put into focus the complexities of further enlargement. The value that Tbilisi and Kiev place on the Article 5 guarantee suggests that they have adopted a far more traditional view of NATO than that currently held by some of its members.

These differences suggest that any estrangement among the NATO allies cannot be attributed purely to the United States or a single individual such as George W Bush. Rather, as the US was charting its own course, especially under the Bush administration, the European countries were similarly thinking about what policies were in their own best interest—both individually and also within the broader context of the European Union, through the processes of the Common Foreign and Security Policy (CFSP) and the European Security and Defence Policy (ESDP).[12]

The election of Angela Merkel in Germany in 2005 introduced a new type of leader to that country, one who was born in the East and has displayed sharp political instincts, which not only led her to the chancellorship but also helped her to chart a new and more self-assured course for Germany. Similarly, the election of Nicolas Sarkozy in France promised a new direction for that country. That promise went far beyond France when Sarkozy, under the auspices of the rotating presidency of the European Union (EU), called a summit to set up a Euro-Mediterranean partnership whose membership would, by virtue of geography, exclude the United States. Even the two countries closest to the United States and to one another in both culture and geography, Canada and the United Kingdom, have been moving in different directions.[13] And these are but a few examples of the divergence in policy interests among the countries on both sides of the Atlantic.

The divisions that have emerged among these various allies have been the result of a number of factors: different understandings and definitions of the threat that emerged after 9/11, and concomitant with that, different ideas of how to respond to that threat; changing domestic politics that have led to changing priorities; altered relationships among the various countries of the Atlantic Alliance due, in part, to the strengthening of the EU; different understandings of the role of the military and of each country's commitment to a common security policy; the emergence and strengthening of new or existing alliances that compete with—or complement—NATO; and changing perceptions of the United States, to name but a few.

Clearly, long-standing and important ties exist between the United States and its allies in Europe. It was US President Bill Clinton who first talked about NATO's enlargement as a question of "not if, but when," as he envisioned a world after the Cold War. And the economic and social conservatism of President George W Bush complemented the approach advocated by British Prime Minister Tony Blair and eventually German Chancellor Angela

Merkel. Nonetheless, the unilateral approach to foreign policy that the Bush administration ultimately pursued undercut many of the features that had brought the United States and the European allies together. It should not then be unexpected that the leaders of the other countries under discussion in this volume have similarly chosen to pursue policies that often diverge from the priorities of the United States.

It is important to note here that this volume is not a condemnation of US foreign policy under the administration of George W Bush. Rather, it seeks to explain, from multiple national perspectives and points of view, *why* there has been so much divergence in the approaches the various countries have taken. And it seeks to raise questions about what those divergent paths might mean for the future of transatlantic relations. A 2007 *Adelphi Paper,* published by the International Institute for Strategic Studies (IISS) and titled "Repairing the Damage: Possibilities and Limits of Transatlantic Consensus," hints at the potential for rebuilding consensus, but also at the fact that doing so will not necessarily be an easy task. The authors identify two conditions that they feel are necessary "for the alliance to survive, much less thrive, in this new and more demanding context." First among these, "Europe and the United States will have to develop compatible strategic frameworks within which to operate and, more importantly, select the issues for which their new à la carte alliance can be of relevance." A corollary to that is that the allies "should learn how not to agree, and even strongly disagree, on those issues on which they have chosen not to act jointly." In other words, the differences that have emerged are not irreconcilable or so deeply rooted as to rip the alliance apart. In fact, the authors argue, "properly managed, the differences could be turned into a beneficial complementarity, once the main points of contention have been overcome."[14] However, the case of Afghanistan has raised the question of NATO failure and the implications it would have for the alliance and trans-atlantic relations.

It is our contention that transatlantic relations are at a turning point. As we suggest above, there are deep divisions among the nations in the transat-lantic alliance, but we, unlike Kagan, believe that as long as these divisions are recognized and respected, there is actually great potential for the relationship to strengthen. A number of Europe's long-standing leaders have left office (Blair, Chirac, Schroeder) whilst others (Brown, Merkel, Sarkozy) have come to office apparently intent on redefining policies, relations and priorities. The United States is undergoing a major shift in policy as it moves from eight years of the Bush administration to the Obama presidency. First appearances indicate that these changes will bode well for the transatlantic partnership, since they could mitigate the polarization of the war in Iraq and the variable support for the war in Afghanistan. Still, there remain significant differences in the ways in which the various countries, all nominally allies, perceive the issues that are most important to them and the ways that those perceptions then become translated into policy decisions. If the countries focus on what separates them, rather than recognizing the many areas that they have in common, then the possibility of "repairing the damage" remains uncertain. However, if the various leaders can face the challenges and are able to recognize their areas of common concern, then the promise of a relationship built on complementary and supporting policies remains.

The Theoretical Framework

Classical realist international relations theory suggests that countries will join together in pursuit of common goals when it is in their perceived national interest to do so, and will remain in an alliance relationship as long as their mutual interests converge.[15] The assumption is that countries will maximize their power by working together, and, by so doing, be able to deter, or if necessary defeat, a common threat. For any relationship to endure and grow, there must be a sense of reciprocity in what each country hopes to derive from the relationship, and also in what each expects to be the outcome of decisions that are made. There must be a sense of mutual benefit, and the belief that in any cost-benefit analysis, the benefits will outweigh the costs. This suggests that the countries involved must believe that they are gaining more from continuing in the relationship than they would gain if they acted alone. What remains unclear is what shape this relationship will take when an individual country's needs and priorities change, and when the relationship is reassessed and possibly reconfigured in the future.

That theory would also suggest that countries are constantly balancing a range of variables in order to make effective foreign policy. Variables include not only the perception of the threat but also domestic priorities (for example, guns vs butter); the role of public opinion; the size, effectiveness and readiness of the military; geographic realities; and traditional ties and relationships, to name but a few. Furthermore, even countries that are close allies or have a close relationship are constantly reevaluating their relationships in light of these critical factors. Thus, understanding foreign policy relationships means understanding the domestic and international context within which various decisions were made. This process is dynamic, and involves a network of ever-changing factors. However, in the case of nations on different sides of the Atlantic, whatever other factors were present, they were superseded by the presumed priority of the transatlantic relationship. As long as those countries were facing a common enemy and perceived a common threat, they were willing to overlook not only differences but transgressions that in other settings or contexts would have driven them apart.

Hence, for example, the Suez Crisis of 1956 presented a challenge to the closest of allies—the UK, France, Israel and the United States—yet one that could be weathered in light of the larger picture that held this group of countries together. Similarly, consider the Enhanced Radiation Warhead (neutron bomb) debacle of 1978, West German Chancellor Helmut Schmidt's famous speech in 1977 questioning the resolve of the United States and Ronald Reagan's 1983 Strategic Defense Initiative (SDI), commonly referred to as "Star Wars"—all resulted in periods of estrangement across the Atlantic.[16] More recently the decision of the United States and some European countries in 2003 to go to war against Iraq led to a serious rift between nations. The difference between these earlier cases and the more recent one is the absence of a common threat. Europeans and Americans could work together and work through the issues that separated them as long as they had a good reason to want to remain allied, and that reason was the Soviet Union. Once that threat was removed, each country had to rethink its priorities, the role of the military and, most important, its defense and security posture in light of a changing world.

This is not to suggest that today there are no threats facing these countries; in fact, there are many. However, they are not as focused or directed as the single and overwhelming threat posed by the Soviet Union during the Cold War. Nor is there even agreement as to the magnitude of these threats, or the priority that should be given to the possible range of threats, let alone how countries should counter them. This lack of agreement, too, has served to divide the countries of the alliance rather than bring them together.

As a result of these factors and others, these countries now face new challenges that threaten their relationship. What are their common interests and concerns, and are these enough to overcome the differences that seem to separate them? As the Europeans think more about the EU and look elsewhere for allies, such as the Mediterranean, what role do they see the United States playing in their future? And as for the United States, which for eight years took a perverse pride in charting its own course, what global role does it see itself now playing?

In order to answer these questions, we need to examine the critical actors as individual case studies and from those, draw some general conclusions about the future of transatlantic relations.

An Overview of the Transatlantic Relationship

NATO celebrated its 60th birthday in April of 2009. It is easy to overlook the history of the alliance, which has been somewhat strained at times. It is important to remember, furthermore, that NATO is only one part of a much larger relationship that transcends the countries on either side of the Atlantic and includes other countries in the English-speaking world such as Australia and New Zealand, as well as extending into parts of the former Soviet Union and Eurasia. It is virtually impossible to understand transatlantic relationships without also looking at the relationship between NATO and the EU; the latter has also been a point of contention as it works toward a common foreign and defense policy. And one cannot adequately address transatlantic relations without also looking at the often-strained relationships between the countries on both sides of the Atlantic and Russia, at a time when Russia seems to be becoming more assertive.

Looking at the transatlantic relationship another way, we need to consider the breadth of the relationship, which goes far beyond security defined in terms of defense and the military. Rather, as the economic downturn that started in 2008 shows clearly, these countries are tied economically through trade and financial policies and institutions, a point that has directly affected their interaction in a less-than-positive way. In addition, each of the countries involved has domestic political issues that it must consider which affect the relationships as well.

Given all this, however, the most important point and the one that ultimately affects the relationship the most is history and the shared values that have held this group of countries together and have allowed them to transcend some of the schisms that have threatened their cohesions-and the Alliance—in the past.

NATO: A Brief History

This brief overview will help set the stage for what had been thought of as the "norm" in transatlantic relations. US involvement with the European allies can be traced to the First and Second World Wars, when the US military became a critical part of the Allied victories. However, it really was not until the end of the World War II and the start of the Cold War that the critical role that the United States would play vis-à-vis Europe would become most apparent. The Truman Doctrine, articulated in 1947, made it clear that the United States was willing and able to play both an economic and a security role in Europe, particularly when it came to defending the allies against the forces of communism. President Harry Truman's speech to the Congress in March of 1947 affirmed U.S. policy: "I believe that it must be the policy of the United States to support free peoples who are resisting attempted subjugation by armed minorities or by outside pressures."[17] But this speech also denoted an important shift in relations between the United States and Europe, and, more important, in the role of the United States as a world leader.

With the implementation of the Truman Doctrine, the United States superseded Great Britain as the major western military and economic power. This 1947 speech by Truman concerning the provision of aid to war-torn Greece confirmed the ascending US role in Europe vis-à-vis Britain: "No other nation is willing and able to provide the necessary support for a democratic Greek government. The British Government, which has been helping Greece, can give no further financial or economic aid after March 31. Great Britain finds itself under the necessity of reducing or liquidating its commitments in several parts of the world, including Greece."[18] Once Congress authorized the funds, the role of the United States as the defender of countries fighting communism was established. The Truman Doctrine was followed shortly thereafter by the passage of the European Recovery Act, known more commonly as the Marshall Plan, which became law in April 1948. This more firmly linked the United States with the countries of Europe by providing infusions of money to help them recover from the war. In addition to further solidifying the role of the United States as a global leader, it also forced the European countries to work together, thereby helping to create the framework for what would ultimately grow into the European Union. In fact, the United States' goals in helping Europe recover from the war were not altogether altruistic, nor were they tied solely to the need to stop communist aggression.

Underlying the US's motives was also the desire to have a strong Europe as a trading partner, which would be mutually beneficial to all concerned.

Nonetheless, the precedent was set not only for US leadership, but for a solid relationship between the United States and the countries of Europe that was tied to security writ large. The underlying assumption was: only if countries were stable economically could they resist Soviet aggression and have the wherewithal to build the strong military necessary to defend themselves, should that become necessary.

These goals were ultimately embodied in the NATO treaty, which linked the then-democratic countries of Western Europe, the United States and Canada in a collective defense agreement (Article 5) as well as stressed political and economic collaboration (Article 2). [19] NATO formalized the relationship and firmly put the US nuclear arsenal at the heart of the NATO military structure to serve as a deterrent against Soviet aggression against the US or its allies.

From the time that it was created, NATO was designed to ensure that all member countries, large and small, powerful and less so, would have an equal say in decision making. The *NATO Handbook* states explicitly that "all . . . member countries of NATO have an equal right to express their views around the Council table. Decisions are the expression of the collective will of member governments arrived at by common consent [i.e., consensus]."[20] The reality differed from the theoretical ideal, however. The United States, with its nuclear arsenal and superpower status, emerged as the "first among equals," and it quickly became the de facto leader of the alliance, enhanced by its "special relationship" with Britain. In fact, the overwhelming military as well as economic power of the United States made this role the logical one for the United States to play. Even after Britain and France developed their own nuclear weapons, in 1952 and 1960 respectively, it was the nuclear arsenal of the United States that remained the major deterrent against Soviet attack.

As any number of histories of the NATO alliance have noted, relations among the NATO nations have not always been easy; a number of internal conflicts and disagreements have shaken the alliance during its history. In addition to the Suez Crisis of 1956, these conflicts included "the Thor-Jupiter decisions of 1957–1960 followed by the multilateral force discussion, De Gaulle's decision to withdraw France from the NATO unified military command structure in 1966, the Helmut Schmidt speech of 1977, followed by the dual-track decision of December 1979."[21] Alliance unity was put to the test at various other points as well: objections over US involvement in Vietnam, Britain's decision to use force in the Falklands Conflict of 1982 despite some allies' objections and the US bombing of Libya in 1986 (supported only by Britain), are but a few examples of one country's foreign policy decisions not being supported by, or being enacted over the objections of, its allies.

The end of the Cold War and the collapse of the Soviet Union in 1991 brought with them a sense of jubilation but also raised a number of other challenges not anticipated by the alliance. As NATO moved toward enlargement and the inclusion of new members from the former Eastern Bloc, it also had to confront the conflicts in the former Yugoslavia, which proved to be a challenge to the cohesion of the European Union as well as NATO.

NATO Enlargement Issues and the Former Yugoslavia

Early in President Clinton's first term in office, his administration identified Europe as one foreign policy area in which he could have a significant impact; specifically, there was a decision to expand NATO eastward to incorporate the former communist countries of Central and Eastern Europe as real partners.[22] Both Czech President Vaclav Havel and Poland's President Lech Walesa took advantage of a meeting in Washington in March 1993 to press for NATO expansion eastward, "to include the new democracies of Eastern Europe as an affirmation of shared values and common defense (i.e., Article 2)." According to the story, before the day was over, President Clinton "is reported to have accepted the logic of expanding the Alliance eastward into central Europe, and by the end of that year, the movement toward NATO enlargement was gaining momentum."[23]

The decision was not without controversy, however. Some in Europe felt that the initiative was being pushed by the United States without adequate consultation with its allies. France and Britain were especially wary of enlarging the alliance, in part because of their concern that an expanded membership would disturb its already-delicate decision-making balance. But even Michael Mandelbaum, one of the most outspoken critics of enlargement, noted that "the extension of NATO eastward is thus necessary to fill what the end of East-West rivalry has created: a vacuum."[24]

One of the factors complicating the discussion for NATO enlargement was the war then raging in Bosnia without any NATO involvement. In fact, by that time, the EU had already sent in peacekeeping troops in what was to become the first test of EU security policy. The short-lived EU mission was succeeded by an equally ineffectual UN mission. But it soon became clear that what was needed was NATO intervention including the United States.

Issues related to NATO enlargement coupled with the conflict in the former Yugoslavia and if and/or how NATO should respond dominated the NATO agenda for the remainder of the Clinton administration (until 2000). History has shown that NATO did move forward to enlargement. It now includes 28 member countries that go up to the borders of Russia; 50 countries comprise the broader Euro-Atlantic Partnership Council, including Russia. The enlargement issue remains difficult and controversial to the present, with ongoing discussions about the possibility—or wisdom—of admitting former Soviet Union (FSU) countries including Ukraine and Georgia. This possibility has enflamed Russia, which had always been skeptical of NATO enlargement, and increased the tension between Russia, those countries, and the NATO nations as a whole.

Similarly, the decisions to take action first in Bosnia and then against Serbia over Kosovo in 1999 were also divisive; they illustrate clearly the differences on the two sides of the Atlantic regarding the use of force. But, once the decisions were made, they also show clearly that the alliance would be willing to take military action beyond the traditional NATO Guidelines Area, that is, to go "out of area"; this helped set the precedent for the military action under way in Afghanistan as this volume goes to press.

For all its divisions, NATO was absolutely united in its decision to invoke Article 5 after 9/11 for the first time in its history. On September 12, according to its official web site, the North Atlantic Council "met in response to the attacks and agreed that if it is determined that this attack was directed from abroad against the United States, it shall be regarded as an action covered by Article 5 of the Washington Treaty, which states that an armed attack against one or more of the Allies in Europe or North America shall be considered an attack against them all."[25]

That unity was short-lived, however, as the United States under George W. Bush made the decision to move forward with—or without—the aid of its allies. Any divisions among the alliance members to that point paled in comparison to the objections raised and the schism that resulted because of the US decision to invade Iraq in 2003. It is that deep division that remains and that the United States must now confront if it is to rebuild relations with its allies on the other side of the Atlantic.

All the enmity that resulted from that decision, however, must also be weighed against the initial support given to the NATO mission in Afghanistan. However, that unity, too, seems to be waning in light of the ongoing war. What will be more telling from the perspective of the alliance, however, is what will happen to that unity and sense of common purpose after the war in Afghanistan ends.

The Relationship between NATO and the EU

In January 2001, NATO and the EU recognized their shared common strategic interests through an exchange of letters between the NATO secretary-general and the EU presidency that defined "the scope of cooperation and the modalities of consultation between the two organizations."[26] In December 2002, the two groups signed the NATO-EU Declaration on European Security and Defence Policy (ESDP), which strengthened the relationship, and included the basis for practical work in crisis management, combating terrorism, conflict management, as well as increased consultation and cooperation.[27]

These goals were codified in the so-called "Berlin-Plus" arrangements, adopted on 17 March 2003, that provide the basis for NATO-EU cooperation in crisis management by allowing EU access to NATO's collective assets and capabilities for EU-led operations. In effect, these arrangements allow the alliance to support EU-led operations in which NATO as a whole is not engaged. Subsequently, the ties between the two organizations have been strengthened through ongoing meetings between the leaders of each organization and through meetings held regularly between the North Atlantic Council and the EU Political and Security Committee. Since the 2004 round of enlargement of both organizations, 19 countries are members of both the EU and NATO (see institutional map on page xiv).

For the purposes of this volume, however, the NATO-EU relationship not only reinforces the need to understand in broad terms the notion of "transatlantic," but also raises in stark relief the precarious role that some of the countries included here play, further underscoring our decision to include them. Paramount among these is Turkey, the only predominantly Muslim nation in NATO and a country with a critical geostrategic location. Turkey has been in accession talks with the EU since 2005, and President Bush actively supported its membership. However, talks remained stalled officially because of Turkey's relationship to Cyprus, a relatively recent EU member, although clearly there are other issues that work against Turkey's membership.

The leaders of both Ukraine and Georgia have indicated their desire to see their respective countries included in both NATO and the EU. However, Moscow has made it clear how much it objected to these possibilities. Russia's decision to cut off the flow of oil to Ukraine most recently in January 2009 also served as a stark reminder of the power that Russia has because of oil. Both Ukraine and Georgia seek further ties with the West, seeing themselves more closely allied with the NATO/EU countries at this point than with their former parent. But the political as well as military costs of admitting one country or both could be severe, and the discussion alone could further undermine, rather than strengthen, the relationship among the countries of the Atlantic region, broadly defined.

As we consider the various countries in the transatlantic region and the relationships between and among them, it is important to look at the juxtaposition of the priorities of each country as they are balanced against those of the whole. Ultimately, that balance is what will help determine the future of the transatlantic relationship.

The Approach of the Volume

In many ways, it would be virtually impossible for any one person to address the range of critical countries involved given the unique perspective that each has, let alone do a significant job of addressing the important issues that affect each country and the overall relationship. Thus, in this volume we bring together country experts from both sides of the Atlantic to address some of these issues. Each of the contributors has produced a chapter built around a set of themes that we think are most salient in understanding that country's perspective. In order to provide a uniform basis for comparison, all of the contributors have been asked to address certain common issues, and then to note how and in what ways the country that they are studying brings other factors to bear that could affect the relationship. For example, in order to get the most comprehensive understanding of each country's perspective, all contributors were asked to provide historical background on the domestic context within which security and foreign policy decisions are, and have been, made. This would include the role of public opinion, as well as domestic politics. Each was asked to describe the security dimension within the country studied, including the changing nature of the threat and the role of the military as a decision maker or "stakeholder" in affecting the policies developed to meet that threat. All chapters give some background on the various alliances or relationships with which that country is involved, not only NATO but beyond, and how those relationships have played a role in influencing the emerging foreign and security policy of the nation.

More specifically, among the overarching themes that each contributor has been asked to address are the following: differing and changing perceptions of "threat" and terrorism since 9/11; the role of domestic politics and policies in determining or affecting transatlantic relations; the role of the public and the media within each of these countries; the strategic culture, including the role of the military and the use of force as well as the evolution of the country's security policy and posture; evolution of the security dimension, broadly defined to include military/security, but also to include what can be broadly termed "human security," such as the environment, economic well-being and the like; responses to the threat and the changing notion of security, including the country's relations to other actors; and finally, some conclusions about the future of transatlantic relations from the perspective of that country, given the points discussed above.

Given all this, each contributor was asked to speculate on what s/he sees as the future of transatlantic relations from the perspective of that country. Our goal is to use the ideas put forward in these chapters and the country experts' analyses to draw general conclusions about the future of the transatlantic relationship.

Chapter 1 reviews how transatlantic relations have been viewed within international relations theory. The book then takes a North American perspective, with chapters viewing these relations from the point of view of Canada and the United States. This is then followed by the European view, again subdivided into various national perspectives encompassing a range of nations drawn from the principal European EU/NATO members (France, Germany and the United Kingdom) to NATO's sole predominantly Muslim state (Turkey) to nations that were formerly part of the Warsaw Treaty Organization (Poland) or Soviet Union and are seeking greater integration within Europe (Ukraine and Georgia), and finally Russia. The final chapter then undertakes a comparative analysis and draws some general conclusions.

1 Transatlantic Relations

A Theoretical Framework

Serena Simoni

Introduction

For many years international relations practitioners and policy-makers on both sides of the Atlantic have tended to dismiss potentially poisonous crises in transatlantic relations (e.g., the Suez crisis, the Gaullist challenge, criticism of the Vietnam War, the clashes caused by Reagan's policies of the early 1980s) that could lead to a significant change in transatlantic relations. These disagreements were considered "little family spats",[1] rather than indicating a major or long-term problem. For, as the Latin locution goes, *ubi maior minor cessat.*[2]

Indeed, during the Cold War, the Euro-Atlantic partnership seemed almost unbreakable; as long as the US and Europe had a common enemy in the USSR, it was generally assumed that their alliance would endure. The East-West rivalry did not seem to offer any other alternative for America and Europe but that of collaboration to counter the Soviet Union. As it was initially conceived, this relationship was predominantly focused on the military dimension, but it soon broadened to include economic and political elements where differences were resolved and discrepancies settled.

However, with the disappearance of the Soviet threat, this once-strong partnership had its foundations shaken. The consequences of the removal of the Soviet threat for the future of transatlantic relations have been much debated amongst practitioners and scholars in the light of changing priorities and the loss of the Cold War "glue".[3] The nature and dynamic of this evolving debate were epitomized by the US's decision to invade Iraq in 2003 and the open opposition of Belgium, France, Germany and Luxembourg to that decision, as well as the opposition of public opinion in the United Kingdom and Italy, two Western European governments that did accommodate the Bush doctrine.[4]

The invasion of Iraq magnified concerns over the future of the Atlantic community. America appeared to be out of sync with its Western European partners, and major divisions amongst the Europeans seemed to further reiterate the possibility of transatlantic separation. Was the conflict over Iraq the validation of John Mearsheimer's argument that the absence of a common threat would lead the US to withdraw from Europe, and that, as a result, Europe would return to power politics?[5] Or was it just another "family spat," leaving unaltered the prospect of continued transatlantic cooperation, even in the absence of a common threat?

This chapter examines the growing body of literature focusing on the policy disputes between the United States and Europe and constitutes an attempt to clarify, synthesize and rationalize the central argumentative positions taken in the debate on the future of the transatlantic relations. It does so by offering an overview of how studies concerning transatlantic relations are framed and by identifying the underlying assumptions of such positions. Rather than setting forth any set of specific hypothesis to be tested, this chapter constitutes the analytical framework that synthesizes the various approaches to thinking and writing about transatlantic relations and serves as a foundation for the analysis that follows in the book. Moreover, countering those scholars who tend to consider Atlantic relations as less theoretical,[6] this chapter puts forward the argument that indeed there is no shortage of theoretical vibrancy in the study of the relationship between the US and Europe. To that extent, the chapter also argues that the theories used, mainly neo-realism and neo-liberalism, are less equipped than others such as constructivism to account for an ever-evolving transatlantic relationship. Accordingly, this chapter is divided into three parts. The first part introduces the primary analytical frameworks that have been used to inscribe and transcribe transatlantic relations, neo-realism and neo-liberalism, and shows what each of those theoretical accounts expect with regard to transatlantic relations, given the end of the Cold War. Part two then offers a comparison of the contending Neo-Realist and Neo-Liberal arguments. Finally, part three draws upon the shortcomings of the neo-realist and neo-liberal arguments, to reflect on the usefulness of other theories such as constructivism to explain the development of transatlantic relations.

The Debate: Neo-Realist Account

In the two decades since the end of the Cold War, the debate on the likely future of transatlantic relations has continued to thrive. Articles and books have generally stressed that transatlantic relations are in a state of inevitable decline, although there is some dissent among those who hold this view.[7] An analysis of the debates in the decade that followed the end of the East-West rivalry reveals that the debates are theoretically grounded and that such theoretical understandings permeate the various discourses about the future of the Atlantic community. Moreover, questions about the future of the transatlantic relations were not triggered by the Iraq War in 2003 exclusively; as stated before, the trigger was in fact the collapse of the Soviet Union in 1991. Against this backdrop, this chapter sets out to take a look at the proliferation of scholarly works on transatlantic relations prior to the political storm of 2003 to explicitly uncover some of the theoretical assumptions underlying the discussion of transatlantic relations in a decade not defined by a perceived common threat that could drive the US and Europe into a military-political-economic partnership.[8] Details about specific countries and their policies towards transatlantic relations, especially in the wake of the 2003 invasion of Iraq, can be found in the national case study chapters, which follow this chapter.

In public and academic circles, experts have tended to rely on two well-established theories in attempting to understand the dynamics and realities of international relations: neo-realism and neo-liberalism.[9] An analysis of the debates on the future of transatlantic relations in the interim period between the end of the Cold War and 9/11 reveals that international relations scholars were sharply divided on the likely future of the Euro-American partnership. Neo-realists, in fealty to their belief that balance-of-power politics is the main determinant of international relations, expected a worsening of Euro-American relations, while neo-liberals, following their core belief in the power of institutions, maintained a more optimistic outlook.[10]

As stated earlier, neo-realist academics such as John Mearsheimer and Stephen Walt have contended that the end of the Cold War removed the ideological "glue" that made for unity in transatlantic relations.[11] Most of those who ratify Mearsheimer's contention share a common set of basic assumptions associated with the realist position, namely that states are the main actors in international relations and their actions are motivated toward their own survival.[12] In addition, the realist world view also suggests that states can harm or even destroy one another. Furthermore, the realist position contends that the principle that governs relations between states is anarchy (i.e., the absence of a central authority that regulates their interactions and therefore protects them if another state threatens or attacks them).[13] Finally, neo-realists share the belief that states live in an uncertain realm wherein they do not know the intentions and capabilities of other states. Therefore, they claim that states are constantly insecure and war is always possible. Consequently, these scholars believe that security is one of the primary and continual concerns of the state.[14] Within the neo-realist literature, one set of arguments largely employs the balance of power theory to offer an explanation of transatlantic relations vis-à-vis the end of the Cold War.[15] These theorists claim that states seek to balance the power of threatening states.[16]

Such acts of balancing can take the form of unilateral action or military cooperation, but they can also lead to other forms of cooperation, such as economic cooperation, because when states combine their economic advantages, they ultimately enhance their power overall. Correspondingly, the demise of a common external threat can undermine the types of cooperation, including military and economic, as described above. Within the dynamics of the latter scenario, neither military nor economic cooperation would be of overriding interest, and either one could possibly be perceived as risky, since such a partnership could enhance the relative military power of either partner, as a result of the economic gains achieved through the partnership.[17]

As I stated earlier, the underlying premise behind neo-realist explanations of the future of transatlantic relations, in particular their cooperative efforts, is the perception of, and reaction to, a commonly perceived threat. Historically, theorists argue, the fear of the Soviet Union induced the United States and Europe to form a powerful military alliance, NATO. The economic cooperation between the core transatlantic states, they claim, was a consequence of the military collaboration. In short, NATO augmented their combined power. These theorists seem to agree that the overriding security interest kept the transatlantic core states together in a political alliance. In essence, during the Cold War, security interests superseded ideological divergences, which did indeed exist at the time.[18] Thus the presence of the Soviet threat was seen as the

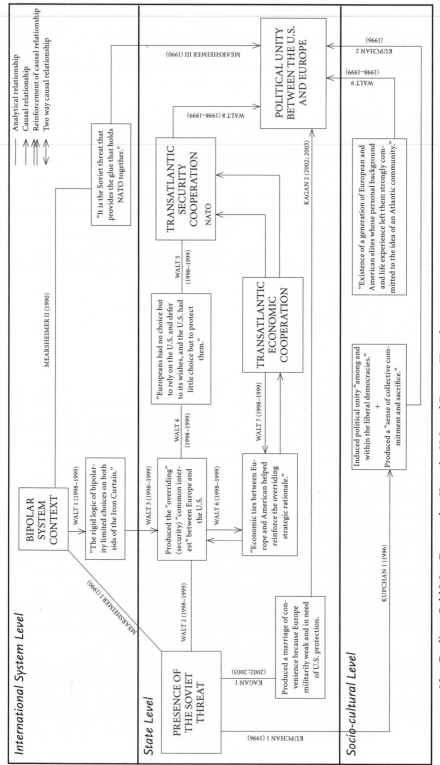

FIGURE 1.1 Neo-Realists. Cold War: Factors that Kept the U.S. and Europe Together.

leading cause for political unity. Some have conceptualized transatlantic relations within a bipolar system[19] and further conceive the threat that had been constituted by the Soviet Union as the most important factor.[20]

It is worth noticing that the neo-realist argument has been used very consistently over the years. All these scholars tend to agree that the end of the Cold War should have attenuated Euro-American military and economic cooperation. For example, John Mearsheimer, in his often-cited article "Back to the Future: Instability in Europe after the Cold War," argued that NATO would, at best, become an empty shell.[21] He went on to argue that if the Cold War came to a complete end, the United States would abandon Europe completely, provoking the end of a stable bipolar order.[22] Mearsheimer has claimed that the stability of bipolarity would be replaced by the instability of a multi-polar structure.[23] He has maintained this pessimistic argument over the subsequent decade, suggesting that without the US, or the American pacifier, Europe would revert to power politics, with Germany as its military fulcrum.[24] This prediction of separation and rivalry is commonly shared within neo-realist scholarship. Owen Harries, for example, in his article "The Collapse of the West," reinforced this point by arguing that the West could not endure the collapse of the Soviet Union, because the concept of the West was constructed out of "desperation and fear," not "natural affinities." In addition to the anticipated split of the military alliance, other neo-realists such as Stephen Walt have argued that given the absence of a common threat, there could also be an end to economic cooperation.[25] Like other neo-realists, Walt recognizes that the US and Europe were brought together by the fear of the Soviet threat; however, he further underlines that it was economic ties during the Cold War which reinforced the military cooperation.[26] In other words, the common threat induced economic cooperation, which produced economic gains that ultimately enhanced the combined powers of the partners. Conversely, Walt argued, the end of the Cold War would eliminate the overriding common security interest and consequently loosen economic ties as well.[27] In fact, Walt already sees the signs of this trend in the US shift in economic activity from Europe to Asia; he warns that such a shift "will inevitably lead U.S. policymakers to devote more energy and attention to the latter [meaning Asia]".[28] In addition, the expansion of the European Union, he suggests, will create further tensions. The euro, Walt explains, has the potential to challenge the dollar as the principal international reserve currency.

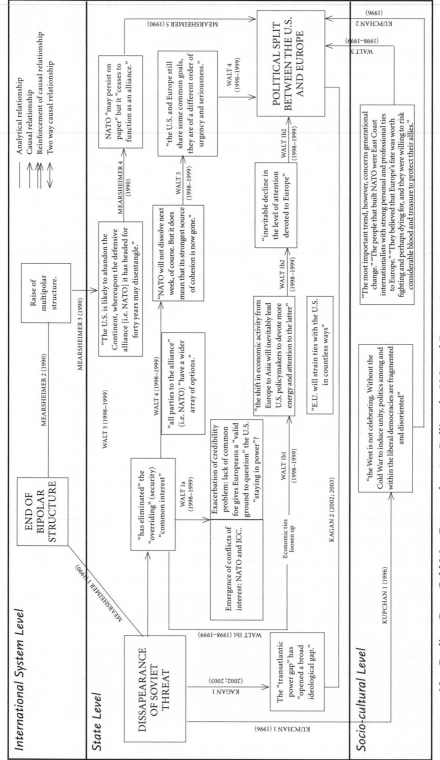

FIGURE 1.2 Neo-Realists. Post–Cold War: Factors that Are Pulling the U.S. and Europe Apart.

A further element inducing fragmentation and disorientation in transatlantic relations, Walt argues, is the decline of a sense of commitment to the Atlantic community.[29] Americans are no longer willing to sacrifice for Europe, Walt contends, because of a generational change. "The people that built NATO were East Coast internationalists with strong personal and professional ties to Europe . . . They believed that Europe's fate was worth fighting and perhaps dying-for, and they were willing to risk considerable blood and treasure to protect these allies."[30] But, he concludes, this is no longer the case. The end of the Cold War is thus producing a transatlantic split.

The aftermath of 9/11, and the ensuing debates over the legitimacy of attacking Iraq, has produced relevant scholarly debates that reduce the current "world disorder" to a division between the US and Europe, based, yet again, on military and economic reasons.[31] Kagan writes: " . . . the U.S. is quicker to use military force, less patient with diplomacy, and more willing to coerce (or bribe) other nations in order to get a desired result. Europe, on the other hand, places greater emphasis on diplomacy, takes a much longer view of history and problem solving, and has greater faith in international law and cooperation."[32] His highly controversial argument has been that on major strategic and international questions, "Americans are from Mars and Europeans are from Venus." Kagan argued that powerful states (i.e., the US) see the world differently from weak states (i.e., Europe) because of their power difference.[33]

Kagan's generalization assumes that any change in the relationship between allies is due to a shift in the balance of power. In his view, Europeans want to rebalance American hegemony by empowering international organizations. The assumption is that since Europe was unable to influence the US after 9/11, Europeans must deploy the inherent power of international organizations to balance against, and thus limit, American power.[34]

In addition to 'power' and 'weakness' as determinants of states' behavior, Kagan explains that conceptions of power and power dynamics also influence how much power one state may pursue.[35] For Kagan, Europeans have a Kantian vision of the world, in which force is unnecessary and counterproductive in solving disagreements. Conversely, Americans have a Hobbesian view, and think that the world is a dangerous place and that states always need to keep the use of force as an option.

A less catastrophic, but nonetheless equally pessimist, view has been forwarded by Ronald Asmus and Kenneth Pollack, who observe that the emergence of new threats such as terrorism, weapons of mass destruction, mass migration and rogue states will make the United States and Europe "rethink the purpose of the transatlantic relationship."[36] In sum, for Asmus and Pollack the rise of a new threat will once again produce transatlantic political unity. Their conclusion is not shared by some, however. For instance, Ivo Daalder claims instead that 9/11 "reinforced America's strategic shift away from Europe."[37] The fundamental consequence of the end of confrontation with the USSR, he argues, is that America's and Europe's security concerns diverged exponentially. The United States focused globally and Europe locally. In other words, while the US engaged in global leadership Europe concentrated on regional leadership in its immediate backyard (i.e., the former Soviet satellite states in Eastern Europe). These differences, Daalder points out, only intensified over the course of the years, especially under the George W. Bush administration. This sample of the various positions within the neo-realist camp helps to illustrate the level of theoretical disparity that continues to infuse the debate about the future of the transatlantic relations. In the neo-realist view, the overriding interest in preserving security is the building block of the trans-Atlantic community.

The Debate: Neo-Liberal Account

Contrary to the neo-realist position in fundamental ways, neo-liberals argue that the US and Europe will keep cooperating because even absent a common threat, the transatlantic partners share security and economic interests, norms, values, political identities and membership in public institutions. These factors, they claim, have been and will be the basis of transatlantic cooperation.[38] Such ongoing shared elements, they claim, will decrease the chances of separation while stimulating cooperation. The neo-liberals' assessment of the future of transatlantic relations is based on a three-fold understanding of the shared constitutive elements that in their view form the Euro-American partnership, namely: (1) common security, (2) common economic interests and (3) common values and political identity.

In the post-Cold War era, neo-liberals claim, transatlantic relations will still be characterized by military cooperation. In 1993, James Elles wrote that "Europe is America's natural partner by virtue of its actual military capability."[39] John Duffield, in an article published in 1994, stressed that there was still a solid consensus between the US and Europe on the need to preserve NATO. The alliance, he emphasized, "continues to enjoy generally strong support from its member states."[40] Robert Blackwill in 1999 wrote that "the two sides of the Atlantic continue to share enduring vital interests and face a common set of challenges both in Europe and beyond."[41] These challenges, he underlined, are many and diverse (e.g., slowing down the spread of weapons of mass destruction or avoiding the emergence of a hostile hegemony in Europe) and cannot be adequately addressed by either the US or Europe alone. Thus, he concluded, the Euro-American partnership will endure even in a world without the specificity of the Soviet threat. Joseph Nye also predicted that NATO will keep playing an important role because Europe has not been capable of solving the Balkan problem on its own, for example.[42] In short, neo-liberals contend that transatlantic relations will not and have not been jeopardized by the collapse of the Soviet Union. These scholars tend to see the transatlantic axis as a concern of security, independent of other challenges that the extant alliance may face (or had built upon initially). This view is closer to the Deutschian concept of the North Atlantic area as a security community that has developed a spirit of its own.[43]

The neo-liberal argument, however, also points at common economic interests that will guarantee cooperation in the Atlantic community. James Elles identifies Europe and the US as natural economic partners by virtue of their economic weight.[44] Daniel Deudney and John Ikenberry observe that "the business of the West is business."[45] They claim that American and European societies are "permeated by market relations, mentalities and institutions" and, they add, "as the importance of the markets grow in these societies, their characters converge."[46] Joseph Nye warns us not to listen too much to the "doom-sayers." In fact, he underlines that "while American trade with Asia has surpassed the one with Europe, American trade with Europe is still more balanced."[47] He also points out that "American foreign investment in Europe still exceeds that in Asia."[48] Similarly, Anthony Blinken in 2001 emphasized that "American investment in Europe has increased seven-fold over the past six years."[49] This, in his view, is a sign of a strong relationship not weakened by the end of the East-West rivalry. Indeed, the current economic meltdown has emphasized the transatlantic economic interdependence, and policymakers across the Atlantic seem to hold the view that cooperation is the only way to end the crisis. Therefore, the economic meltdown could prove to be an element of unification. For example, at the London summit on April 2, 2009, the G20 announced that the leaders had committed to $1.1 trillion in new funds to increase the capital available to the International Monetary

Fund (IMF). The goal was the revival of trade, which was expected to lessen in 2009 for the first time in thirty years.[50] The G20, an institution that is heavily biased in terms of transatlantic membership, could be seen as bringing together the leaders of the world's major economies to take collective action to stabilize the global economy and rescue jobs.

Finally, neo-liberals emphasize that shared norms, values, political identities and membership in common public institutions will continue to foster cooperation between the US and Europe. Deudney and Ikenberry underline that the West is "bound by a web of complex institutional links and associations," which created what they call the spirit of the West."[51] Such spirit, they claim, is made of common norms, public mores and political identities. Because the US and Europe share this common spirit, within an international institutional framework, they are likely to keep cooperating. Thus the transatlantic relationship, from the neo-liberal perspective, seems likely to survive because it is deeply embedded in international (transatlantic) regimes such as NATO, the G20 and the G7.[52]

In this world view, international institutions such as NATO embody common Western values and political identities, and since those institutions are also an integral part of US and European domestic and international politics, an institution like NATO cannot be considered as merely instrumental, but rather as the cornerstones of Western cooperation. James Elles, for example, claims that there is no reason to be pessimistic about the future of transatlantic relations because the US and Europe share the common values of democracy and a market economy.[53] Furthermore, he stresses that they have also created "mechanisms, procedures and institutional and personal relationships for coordinating positions and resolving differences."[54] Charles Kupchan is of the same opinion when he claims that "shared norms are working together to produce the cohesiveness of the transatlantic community."[55] Joseph Nye identifies the transatlantic communality of values in democracy and human rights, and claims that the US shares such values more thoroughly with Europe than with most other states.[56] Finally, Anthony Blinken argues that there is no values gap between Americans and Europeans and that "the U.S. and Europe are converging culturally."[57] As evidence, he observes that while support for the death penalty is decreasing in the United States, it is increasing in Europe. As a result of such observable social phenomena, Blinken concludes, transatlantic values are converging, rather than diverging.[58] More recently, Tod Lindberg endorsed Blinken's argument by claiming that Ameri-

FIGURE 1.3 Neo-Liberals. Correlation of Post–Cold War arguments.

cans and Europeans share political and moral matters and indicate similar public policy preferences as well.[59] In essence, disagreements among the alliance take place within a larger framework of agreement about "fundamental values." It is worth noticing here that while in the last twenty years many scholars have grappled with the question of the future of the transatlantic order, what emerges from the theoretical debates is a definition of "transatlantic relations" that largely leaves Canada out of such a political order. In fact, all of the authors in this literature review seemed to have a "narrow" idea of transatlantic relations which is by and large confined to the United States and Europe. Whether this can be interpreted as a sign of American cultural blindness or not remains yet to be verified. Certainly, under any set of circumscribed arguments, Canada is a leading actor in the "trans-Atlantic" community and there appears to be no rational reason for its exclusion.

Assessment of the Debate

In the previous discussion, I have attempted to summarize how neo-realists and neo-liberals view transatlantic relations from different perspectives and reach almost diametrically opposed conclusions about its future. From a neo-realist perspective, the end of the Cold War was supposed to lead to the end of the transatlantic security effort. For neo-liberals, shared economic interests and political identities (i.e., democracy and free-market economies) as well as membership in public institutions such as NATO, WTO, IMF and G7 continue to constitute a stable basis for transatlantic cooperation. The absence of a common threat and the presence of such shared elements, neo-liberals have argued, decrease the likelihood of separation between the transatlantic allies.

Two decades of empirical records have shown that military cooperation between the United States and Europe has continued. Clearly, NATO has survived the disappearance of the external threat that had prompted its initial creation in the first place, and remains as the key security organization for its members. However, subsequent to the disappearance of the Soviet threat, each party has emphasized different means for achieving the newer and evolving goals of the alliance over time. Primarily, this harmony within the alliance was accomplished by redefining the members' transatlantic interests on humanitarian grounds. The Kosovo War offers a revealing example of the reshaped moral identity of the transatlantic leaders.[60] The character of this "renovated West" is deeply normed or value-laden since the frictions that occurred in the 1990s were reconciled through a reborn sense of Western identity, which developed with the protection of human rights as a unifying principle.[61] Thus, even militarily, the unity and self identification of the post-Cold War West are adjudicated by the common perception that human rights must be defended.

However, in predicting the probability of a troubled transatlantic relationship, neo-realists have also been reasonably accurate: since the 1990s, the transatlantic relationship has indeed been characterized by internal clashes. The US and Europe have been at odds on security, and these policy disagreements can justifiably be interpreted as a political split. The flaw within the neo-realist view rests, rather, in its inability to predict how the evolution of norms could contribute to avoiding a more serious split.

The same empirical record (e.g., the Kyoto Protocol in 1997, the Ottawa Treaty in 1997, the Rome Statute in 1998 and most recently the invasion of Iraq in 2003) also highlights flaws in the neo-liberal approach.[62] Such an account, with its emphasis on cooperation based on shared values, has been flawed by not having taken into account the evolution of transatlantic relations in the 1990s. In this case, oversimplification in theorizations impeded neo-liberals from explaining the evolution of the disagreements which have emerged in a post-Cold War world. Conversely, the theory also needs to draw attention to the members' conflicted relations, emphasized by several disagreements that have arisen from the increasing differences in the members' understanding of some specific values. This is not inconsistent with my critique of the neo-realists' analysis, because on a broader scale, while it is clear that both the US and Europe do share the common value of protecting human rights, there is fundamental disagreement on how to prevent such violations and on how to punish those who violate such rights.[63]

Without an understanding of how changing norms of behavior have influenced the redefinition of the West, even in terms of security issues, it is impossible to comprehend why those disagreements did not bring about a total split in transatlantic relations. In essence, while it is evident that the 1990s and the 2000s were years of change, characterized by disagreements within the transatlantic partners, changes in values, such as the need to protect human rights, are redefining the West beyond the traditional commonalities of capitalist democracies emphasized by neo-liberals.

An Alternative Framework: Constructivism

A constructivist approach provides alternative understandings of mainstream international relations issues by privileging the concept of "identity" in world politics and culture within international relations theory. One of the main questions for constructivists is "how much do structures constrain and enable the actions of actors, and how [far] can actors deviate from the constraints of structure."[64] Within the constructivist view of world politics, a "structure" is a set of unchangeable norms and principles that constrains the behavior of states. One of the critically important questions for constructivism is how a given action may or may not (correspondingly and/or simultaneously) reproduce both the state and the structure. For example, to the extent that Franco-German opposition to the invasion of Iraq was plausible because of France and Germany's identity as "middle powers," that action also correspondingly constituted France and Germany as "middle powers" for the very use of, and preference for, diplomacy. Conversely, with reference to the invasion of Iraq, non-military intervention was an inconceivable option for the US because of the conceptualization of US identity as a "great power." Once again, correspondingly, it was the military intervention itself that reflexively constituted the US as a great power.[65]

As Ted Hopf explains, "meaningful behavior, or action, is possible only within an inter-subjective social context. Actors develop their relations with, and understanding of, others through the media of norms and practices. In the absence of norms, exercises of power, or actions, would be devoid of meaning. Constitutive norms define an identity by specifying the actions that will cause Others to organize that identity and respond to it appropriately."[66]

Answering questions about the future of the Euro-American partnership requires the consideration of two factors: an understanding of the fluidity of the transatlantic relations within the social context and an assessment of the ongoing debates on the future of the transatlantic relations.

Given what constructivism brings to our understanding of world politics, determining the future of transatlantic relations will require knowing more about the situation (i.e., culture, norms, institutions, procedure, rules, and social practices) that constitutes the US and Europe as well as the inherent "structures" that define them. Therefore, we need to investigate the social practices of the US and Europe as constitutive practices.[67] In short, we need to employ a constructivist approach, which will better enable us to predict the future of the partnership because the US and Europe behave and act within a prescribed social context. Consequently, an approach that considers these interactive exchanges or "inter-subjective" actions within a social context will give us insights into how their interests are changing and how changing interests are shaping their behavior.[68]

Given that for constructivists, "identity" has a unique and specific meaning, indeed it is important to consider US and European political identity as discrete, and investigate how their identity affects their behavior and consequently their relations. The identity of a state entails, as Ted Hopf puts it, "its preferences and consequent actions." And it is important to note further, that *each state defines others according to the identity it ascribes to them.* This process is rendered even more dynamic because the state also constructs its own identity thorough continuous daily practice. Indeed, the way the state perceives others and itself determines its self-identity, as well as the preferences which ultimately result in actions the state will choose to exercise. In essence, if a state identifies itself as a "great power," it will have a different set of preferences or interests than one which identifies itself as a middle power.[69] These types of considerations enable us to understand why the US and Europe seem to be headed in different directions. The Atlantic partners simply have different preferences due to self-defined identities within the larger international and transatlantic context. It is the social construction of their identities that determines diverging interests, not the gap in military capabilities as Robert Kagan would have us believe.

Lastly, we need to employ the constructivist approach because neo-realism and neo-liberalism seem to be inadequately equipped to explain the fluidity of the transatlantic partnership. A relationship that is changing and constantly evolving cannot be analyzed by theories that tend to explain and perceive international politics as static. Such an analysis will not be able to capture elements of change, because it does not conceive change as a constitutive factor. Constructivism, in contrast, allows for an analysis of the interactions, or praxis,[70] of the United States and Europe within international institutions. Providing evidence for their behavior,[71] such an analysis would show the validity and usefulness of both the neo-realist and the neo-liberal predictions for the future of transatlantic relations. Further, it would tell us which predictions have thus far been more accurate and insightful and would expose the underlying general theoretical assumptions of each approach with respect to a trans-atlantic partnership between the two powers. Additionally, such an analysis would offer an understanding of what issues the United States and Europe would consider worthy of cooperation in, and therefore allow for more accurate predictions on the future of the transatlantic relations.

Conclusions

This chapter has examined two of the most important and controversial theoretical approaches in the study of transatlantic relations—neo-realism and neo-liberalism—and has suggested an alternative theory to analyze them: constructivism. Balance-of-power theory does not seem to be able to explain either the preservation of NATO or its enlargement or its new out-of-the-region missions; but its long-term prediction of a troubled partnership thus far seems to hold true. Conversely, neo-liberal theories seem to be able to explain NATO's persistence, but not how transatlantic relations are evolving and why the allies are often at odds. Neo-liberals have led us to believe that there is almost a natural inclination toward cooperation in the trans-Atlantic arena. However, there is nothing truly "natural" or innately predictable about international politics. International as well as transatlantic relations exist within a context that is socially constructed. In other words, the evolution of a state's identity carries on to the international arena and affects state relations because these changes in identity are correspondingly, constantly, reformulating their interests. In addition, interactions between states also have an impact on both their identity and their normative behavior; such behavior is also constitutive of identity. In this scenario, what needs to be analyzed is the evolution of American and European identity within the context of transatlantic relations, which can offer an explanation as to where the relationship is headed. We need to recognize change both in their relations and in their ever-evolving notions of self-identity. Thus, because so far it is the only theory that can offer a dynamic account, we need constructivism to analyze transatlantic relations. Scholarly works on this subject will move forward the debate on the future of the Atlantic community and will enhance our knowledge of the explanatory power of theories.

2 The Future of Trans-Atlantic Relations

A View from Canada

David Rudd

Introduction

NATO's 60th birthday in April 2009 found Canadian policy-makers pre-occupied with issues close to home, even as the Canadian Forces (CF) prosecutes its most complex and dangerous overseas mission since Korea.[1] At the time of the NATO summit the Government of Canada had not articulated a comprehensive policy tackling the myriad issues in the trans-Atlantic file. But two macro policy issues—the mission in Afghanistan and military transformation—are receiving significant, on-going attention. The former, particularly, is notable in that it has acted as a catalyst for the latter, while at the same time sparking debate on Canada's security "culture." It remains to be seen whether public unease over the human and material costs of the Afghanistan engagement will alter perceptions of the value and purpose of the trans-Atlantic security relationship.

Following an examination of recent political developments, this chapter will explore how Canada's domestic political landscape, strategic culture, and external relations shape current policy. The picture that emerges is twofold. First, even though Afghanistan dominates the agenda, trans-Atlantic relations are multi-dimensional. Second, Canadians are internationalist by inclination but remain quite continentalist in practice. The country values its membership in the United Nations (UN), NATO, and the Group of Seven most industrialized democracies (G-7). It is also committed to advancing the cause of global governance, as witnessed by strong support shown for the UN's Responsibility to Protect principles and the International Criminal Court. But Ottawa is clearly pre-occupied with bilateral trade and security arrangements with its southern neighbour. It is also devoting greater attention to security in the High Arctic. This emphasis will not change; indeed, it may become more acute in the short term, especially as the minority Conservative government sizes up the Obama Administration, looking to it for support on key bilateral issues. It also will not change because Europe is unlikely to change. Perennially focussed on the evolution of the European Union (EU), Canada will continue to be at the very edge of Europe's political radar screen. Still, it is quite possible to fashion a productive trans-Atlantic security relationship—one in which Canada should make its voice heard.

Recent Political Developments

Mid-2009 found Canada with a minority Conservative government of uncertain longevity, grappling with restive opposition in parliament, economic turbulence caused by the global credit crisis, uncertainty over the direction of the new US administration, and significant public unease over the war in Afghanistan. At the time of writing, prospects of a change of government look unlikely; a decision by the opposition parties—the largest of which is headed by a pragmatic internationalist[2]—to not topple the government ensures that a re-evaluation of Canada's international engagements is not in the offing. This would be unlikely in any case, as the Liberal Party originally committed Canada to its present engagement in Afghanistan's volatile Kandahar province in 2005. The party has also been the chief architect of Canada's post-1945 internationalist security policy.

Canada has deployed 2,800 military personnel from all three services to the NATO-led International Security Assistance Force (ISAF) in Afghanistan. It is the fifth-largest contingent among the participating nations and one of relatively few to engage in combat against the insurgency. It comprises a sizeable ground and supporting air component in southern Afghanistan plus a forward support element in a nearby Middle Eastern country. In addition, from June until September 2008, a three-ship task group from the Canadian Navy formed the command element of Combined Task Force-150, a multinational naval coalition patrolling the Arabian Sea to guard against terrorism and other illegal activity. Ottawa's commitment to ISAF received a boost early in 2009 by the deployment of additional capabilities identified by the Alliance as critical to mission success-namely, heavy-lift Chinook helicopters and un-manned aerial vehicles (UAVs) for air-to-ground surveillance.

But while the military dimension of the trans-Atlantic partnership has virtually monopolized public attention in Canada, collaboration is also hap-pening in other areas. Law enforcement and intelligence co-operation with major partners (especially the United States and the United Kingdom) con-tinues, and was recently on display in the trial of Mohammad Khawaja, a Ca-nadian software engineer of Pakistani origin who was convicted in October 2008 of providing technical assistance to UK-based jihadists planning bomb attacks.

That same month, discussions were launched on an ambitious trade deal between Canada and the 27–nation EU. A notional accord would liberalize trade in goods, services and investment. But what would distinguish it from the tripartite North American Free Trade Agreement (NAFTA) is a proposal to allow the free flow of labour and an open market in government services and procurement.[3] Although short-term prospects for a deal are uncertain in the face of inter-provincial trade barriers, European reluctance to grant privi-leges to Canada that may ultimately have to be extended to the US, and rising protectionist sentiment among G-8 nations, a significant trans-Atlantic eco-nomic relationship exists. The EU is the second largest destination for Cana-dian exports, albeit by a distant margin. According to a study by the German Institute for International and Security Affairs (SWP), "Foreign direct invest-ment has become, over the years, the strongest element of the trans-Atlantic relationship: both FDI [foreign direct investment] stocks held by the EU in Canada and Canadian FDI in the EU more than tripled from 1995 to 2006."[4]

One of Canada's leading national dailies, *The Globe and Mail*, reported on the political importance attached to trans-Atlantic trade talks, noting that "although Ottawa's list of foreign-policy priorities does not include European issues, European and Canadian officials say that [Prime Minister Stephen] Harper has been heavily engaged with the proposed trade pact."[5] Thus while the US remains both the target and the source of Canadian commerce, diver-sification is clearly priority for Canada as it holds prospects for future growth once the global recession abates. In the meantime, smaller bilateral trade ini-tiatives are coming to fruition. In December 2008, Canada and Europe con-cluded an air transport agreement allowing each party unrestricted direct air services in each other's markets.

Much of this trans-Atlantic activity takes place outside the public eye, but it is clear that the relationship is more than a military one. Perhaps more by default than design, it has come to reflect the goals set out in the little-known Article 2 of the Washington Treaty, which calls upon NATO members to "encourage economic collaboration between any and all of them."[6] But insofar as Canadians think about the relationship there is little doubt that they currently see it through the prism of the "hard" security provided by NATO, and by inevitable extension, Afghanistan. It is not difficult to discern why. By the spring of 2010, 142 Canadian troops and one diplomat had lost their lives in that benighted country—a steep price for a small military and diplomatic power to pay.

Canada has been a supporter of NATO enlargement, recently ratifying accession protocols for Albania and Croatia. Ottawa has also expressed support for Georgian and Ukrainian membership prior to the former's short war with Russia in August 2008. Since then there have been no official pronouncements as to how membership prospects can (or should) be reconciled with Russia's well-known opposition to membership for these two former Soviet republics. But Foreign Affairs Minister Lawrence Cannon alluded to the desirability of further expansion, saying that the admission of the two Balkan states "sends a clear message that will inspire other NATO aspirant countries to continue on the path of integration and reform."[7]

Beyond enlargement, Canada has expressed support for transformation goals outlined in the Prague Capabilities Commitment (PCC) of 2002. The latter seeks multinational solutions to deficiencies in key military capabilities. Allies are encouraged to re-prioritize national requirements and to pool resources to acquire capabilities which would otherwise be too expensive to acquire, operate, and maintain.[8] Canada participates in the Strategic Airlift Interim Solution (SALIS), which has seen the pooling of funds by several allied nations to charter Antonov-124 transport aircraft at a usage rate of 2,000 hours per year until 2012.[9] Other commitments include the provision of strategic sealift.

But despite some progress on capability development within NATO and a few cryptic statements on enlargement, there is little indication as to whether Canada has a coherent vision for the future of the security relationship as NATO enters its seventh decade. Afghanistan seems to dominate Ottawa's strategic horizon, and that horizon may not extend further than 2011, when the combat mission is scheduled to end. Does this apparent omission indicate a lack of strategic thought on Canada's part, a disinclination to believe that small- or medium-sized powers can articulate a grand strategy? Does it speak to domestic politics—particularly an inability to forge a strong consensus on what the ends of Canada's foreign and security policies should be, and what should be the means to achieve them?

Canada's Strategic Culture

Strategic culture refers to "a set of normative and cognitive beliefs evolved from experiences held by a collective (usually a nation) about the use of force in international politics."[10] To this we should add the principles upon which a nation's security policy is built and the tools and organizations employed in its name. For Canada, force is not at the center of policy, although it remains a necessary tool.

The principal hallmarks of Canada's strategic culture include a commitment to liberal internationalism and multilateralism, including the upholding of international norms and a commitment to expanding the body of international law. These sentiments ensured that Canada would not retreat into a North American redoubt after the end of the Second World War. Enthusiastic support was shown for the formation of international bodies (i.e., UN, NATO) and the establishment of international financial institutions for reconstruction and development. There is broad consensus on the utility and wisdom of multilateralism in the Canadian body politic.

On the "hard' security side, visible manifestations of Canada's strategic culture include support for those principles articulated in the UN Charter dealing with the right to individual and collective self-defence, the duty of the international community to intervene in times of gross human rights violations, as well as the mutual defence clause (Article 5) of the Washington Treaty.

Each of these statutes and principles envisions (and legitimizes) the use of military force. Nevertheless, few would argue that the use of force occupies a place of primacy in Canadian policy or in the public mind, except under exceptional circumstances.[11] Despite active participation in numerous armed conflicts since 1945, as well as expensive and elaborate preparations to deter (and to fight) a war with the Soviet-led Warsaw Pact, many Canadians have associated their country (and their armed forces) with UN peacekeeping,[12] or operations at the lower end of the conflict spectrum. That this image persists in many quarters, despite the noticeable decline in such activities since the mid-1990s, illustrates another aspect of strategic culture—namely that it encompasses "a range of predispositions with observable manifestations in policy that are semi-permanent, lasting beyond the era of their original conception."[13]

Key foreign and defence policy documents of recent times consistently cite these enduring aspects of strategic culture, even as they identify new security risks and explore new strategies to deal with them. The Liberal government's 2005 International Policy Statement (IPS), an innovative document which sought to integrate Canada's defence, diplomatic, and overseas development efforts, cited multilateral co-operation as "the foundation of a stable and peaceful international system. Our country has stood by this principle for more than five decades, and we have been at the forefront of efforts to establish and strengthen multilateral institutions. The nature and complexity of the threats facing us, from failed states to terrorism, require a co-ordinated approach . . . "[14] The importance of the trans-Atlantic partnership, both as a reflection of strategic culture and a means of achieving policy goals, was evident in the declaration that "the Canadian Forces will . . . maintain their contributions to international institutions such as the United Nations and the North Atlantic Treaty Organization. Membership in both these organizations continues to serve Canadian interests and reflects our values."[15] The IPS repeatedly mentioned the need for a combat-capable military, and nodded its head to the salience of force in international relations, saying that "while diplomacy remains the preferred tool in the pursuit of international peace and security, our country must possess the hard military assets necessary to achieve foreign policy goals. This includes using lethal force when necessary."[16]

The Conservative government's 2008 Canada First Defence Strategy (CFDS)—a somewhat less ambitious document with a heavier emphasis on the re-capitalization of the CF—also devoted space to the importance of multilateral action and the trans-Atlantic link. Like its 2005 predecessor, it stressed the importance of the Arctic as a theater in which non-traditional security threats could emerge and pledged to increase surveillance of the area. But in a departure from previous practice it specified a clear (and robust) role for the Canadian Navy in the region. Pledging to add six to eight armed, ice-strengthened patrol vessels to the fleet,[17] the government envisions transferring some responsibility for the patrol and stewardship of Arctic waters away from the civilian agency that has for decades been their main custodian: the Canadian Coast Guard.

In an oblique reference to Canada's tradition of multilateralism, Prime Minister Stephen Harper boldly declared in the opening remarks of the CFDS that Canada would "return to the international stage as a credible and influential country, ready to do its part."[18] This statement indicates a perception that Canadians had been living off of past glories, aspiring to a position of prominence which did not correspond to their actual contributions to peace and security. According to this viewpoint, Canadians were not in tune with their strategic culture; they spoke the language of internationalism but were at pains to realize that they could not lead by words (or peacekeeping) alone. The CFDS aimed to put that right, declaring that "leadership requires the ability to deploy military assets . . . In concert with allies, Canada must be prepared to act and provide appropriate resources in support of national interests and international objectives."[19]

Culture and Its Discontents

Seldom has the promulgation of foreign or defence policy caused significant political upheaval in Canada. This may be attributed to bipartisan support of the two main political parties (the center-left Liberals and the center-right Conservatives) for the basic tenets of Canada's security culture. Canada's membership in collective defence and security bodies and the paying of membership dues in these clubs are never an election issue; neither the IPS nor CFDS drew heavy attention let alone criticism from Canadian civil society when they were tabled in parliament.[20] Professors Dan Middlemiss and Joel Sokolsky have sought to explain this phenomenon, noting that an informal consensus is apparent in Canadian defence policy—one which favors international engagement, arms control, and an adequately-equipped military. They question whether this is the result of public consideration of the alternatives, or of "passive acquiescence or even indifference and apathy about policies decided by the government."[21] They conclude that while there are nuances in public opinion, and while the latter may shift according to individual issues that crop up from time to time, "there has been a significant degree of agreement among [the attentive and general] public regarding the fundamental orientation of postwar Canadian defense policies."[22]

This is not to say that there are no cleavages or dissenting views over how best to foster security at home and abroad. Dissent does occur, often emerging along party or regional lines. The French-speaking province of Quebec has, in minds of many Canadian scholars, stood apart from the rest of the country in matters of defence and security. Quebecers have historically shown less support for overseas military operations than the rest of Canada—a fact reflected in their opposition to conscription during the world wars and to the current mission in Afghanistan.[23] Jean-Sébastien Rioux of Laval University has theorized that Quebec's unease stems from a deeply-held suspicion that English-speaking Canada has been too quick to associate the interests of the "imperial" power of the day to its own, entering into conflicts in which Canada had no clear stake. From the South African War to the Second World War, that power was Great Britain; in recent years it has been the United States.[24] However, this strategic "sub-culture" has not prevented Quebecers from endorsing the use of force when they perceive a humanitarian imperative. For example, support for intervention in strife-torn Haiti (1995) and in Kosovo (1999) was noticeably high. Indeed, Quebecers see themselves as internationalist and support membership in the UN and NATO. Rioux, however, suggests that that province's internationalism has clear limits:

> Quebecers and English Canadians often disagree on the nature and level of Canadian commitments, with the former clearly favouring action with the United Nations yet not necessarily ready to pony up, while English Canadians are generally more willing to send troops abroad. For example, a 1994 Gallup Canada poll confirms . . . that French Canadians agree on collective security *in principle*, but are against concrete military commitments . . . [25]

The left-wing New Democratic Party (NDP)—the smallest of the four main parties in Canada's parliament—might lay claim to the tile of strategic "counter-culturalist." While supportive of liberal internationalism and membership in the UN, it maintained an official position of hostility to Canada's membership in NATO during the Cold War. This posture was quietly jettisoned in the 1990s, and the party joined the chorus of voices calling for action to prevent another slaughter in Kosovo. But a long history of subtle anti-Americanism and more recent (and strident) opposition to perceived US imperial ambitions during the administration of George W. Bush have colored the party's view of the ISAF mission in Afghanistan. Although it is a clearly multilateral undertaking, legitimized by the UN Security Council to advance a progressive cause, it is also one in which the US has a controlling stake. This, along with the perceived militarization of the mission at the expense of development and reconstruction, discredits it in the minds of most party members. Calls for an immediate end to combat duty—a position supported by the third party in parliament, the separatist Bloc Québecois (BQ)—have so far gone unheeded by the Harper government.

The point to be made here is that these political forces can have an impact on Canada's strategic behaviour when the ruling party does not command a majority in parliament. The decision by the Harper Conservatives to table a motion in 2007 extending the mission to 2011 was in the minds of many an attempt to remove Afghanistan as an election issue should the government fall to a vote of non-confidence. Had the Conservatives been replaced by a coalition of Liberals, NDP and BQ, the duration and/or configuration of Canada's ISAF commitment may well have been altered.

A "Culture" of Peacekeeping

Consistent and widespread public support for membership in international organizations as vehicles for tackling a multitude of security problems is mirrored by considerable support for overseas military operations at the lower end of the conflict spectrum. Peacekeeping, especially under UN auspices, has long been seen, however misguidedly, as a uniquely Canadian undertaking—one that fosters a positive self-image and bolsters a sense of distinction from (and superiority to) Canada's southern neighbor.[26] Consistent participation in such operations from the mid-1950s to the mid-1990s has given rise to what some have called the "myth" of Canada as a "peacekeeping country"—a de-militarized (or at least non-militarized) society that does not engage in offensive military operations to protect national interests, but instead intervenes altruistically and without prejudice where combatants request assistance or where a more nebulous international interest is at stake. Joseph Jockel, an American scholar and long-time observer of Canada's defence effort, offered this by way of disagreement:

> There have been other, important motivations that have reinforced altruism. It was frequently argued during the cold war that peacekeeping reinforced Canada's physical security. This was a result of both Canada's proximity to the United States and the leading role of the United States in containing the Soviet Union ... The two superpowers could have been drawn into an escalating

conflict in [which] . . . Canada could have suffered as grievously as the United States.[27]

However flawed, this self-image persisted up to the 1990s, and was reinforced by government to the point where it was virtually ingrained into the national psyche.[28] The erection of the Canadian Peacekeeping Memorial in Ottawa in 1995 and the inauguration of National Peacekeepers' Day in 2008 (celebrated each 9 August) nurtured the "myth" even further, and undoubtedly contributed to the belief that peacekeeping was the primary role of the Canadian Forces on the international stage. (In truth it never was: the human and material resources devoted to the defence of Canada, North America and Europe since 1945 are several orders of magnitude higher than those devoted to peacekeeping.) It should therefore come as little surprise that the rigors of the counter-insurgency campaign in Afghanistan have been something of a shock to many Canadians. But evidence of a new-found pragmatism can be seen in the relative stoicism with which the Canadian public has accepted the steady trickle of casualties from the war zone. Future research may reveal whether this is due to an unspoken consensus that fostering good governance, institutional reconstruction and socio-economic progress in that distant land—even if force must be used in the process—is consistent with Canada's foreign policy tradition and strategic culture, especially if its ultimate goal is a more stable, progressive international order.

Canada's Security Evolution: Transformation in Many Guises

Once a means for ensuring the territorial defense of the West, the trans-Atlantic security relationship has evolved politically and militarily as the various partners perceived the emergence of a new security environment and the criticality of adapting to it. Threats are less existential but increasingly diverse, such that international organizations constituted for narrow purposes risk becoming irrelevant unless they adapt and embrace new ways of doing business.

Although the bureaucratic superstructure of NATO remains largely unchanged since the end of the Cold War, efforts to make the organization more forward-looking and operationally-focussed have resulted in the establishment of new commands such as Allied Command Transformation (ACT) in

Norfolk, Virginia. Canada's recent security policies have mirrored these re-forms. Efforts at transformation created an entirely new military command structure to handle domestic and overseas operations, support functions, and special operations.

But more important than mere institutional reforms are those which speak to the purpose of the trans-Atlantic security relationship. The Comprehensive Political Guidance, endorsed by NATO members at the 2006 Riga summit, emphasized the need to project joint, expeditionary forces, address asymmetric threats, and employ a "comprehensive approach" to crisis management in which military capabilities were brought to bear in concert with those offered by non-military partners.[29] Central to this new tasking is the stabilization of failed and failing states so that they do not become incubators of war, famine or international terrorism, or conduits through which materials needed to fashion unconventional weapons are transferred.

With the IPS and CFDS, Canada has wholeheartedly supported the strategic reorientation (or "transformation") of NATO's raison d'être from pure territorial defense to a new type of forward defense that prioritizes the failed state[30] and requires high-quality expeditionary forces enabled by key technologies and equipment sets, as well as leading-edge doctrine. The need to recapitalize the CF has been recognized by both Liberal and Conservative governments. Since 2005 extra funds for personnel, strategic and tactical lift, surveillance, armour protection and firepower enhancements have been either spent or promised.[31]

The CF has always been expeditionary, but the transformation of mindset and force structure was still considered necessary—especially after 9/11—for the organization to be relevant in an environment characterized by complexity. Accordingly, significant doctrinal reform took place under former Chief of Defence Staff (and ISAF commander) General Rick Hillier. The Canadian military became an initial adherent to the (admittedly land-centric) Three-Block War paradigm, in which troops were expected to undertake combat, stability, and humanitarian operations within the same operating space and alongside other government departments and international and non-governmental organizations. The term given to this by Canadian planners was the "3-D" approach (for defence, diplomacy, and development). It was later amended to "3-D+C" (commerce) to take into account the importance of building a viable economy to ensure the long-term stability of the target country. More recently the CF has widened its operational identity, embracing concepts and doctrine which draw on the capabilities of all three services as well as additional non-military arms of the national security apparatus.[32] Dubbed the "Whole-of-Government" approach, it recognizes that the list of capabilities needed to achieve the desired end-state is non-exhaustive. Theoretically, *any* government department or agency may now be called upon to assist, as the reconstruction or reformation of a target state's vital organs may include, inter alia, the civil service, police, judicial, and education systems.

Progress and Problems

The adoption of the Comprehensive Approach in the Comprehensive Political Guidance (and by Canada in its policy documents) points to the political agility and strategic innovation inherent in the trans-Atlantic security partnership. It also reflects one of the most important strategic developments of recent years: that the myriad problems facing the allies will defy purely military solutions. This, in addition to the halting and uneven Alliance-wide transformation of force structures, will yield forces which can underwrite an "enhanced" multilateralism—one that envisions the partnering of the Atlantic Alliance with non-NATO states and, most notably, with non-military arms of each partner's government, as well as with other international organizations.

However, concerns abound as to whether these new doctrines will have the desired effect. Particular attention has been devoted to the question of whether military forces can or should operate in the same space as non-partisan humanitarian groups. The latter worry that their efforts, as well as the lives of their workers, are threatened by troops undertaking small-scale development projects as a means of winning hearts and minds.[33] For their part, some military forces fear the loss of institutional identity if they are viewed by their publics as anything less than combat-capable.[34] The Comprehensive/Whole-of-Government Approach should therefore be seen as an initial attempt to reconcile institutional preferences with the public's conception of security in the 21st century.

Another challenge is that some security concerns are clearly not covered by NATO. It is uncertain whether the Alliance will have much to say on them, let alone whether the partners will take action as a collective. The Russia-Ukraine spat over natural gas exports in early 2009 unnerved the European allies but not their North American partners. This suggests that the EU may be a better vehicle for addressing the critical question of energy security—at least in that part of the Euro-Atlantic area.

The geographic dispersion of security concerns to places heretofore off the Alliance's radar screen may also hold unforeseen challenges for the trans-Atlantic partners. Canada, the US, and the EU have shown a heightened interest in the Arctic in recent years.[35] This stems from the estimated 25 per cent of the world's undiscovered oil and gas deposits that lie in the region, its potential as a route for maritime commerce, and its potential as a test-case for the international community's willingness to tackle the threats posed by global warming. A maritime boundary dispute between Canada and US in the Beaufort Sea, and its implications for the ownership of undersea resources, may become a serious bilateral irritant. Although policy-makers are loath to admit such linkages, non-resolution of this dispute will be seen in Canada as a threat to national sovereignty—a perennial concern for any Canadian politician. Left unresolved, it may adversely affect the inclination of future Canadian governments to respond positively to American pleas to undertake or maintain commitments to international security operations such as Afghanistan.

Meanwhile, concerns over the effects of oil exploration on climate change may create tension between the North American partners who have not signed recent protocols on global warming, and the more environmentally-minded Europeans who have.[36] Despite their environmental footprint, the Alberta oil sands are a significant source of energy for the US and Canadian markets, potentially holding as much oil as Saudi Arabia. The Conservative government's base of support lies in Alberta, making it unlikely that it will introduce environmental provisions that would prohibit further exploration. That this policy may be applied to the Arctic does not sit well with environmental constituencies.[37] One account is illustrative of Europe's chagrin at Canada's claim to be an energy super-power. Said Petra Dalata-Kreutzkamp of the Free University of Berlin, "Instead of welcoming Canada's energy wealth as a way to tackle energy security, Europe is more worried about Canada's role in the Arctic."[38]

The EU statement on Arctic security[39] recommended the establishment of international governance structures in a region where the vast majority of EU states have no territorial claims or energy resources. This called forth a seldom-seen defiance from an influential Canadian parliamentarian. Writing in a defence and security blog, Senator William Rompkey, Chair of the Senate Standing Committee on Fisheries and Oceans, chastized Europe for its presumption to adjudicate energy issues in the Arctic, and dismissed its claims to environmental rectitude, citing its inability to responsibly regulate the North Atlantic's heavily-depleted fish stocks.[40]

Regardless of how these issues play out, the prominence accorded to the Arctic by the Canadian government in its CFDS is without precedent in the last several decades. It illustrates a further evolution of Canada's security equation. A promise to devote funds for the construction of northern training facilities for the Canadian military, as well as ice-capable naval vessels to patrol the area, indicates that Canada will be devoting a larger portion of its still-modest defence and security resources to assert sovereignty over lands and waterways it claims come under its jurisdiction. It is too early to estimate the effect of this on Canada's ability to meaningfully contribute to security-building efforts in the unstable arcs of the world. But it does illustrate the increasing salience of non-traditional security issues, their capacity to contribute to trans-Atlantic discord, and the (re-)emergence, since 9/11, of North America as a theatre in which those concerns are played out.

Responses and Relationships

Regardless of the issue area, it is clear from current policy that multilateralism will be the preferred means to cope with the variety of security challenges facing Canada. Even in the Arctic—where Canada bristles at the thought of non-polar countries disputing its sovereignty, and where the trans-Atlantic partnership has seldom if ever been the vehicle for joint action or dispute resolution—there will be efforts to forge a multilateral consensus on maritime boundaries, resource exploitation and the environment.

As major stake-holders are beginning to assert interests in the far north (Russia's much-publicized trip to the floor of the Arctic Ocean and its claim to the Lomonosov Ridge is a case in point), some efforts to bring together circumpolar nations to iron out disputes have already been made. The Arctic Council working group was established in 1996 to promote co-operation in sustainable development and environmental protection among eight countries whose territory straddles the Arctic Circle.[41] Although the Council is not a formal international organization, its existence illustrates a perceived need for security dialogue in non-traditional forums.

This is not to de-value existing memberships. Despite a sharp decrease in contributions to UN peace support operations, the UN continues to be a key enabler and contributor to missions supported by Canada, most notably in Afghanistan. Since 9/11 the Canada-US North American Aerospace Defense (NORAD) partnership has expanded its remit from early warning and aerospace defence to include joint warning of maritime threats. The evolution of this partnership is reflected in the IPS, which elevates bilateral co-operation to a new level by recognizing the importance of joint responses to terrorist attacks or natural disasters along the shared 3,000–mile border.[42] The latter may be necessary to ensure that the border remains open so that the flow of bilateral trade—which dwarfs trade with any other country or group of countries and which is key to Canada's socio-economic well-being—suffers no interruptions. Much political attention will undoubtedly be devoted to these domestic and continental matters. Secure trade (including in energy resources), Arctic resource development, and the need for co-operative economic stimulus in a recessionary climate will continue to pre-occupy policy-makers in Ottawa, notwithstanding the considerable attention (and worry) invested in the Afghanistan file.

Having acknowledged that membership in the trans-Atlantic club requires serious commitment, and having made those commitments in Afghanistan since 2002, Canada has begun to ask how much of the collective security burden it should have to shoulder (and for how long) in view of the reluctance of a number of allies to assume the same level of risk. Whereas Canada was once pilloried (not unjustifiably) for being an "easy-rider" on the NATO bandwagon, senior officials, including the current defence minister, have used the pulpit afforded by Canada's sacrifices in Afghanistan to try to persuade allies to do more.[43] Public awareness of European skittishness toward the dangers of combat (although not perhaps the reasons behind it) is manifest in Canadian discourse but has not translated into any deep-seated resentment. If it had been, there is little reason to believe that this would resonate on the other side of the Atlantic. On issues ranging from freer trade to security, Canada is seldom on Europe's mind. Compared to the constant, multi-level and multi-issue interactions between the North American partners, a harmonious but comparatively distant relationship prevails with Europe. Efforts to expand that relationship through a 2005 framework agreement to facilitate Canadian participation in EU-led security operations, or the more recent talks on a Canada-EU free trade accord, have as yet borne little fruit. Meanwhile, the relief which greeted the announcement that President Barack Obama would make his first foreign visit to Canada indicates that Ottawa is counting on the administration to quickly address pressing bilateral issues. It remains to be seen if this popular president will be able to persuade Canada to remain an active participant in his most important foreign policy project after 2011.

Afghanistan: Domestic Pressures and Trans-Atlantic Risks

Following the attacks of 9/11 and the invocation of Article 5 of the Washington Treaty, Canada contributed ground and naval forces to the US-led campaign to rid Afghanistan of the Taliban and al-Qaeda. An initial six-month deployment of troops to the ground battle in 2002 was followed by a deployment of an infantry battle group to the Kabul area as part of ISAF. As the latter began to expand its presence elsewhere in the country and allies responded to calls for forces in the northern and western provinces, the Liberal government agreed to shift the CF to the more volatile south. Forces currently deployed in the vicinity of Kandahar include a combined-arms battle group and supporting units, but also a significant civilian component for reconstruction purposes, illustrating the importance attached to the Comprehensive/Whole-of-Government Approach.

After winning a minority government in early 2006, the Conservatives pledged to keep Canadian forces in Afghanistan until 2009. In 2007, ostensibly to ensure that the mission did not become an election issue if the minority government was defeated on a confidence motion, the government took a resolution before parliament to remain in-country until the end of 2011. Prime Minister Harper secured the support of opposition Liberals, but objections were raised by the BQ and the NDP on the grounds that legislators had inadequate time to debate the topic. They also disputed the commitment on pragmatic as well as ideological grounds. Some parliamentarians wondered if NATO's ambitious objectives could be accomplished at reasonable cost, and whether the apparent focus on combat operations would have the desired result. Others fumed at what was perceived to be another misadventure concocted by the widely-disliked Bush Administration.

While public opinion has been split on the wisdom of Canada's mission in Kandahar, with a slight majority favouring withdrawal in or before 2011, no widespread or sustained "Bring the Troops Home" campaign has yet emerged. Major (print) media outlets have been generally in favour of staying the course until that time. The editorial boards of the two nationally-circulated newspapers—the *National Post* and *The Globe and Mail*—have expressed support for continuing engagement even as casualties have risen and the prime minister has (belatedly) acknowledged that the eradication of the Taliban and the establishment of Western-style democracy is impossible.[44] The editorial board of the largest English-language daily, *The Toronto Star,* is also generally supportive of the mission, although its op-ed writers are almost universally opposed.[45] Quebec's largest English daily, *The Gazette* of Montreal, is also supportive, being part of the Canwest media group that owns the *National Post* and many other (supportive) regional papers.[46]

All this might help explain how despite public nervousness, most Canadians have (so far) been willing to accept the financial and human costs of the Afghan commitment, and why the Canadian military remains among the most respected institutions in the country. As a result, any change in government before 2011 will not likely result in a precipitous withdrawal. At the same time, polling data reveal that most Canadians do not believe that the government has adequately explained the rationale for the country's continuing presence in a country where political progress seems slight, violence is on the rise, and the costs in blood and treasure are steadily mounting.[47] How to explain this apparent contradiction between (élite) media support and public disquiet? Quite possibly it stems from a widespread acknowledgement that having achieved a hard-won political consensus to remain in place to a fixed date, there is little to be gained domestically by departing early. In addition, having made a very public commitment to the allies to remain in place until 2011, any early departure would undermine Ottawa's ability to encourage less-committed allies to take up the slack. The answer may also lie in Canada's foreign and security policy tradition. Even if the current government does not make the link, Canadians implicitly realize that to abandon a blighted country to politically regressive forces is to set back the cause of building a stable, open and inclusive international society. Derek Burney, Canada's former ambassador to the US, and a member of a non-government panel which assessed the future of Canada's role in Afghanistan, summed it up thus:

> To the critics who say fundamentally that we should not be in Afghanistan, I ask the following question: If we are not willing to commit our military resources when asked to do so by the United Nations, for a mission co-ordinated by NATO, in a country whose democratically elected government wants us and whose citizens desperately need us, then precisely where and when would Canada be prepared to do so?[48]

While the use of armed force in a distant, complex environment has tried the patience of a public and political class stubbornly (yet decreasingly) clinging to the memory of the low-risk peacekeeping missions of yore, Canada has partially re-discovered its martial spirit. It has also re-discovered the importance of the trans-Atlantic relationship as a way of sharing risk, although allied reluctance to do more could result in disillusionment. Some, including veteran defence scholar Douglas Bland of Queen's University, argue that regardless of outcome of mission, Canada will eventually eschew any future commitment to joint operations at the higher end of the conflict spectrum.[49] If this were to come to pass, it will have obvious consequences for NATO's mutual defence clause. It might anyway. As the Alliance was conceived to defend Europe and fewer Canadians count Europe as their ancestral homeland, the salience of the trans-Atlantic link may grow weaker in the public mind.[50] On the other hand, a December 2008 poll by the Innovative Research Group found that Canadians strongly support intervention for humanitarian purposes,[51] raising the possibility that framing Afghanistan's plight in humanitarian terms may stabilize public support for continued engagement—something the trans-Atlantic partners would undoubtedly welcome.

The Future of the Trans-Atlantic Partnership

Despite deeply-rooted internationalist traditions, it is anyone's guess how long or to what degree Canadians will value their membership in the North Atlantic alliance. That Canada remains a partner in the absence of an existential threat may be an indication of its faith in that partnership or its inability to conceive of a relationship without Europe to counter the immense geo-strategic pull of the United States. The return of American multilateralism under Barack Obama may make it politically palatable for allies, including Canada, to remain committed to security operations currently underway, or even do more. But this sense of goodwill and optimism sits uncomfortably with what the International Institute of Strategic Studies observed in the preamble to the 2009 edition of *The Military Balance*—namely a "diminishing will-power and capacity among European states for sustained projection of . . . military power."[52] Indeed, the allied response to Obama's plea for more resources for the fight in Afghanistan seemed to fall on deaf ears at the April 2009 summit. Europe's pledge of a few extra troops to provide security for the August 2009 Afghan presidential elections was dismissed by at least one American journal as "a mixture of pacifism and free-riding."[53] Might Canada suffer the same fatigue after 2011? If Afghanistan ends badly or with little sign of progress, political and public opinion may succumb to Professor Bland's pessimistic scenario, resulting in a period of overseas retrenchment that might only be remedied by a "return" to the days of low-risk peacekeeping.

Like its allies, Canada welcomed the surge of US forces into Afghanistan in 2009 and looks forward to learning how much the Obama Administration intends to invest in Afghan reconstruction over the medium to long term. But it is also waiting for the administration to make its views known on how NATO can help foster international security in the 21st century. Questions linger as to how far to the east the alliance should expand and what issue-areas its strategic vision should encompass. Ottawa is unlikely to buck any trend toward restraint in offering membership to aspirants on the borders with Russia, although it could ask for clarity on what political criteria aspiring states must meet in addition to performance criteria. If a sovereign state with strong democratic credentials, lying contiguous to NATO territory, freely expresses the desire to join the organization, can a third party have the right of veto?

Although NATO's 60th anniversary has presented Canada with an opportunity to help revitalize the Strategic Concept, the government has made little effort to articulate its views—at least publicly—let alone engage Canadians on the matter. Admittedly, the notion of Canada as a vocal, proactive modernizer might seem quaint in light of its status as one of NATO's smaller military powers. But as the former US ambassador to Canada, David Wilkins, told Canadian business leaders : "You've earned a vast amount of credibility with the major role in Afghanistan and the heavy lifting you're doing there. This increasing visibility and credibility gives you more standing to talk about issues."[54]

One way to exploit that standing is to pose (and answer) a series of questions. In an era of diffuse and non-traditional threats, what needs does the trans-Atlantic security relationship fulfil? Will it be a mini-UN, one committed to advancing UN principles as the Washington Treaty states? What mechanisms should it adopt to integrate non-NATO EU (and non-EU) states which have similar values and interests and what role should the latter be given in collective decision-making? Is European-style "permanent structured cooperation" in the cards, whereby groupings of states push ahead with defence initiatives without the benefit of a full consensus?[55] This suggests a loosening of the requirement that allies share burdens and risks equitably, although the ISAF experience suggests that this process is well underway.

A related issue involves the definition of security itself. Policy-makers confront a broader range of issues than in decades past. Which of these can be addressed by long-standing organizations such as NATO, and which should be left to other bodies or ad hoc groupings of allied (and non-allied) states? Should energy and cyber security be areas for allied co-operation, or are the partners affected so differently that the topics are best left to other forums? Should Arctic security be an issue, as suggested by former NATO Secretary-General Jaap de Hoop Scheffer?[56] Clearly, stretching the alliance's geopolitical remit to deal with all manner of emerging issues risks diluting its essential purpose. But if the security environment places a premium on issues and capabilities outside of NATO's traditional realm of activity, the partnership will almost certainly lose its value over time.

In the wake of the Russo-Georgian war, should the allies return to first principles and signal a re-commitment to territorial defence? If so, how is this to be done without alienating an already-surly Russia or diminishing its ability to undertake the expeditionary operations that some members see as the best way of keeping the alliance busy and therefore relevant?[57] Is a rhetorical re-commitment to Article 5 all that the alliance's eastern members can expect, as few allied governments are likely to agree to the re-introduction of the large-scale military exercises of the 1980s? Or is the establishment of a cyber-security defence centre in Estonia to counter computer attacks from Russia sufficient, given that asymmetric attacks will be the preferred method of showing displeasure with NATO?

Finally, how can the Comprehensive/Whole-of-Government Approach be further institutionalized so that skills and resources for non-kinetic operations (i.e., those wielded by non-military actors) are in adequate supply and can be deployed as rapidly as military forces? If, on the other hand, the approach is reaping few rewards in Afghanistan, should it be modified or replaced by a more effective doctrine?

The current political situation in Ottawa—where a minority government rules and where domestic/continental economic and security issues will always resonate more strongly with voters—is almost certain to impede efforts to muster the necessary political capital to rejuvenate the trans-Atlantic relationship. A fragile government is unlikely to want to articulate any "big ideas" which may draw fire from opposition parties. But the problem is one of think-ing small and un-strategically. As John Ibbitson of *The Globe and Mail* causti-cally noted, "Canada has a series of positions on things, but, in a larger sense, our country no longer has a foreign policy."[58] The problem is exacerbated by the tendency to accord international security policy a lower priority on the government's agenda. Cabinet shuffles frequently leave finance ministers in place while foreign and defence ministers (there have been seven of the former since 2000) experience greater turn-over, resulting in loss of focus and insti-tutional memory. New ministers require a great deal of time to familiarize themselves with complex issues and re-build working relationships with their allied counterparts.

But even in the absence of such turmoil, Canadians and their leaders would face at least four obstacles to the renewal of the trans-Atlantic security partnership. As previously stated, official Ottawa is necessarily focussed on the policies taking shape south of the border. Border security, the interplay between energy supplies and environmental policy, and the blatantly protec-tionist "Buy American" directive in the Obama economic stimulus plan make for a full in-basket. Second, there is a risk that the trans-Atlantic relationship becomes one-dimensional in the Canadian mind, seen through the lens of Afghanistan rather than one meant to serve a variety of common interests. Policy-makers in Ottawa need to achieve a higher level of literacy vis-à-vis both long-term and unforeseen security risks, and share their thoughts with the Canadian public. A better understanding of Europe's evolving strategic culture and political priorities is also essential if Canada is to achieve key ob-jectives such as freer trade, or head off potential disputes arising from clashes between energy security and environmental sustainability.

Third, as noted above, Canada places rather little value in broadening re-lations with the European Union outside of trade matters. Notwithstanding the 2005 Canada-EU Framework Agreement that would facilitate Canadian participation in EU-led security operations, little interest in implementing the agreement has been shown by either party. As a result, little thought is given as to the desirability of a deeper NATO-EU security partnership where each organization brings distinct but complementary capabilities to the table.

The fourth challenge is that the European partners, pre-occupied with economic uncertainty, EU reform, and strengthening ties with the Obama Administration, display a reciprocal apathy or ignorance toward Canada.

Evidence abounds that discussions on trans-Atlantic relations routinely ignore the non-US half of North America. The German Marshall Fund's 2008 edition of *Transatlantic Trends* reveals that the opinions of Canadians on the major security issues of the day are completely omitted from the research.[59] Similarly, an editorial appearing on the English-language website of *Der Spiegel* provocatively suggested that the US and the EU dispense with NATO in favour of a new trans-Atlantic security architecture designed to address the more numerous non-military threats to global security.[60] No thought is given to Canada's potential role, let alone to the desirability of keeping a committed internationalist and loyal security partner from succumbing to neo-isolationism and continentalism.

Conclusion

Canada and its allies confront a dynamic security environment—one that would tax the analytical and prescriptive abilities of the best strategic thinkers. The trans-Atlantic security partnership has served its members well, and retains a certain degree of utility in the post-9/11 world. Its capacity to adapt to meet some of the new challenges and integrate new partners virtually ensures that it will survive both the difficulties posed by the mission to Afghanistan and the occasional disagreements which pundits seize upon as evidence of imminent collapse. However, the increasing importance of non-military yet strategically important issues such as economic stability, energy security, and environmental protection may oblige the trans-Atlantic partners (and others) to search for other forums in which to discuss and implement solutions. Thus the salience—indeed, the survival—of an organization designed primarily to apply military force in the Euro-Atlantic area should not be taken for granted.

Guided by a strategic culture that has remained largely unchanged over the past several decades, Canada will continue to pay its membership dues in the alliance, while continuing the process of military transformation. However, it will take considerable political energy to both maintain that level of commitment and ensure that the security partnership remains relevant to Canadians over the longer term. It is uncertain whether this will come to pass, as the current government has yet to initiate an internal debate over the Alliance's Strategic Concept. And there can be little doubt that continental concerns will compete for the attention of Canadian policy-makers over the next few years. Canada's partners would do well to take note of its recent contributions to collective security, its commitment to multilateralism, its privileged economic and security relationship with the United States, its awareness of non-traditional security issues, and proactively engage it on these and other topics of mutual interest. The trans-Atlantic community, facing an uncertain future, will surely be the better for it.

3　The United States and the Transatlantic Relationship

A Test for U.S. Foreign and National Security Policy

Joyce P. Kaufman

Introduction

As this chapter was being drafted, the Obama administration was debating what to do about Afghanistan. In September 2009, an unclassified version of the report drafted by General Stanley A. McChrystal, Commander, NATO International Security Assistance Force (COMISAF), was released publicly[1] while the complete classified version of the report was provided to the Obama administration. This report came when the Obama administration was considering its options regarding Afghanistan, and amid growing uncertainty on the part of the European allies about the viability of the mission. In August 2009, President Obama gave a speech to the Veterans of Foreign Wars in which he dubbed Afghanistan a "war of necessity."[2] Even so, that war was also threatening to become the quagmire that Iraq had appeared to be, not too long ago.

Consistent with the Status of Forces Agreement signed in Baghdad in November 2008,[3] U.S. combat forces were being withdrawn from Iraq, and the Iraqis were readying themselves to take over that operation with the U.S. remaining in a "support" role. No such agreement exists in the case of Afghanistan, nor is there any publicly known exit strategy at this time. In fact, the presidential election that was held in Afghanistan on August 20, 2009, which the United States and the other allies had hoped "would deliver a popular mandate for a strong, democratic government able to address the nation's security woes,"[4] has only contributed to the confusion as to the future of the country. With that uncertainty has come further skepticism on the part of those U.S. allies who have contributed to the Afghan effort. While it is the United States who initiated the war against Afghanistan in October 2001 and while the bulk of the troops are U.S. forces, the conduct of the war depends upon the support of the NATO allies, which has been waning over time.

In many ways, the situation regarding Afghanistan stands as a microcosm as well as illustration of the dilemmas facing the U.S. relationship with its traditional allies. On the one hand, the United States has a long-standing and strong political, economic, and military/security relationship with allies on both sides of the Atlantic—Canada is very much one of those countries. But, on the other hand, as the EU has grown in cohesion and strength, and as U.S. leadership has been undermined in part by the United States' own decisions, a schism has resulted.

This schism can be further seen with the United States' decision in September 2009 not to deploy the nuclear missile shield in Poland and the Czech Republic.[5] This plan, which was developed by the Bush administration specifically to counter the perceived threat to Europe from Iranian nuclear weapons, infuriated Russia, thereby contributing to tensions between the United States and that country. In fact, while the allies, especially the Czech Republic, initially were wary of having the system based on their territory, the decision to cancel it was also cause for alarm, thereby putting the United States in another difficult position at a time when it needed allied support.

This chapter will explore in more detail some of the challenges and also some of the options available to the Obama administration in strengthening and rebuilding the transatlantic relationship. The decisions this administration makes and the approach it takes toward its allies will have implications that go far beyond the presidency of Barack Obama, just as the Obama administration has to address the policies made by the previous administrations, especially those of George W. Bush. The chapter will put relations with the United States' closest allies into a domestic as well as international context, something made more challenging in light of the global economic crisis that further limits U.S. options. After addressing the changing concept of the threat, an overview of the strategic culture, and the strains on the U.S. military because of wars in Iraq and Afghanistan, it will draw some general conclusions about the future of the transatlantic alliance from the perspective of the United States.

Transatlantic Relations and the
Obama Administration

In an article in *Foreign Affairs* in summer 2006, Philip H. Gordon wrote: "U.S. foreign policy has historically been marked by regular and sometimes wild swings between internationalism and isolationism, and those swings have been influenced by changes in *threat perceptions*, the amount of *available resources*, and the *level of domestic political support*" (emphasis added).[6] Thus, Gordon identified many of the factors that are directly relevant to the understanding of U.S. policy that have affected its relations with its allies across the Atlantic in the past, as well as those that will inform them in the future.

Also writing in *Foreign Affairs* but more recently, former National Security Advisor Zbigniew Brzezinski noted about NATO and the transatlantic relationship that when the alliance was created 60 years ago, it was the European states which "yearned for guaranteed U.S. power but had no effective power themselves." As a way of mitigating their "collective insecurity," Article 5 committed the United States to their defense. Now, however, the allies feel relatively secure but "it is the United States that needs committed allies in that war [with Afghanistan]."[7] In other words, the relationship has shifted, requiring the United States to rethink and perhaps alter its own approach to transatlantic relations.

Clearly, there has been much analysis of the transatlantic relationship both historically and also more recently in the wake of the decision to go to war with Iraq. What we see today is a U.S. president who came into office with a broader global outlook and understanding than previous presidents have had, but also, as Brzezinski stressed, it is the United States that now needs the allies if it is to accomplish its goals, including its mission in Afghanistan. The balance of power seems to have shifted, and if the United States is to be successful not only in its war in Afghanistan but also in asserting its role as a leader internationally once again, it needs to rethink, reevaluate, and revise its policies regarding the transatlantic relationship.

In his inaugural address on January 20, 2009, President Obama made clear what some of his U.S. foreign policy priorities would be. To all who were watching and listening, he sent these words: "know that America is a friend of each nation and every man, woman, and child who seeks a future of peace and dignity, and that *we are ready to lead once more*" (emphasis added).[8] After eight years in which U.S. influence internationally waned and its power—especially soft power—was undermined, many around the world as well as at home were waiting to hear what the new president would say and to learn in what direction he would take the United States.[9]

As he stated in his address, Obama came into office facing critical challenges to the United States' foreign and security policy. Not least among those would be restoring the relationship between the United States and its European allies, which arguably has been the most critical and enduring facet of post-World War II U.S. foreign policy.[10] In the eight years of the Bush administration, that relationship unraveled, leading to questions about U.S. leadership, commitment, and intentions. If the transatlantic relationship is important to the Obama administration, and all indications are that it is, then one of the administration's highest priorities will be to determine not only how to repair that frayed relationship but also how to ensure that it is a central part of U.S. policy once again. This will not be an easy task, nor will it be possible for the Obama administration to arrive at a blanket policy that covers all the European allies. Rather, what this administration needs to remember is that "Europe" is not one country but many, each of which has its own priorities and national interests, as well as having interests as a collective through organizations such as the European Union and NATO. At a time when the EU in general, and the individual European countries in particular have been moving forward and developing their own policies, the burden will be on the United States to create policies that will once again cement the transatlantic relationship both within and outside formal organizational structures.

Obama actually started to try to rebuild the ties between the United States and Europe while he was a candidate. In a much-heralded trip to Germany in July 2008, then-candidate Obama spoke near the Brandenburg Gate to a crowd estimated at 200,000. In that speech, Obama drew on the past to remind all who were listening about the long history of friendship and support that has characterized U.S.-German relations since the end of the Second World War. And he affirmed the importance of the ties between the two nations, while also acknowledging the need to move beyond the current gulf between them, as seen in this long, but important, excerpt from his speech:

> ... if we're honest with each other, *we know that sometimes, on both sides of the Atlantic, we have drifted apart, and forgotten our shared destiny.*

> ... there have been differences between America and Europe. No doubt, there will be differences in the future. But the burdens of global citizenship continue to bind us together.... In this new century, Americans and Europeans alike will be required to do more—not less. *Partnership and cooperation among na-*

tions is not a choice; it is the one way, the only way, to protect our common security and advance our common humanity.

That is why the greatest danger of all is to allow new walls to divide us from one another.

The walls between old allies on either side of the Atlantic cannot stand.[11]

Obama took the opportunity to travel to France and Britain as well as Germany. According to a Pew poll taken just before his visit in July 2008, in France, "84% of those following the U.S. presidential race say they have confidence in Obama to do the right thing in world affairs; only a third, however, are confident in McCain. The numbers were almost identical in Germany (82% confidence in Obama, 33% in McCain)."[12] This suggests not only that Obama was aware of the need to mend fences even before he came into office—and started to build the groundwork for doing so while still a candidate—but also that the European public was willing to give him the chance, a change from the attitude that they had held about President Bush by the time that he left office.

On his first official trip to Europe as president in April 2009, Obama took additional steps. Polls taken at that time show that not only did the trip affirm the president's popularity abroad, but it helped solidify his position at home regarding foreign policy. By July 2009, a Pew Global Attitudes Poll reported that "the image of the United States has improved markedly in most parts of the world. . . . Improvements in the U.S. image have been most pronounced in Western Europe, where favorable ratings for both the nation and the American people have soared."[13] Going into meetings with European leaders in the fall of 2009 about both the economy and Afghanistan, this surge in popularity put President Obama in a stronger position to request support for his policies. But it was not strong enough to counter the growing doubts of the European public, especially about Afghanistan.

September 11 and the Changing Political Context

Understanding the current situation requires putting U.S. policies into context. In the January–February 2000 volume of *Foreign Affairs,* Condoleezza Rice laid out what she saw as the priorities of the United States in a Republican (George W. Bush) administration. She said: "The United States has found it exceedingly difficult to define its 'national interest' in the absence of Soviet power." But she also noted that such times "of transition" are important because "one can affect the shape of the world to come."[14] While many of the subsequent Bush administration policies were affected by the events of September 11, the article is instructive. Rice proved prescient when she stated: "The president must remember that the military is a special instrument. It is lethal, and it is meant to be . . . it is certainly not designed to build a civilian society." Rather, in her estimation, "Military force is best used *to support clear political goals,* whether limited, such as expelling Saddam from Kuwait, or comprehensive, such as demanding the unconditional surrender of Japan and Germany during World War II" (emphasis added).[15]

At the time of the publication of this article, Rice, and presumably the entire Bush defense and foreign policy team, appeared to be focused rightly on defining national interest in the absence of the Soviet threat. Included among the issues to be addressed were a re-examination of NATO, specifically focusing on what holds the Atlantic alliance together, and a redefinition of its mission in light of changing global priorities.[16]

The attacks of 9/11 significantly altered the priorities of the Bush administration, which came to recognize the "war on terror" as the highest national security priority. From that time forward, all aspects of Bush administration foreign and security policy stemmed from, and were justified by, the need to support the war on terror. It is therefore instructive to go back to the Rice article and note the attention that she paid to U.S. national interest defined "by a desire to foster the spread of freedom, prosperity and peace."[17] It was the desire to "spread freedom" and democracy that ultimately justified the United States decision to go to war in Iraq, eclipsing the initial rationale for the attack, which was "regime change" and eliminating the alleged threat of weapons of mass destruction from Iraq.

It is important to note that the NATO nations were unified in their support for the United States immediately after the attacks, although that unity did not last. On September 12, NATO invoked Article 5 for the first time in its history. The North Atlantic Council issued a press release on September 12, 2001, affirming that Article 5 "stipulates that in the event of attacks falling within its purview, each Ally will assist the Party that has been attacked by taking such action as it deems necessary. Accordingly, the United States' Allies stand ready to provide the assistance that may be required as a consequence of these acts of barbarism."[18] By early October, under the framework of Article 5, NATO had started to deploy Airborne Warning and Control aircraft (also known as AWACS) to the United States. However, this was the only act that NATO took in support of the United States, not because NATO did not want to do more, but because the United States, under the Bush administration, preferred to work independently of NATO or any other formal alliance relationship.

In January 2002, Lord Robertson, then NATO Secretary General, gave a speech in New York in which he affirmed the critical role that NATO *could* play in the strategic context that had arisen as a result of the September 11 attacks. He invoked Article 5 and the importance of the rapidity with which the Allies made the decision to respond as a group. According to Lord Robertson, that decision "demonstrated that the mutual trust and commitment on which the Alliance has been based for 52 years remain tangible, real and reciprocal." And he reaffirmed that NATO "remains the pre-eminent and unrivalled forum for preserving the security of all its members." He also quoted President Bush as saying: "This has never happened before, that NATO has come to help defend our country, but it happened in this time of need and for that we are grateful."[19] What is now striking is how quickly, after such a strong and unified beginning, the NATO nations became divided after the United States moved to chart its own course of action irrespective of the Allies.

It is well known by now that the decision to invade Iraq had a devastating effect on the relationship between the United States and its allies. NATO was deeply divided, with Great Britain remaining one of the United States' strongest allies, but Germany and France were united in their opposition. Increasingly Germany and France, often joined by Belgium and Luxembourg, were vocal in their opposition to the U.S. policy decisions surrounding the invasion of Iraq.[20] Unlike the situation for President Bush's father, who had been able to build a "coalition of the willing" to help the United States fight against the forces of Saddam Hussein in the first Persian Gulf War in 1991, this time the number of countries willing to support the United States was far smaller. But of greater significance is the fact that many of the countries which most vehemently opposed the United States' decision to invade were among the United States' closest allies. In fact, the U.S. decision to invade Iraq without a UN Security Council resolution deeply divided NATO, with lines especially drawn between a Franco-German alliance versus the traditional Anglo-American one.

In February 2003, France, Germany and Belgium decided not to support the Bush administration's request under Article 4 of the NATO Treaty to prepare for the defense of Turkey in anticipation of a possible spread of the conflict. This action raised serious concerns about alliance unity, especially if NATO needed to respond to an attack on Turkey using Article 5 once again. The issue ultimately was resolved when the discussion was moved to the Defense Planning Committee, where France did not have a vote.[21] But it also illustrates the level of division already apparent.

Serious strains between the United States and Turkey emerged, in part as a result of this, but also because of the pressure the Bush administration put on the Turkish government for permission to use Turkey as a staging area for the attack on Iraq, which threatened to incite anti-American sentiment among the public. As discussed in the chapter in this volume from the Turkish perspective (Chapter 7), the United States has long appreciated the importance of Turkey as an ally because of its strategic position as well as its role as an Islamic nation straddling Europe. In this case, as in others, it was left to the Obama administration to rebuild this relationship. The U.S. made strides in doing so when Obama visited Turkey and addressed the parliament in Ankara. But this serves as yet another example of the divide that has emerged in NATO, and what the United States and the Obama administration need to do to repair the frayed relationship often working country-by-country.

The decision by the United States to invade Iraq over the objections of its allies and absent full NATO support can be seen as the start of the transatlantic schism that the current administration must confront. But perhaps even more critical, this can also be seen as the point when U.S. leadership internationally started to erode.

Changing Perceptions of the United States

The decline in the European public's perceptions of the United States following the invasion of Iraq can be seen dramatically both in the findings of the Pew Global Attitudes Project[22] and in the Transatlantic Trends survey published by the German Marshall Fund.[23] In both cases, the European and the American public shared some common concerns, especially about the threat posed by a nuclear Iran, by Islamic fundamentalist extremists, and by instability in the Middle East. However, what is more important from the perspective of U.S. relations with Europe is the decline in Europeans' positive views of the United States, although the extent of this decline did vary by country.

The Transatlantic Trends survey found that "the proportion of Europeans who view U.S. leadership in world affairs as desirable has reversed since 2002, from 64% positive to 37% this year [2006], and from 31% negative to 57%. Among European countries, the greatest decline was in Germany, from 68% positive in 2002 to 43% in 2006." The survey also noted that only three countries, the Netherlands, Romania and the United Kingdom, "view U.S. leadership more positively than negatively," and even then, the findings were moderate.[24] These negative opinions about the United States and its role as a global leader were also reflected in a decline in European support for NATO, which is heavily perceived as tied to the United States. In that area, "European support for NATO has declined from 69% in 2002 to 55% in 2006, with large declines in countries traditionally perceived as strong supporters of NATO— Germany, Italy, Poland and Turkey."[25]

A 2008 Pew poll found very clearly that "the U.S. image is suffering almost everywhere," and that part of this is due to the fact that "in the most economically developed countries, people blame America for the financial crisis." In addition, "opposition to key elements of American foreign policy is widespread in Western Europe, and positive views of the U.S. have declined steeply among many of America's longtime European allies."[26] What this poll further underscores is the interrelationship between the United States' economic situation and that of the rest of the world, resulting in a further undermining of the role of the United States internationally.

It is also possible to look back and gauge the anger that many in the United States felt toward the Europeans, who did not support the United States decision to go to war with Iraq. Perhaps the embodiment of this was the decision to rename "French fries" as "freedom fries," and "French toast" as "freedom toast," as was done in cafeterias of the House of Representatives in March 2003. "'This action today is a small, but symbolic effort to show the strong displeasure of many on Capitol Hill with the actions of our so-called ally, France,' said Rep. Bob Ney, R-Ohio, the chairman of the Committee on House Administration." Ney, who chaired the committee which oversees the cafeterias, said that the decision came after other colleagues also requested the change.[27] (Three years later, in August 2006, the original names were reinstated.) Although apparently small and superficial, the change in names reflected American public opinion. The 2006 Pew Global Attitudes survey revealed a change in U.S. perceptions of France from time of the beginning of the war in Iraq. As of 2006, 52% of Americans surveyed "had a favorable impressions of France, still below the pre-Iraq War level of 79% in February 2002, but up from 46% last year [2005]."[28]

Of course, further changes in U.S. attitudes and public opinion can be seen more recently. Domestically, the growing displeasure of the United States public with the decisions of the Bush administration could not be demonstrated any more clearly than in the outcome of the election of November 2008, which not only brought Barack Obama to the presidency but also handed both houses of Congress to the Democrats. Although by election day the dramatic decline in the economy had eclipsed the issue of the Iraq War, all indications were that up to that point, Iraq was the major foreign policy issue for the American public.

And, as is noted in the Pew polls above, the efforts that Obama has made thus far to rebuild the ties with Europe are having an impact. However, the Pew poll also found that "sending more troops to Afghanistan is the only policy that does not engender broad global support. In fact, majorities in most countries oppose the added deployments. This includes the publics of several NATO countries—such as Britain, Germany, Spain and Canada—most of which in recent years have called for removing troops from Afghanistan."[29]

Polls taken in late summer to early fall of 2009 have shown that the American public in general approves of the way in which the president is handling the situations in both Iraq and Afghanistan. For example, one public opinion poll released by Fox News, which tends to be conservative and anti-Obama in general, found virtually no change in his rating regarding Iraq, and a slight drop (from 56% to 49%) in his approval of his handling of Afghanistan since July.[30] A *Washington Post* poll taken in August 2009 surprisingly showed the strongest support coming from Republicans; 70% said that the war is worth fighting.[31] In short, Obama will need to convince the American public, even those who were supporters who voted for him, as well as the allies about the wisdom of the course of action that he is pursuing regarding the war in Afghanistan. Convincing either constituency will not be an easy task.

NATO in Afghanistan

While it is clear that the U.S. decision to go to war against Iraq in 2003 had a deleterious effect on transatlantic relations, the initial decision to attack Afghanistan, one of the bases for Al Qaeda, was seen as justified and was greeted positively on the whole. The initial attacks, on October 7, 2001, were supported by the British in what then-Prime Minister Tony Blair described as "acting in Britain's national interest." Initial estimates were that two hundred Britons were killed in the attacks of 9/11, although the actual number turned out to be far lower.[32] However, Blair also said that "even if no British citizens had died, it would be right to act. This atrocity was an attack on us all."[33]

Despite popular support for the attack on Afghanistan, according to a news account printed just prior to that attack, the Bush administration made the decision to limit the consultation and involvement of other nations initially, with the exception of the British. According to one senior administration official, "the fewer people you have to rely on, the fewer permissions you have to get." And another sign that the U.S. wanted to act independently was "its rejection of the United Nations Secretary General Kofi Annan's entreaties that any American military action be subject to Security Council approval . . ."[34] A few months later, the war expanded, other countries were included, and ultimately it became a NATO mission. Even with NATO support, the longer the war continued with little apparent progress, the more it too started to divide the allies.

The UN created the International Security Assistance Force (ISAF) after the ousting of the Taliban regime in December 2001 as a UN-mandated international force. "ISAF is not a UN force, but is a coalition of the willing deployed under the authority of the UN Security Council." ISAF was created initially to assist the Afghan Transitional Authority reconstruct the country. Since August 2003, "ISAF is supported and led by NATO, and financed by the troop contributing nations. The Alliance is responsible for the command, coordination and planning of the force."[35] According to an analysis by the Congressional Research Service, the NATO mission in Afghanistan "is a test of the allies' military capabilities and their political will to undertake a complex mission." In NATO's first "out of area" mission that takes it beyond Europe, the report continued, "the allies wish to create a 'new' NATO, able to go beyond the European theater and combat new threats such as terrorism and the proliferation of weapons of mass destruction (WMD)."[36] This mission was a test of the "new NATO" but also of U.S. leadership, at a time when it was being questioned.

NATO's role in Afghanistan has been described as three-fold: first, through ISAF, it "assists the Afghan authorities in extending and exercising its authority and influence across the country, creating the conditions for stabilization and reconstruction"; second, it provides a Senior Civilian Representative, who, among other things, is "responsible for advancing the political-military aspects of the Alliance's commitment to the country"; and third, in cooperation with Afghanistan, it has a program that involves defense reform, defense institution-building and "the military aspects of security sector reform."[37] It is the latter role that is most contentious.

There are currently five regional commands in Afghanistan, each headed by a lead nation including Germany, Italy, France, Canada and the United States, and all under ISAF operational control. In total, 40 countries are involved with the ISAF mission in Afghanistan; the United States has the largest number of troops deployed, followed by Britain, Germany and Canada. After the United States, Britain and Canada have sustained the greatest number of losses: these losses have contributed to questions about the NATO's role and mission, as well as its likelihood of success.[38] Troops from various nations may operate under "national caveats," which are specific restrictions or limitations imposed on the tasks that those forces can engage in. "At the NATO summit in Riga, Latvia, in November 2006, allied leaders sought to reduce the caveats in Afghanistan." Some forces have done so; however, others remain under the decisions of their capitals.[39]

With the passage of time, it has become more difficult to raise forces from the allies. This had led to criticism of the allies by Defense Secretary Robert Gates, but after the NATO Defense Ministers' meeting of December 2007, "he acknowledged that domestic political problems are preventing some allies from increasing their force levels in Afghanistan." According to information obtained in interviews, Congressional Research Service (CRS) analyst Paul Gallis wrote: "Allied government officials state privately that their populations are reluctant to follow the Bush Administration, largely due to the U.S. invasion of Iraq and subsequent criticism of the United States in Europe and the Middle East."[40]

Clearly, the difficulty in raising forces in continuing support of the ISAF mission is only one of the issues that divides the United States from its allies. At a time when other countries had decreased their troop strength in Afghanistan, or were threatening to withdraw them altogether, the Obama administration initiated a policy decision to increase its forces there, in a move that can be seen as parallel to the 2007 surge in Iraq. However, that policy is now being questioned as the Obama administration must decide how to respond to General McChrystal's report and the request to increase U.S. troop strength still further at a time of growing U.S. and European skepticism about the mission.

In his comprehensive report on NATO and Afghanistan written in 2008,

Paul Gallis documents growing divisions over mission, merging of commands, and even how best to accomplish the agreed-upon mission. The differences were exacerbated by a surge in Taliban activity and increasing casualties, which contributed to a concomitant decline in the publics' support for the mission. Although Gallis notes that "the governments of the United States, Britain, and Canada share similar views on how ISAF should fulfill its mission"[41] and they have all sent combat forces to the most unstable parts of the country, in the case of Canada, especially, public support for this mission has eroded.[42] As one U.S. newspaper report about the growing strains in the alliance noted, "stress has grown along with casualties, domestic pressures and a sense that the war is not improving, according to a wide variety of senior U.S. and NATO-member officials."[43]

The disparity in casualties concomitant with the U.S. call for more troops has furthered the tensions among the allies over Afghanistan.[44] Again, according to one news report, "while Washington has long called for allies to send more forces, NATO countries involved in some of the fiercest fighting have complained that they are suffering the heaviest losses. The United States supplies about half of the 54,000 foreign troops in Afghanistan, they say, but the British, Canadians, and Dutch are engaged in regular combat in the volatile south."[45] What that means is that "the Canadian death rate, proportional to the overall size of its forces, is higher than that of U.S. troops in Afghanistan or Iraq, a Canadian government analyst concluded last year."[46]

Clearly, what can be seen is an alliance that initially agreed to the basic purposes of the mission in Afghanistan but has differences regarding how best to implement and sustain that mission. Further, continued support for the Afghan mission has been eroding among the allies' publics at a time when the United States under Obama is starting to direct more attention to Afghanistan. European leaders feel the pressure from their own public at the same time that the United States is committed to increase its efforts in Afghanistan as it draws down in Iraq.

What is more telling about this particular situation is that the role of the United States within NATO and its relationship with its allies are bound up, in part, on the success of the mission in Afghanistan. That, in turn, depends on the domestic political situation within the various NATO allies, the circumstances of which the United States has little control over, and whether they can be persuaded by the Obama administration to continue to support ISAF and the agreed-upon mission in Afghanistan.

U.S. Defense and Security Policy
and Transatlantic Relations

The attacks of 9/11 altered U.S. defense and security policy significantly. From that point on, and for the duration of the Bush administration, U.S. national security policy was "founded on two pillars: promoting freedom, justice, and human dignity by working to end tyranny, promote effective democracies, and extend prosperity; and confronting the challenges of our time by leading a growing community of democracies."[47] Virtually every aspect of U.S. security, military and even foreign policy was designed to support these two broad goals. Militarily, the focus was on fighting the "war on terror," a vague concept that was tied to the need to find, ferret out and destroy those groups or individuals who allegedly were tied to Al Qaeda. This led the United States into alliances with countries such as Pakistan, which, by virtue of geography, became a critical front line in the war on terror. At the same time, it led the United States to disregard or actually alienate its traditional allies or any country that did not support the U.S.'s goals. It also required a significant rethinking of the use of U.S. military force to be more responsive to this new type of warfare against a vague enemy not tied to any nation-state, but capable of ignoring national borders.

To meet this need, and after the wars in Afghanistan and Iraq were well underway, on August 24, 2004, President Bush announced "the most comprehensive restructuring of U.S. military forces overseas since the end of the Korean War." The changes in U.S. force posture grew out of the belief that the then-existing posture was too steeped in Cold War thinking and that the military had to change to take advantage of new technologies as well as current realities.[48]

In his 2001 Quadrennial Defense Review (QDR), issued on September 30, 2001, then-Secretary of Defense Donald Rumsfeld noted that even before the attacks of 9/11, "the senior leaders of the Defense Department set out to establish a new strategy for America's defense" to refocus and guide "the development of U.S. forces and capabilities, their deployment and use."[49] The changes outlined in 2001 were reassessed and updated in the successor document, issued in February 2006. Where the 2001 document began to anticipate U.S. responses to the attacks, as Rumsfeld made clear in the preface to the subsequent document, "this 2006 Quadrennial Defense Review is submitted in the first year of this long war" (i.e., the wars in Iraq and Afghanistan).[50] It is also clear from the 2006 document that the transformation in the U.S. military that Rumsfeld outlined is consistent with his vision of what the military *should* look like, although with the advantage of hindsight, it was also clear that the current U.S. military force was inadequate to meet the larger set of tasks it faces and will continue to face.

Rumsfeld also noted that in order to realize the goals outlined, "the Department stands ready to join in a collaborative partnership with key stakeholders in the process of implementation and execution—the Congress, other agencies of the Executive Branch and alliance and coalition partners."[51] Approximately nine months after this document was issued, Rumsfeld was removed from office, to be replaced by Robert Gates. Rumsfeld's dismissal, which many had called for far earlier, was due, at least in part, to the waning of support at best, or to the outright enmity of many of those same stakeholders, brought about by the lack of progress in Iraq and Afghanistan.

In June 2008, Secretary Gates issued a National Defense Strategy (NDS) document for the United States. This document built on President Bush's 2006 National Security Strategy (NSS)[52] and the 2006 QDR by identifying lessons learned from Iraq and Afghanistan, but it was also blunt in stating that "the United States will soon have a new President and Commander-in-Chief, but the complex issues the United States faces will remain."[53] To get a more complete picture of U.S. security policy especially as it pertains to transatlantic relations, the NDS must be seen in conjunction with the National Security Strategy document.

It is important to note at the outset that the NSS document reflected the views and priorities of the Bush administration and no doubt will be amended to reflect the priorities of an Obama presidency. Nonetheless, the 2006 NSS provides some understanding of the current relationship between the U.S. and its European allies including the perspective that the Bush administration had in that regard.

The document has one section devoted to "Europe."[54] The description in this section reflects the importance of NATO as "a vital pillar of U.S. foreign policy." And it reaffirms that "Europe is home to some of our oldest and closest allies. Our cooperative relations are built on a sure foundation of shared values and interests."[55] However, it paid little attention to the ways in which the United States was going to nurture these relationships, especially in light of the growing rifts. In fact, it is also instructive to note that this document was released virtually simultaneously with the 2006 Pew Global Attitudes poll and German Marshall Fund survey, both of which showed a decline in positive attitudes toward the United States by the European public.

The National Defense Strategy of 2008 does not specify countries or regions but instead addresses the general need to "strengthen and expand alliances and partnerships." Europe is implicit in this call, especially in the recognition that the U.S. alliance system "has been a cornerstone of peace and security for more than a generation and remains the key to our success, contributing significantly to achieving all U.S. objectives. Allies often possess capabilities, skills, and knowledge we cannot duplicate."[56]

U.S. Decision on Nuclear Missile Shield: Implications for Transatlantic Relations

One of the policy decisions made by the Bush administration was to deploy a missile shield in Eastern Europe specifically to counter the threat of proposed Iranian nuclear missiles. The decision was announced in 2007, and, prior to leaving office, the Bush administration pushed negotiations with Poland and the Czech Republic to get agreement on its deployment. While the decision was greeted positively by the publics in both countries, there was a mixed reaction from the governments. The Czech government indicated that as long as there was a strong NATO requirement, then Czech security would not be undermined by the decision. Poland similarly affirmed U.S. security assurances.[57] NATO Secretary-General Anders Rasmussen welcomed the subsequent shift in U.S. policy under Obama, and indicated that he felt that the decision would lead to a greater degree of involvement of NATO regarding security decisions in the future.[58] Russia, too, reacted positively to the decision; no doubt it contributed to that country's willingness to support Obama's intention to ask for the imposition of economic sanctions against Iran in response to the revelation of a nuclear processing site near Qom. This suggests that in the reversal of that one policy decision, Obama was able to begin the process of easing tensions between the U.S. and Russia, potentially gaining that country as an ally.

Mending Fences?

The Bush Administration

In his book *Winning the Right War*, foreign policy analyst Philip Gordon notes that the Bush administration, early in its second term, started to recognize the reality that an America "that is popular, respected, reliable, and admired has a far better chance of winning needed cooperation than an America that is not." He also contends that the administration was aware of the high price it paid "for gratuitously alienating allies and that diplomatic efforts to repair relations were worthwhile."[59] This awareness resulted in an effort by then-Secretary of State Rice to begin to mend relations with the allies by traveling to Europe followed, shortly thereafter, by a trip by President Bush.

This effort to reach out to the European allies continued through Bush's second term in office, including a "farewell tour" to European capitals in June 2008. According to one account of the visit, "the question of his legacy hangs over his eight-day visit to Europe." But the same account also notes the fact that the war in Iraq "did more to strain relations with Europe—not to mention with the Muslim world—than any issue since Ronald Reagan deployed intermediate missiles in Europe in 1984 at the height of the cold war. As a result, he [Bush] remains deeply unpopular in Europe, as he does at home."[60]

In his visit, Bush himself referenced previous disputes that divided the United States and Europe, specifically the Suez Crisis and the basing of missiles in the 1980s, but claimed that "with the distance of time, we can see these differences for what they were: fleeting, disagreements between friends."[61] He also said, optimistically, that "when the time comes to welcome the new American president next January, I will be pleased to report to him that the relationship between the United States and Europe is the broadest and most vibrant it has ever been."[62] However, a lot of work and fence-mending needs to be accomplished before this statement is an accurate reflection of reality.

Gordon claims that the new administration will have to go much further than Bush's relatively newly found commitment to multilateralism and recognition of the fact that "the United States needed more international support, and that such support was not automatic."[63] However, Gordon also notes that simply "having a new face in the White House will itself do much to restore many allies' disinclination to work closely with the United States."[64] At this time, the United States needs the allies' help in Afghanistan. And there are other issues that will be best met as a unified bloc, such as how to confront and deal with Iran and North Korea as they move forward with their own nuclear plans. Although President Obama's popularity may be waning comparatively at home, he remains extremely popular in Europe and therefore is uniquely positioned to draw upon European good will to address some of these contentious issues.

To be effective, what will be necessary are policies that not only reverse some of the Bush administration's policies most reviled by the allies—ending the war in Iraq, closing Guantanamo, repudiating any policy that supports torture, to name but a few—but actively reach out to allies and indicate a willingness to listen to their viewpoints as well as to work with them on assigning priorities that are mutually important. But perhaps even more important is the idea that re-visioning the U.S.' relationship with its allies from one that has been largely negative to one that is more positive must take place within the broader context of rethinking of U.S. foreign policy after the war on terror.

Obama and Transatlantic Relations

One conclusion drawn by the Transatlantic Trends survey is that "the prospects for transatlantic cooperation will be shaped in part by domestic developments within the United States and Europe."[65] Taking that assumption forward, the change from the Bush administration to an Obama presidency has the potential to alter relations positively.

Writing in *Foreign Affairs* in 2007, then-candidate Obama confronted the failures of American leadership, and issued a call for the U.S. to "rebuild the alliances, partnerships, and institutions necessary to confront common threats and enhance common security." Speaking specifically of the European allies, he noted how "in the case of Europe, we dismissed European reservations about the wisdom and necessity of the Iraq war" and called attention to the need to "rebuild our ties to our allies in Europe."[66]

Obama echoed many of those same themes in his speech in Berlin in July 2008, when he said: "we know that sometimes, on both sides of the Atlantic, we have drifted apart, and forgotten our shared destiny." He then continued:

> In Europe, the view that America is part of what has gone wrong in our world, rather than a force to help make it right, has become all too common. In America, there are voices that deride and deny the importance of Europe's role in our security and our future. Both views miss the truth—that Europeans today are bearing new burdens and taking more responsibility in critical parts of the

world; and that just as American bases built in the last century still help to defend the security of this continent, so does our country still sacrifice greatly for freedom around the globe.[67]

What is perhaps most instructive about this speech is the way in which Obama started to set the stage for reconciliation between the United States and the European allies. For example, he recognized the fact that "there have been differences between America and Europe," but said that "the burdens of global citizenship continue to bind us together." And he acknowledged that "America has no better partner than Europe. Now is the time to build new bridges across the globe as strong as the one that bound us across the Atlantic."[68] Clearly, this is a start, but it is only a start. And the question is what actions will all the major actors have to take to begin to rebuild the relationship—if, in fact, all deem it worthwhile to do so. In that sense, the president's trips to Europe in April 2009 for the G-20 and NATO meetings, and subsequent trips to help build support for the U.S. mission in Afghanistan have reinforced his willingness to reach out to the European allies and move past the policies of the previous Bush administration.

While candidate Obama talked frankly of the failings that led to the estrangement across the Atlantic, he was addressing in broad political terms not only the differences between them, but also the ways in which Europe and the United States could reconcile. What he did not address, and what threatens the relationship as well, are the current economic situation and the differences not only in the perception of "threat" in general, but the ways in which both sides choose to deal with these problems.

Economic Crisis

Rightly or not, the Pew polls show that the United States is being blamed for the economic crisis that is affecting not only that country, but most of the rest of the world. Historically, one of the reasons that the United States was able to emerge and remain an international leader was the strength of its economy, as well as its military. The weakened economy is casting further doubt on the U.S.'s global leadership role. For example, in a December 2008 column in *The Wall Street Journal*, Gerald F. Seib wrote: "The meltdown in financial markets hasn't simply damaged the American economy. It has also tarnished the U.S. economic model, and threatens to reduce Washington's ability to exert influence around the globe."[69] Although here Seib is referring specifically to economic issues, the United States' role politically ties directly to its role as a global economic leader, a point that he also makes. The need to deal with the economic crisis, and the apparent differences in perspective on the best way to do so, has been a critical part of the talks between the United States and its allies at various international meetings.[70] By the middle of 2010, as the U.S. economy was starting to show signs of recovering, the EU had to deal with severe economic crises among member nations, especially Greece and Portugal. This shifted some of the emphasis away from the U.S. onto the EU to determine how best to deal with its own economic issues.

Another factor that must be considered regarding the economic downturn and the changing role of the United States is that the Obama administration will have to confront some serious realities, specifically, regarding assigning domestic priorities which will eclipse the role of foreign policy. At a time when the U.S. military is already stretched thin because of the war in Iraq, funding for security will have to come at the expense of other items, a classic "guns versus butter" dilemma. The choices that the administration makes have implications not only for the future direction of the U.S. military, but also for transatlantic relations.

Changing Nature and Perceptions of "the Threat"

Despite what Condoleezza Rice wrote in 2000 about the need for the U.S. to redefine its national interest absent the Soviet threat and the Cold War security framework, the reality is that subsequent to 9/11, U.S. national interest was directed toward the war on terror and the threat from terrorist attacks against the United States and its citizens. Here, too, the Bush administration diverged wildly from its allies, who were starting to redefine the notion of "threat" not just in traditional military terms but also in terms of human security, addressing those issues that threaten human beings and their existing way of life.

While few would deny that the Europeans are unaware of the threat posed by terrorist groups—witness the Madrid train bombings in March 2004, the attacks in London in July 2005 and in Glasgow in June 2007, for example—they also have been far ahead of the United States in redefining security to encompass other threats to human life. For example, the U.S.' European allies have led the way in recognizing the threat posed by Europe's dependence on foreign oil and in addressing solutions in the form of alternative energy sources. Where the Europeans have long faced gasoline prices that are very high by U.S. standards, and have manufactured smaller and more fuel-efficient cars, the United States continued to produce sport utility vehicles, trucks, and other "gas guzzlers" that have now led the major U.S. automobile makers into near-bankruptcy.

Similarly, European countries such as France have led the way in turning to nuclear energy, which is far cleaner and more efficient than the coal and other fossil fuels that the United States relies upon. Under the Bush administration, the United States also differed with its allies about the causes of climate change, let alone about how to address this issue that threatens the entire planet.

What these examples suggest is that the United States needs to look to, and learn from, its allies on many of the broad "human security" issues. This suggests a collaboration, not a competition, as well as a recognition that the United States may not always be the leader in all things. Recognizing that is not an indication of weakness but of humility, which might, in turn, contribute to improving transatlantic relations.

The Future of Transatlantic Relations: The U.S. Perspective

If transatlantic relations are really to improve, then the United States must go beyond reaching out to Europe as a whole through NATO and the European Union; it must also work directly with individual countries to assuage their particular concerns. The United States must also work to repair relations with Canada, a NATO ally as well as a neighbor, but one whose public has been swayed against the United States by a growing number of casualties in Afghanistan. President Obama took a significant step in this direction by making the decision to make Ottawa his first foreign visit as president. While Canada has been more closely aligned with the attitudes of the European countries than with those of the United States, thereby creating an important counterweight to the United States within NATO, it also has come forward and aided the United States economically by contributing to the "bailout" of the major car companies. This clearly is in Canada's best economic interest, as well as the United States', and it shows how intertwined the two countries are economically and how important it is for relations between them to be strengthened. Again, this means not only winning over the leaders of Canada but also the public, who remain skeptical of the United States and the impact of U.S. policies on them.

Obama's speech in Ankara seems to have started to repair the frayed relations with Turkey, and the Pew Global Attitude Poll of July 2009 suggests that the president's popularity might help him build bridges. But this must be done country-by-country, as each individual leader has to deal with the pressures brought to bear by his or her own public. It appears that Obama understands and appreciates that; however, this outreach cannot come at the expense of the American public, which has its own issues and concerns.

In sum, transatlantic relations, which were at a low point when Obama came into office, are starting to be rebuilt. But doing so means that the United States needs to recognize what brought the relationship to that low point initially, and take responsibility for rebuilding and strengthening it. Doing so will also require an assessment of U.S. foreign and security policy with a realistic understanding not only of the role that the United States has played in Europe, but also of the support that the United States has received from the European allies as well. This is not an easy task for the United States, which is used to seeing itself in the leadership role. If the relationship is deemed important to the United States, and is to be rebuilt, however, it is essential.

4 Transatlantic Relations

The United Kingdom

Andrew M. Dorman

Introduction

The issue of transatlantic relations has been a source of challenge for successive British governments ever since the founding of America and the first settlements at Plymouth Rock.[1] The relationship is more than that between two governments, for Canada has always played an important part, as have British interests in the Caribbean and Latin America. In addition, much of the relationship has been defined in the last century by issues with other nations around the globe, for example Hitler's Germany, the Soviet Union and more recently Iraq and Afghanistan. Moreover, these relations have also stretched far beyond the formal interaction between states to the personnel dynamics of the relationship between the Prime Minister and President, shared language and culture and ideas of the 'English speaking people,' and French fears about an Anglo-Saxon hegemony.[2]

With this as a backdrop there has been the question of what the United Kingdom is. For over half a century the United Kingdom has struggled to redefine itself. It is clearer what it was—one of the world's greatest empires spanning the world and exerting power, patronage and influence to an unprecedented extent.[3] However, that is no longer the case, and Dean Acheson's often quoted comment that 'Great Britain has lost an Empire and has not yet found a role' continues to ring true for many.[4] In this sense the United Kingdom is very similar to Russia today, in that it similarly wrestles with its own identity and its journey through history.

In response, successive British policy-makers from the 1940s onwards have emphasized the British role as that of the principal advisor to the United States government and the conduit or bridge between America and Europe.[5] This has played out as part of the concept of the so-called 'special relationship', a relationship that appears to ebb and flow over time.[6] Nevertheless, there continue to be a significant number of areas of common ground between Britain and the United States, ranging from resuscitating the banking sector and general trade to intelligence sharing and NATO's war in Afghanistan, that suggest that the United States and the United Kingdom will continue to be close partners for some time to come.[7] Moreover, the importance of the other North American partner, Canada, has grown from a British point of view along with that of Australia and New Zealand, as part of what George W. Bush referred to as the 'Global War on Terror.' There has therefore been a re-emphasis on the idea of the nations of the 'English speaking world' as the default coalition of the willing, with Denmark and the Netherlands becoming honorary 'English-speaking' partners.[8] This is based on the ABCA (Australia, Canada, Britain and America) program: set up to provide defence standardization amongst the partners armies (now land forces), it dates back to 1947, with New Zealand joining in 2006,[9] and is mirrored by a similar intelligence relationship.

At the same time, Britain remains a European state as a result of its geographical location, its alliance agreements and its trading links to the European mainland. Whilst the United States may be Britain's largest trading partner and its banking sector may be global, Europe remains the major area for British trade. The 2009 demonstrations across the United Kingdom about foreign workers re-emphasized Britain's role as a member of the European Union and the reality that Britain remains a European power geographically, if not emotionally.[10] Moreover, British foreign and defense policy has for centuries been dominated by the idea of a 'balance of power' in Europe as a mechanism of providing for Britain's defense and allowing it to engage in trade across the globe.[11] The creation of NATO was a manifestation of this; for Britain the role of NATO was to tie America into the defense of Western Europe and thus serve as the counterweight to the Soviet Union just as the United States had its reasons for wanting to be more firmly tied to Europe[12] For Britain there is, therefore, both a transatlantic and a European pull and, according to Michael Portillo:

British post-war foreign policy has generally been pragmatic and can be defined in a phrase: never chose between America and Europe. The policy perfectly suits our geography and culture. Anthony Eden clashed with America over Suez and it finished him. Ted Heath galloped towards Europe, and Thatcher in her last years galloped away from it, and neither was a good example.[13]

In examining transatlantic relations from the perspective of the United Kingdom the chapter has been divided into five parts. The first section considers the domestic political context outlining who the main stakeholders are and what are their respective agendas. The second part analyses Britain's strategic culture and how Britain views the role and use of armed force. The third section examines the evolution of its security and defense policies and the impact of transatlantic relations upon them. The fourth part reviews the United Kingdom's responses to the changing security agenda, its bilateral, multilateral and alliance relationships and the transformation of its armed forces. Finally, the chapter will conclude by considering the future of transatlantic relations from the perspective of the United Kingdom.

The Domestic Political Context

With the inauguration of every American president a great deal of effort is put in by the Whitehall elite to ensure that the British prime minister is the first European, and ideally the first world leader, to formally meet with the new president. The Obama administration was no different, and as a first step within a week of Barack Obama's becoming the 44th president, the British foreign secretary, David Miliband, successfully beat his German counterpart to be the first foreign minister to meet the new US secretary of state, Hilary Rodham Clinton.[14] In the subsequent press conference the usual pleasantries were made, with the US secretary of state uttering the magical phrase of the 'special relationship' and thus no doubt providing relief to the British delegation.[15] However, it was ex-British Prime Minister Tony Blair, rather than Gordon Brown, who was the first to have a meeting with the new president. At one point it looked as though the situation could get worse for Brown. There was a real concern that the French president would be invited to Washington ahead of him and what this might symbolize for future Anglo-American relations, thus reflecting some of the paranoia that often is associated with this personal relationship.[16] Fortunately for Brown he was invited to meet the new president ahead of his French counterpart and on cue Barack Obama made reference to the special relationship between the two states, saying that the relationship would only get stronger.[17]

This highlights that at one level transatlantic relations are deeply personal and are in part dependent on this relationship. The ebb and flow of this personal dynamic between prime minister and president significantly influence the relationship between the two states on the world stage. John Major, as prime minister, made the mistake of backing the incumbent president, George H. W. Bush, in the 1992 presidential race and when he lost, Bush's successor, Bill Clinton, initially snubbed the Major administration.[18] Later many commentators and officials wondered how the Bush-Blair dynamic would work, given the previous close partnership of Clinton and Blair. On leaving office Bill Clinton advised Tony Blair how to gain access to his successor, George W. Bush.[19] Ironically, it would be Blair's strong links to Bush that would do so much damage to him domestically.[20] Yet British public opinion struggled to comprehend why George W. Bush was elected as president rather than Al Gore, and Blair's subsequent close allegiance to Bush did immense damage to Blair. Michael Portillo, former Conservative minister, argued that:

> The prime minister has sacrificed his career by supporting George W. Bush. He has humiliatingly offered to fly around the world preparing the way for Condoleezza Rice, the Secretary of State. British body bags continue to arrive back from Iraq and Afghanistan. Blair has nothing to show for it.[21]

It was therefore entirely predictable that this relationship would again evolve as both Blair and Bush have been replaced, with Gordon Brown succeeding Tony Blair in the United Kingdom and Barack Obama succeeding Bush in January 2009.

When Gordon Brown succeeded Tony Blair in June 2007, it quickly became apparent that the new prime minister would seek to define the bilateral relationship in a way that would work for him.[22] As the 'War on Iraq' and Blair's close relationship with George Bush had done him immense damage domestically, it was clear that for political reasons Brown would want to be seen to be less of a 'poodle' than his predecessor, and he was placed under enormous pressure to reduce the British military involvement in Iraq.[23] However, despite promises of an early draw-down in British troops in Iraq, Brown did not pull out the troops under pressure from Washington.[24] Moreover, once his first party conference as leader was over in September 2007 he began to back-track on his earlier pledges. In his November 2008 speech at the Mansion

House he reiterated the importance of the US and tried to apologize to Bush for threatening to pull British troops out of Iraq.[25] Instead, it was only with the reluctant agreement of the US administration that British forces began to be drawn down in 2009 ahead of their American allies.[26] Questions about the British military's ability to sustain casualties have emerged as a result of their relative inaction in Basra, and a series of pieces in the summer 2009 edition of *British Army Review* raised disquiet about the reputation of the British military.[27] At the same time, the Brown government came under increasing pressure to significantly increase its commitment to Afghanistan from the previous temporary level of 9,000 troops as other allies decline US calls. The Obama administration has pressed for the deployment of a second brigade of some 4,000 personnel but the Brown government has sought to both appease the US and its own domestic public opinion, which is against the war, by providing some 500 additional personnel.

The economic downturn in Britain drew Brown towards similar measures to those taken by President Obama. A resurgence in popularity that followed from the initial collapse in the autumn of 2008 was replaced by significant criticism of Brown's handling of the crisis and a questioning of his previous performance as chancellor of the exchequer under Blair during the years of plenty. Brown's previous promise to be the chancellor who would end the cycle of boom and bust in the British economy looks exceedingly hollow.[28] With a general election called for in May 2010, Gordon Brown became increasingly desperate in his search for a solution to the depression that continued to confront the British economy. The ability of the Obama administration to rapidly revive the world's economy was therefore vital to Brown's chances of re-election and partially explains Brown's support for further spending along lines similar to the US at the G-20 meeting in London in April 2009.[29] Brown proved unsuccessful in the May 2010 general election and his government was replaced by a Conservative-Liberal Democrat coalition led by the Conservative David Cameron. The first international statesman to congratulate him on his success was the US president, who invited him to visit the US within two months. In the meantime the new British foreign secretary flew to meet his counterpart, Hilary Clinton, during the first week of the new government.

In general, Britain's Labour Party has traditionally had far closer links to the US Democrats, whilst the British Conservative Party has stronger links to the Republican Party. Yet, in many ways both parties are more Democrat in outlook and understanding. This is reflected in British society: in polls of the British electorate prior to the 2000, 2004 and 2008 presidential elections the Democratic runner has always had a far greater level of support. In this respect, British society is entirely in tune with its European counterparts and has struggled to understand the appeal of Republican candidates such as George W. Bush in 2000 and 2004 or John McCain's running mate Sarah Palin in 2008.

Although now physically connected to the European mainland by the Channel Tunnel, the United Kingdom remains an island nation. This physical separation has allowed its population to remain semi-detached from the rest of Europe, despite becoming increasingly interconnected with it economically; its history although closely linked to Europe stretches significantly beyond Europe. The migration of Britons over the years to North America, Australia etc, together with colonial roots and ongoing immigration, which can be traced back over the centuries, has given it a far more cosmopolitan view than many states have. This is reinforced by the many family ties that stretch across the globe.

This perspective has had other consequences and is linked with increasing moves towards greater independence of parts of the union. Scotland, Wales and Northern Ireland have varying degrees of local rule, whilst England remains administered from the center. This is becoming increasingly problematic, as the Conservative Party is now being viewed as an almost entirely English party, with Wales and Scotland both dominated by the Labour Party. The issue of identity has also led to differences in attitudes towards Britain's armed forces and raised concerns about Britain's security at home. For example, the parade of the returning 2nd Battalion, the Royal Anglian Regiment, in Luton was marred by a counter-protest drawn from within some of Luton's Asian community. This was condemned by both the United Kingdom's political elite and other elements of society.[30] This, in part, reflects the ongoing changes to British society, which is witnessing significant shifts in the relative size of the various communities that comprise it and in their willingness to be more visible and vocal.

Within Whitehall, the wider policy think-tanks and academia there has long been a debate about the so-called special relationship between the United States and United Kingdom. Much has been written on the subject and questions have been raised about the extent to which the relationship is one-sided.[31] All have been full of advice for the new US administration. Yet within Whitehall the emphasis remains on three traditional areas—the intelligence relationship, the nuclear dimension and wider defense and security—and one new area, the global recession and the collapse of the international banking system.

It is the intelligence relationship that highlights most clearly that the special relationship is not merely about the interaction of two states but varies in its definition. In 1947 the UKUSA agreement formally tied together the signals intelligence organizations of the United Kingdom, United States, Australia, Canada and New Zealand.[32] In the 1980s, access for New Zealand was restricted in response to their anti-nuclear policies, but the New Zealand government in recent years has quietly re-engaged in this partnership quite significantly. The size of this operation is substantial with the United Sates funding upwards of 90% of the total cost. Writing in 1990, Richelson and Ball commented:

> The UKUSA security and intelligence community, with more than a quarter of a million full-time personnel and a total budget of 16–18 billion (US dollars), constitutes one of the largest bureaucracies in the world. As such, it not only wields enormous political power and influence, but exhibits most of the typical attributes of large bureaucratic organizations, including a tendency to define and pursue bureaucratic objectives which are not necessarily in complete concordance with the national interests of the five UKUSA countries themselves.[33]

The continuing of the relationship was particularly evident post 9/11 when the heads of MI6, MI5 and GCHQ were flown in the first aircraft to re-enter US airspace after the attacks.[34] This intelligence relationship is not without controversy, especially in the construction of the case of Iraq weapons of mass destruction[35] and more recently in the case of Binyam Mohamed, an ex-Guantánamo Bay resident, whose trial in the United Kingdom included the use of US intelligence, which the judges prevented from entering the public domain on the grounds that it would be prejudicial to the intelligence relationship.[36]

The nuclear relationship remains close and dates back to collaboration between the US, United Kingdom and Canada on the Manhattan project, which led to the development of the atomic bombs that were dropped on Hiroshima and Nagasaki in August 1945.[37] In the aftermath of the war, and with the passing of the McMahon Act by Congress in 1946, the US and UK went their separate ways in nuclear development. However, over time their nuclear interaction returned and the McMahon Act was finally repealed in 1958. This closeness has meant that since the 1962 Nassau Agreement the United Kingdom has been able to acquire successive generations of strategic nuclear delivery systems from the United States.[38] Interaction has reached the point where the US and UK own shares in a common pool of Trident missiles, from which they draw when their respective submarines deploy on patrol. Within Britain there remains a debate about the relative advantage this element of the relationship gives to the United States.

On the wider defense and security front the relationship remains close. For Britain's military the United States remains the ally of choice and one whom they aspire to continue to operate with. In fact over the years the various government moves towards improving the rest of Europe's militaries have been generally met with disdain within Britain's armed forces. Since the end of the Cold War, British forces have always deployed alongside their American counterparts, with the single exception of Somalia. In both the 1991 Persian Gulf War and 2003 Iraq War Britain deployed a division to ensure that it had sufficient representation within the American-led coalitions, whilst in Kosovo in 1999 and Afghanistan in 2001 the campaigns were started with a joint UK-US cruise missile strike and the British featured prominently. In the case of the former there was considerable tension between the US NATO commander, General Wesley Clark, and his British subordinate, land commander Lieutenant-General Mike Jackson, especially over the Russian deployment of troops to Pristina Airport. More significantly, the most recent British defense policy statement—'Delivering Security in a Changing World'—concluded that Britain would no longer engage in any large-scale operations without the express involvement of the United States. This closeness was reinforced in 2006 when NATO expanded its operations to the whole of Afghanistan. The US was content for their Operation Enduring Freedom to be incorporated under NATO command because the NATO commander was British.[39] Indeed the need for the United Kingdom to be in a position to influence US decision-making has led its armed forces to adopt an informal 15% rule, whereby the United Kingdom seeks to deploy a force amounting to at least 15% of the US force.

However, there have been some tensions between the respective militaries over operations in Iraq and Afghanistan. The US has rightly raised questions about the commitment of the British government and armed forces in terms of their willingness to deploy forces and accept casualties. There has also been anger about the British military's views of the US military. The criticism of the American approach to the counter-insurgency campaign built up from

2003, with a number of officers still arguing that the British know best and referring incessantly to the Northern Ireland experience. Brigadier Nigel Aylwin-Foster's Seaforth House paper, published in *Military Review*, helped to bring this to a head but also supported the changes that the Americans themselves put through under the auspices of General David Petraeus.[40] The British certainly did have more experience of counter-insurgency operations at the start of the war in Iraq, and the US did make a number of mistakes.[41] However, there is certainly evidence to suggest that the British grew complacent, not to mention condescending, whilst the US forces transformed their forces.[42] The subsequent failures of the British in both Basra in Iraq and Musa Qala in Afghanistan have raised serious questions about British capabilities, and both are areas the British military wish to address.[43] However, this has not prevented some senior British commanders from continuing to refer to the Northern Ireland experience against all evidence to the contrary.

The problem is that in Afghanistan, as in Iraq, British policy has, in the words of Simon Jenkins, 'detached itself from reality'.[44] The government wants both to defeat the Taliban and to eradicate the poppy crop, goals that many pundits see as diametrically opposed to one another. Moreover, the perceived failings in both Iraq and Afghanistan are raising serious questions about the credibility of the United Kingdom's armed forces, especially given the relative paucity of the UK's defense spending and lack of domestic support.[45]

The one area of defense where cooperation has been consistently poor has to do with the considerable obstacles that lie in way of US-UK defense trade. Over the last two decades the United Kingdom has led the way in opening its defense market to others, with many US defense companies opening offices in the UK and acquiring smaller British defense companies. Likewise BAE Systems, Britain's largest defense provider, has invested heavily in acquisitions in the United States to the point where the US, rather than the United Kingdom, represents its main market.[46] This integration, matched to the increasingly close working relationship of the British and American militaries, has raised the idea of an International Traffic in Arms Regulation (ITAR) waiver for the UK (and Australia) to get around limitations in technology transfer from the US to the UK. Unfortunately on Capitol Hill the waiver has become a political football that has not been resolved.[47] At one point the former minister for defense procurement, Lord Drayson, even threatened to cancel the British involvement in the Joint Strike Fighter program. However, despite subsequent agreement between the US and UK governments, the waiver remained un-signed during the Bush administration and has been passed on to the new Obama administration.[48]

The new area for cooperation lies in confronting the challenge of the global economic downturn and problems with the banking sector. The collapse of the US sub-prime mortgage market brought a number of British financial institutions close to collapse, and the government has had to intervene to keep a number of them afloat. The nationalization of the Northern Rock Building Society was just the start.[49] Brown has sought to rally and cajole his European counterparts and other G20 members to try and reduce the economic downturn, which has left the United Kingdom particularly exposed, as the fall in the value of sterling against the Euro and US dollar has shown. How this will unfold in future is still to be seen and the degree of international cooperation remains unclear.[50] Moreover, whilst the rest of Europe appears to have begun to come out of recession, the United Kingdom has not.

Strategic Culture

The Cold War period witnessed quite profound challenges for the United Kingdom. By 1989 only a few vestiges remained of what was once the world's largest empire. Europe, rather than the Empire, had become the focus of British foreign and defense policy. Within this transformation four inter-linked assumptions remained constant: the hostility of the Soviet Union, the 'special relationship' with the United States of America,[51] the creation and maintenance of a nuclear deterrent, and the ambition to maintain the ability to influence decisions on the world stage.[52]

The first three elements were deeply intertwined. Fear of the Soviet Union and the destabilization of the relative power balance in Europe had driven the early post-war policy-makers to push for the creation of NATO to tie the United States directly into the defense of Europe in order to act as a counterweight to the Soviet Union and the guarantor of Western Europe's independence.[53] The third element, the nuclear deterrent, reflected a British distrust of others, even the US. Only by the possession of a nuclear deterrent could the United Kingdom ultimately guarantee its independence from Soviet dominance and maintain its status as a 'world power'.[54]

The last assumption, the ambition to maintain the ability to influence events on the world stage, has remained. This links back to the Acheson quote in the Introduction and was encapsulated in the 1948 Defense Estimates: 'the United Kingdom, as a member of the British Commonwealth and a Great Power, must be prepared at all times to fulfill her responsibility not only to the United Nations but also to herself.'[55] This thinking has remained part of the psyche of the political elite and domestic public opinion, and it can be seen within the 2006 Defence White paper outlining the case for a new generation of ballistic missile submarines.[56]

Up until the late 1960s, successive British governments had shown a remarkable propensity to use military force in pursuit of the national interest. For much of the period after 1945 this had been part of the process of decolonization, and the period from the early 1970s to the end of the Cold War witnessed comparatively few foreign adventures, with the notable exception of the 1982 Falklands Conflict. Again US support for the British was crucial, with the US Department of Defense providing significant material assistance to the British Task Force, whilst the State Department initially sought to adopt a more impartial line.[57]

Since the end of the Cold War there was an increasing willingness to use the armed forces in support of Britain's foreign policy, culminating in Tony Blair's time in office (1997–2007).[58] This began under Margaret Thatcher, who committed British forces to the 1991 Gulf War. Subsequent deployments, particularly to the Balkans under the leadership of her successor, John Major, were used as a means of gaining and maintaining influence, and there was considerable discussion about the idea of Britain 'punching above its weight'. In other words, the armed forces were increasingly seen as an important mechanism to counter the UK's other perceived weaknesses and maintain its place in the world, with reference frequently being made to 'a force for good'. This line of thinking developed further under Tony Blair. Geoffrey Wheatcroft, in his book *Yo! Blair*, dubbed him a 'War Prime Minister',[59] whilst Blair himself argued the case for humanitarian intervention in his often quoted speech on the 'Doctrine of the International Community'.[60] At the time this resonated with public opinion, and in his first six years in office Blair used armed force five times (*Operation Desert Fox* against Iraq in 1998, Kosovo 1999, Sierra Leone 2000, Afghanistan 2001 and Iraq 2003), and that excluded the deployment of forces in support of the United Nations' mission to East Timor in 1999 and elsewhere.[61] The Iraq controversy meant that in his subsequent four years in office there were no new wars apart from NATO taking over responsibility for the war in Afghanistan from the US-led coalition (of which the United Kingdom was a part) and the deployment of troops to southern Afghanistan. Currently, there is evidence to suggest that there is at least a temporary downturn in the public's and political elite's willingness to use armed force, and it is not clear how long this is likely to last.

As part of a valedictory series of lectures, Blair's January 2007 speech on defense articulated the continuing case for a proactive foreign and defense policy, which would continue to include the use of hard power along with soft power. In that speech he argued that 'there are two types of nations similar to ours today. Those who do war fighting and peacekeeping and those who have, effectively, except in the most exceptional circumstances, retreated to the peacekeeping alone. Britain does both. We should stay that way.'[62] Despite early indications that Brown would be less keen to engage in military adventurism than Blair was, he soon made enquiries about military options following the outbreak of communal violence in Kenya after the elections in December 2007. In this case he was informed there were no forces available because of existing commitments. Similar discussions have been held periodically with reference to Zimbabwe and Darfur, again without success, and it looks as though Afghanistan is fast becoming Brown's war. What the new Cameron government will do remains open to question, but it does seem certain that Afghanistan will quickly become that administration's war.

Evolution of the Security Dimensions

Despite the great emphasis on the use of the military overseas, it was not until March 2008, some six and a half years after the attacks on America, six years after the publication of 'SDR: New Chapter',[63] five years after the invasion of Iraq, and two and a half years after the attacks on the London transport system, that Gordon Brown launched the 'National Security Strategy of the United Kingdom', Britain's first national security statement.[64] Despite the wait, the resulting document was immensely disappointing. Ann Fitz-Gerald rightly commented that the British 'government continues to pursue national security objectives devoid of a 'grand design'.'[65] The new strategy listed a whole range of security challenges without any form of prioritization or comment on how many could be engaged with at any one time. It concluded that Britain should remain close to the United States, but not much else. In launching the document Brown's first two major substantive points were to provide an additional £2m for military recruitment and £20m to provide a home purchase fund for members of the armed forces.[66] It was hardly surprising that the leaders of the opposition parties were quick to find fault.[67] Privately the weakness of the new strategy has been acknowledged, and a second edition was published in June 2009. It aimed at appearing to be an update whilst in fact seeking to provide an intellectual foundation to the earlier document, albeit with little additional substance.[68]

The evolution of British security policy has been a slow process. Up until the end of the Cold War, successive governments articulated a foreign and defense policy predicated on the four interconnected threads outlined in the previous section. With the end of the Cold War a security debate emerged between the Foreign and Commonwealth Office (FCO) and the Ministry of Defence (MOD). This could be seen in the speeches of the various Conservative ministers concerned.[69] The FCO argued in favor of a much broader definition of security expanded beyond the traditional political and military dimensions, whilst the MOD sought to contain this expansion. The FCO ultimately won this debate and the 1998 'Strategic Defence Review' introduced by the new Labour government embraced the FCO's agenda, whilst a later defense white paper was entitled 'Delivering Security in a Changing World'.[70]

However, the Blair government went much further than the FCO had wanted and created the Department for International Development from the old Overseas Development Administration, which had traditionally been a subordinate part of the FCO. The result has been a significant turf war, differences over future policy and in particular the role of Britain in Iraq and Afghanistan, and a stasis in policy development as disagreement over the various aspects of policy has combined with failures in Iraq and Afghanistan and an internal fight for resources in Whitehall. Thus, there is much discussion about the idea of a 'comprehensive approach' but little agreement on what that actually means.

Responses of the United Kingdom

The United Kingdom has successfully retained membership of the major international organizations including the United Nations Security Council, where it jealously guards its status as a permanent member with veto rights. Successive British governments have sought to protect that status and have emphasized Britain's role as a 'good citizen' and 'a force for good', thus involving themselves in the majority of UN peacekeeping missions. The extent to which the government can maintain this position remains open to question.

The issue of European security and the respective roles of NATO and the European Union (EU) remain central to British security policy. Since its inception, NATO has always been Britain's alliance of choice as it has a North American dimension and the relative power balance within it has suited British interests. With the end of the Cold War successive British governments sought to maintain NATO's relevance and the UK's standing within it. Three elements have been central to this British policy: who controls the various key command posts, the need for the NATO members to transform their respective militaries, and the creation of an autonomous European defence capability without US disengagement.

In many respects in the immediate aftermath of the Cold War the command post issue was resolved from a UK perspective. The loss of the Cold War NATO Channel command post (CINCCHAN) left only the US with control of the Supreme Allied Commander posts (Europe and Atlantic), but the British government successfully fought off the German government for control of the new Allied Rapid Reaction Corps.[71] Not only did this mean that the British Army could retain a corps-level capability; it also meant that the British had control of any NATO deployment and the post of their commander on the ground.

Subsequent reviews, such as the 'Defence Capabilities Initiative' and 'New Strategic Concept' developed by NATO, all supported Britain's desire for the alliance and its European members to reform and latterly transform their military capabilities. Partly this has been seen as a way of ensuring that NATO remains important to the United States, and thus to maintain the US commitment to the alliance. It was also viewed as a mechanism to discourage the creation of an autonomous European capability. This attempt was only partially successful and under Blair it was changed. There is now a greater British willingness to accept autonomous European capabilities, focused initially on revisiting the Yugoslav Wars (1999 Helsinki Headline Goals) and more recently on deploying to Africa (2003 EU Battlegroup concept). In other words, these allow Europe to develop independent capabilities to fill gaps where the US has no strategic interest, but Britain does.

Beyond the European organizations there have also been changes. In announcing the 2003 defense white paper the then defense secretary, Geoff Hoon, referred to Britain having two special relations, the traditional one with the United States and a second one with Australia. What this reflected was a British shift away from NATO towards a more traditional informal alliance involving states such as Australia, Canada and New Zealand working alongside the United States: in other words, a return to its more traditional alliances based on the English-speaking world and those nations that share a particularly close intelligence partnership with the United Kingdom. It also reflected the operational realities on the ground, where British forces found themselves working closely with these partners along with the Dutch and the Danes, who have become honorary members of the 'English-speaking' club.

In terms of Britain's armed forces adjusting to the changing security environment, there have been three waves of change that have led to the current strategic meltdown.[72] In the initial wave of post-Cold War change, they continued to adopt a threat-based approach fearing some form of resurgent Soviet Union and compromised.[73] Britain's armed forces focused on three defense roles.[74] Defense role 1 was largely about home defense and the defense of Britain's dependent territories. Defense role 2 proved to be the main role and focused on the defense of Europe through NATO. Defense role 3 swept up the remaining missions, in particular the out-of-area role and support for UN peacekeeping missions. It was viewed as the least important, although, ironically, it would prove to be the most significant in terms of operational deployments and long lasting commitments.

The second wave of reform linked directly to Labour entering power in 1997 and lasted until the 9/11 attacks. The 1998 'Strategic Defence Review' (SDR) represented a shift away from specific threat-based planning towards a more capabilities-based approach.[75] The armed forces were no longer to be constructed to deal with specific threats, such as that from the Soviet Union or a nuclear attack against NATO. Instead they were to have a series of capabilities that would enable them to be used in a variety of circumstances. However, the type of operation which these were aimed at was entirely predictable. The large-scale operation focused on a re-run of the 1991 Gulf War, and the medium-level deployments were based on the deployments to the Balkans. In other words, they represented what had happened before rather than any consideration of what might happen in the future.

The third wave of reform developed after the 9/11 attacks and built on the various operations in which Britain had been involved, principally Kosovo (1999), Sierra Leone (2000), Afghanistan (2001–2) and Iraq (2003). Although the 'Strategic Defence Review: A New Chapter' of 2002 took a number of steps forward, notably embracing the US defense transformation agenda and the threat posed by asymmetric warfare, it did not fully embrace the concept of effects-based warfare.[76] This change was not fully undertaken until the two-part defense white papers, titled 'Delivering Security in a Changing World', which followed in 2003 and 2004.[77] Amongst the changes were a shift of focus away from Europe and an 'arc of concern' stretching from North Africa to the Middle East towards a global approach. There was also a move towards the US and away from a European focus. The new working assumption is that any European involvement will most likely be on a much smaller scale in Africa, which explains the British emphasis on the Anglo-French initiative to create rapidly deployable EU battle-groups of around 1,500 personnel.[78] Less publicized has been the shift towards more informal alliances outlined above.

The problem has been that the level of resources put into defense has not been commensurate with the level of engagement that the armed forces have found themselves committed to. As a result, as the government sought to focus its efforts on the war in Afghanistan whilst making cuts to the level of defense spending, the procurement program collapsed. Eventually, Gordon Brown's new defense secretary, Bob Ainsworth, announced that a defense review would be forthcoming but not until the next parliament.[79] A defense green paper was published in February 2010, and was met with general approval. Nonetheless, all three main political parties entered the May 2010 general election promising a defense (and security, in the case of the Conservatives and Liberal Democrats) review. All implicitly accept that defense spending will have to be reduced to help alleviate the fiscal pressure currently confronting the nation. The question is what direction the new Conservative-Liberal Democrat coalition will seek to take defense in and the implications this will have for the armed forces.

Future of Transatlantic Relations

The price of the transatlantic partnership has been high in recent years, and not just in terms of British service personnel lost in operations in Iraq and Afghanistan or the scale of the ongoing British commitment to NATO operations in Afghanistan.[80] Questions have been raised about the increased vulnerability the United Kingdom now confronts as a result of these operations and its association with the United States, the potential long-term loss of credibility for the UK and NATO should the Afghanistan operation result in failure, and the price in terms of civil liberties that the UK is paying to maintain the intelligence relationship. Perhaps more significant, but yet to be fully determined, is the price the British economy will pay from its integration into the American economy, especially in the banking sector. The British economy is almost entirely dependent on the Obama administration's finding the right answer to the global recession and preventing a global depression.

Much of the above are potentially only short-term bumps in the road, and the wars in Iraq and Afghanistan have reinforced more traditional partnerships. Moreover, the ongoing relationship with the United States has continued to allow the British political elite to talk of 'punching above its weight', being a 'force for good' and other such phrases that encapsulate playing on the world stage whilst ignoring the future direction of the United Kingdom and its place in the world. In other words, the United States may have permitted the United Kingdom to avoid finding the role that Dean Acheson implied it needed to find. The relationship has also allowed successive governments to ignore or at least delay answering the question of Britain's long-term relationship with the European mainland, and particularly the future of the European Union. Thus, the transatlantic partnership remains absolutely pivotal to the future direction of British foreign, defense and security policy for some time to come. The key for successive British governments will be to balance the demands of the United States, Europe and its own public opinion.

5 France and Transatlantic Relations

Adrian Treacher

Introduction

Strasbourg was the venue for France's formal reintegration, after over forty years, into NATO's integrated military structures in early April 2009. This is the most recent key development in a Franco-American relationship that has been colorful, certainly, often turbulent, and characterized more often than not in the contemporary general psyche, in public at least, by competition more than cooperation. This latter perception, primarily associated with General Charles de Gaulle's presidential tenures at the Elysée from the late 1950s through the 1960s, was reasserted in 2003 when President Jacques Chirac's France vehemently and vocally opposed the American-led invasion of Iraq. However, in the last third of the eighteenth century, the initial formalization of Franco-American relations could have been associated with the crucial French military, notably naval, support, albeit for national strategic reasons, for the American colonists successful bid for independence from British rule.

In European terms, the nineteenth century marked a general decline in French power and influence, from the apogee of Napoleon Bonaparte's conquests to the humiliation of Napoleon III's defeat by Bismarck's Prussia at Sedan in 1870. The newly created state of Germany would then humble France twice more in successive world wars in the first half of the twentieth century. Concerning the transatlantic dimension, the latter two military defeats were certainly blamed by many in France on US tardiness in intervening on the side of the Allies.[1] Put another way, from a French perspective, the failure of alliances (prior to World War I) and of collective security (prior to World War II, with the United States remaining outside the League of Nations) meant that France had to henceforth unilaterally secure its own interests without automatic reliance on any external benefactor.

The fact that France's early post-1945 years were then marked by weak government in Paris, economic reliance on American Marshall Aid, and a preoccupation with security guarantees against Germany, and then West Germany (which was a founding member of NATO and the Western European Union and proposed the ultimately rejected European Defence Community), only compounded the urgency. This general sense of helplessness and reliance on others was then compounded by the humiliating collapse of French colonial ambitions in Indo-China in 1954 (with French forces belatedly being replaced by American ones), the Suez embarrassment of 1956 and the Algerian crisis, which significantly contributed to the collapse of the Fourth Republic. John Gaffney refers to this sense of vulnerability becoming a cultural fact and serving to fashion the French strategic imagination.[2]

It was in this climate of national self-doubt that de Gaulle came to the presidency in 1959. It is almost as though he then, single-handedly, re-established national confidence and reasserted France's position as a global power, helped admittedly by *les trente glorieuses* (a period of dramatic economic growth). A key external reference point for all this was the United States, and de Gaulle's attempts to move his country away from a position of total reliance to one of non-dependence. This principle, and de Gaulle's reform of the Constitution, would guide all of his successors at the Elysée and is crucial to understanding France's approach towards the US throughout the lifetime of the Fifth Republic.

The Domestic Contest

French foreign policy during the Fifth Republic is consistently described as being based on *Gaullist* principles (associated with the first president of the Fifth Republic, Charles de Gaulle). Just what *Gaullism* actually means, or stands for, is contested, but its principles were adhered to with an unwavering, instinctive devotion by all of France's subsequent foreign policy-makers regardless of political affiliation. For this author, these principles, if vague, are fundamental, fixed, universally accepted (within the national political elite) and go to the very core of French identity (at least as far as the elites are con-cerned). I have, elsewhere, referred to them as intransigent *strategic* objectives and argued that there have been several *tactical* adjustments made to achieve those objectives; the objectives themselves have, however, remained largely unchallenged despite France's relative loss of real global power.[3] De Gaulle crystallized these, to use Gordon's term[4], as the claim to, and evocation of, continued national *grandeur*, or greatness, and the relentless pursuit of an el-evated global standing, or *rang*, for the country; together, they formed the *grandes lignes* of French foreign policy.

During de Gaulle's presidential era, these *grandes lignes* were developed not so much in terms of fervent anti-Americanism as might have been as-sumed from his provocative Québec speech[5] or his engagement with Latin America in Washington's backyard, but more on a claim of non-dependence on *either* superpower and a claim to an alternative pillar, or third way, of global influence. What de Gaulle, and his successors, sought was a certain freedom of maneuver on the international stage. As noted below, this public presentation did, however, somewhat hide a rigid commitment to the cause of the West, should the superpower stand-off ever escalate. But during the *détente* periods, particularly in the mid to late 1960s, France was globally able to act out a type of privileged part, playing one superpower off against the other. To some extent then, the Cold War-era bipolar nuclear stand-off served the French pursuit of the *grandes lignes*.[6] That said, as mentioned above, the perceived delay in American military intervention on France's behalf in both world wars (of three years and two years, respectively) dug deep in the subse-quent French political elite psyche. For Pierre Lellouche, the Gaullist conclu-sion was thus distinct from other west European countries in that France's defense could not be guaranteed by any other power; rather, defense was something for which each state should be directly and solely responsible.[7] The bitter lesson learnt was that a militarily weak France, reliant on others for its security, was an enslaved and vulnerable France. Part of this painfully drawn conclusion was, simultaneously, that, despite the mutual defense guarantee supposedly enshrined in the NATO Charter, there was actually no such au-tomatic guarantee in an era of a superpower nuclear stand-off; France, as an inherent Great Power, thus had to have its own nuclear weapons capability.

Another key external reference point for French foreign policy was the neighbor across the Rhine. There has been a determination to either contain or balance German power ever since the rise of Bismarck in Prussia in the mid-nineteenth century. Anti-German sentiment had been based on territorial proximity, military conflict, cultural and religious opposition, economic rivalry and ideological cleavages.[8] It became a French political maxim that the (regional) hegemony, prosperity and unity of France depended on relative German weakness, the lesson being that when it was politically united, Germany invaded France. Hence, coming out of World War II, a single Germany was not deemed to be in French interests. In the subsequent divided Europe, West German ambitions had to be tamed and French leaderships undertook this mission through a variety of bilateral and multilateral arrangements by which Paris could influence developments.[9] What emerged, at least from a French perspective, was an implicit French assent for West German economic leadership in Western Europe in return for support from Bonn on issues of *grande politique*. In this way, France gained greater international maneuverability than it might have had due to the external and internal constraints placed on its West German neighbor. For Patrick McCarthy this was not, initially at least, an alliance of two friendly powers against outside forces; it was more the means for one power to control the other and for the other to control itself as it had not done in the first half of the twentieth century.[10] According to Julius Friend, meanwhile, 'Gaullist policy since the mid-1960s had operated on the unspoken premise that since West Germany was utterly loyal to the United States, France could afford to dance out of line, remaining loyal to the Atlantic Alliance but in its own independent and idiosyncratic way'.[11]

Central to French ambitions for continued Great Power status has been a prioritization of the UN as *the* primary authority on global issues. Clearly, retention of the permanent seat on the UN Security Council is paramount, but the role of *la francophonie* should also be acknowledged in this regard. De Gaulle had initially been dismissive of the organization, perceiving it as an instrument of American pretensions for global hegemony, and he resented what he saw as UN interference in his country's decolonization process. However, he came to appreciate the potential utility of the organization for his *grandes lignes*; as did subsequent presidents.

Perhaps more than any other west European country, at least until Tony Blair's UK and the 2003 Iraq crisis, French foreign policy has been characterized by a strong declaratory element and an emphasis on grand public gestures designed to demonstrate that France retains *rang* and *grandeur* on the world stage. Behind this facade, however, the *actual* policy had often been somewhat different. De Gaulle, for example, though associated with his substantive challenge to American hegemony in the West, was the first ally to stand by President Kennedy during the Cuban Missile Crisis.[12] Moreover, although he had ordered France's partial rupture with NATO in 1966, behind the scenes talks immediately followed in order to establish France's role in the Alliance's response to the expected Red Army attack across central Europe.[13] Even during the post-Cold War debates on a European Security and Defense Identity (ESDI), French representatives, rather than fearing that American hegemony in Europe would be rendered unjustifiable by the end of the Cold War, became keen not to encourage a full American military withdrawal from Europe because they knew the Europeans were not collectively ready to fill the vacuum.[14] In addition, however, French leaders (meaning presidents) have perhaps been more prone to use the public platform to drive forward foreign policy debate.[15]

It is clear from the above discussion that the president plays a central role in French foreign policy making. Indeed, on frequent occasions, this observation actually underplays the defining role played by the Elysée; presidential power regarding foreign and security policy obtained, in reality, the potential to be virtually unrestrained. As noted by John Gaffney, de Gaulle, firstly by force of character and then by constitutional reform, 'radically personalized'[16] the French state around one individual. In stark contrast to its predecessors, the 1958 constitution, which created the Fifth Republic, marked an emphatic reorientation away from political parties and towards the presidency. At a famous press conference in 1964, de Gaulle encapsulated this vision. There could, he argued, be no duality of power at the summit of the State, and as a result it is the president who is *l'homme de la Nation*, who is the source and holder of national power.[17] Hence, the presidency, particularly with regard to foreign and security policy, was endowed with the predominant position in French politics at the expense of the National Assembly and other political actors like the foreign and defense ministries. On paper, the constitution provided for a balanced division of power between executive and government. In practice, it has clearly been seen to favor the former, particularly after 1965 and the introduction of presidential election by universal suffrage, which thereby forged a direct link with the people and provided the incumbent with power and legitimacy of unrivalled quality within the Hexagon. Other key constitutional amendments in this vein were de Gaulle's January 1964 decree bestowing the president with sole authority on the use of nuclear force and President Georges Pompidou's December 1971 decree placing the joint chief of staff under the authority of the president.[18] In effect, the president is the real defense minister, with the defense ministry largely having little significant input in the formulation of national strategic and security policy or in the decision-making process. The foreign ministry has been equally subservient. Indeed, François Mitterrand, as president, defined the role of the latter as not to define policy but to act as 'a powerful and efficient instrument' implementing policy designed at the Elysée.[19] Prime ministers, meanwhile, also played a junior role, reliant as they were on presidential patronage. This dynamic was disrupted in 1986, when legislative elections produced a government of the center-right in opposition to the incumbent Socialist Mitterrand as president. This, and subsequent periods of *cohabitation*, demonstrated that presidential power can be constrained by political circumstance. That said, the impact on French foreign and security policy has been minimal as a result of all governments and presidents sticking uniformly to the Gaullist *grandes lignes*.[20]

Elsewhere, the general absence of anything approaching a popularly supported alternative to the *grandes lignes* and France's claim to a universal mission has given the presidency an even freer rein. No grass-roots social movement has been able to overcome the huge systemic obstacles and emerge with sufficient influence to challenge the monopoly of security policy specialists over decisions concerning vital strategic questions and to foster political change. Barbara Balaj, writing in 1993, noted that French policymakers refer to a 'broad public consensus' on foreign affairs and consider themselves removed from public opinion and interest group pressures. She added that they deem themselves to be the arbiters of the national interest.[21] Moreover, the very vagueness surrounding just what Gaullist policies are, summarized by Pierre Hassner as 'strategic simplicity, diplomatic flexibility and political ambiguity',[22] may have actually facilitated the emergence of a broad agreement regarding France's position in the world.[23]

Strategic Culture

French experiences in the 1991 Gulf War served as a huge wake-up call regarding the realities of the new post-Cold War security environment and of France's potentially marginal role within it. Only 12,000 troops could be mustered from the conscript army, equating only to some 3 per cent of the American contribution.[24] Here was a stark illustration of the extent to which France's conventional forces had suffered decades of neglect and underfunding, with priority being given to the nuclear weapons program, the *force de frappe.*

Once at the Elysée, de Gaulle had instinctively chosen to accelerate the national nuclear weapons program. For him, this step was logical and fundamental to the pursuit of the *grandes lignes.* He argued that as soon as the US, and then the Soviet Union, attained a nuclear weapons capacity, France's strategic outlook would be transformed. The reality was now that 'all forms of force, other than the nuclear, would be so constrained by international restrictions that subordination to the US in the foreign and defense field, thereby leading to political subservience, would be inevitable'.[25] From this perspective, the French thus had to carve for themselves a nuclear niche out of the bipolar superpower rivalry in order to derive maximum political and military leverage, thus keeping France on the top rungs of global power. It was simply not enough to rely on the supposed security guarantee proffered by the US to its Atlantic Alliance partners. For Lawrence Freedman, de Gaulle came to perceive the American nuclear guarantee as 'a flimsy foundation for security, much inferior to a national effort'.[26] To this end, de Gaulle talked of nuclear *sanctuarization.* He would, according to Gordon, 'endow France with a powerful and invulnerable nuclear force that would make it possible for his successors—if warranted by events—not to follow quietly the policies of their protector, the United States'.[27] From Gregory's perspective, meanwhile, past national humiliations, as referred to above, made it imperative that the country now be at the forefront of any technological and tactical advances such as nuclear weapons.[28] That said, the *force de frappe* could equally be understood as 'the ultimate political symbol and instrument of national independence from America and of global standing rather than as a military weapon directed at the USSR'.[29] For de Gaulle, the diplomatic significance of an autonomous nuclear capacity outweighed any strategic importance; it was to be used to regain for France Great Power status and to mitigate the psychological damage created by relative national decline.

De Gaulle's successors were to share the view that the price, a considerable proportion of the defense budget devoted to the *force de frappe* to the detriment of conventional forces (increasingly assigned a support role), was one worth paying. The 'conversion' of the Communist and Socialist parties in the late 1970s meant that all the major political parties supported the national nuclear deterrent as the ultimate guarantee of France's elevated rank through the independence of defense. As a result, there was minimal space across the political spectrum for alternative policies to receive an airing. The Socialists, for example, subordinated their rhetoric on disarmament to the Left's strong tradition of defending *la patrie* dating back to the aggressive patriotism of the revolutionary era.

The end of the Cold War did not initially herald a serious and public debate on the continued utility of the *force de frappe*. Retention seemed almost instinctively obvious to the relevant decision-makers. Gregory noted that there were still viable justifications for retention that could be put forward, such as the unpredictable situation in Russia, possible further proliferation around the world and the continued international leverage that a nuclear weapons capability could accord.[30] That said, budgetary constraints were kicking in by this time; indeed, spending on the *force de frappe* actually began to fall in 1988. In the first few years of the post-Cold War era, it would, however, continue to be prioritized, although demands on other aspects of France's military capacity, namely retaining the ability to project force around the world, were rising dramatically. Indeed, while defense spending between 1985 and 1994 fell by 17–21 per cent in Britain, Germany and the US, it actually rose by 2 per cent in France.[31] Hence, France was the last Western state to draw its budgetary conclusions from the collapse of the Soviet empire and the end of the Cold War.[32] Mitterrand postponed major decisions and chose to persist with costly, and possibly anachronistic, procurement schemes. It wasn't until the middle of the 1990s that defense spending began to be cut, not least due to the EU's convergence criteria for Economic and Monetary Union.

Another key strand of French strategic culture during the Fifth Republic has been a nationalist approach to defense procurement. By the 1990s, the country had achieved a level of self-reliance in defense manufacture of nearly 96 per cent (second only to the US among then NATO members).[33] But this sheltering of French defense manufacturers, predominantly part of the public sector, from the exigencies of the competitive global costs, such as the need to reduce costs, was now clearly producing negative results. There now, for instance, appeared a distinct lack of quality on offer for export in the conventional side at least. Elsewhere, the incompatibility of much of the French equipment with that of NATO allies, combined with the Armed Forces' general unfamiliarity with NATO military procedures, led to a certain marginalization of France in the first major conflict of the post-Cold War era, Iraq's invasion of Kuwait and the subsequent American-led Operation Desert Storm. Belatedly, France's heavily protected domestic armaments industry was re-structured, partly denationalized and allowed to engage in transnational co-operation and mergers.

Conscription is the final component of the Fifth Republic's strategic culture to be covered here. Calls for its removal were becoming more numerous by the end of the 1980s, but they were repeatedly resisted on the grounds that they represented a renunciation of the tradition of the citizen in uniform. This tradition dated back to the *levée en masse* of 1792 and the subsequent victory over a seemingly invincible Austro-Prussian army that was deemed to have saved the revolution, and it was formalized in 1905. National Service thus persisted due, in large part, to the French belief that it preserved the crucial link between army and nation and it served to perpetuate ideas associating the people with the defense of *la patrie*. So it was not until early 1996 that Jacques Chirac, as president, felt able to announce the abolition of conscription in favor of a fully professional army. He justified this transformation on the grounds that the country no longer faced a ground threat and that the bulk of French military activity was now overseas. Professionalization was essential, he argued, if France was to be able to project significant troop numbers into conflict zones as part of multinational peacekeeping and humanitarian operations. Here then was another key indicator that France was moving away from a focus on self-reliance and non-dependence to more openness to cooperation with allies and partners.

Post-Cold War Foreign and Security Policy

As the post-Cold War era unfurled, French foreign policy-makers were presented with a series of challenges in a new global security order unfettered by nuclear superpower bipolarity. But it was clear from the outset that the conviction these elites held for the Gaullist strategic objectives remained unshaken; all that was needed were some tactical adaptations. In particular, with the reunification of Germany a rapid process following the collapse of the Berlin Wall in 1989 over which Mitterrand's administration had limited influence, and with the perceived devaluation in the utility of nuclear weapons, it was paramount that they made a maximum effort to avoid the country's international political marginalization. In this context, with everything turned upside down, it seemed almost instinctual to turn, as a tactical shift, to the UN as a primary vehicle as a future guarantor of France's *grandes lignes*.[34] Hence, President Mitterrand, by the early 1990s, was 'showing every endeavor in placing France at the very center of UN proceedings, making it a driving force as the Organization re-launched itself in response to the "new world order".[35] The now 'unfrozen' UNSC became the conduit by which pronouncements were made in the name of France on all major crises and issues around the world. Concurrently, France took on a disproportionate share of the UN's peacekeeping burden. Significantly, President Chirac would then further encapsulate this newfound embrace of UN-based multilateralism in France's traditionally perceived *pré carré* (backyard) of sub-Saharan Africa in the late 1990s following the sudden demise of long-time Paris client Mobutu in (what was then) Zaire.

In the European context de Gaulle's pursuit of the *grandes lignes* rested on the acknowledgement that, alone, France simply lacked the resources to achieve these fundamental goals. However, rather than modifying these goals to reflect the country's resource limitations, France transferred its national strategic ambitions onto its west European partners and focused on attempts at mobilizing them into a cohesive global political actor under implicit French leadership. For decades, de Gaulle and his successors had been making no distinction between French and European interests. As Alistair Cole put it, 'Europe was to be led to independence from American hegemony under France's enlightened military and political leadership. Only France, the lone continental European nuclear power, was strong enough to provide an alternative to American leadership'.[36] To this end, Jonathan Eyal observed the remarkable ability of France's leaders 'to portray their country's national interests as Europe's fundamental imperatives'.[37] Becker, meanwhile, referred to French ideas for the European security architecture as the projection of national aims on a larger scale.[38] Nevertheless, even prior to the end of the Cold War, the Paris policymakers were recognizing that this tactical approach was making only limited headway and that a change was required; when it came, the end of the Cold War then acted as a catalyst for this change.

After initial failed attempts to revive the concept of an independent European security system from which NATO and the US would be excluded, it was clear that France's European partners, including, crucially, Britain and Germany, did not, yet at least, share the French vision of an EU acting as an autonomous security actor on the world stage. This lack of consensus was graphically illustrated by the stumbling, incoherent and ultimately vacuous European response to the break-up of Yugoslavia in the early 1990s. This crisis served as a testing ground for the French vision,[39] and it was duly found to be isolated and hence unworkable. By seeming to hold up the Western European Union (WEU) and 'Europe' in opposition to American-led NATO, French leaders had become somewhat politically isolated. For Jacques Baumel, '[w]e desire the emergence of a European security and defense pole, but we are virtually the only ones to really wish it'.[40] Indeed, French political and military leaders had to acknowledge that, in this crisis at least, NATO was proving far more effective than the UN.[41] Nevertheless, France's role, albeit marginal, in *Desert Storm* and its subsequent more effective contribution to the multinational military efforts in the former Yugoslavia led to a certain warming of attitudes towards this European maverick and an appreciation of it as a willing partner.[42]

By the time of Jacques Chirac's arrival at the Elysée in mid-1995, France's relative isolation in the European security dialogue had produced a simple reasoning: 'the "European defense identity" will be built within NATO or will not be built at all'.[43] Key decisions about the future of European security management were now being made by the alliance, often in a forum from which France had withdrawn itself since 1966. In order to influence this dialogue, Chirac thus swiftly authorized a certain *rapprochement* with NATO by seeking to bring France partially back into some of these NATO fora. But once again, French aspirations for a European Security and Defence Identity (ESDI) were to be frustrated. Then, an attempt in 1997 to integrate the WEU into the EU was blocked by the newly incumbent Blair administration in London. So it was with an overriding sense of disillusionment regarding ESDI that France's leaders entered the last quarter of 1998.

Regarding European security management, the convention has been to split EU members into three broad groupings: the Atlanticists, led by the UK (favoring the primacy of NATO and a leadership role for the US); the Neutrals including Ireland and Sweden (opposed to the coercive use of military force); and the Europeanists (promoting a leadership role for the Europeans themselves as an alternative to American primacy). As indicated above, France has been the champion and most vocal advocate of this last grouping. So when, in October 1998, Tony Blair's Labour government, after only 18 months in power, announced its predisposition to an augmented, and *autonomous*, European military capacity, Chirac and his advisors naturally suspected an Atlanticist plot; it took them a while to recognize the initiative as being serious and to appreciate just what a policy shift was taking place in Westminster. Given all this, Franco-British cooperation on the ensuing ESDP (European Security and Defence Policy), which emerged out of the Franco-British St Malo Declaration of December 1998 and was then ratified by the European Council meeting in Cologne in June of 1999, has been quite remarkable, and often unreported.

However, there remained a serious divergence over the long-term vision for the project, and it rested, as ever, on the part to be played by the US. The key question was whether ESDP was to be developed as an alternative or a complement to NATO. Although undoubtedly a watershed, St Malo had inevitably been a compromise between 'French desires to boost the profile of the EU and British concerns that any augmenting of European defense capabilities should proceed under the umbrella of the Atlantic Alliance'.[44] As Howorth noted, while the French leadership, post-St Malo, consistently acknowledged an American role in ESDP, it was, nevertheless, intended to be a solely European initiative, with the US in a supportive role.[45] Moreover, French ambitions for ESDP were *global*, as they had been for the EU more broadly, even back to de Gaulle's time. Following Cologne, on paper at least, it seemed that, after years of frustration, French strategic ambitions centered on the EU were coming to fruition, the possibility of a 'common defence policy', as mentioned in the Maastricht Treaty, was now being discussed as something both concrete and realizable. Militarization of the EU was finally underway, and French leaders could realistically contemplate a credible European alternative to American global hegemony. The embarrassment of the meager European contribution to NATO's military campaign in the 1998–9 Kosovo crisis then served to stiffen the resolve of some 'waverers' among the then-EU15. Graham observed that there was now a general conviction that Europe must 'move rapidly to acquire the means to act independently of the US since the EU has increasingly a different set of priorities from that of Washington and may become willing to intervene where the Americans are reluctant'.[46]

As mentioned above, the role of the US in the management of west European, and then pan European security has been a constant preoccupation of the Fifth Republic's policymakers. The traditional mantra, going back to de Gaulle, was that, at some moment, the Americans would quit their European security management role and that, therefore, the (then) West Europeans should collectively prepare for that day by building up their own autonomous (meaning without the US) military capacity. Moreover, this mantra held that the emergence of a functioning autonomous (west) European capability would serve to 'consolidate and enhance a more balanced' Atlantic Alliance.[47] In contrast, the UK, as the other key player in West European security management, held that if the region started to prepare for an American withdrawal, the US would then actually order such a withdrawal, retreat back into isolationism and thereby engender the collapse of the alliance.

Official American reactions to the ESDP process remain a mix of approval and concern. One major bone of contention between Paris and Washington, DC, has been the question of *duplication* as highlighted by then-Secretary of State Madeleine Albright.[48] The American line went, and remains: why do the Europeans need to duplicate the capabilities that NATO can already offer? For their part, the French countered with the question: how could the Europeans ever achieve autonomy (from the US) without duplication?

Franco-American Relations Post-9/11

In the immediate aftermath of the 9/11 tragedy, NATO, in an unprecedented move, invoked its Article 5 mutual defense guarantee. However, this gesture would be largely ignored in Washington, and it would be demonstrated that the US did not formally need its alliance partners in order to respond militarily to the attacks on its soil. The American administration was determined not to go through a repeat performance of the Kosovo campaign, in which targets had had to have been agreed by all 19 members of the alliance. It would not be put into a similar situation of conducting a war by multinational committee.

The resultant largely unilateral American response can only have heightened French concerns at what they perceived as the growing hegemonic preponderance of the American *hyperpuissance* (hyperpower). The US-led military Operation Enduring Freedom in Afghanistan ran completely counter to the French multipolar vision for global management. And worryingly for this vision, the EU, the principal focus for French ambitions, was noticeably absent from the crisis. Despite this, the decision-makers in Paris still instinctively sought to preserve the *grandes lignes* in what was now America's global 'war on terror'. To this end, both Chirac and Prime Minister Lionel Jospin pledged political and military support to the Bush administration and Chirac won the race to be the first foreign head of state to get to the White House. But, initially at least, and in contrast to the US's specially selected privileged partners at this time (Australia, Canada and the UK), there would only be token French participation in Enduring Freedom.[49] A more significant French military contribution was, however, announced at the NATO April 2008 Bucharest Summit, in which France committed over 2,800 troops by the end of 2008.

More generally, although not alone in doing so, French foreign policy makers, with their reliance on multilateral structures or coalitions as vehicles for the promotion of the *grandes* lignes, were becoming increasingly anxious at the unilateralist tone of the George W. Bush administration that had been inaugurated at the start of 2001. Moreover, in the context of the 'war on terror', government officials in Paris actively attempted to counter the 'anti-Islam' tag increasingly being associated by many in response to developments in Afghanistan, both in order to preserve Franco-Arab relations (read French international influence) and to assuage potential domestic agitation among France's Muslim population.[50] However, as John Vinocur noted, the French foreign policy machine at the time was constrained on this issue by a period of *cohabitation* (in this instance, a president [Chirac] from the center-right and a prime minister [Lionel Jospin] from the center-left) and so struggled to come up with a singular approach/response to the 'war on terror'.[51] Moreover, as Lansford noted, instinctive French attempts to be at the top table of decision-making in this crisis were further thwarted by Tony Blair's emergence 'as the European leader with the most influence in Washington'.[52] And Lansford added that, perhaps, the French military contribution to Enduring Freedom might have been more substantial had Chirac's insistence on a multilateral command structure (clearly an anathema to the Pentagon after its Kosovo experience) not been rebuffed by the Bush administration.[53]

These Franco-American tensions concerning European and global security management were to then spiral into a very public diplomatic stand-off over Iraq. In an interview in March 2003 (before the war), President Chirac repeated his conviction that Iraq obviously possessed weapons of mass destruction (WMDs) and that it was essential that Saddam Hussein's regime be disarmed of them.[54] Moreover, Chirac was prepared to use military force to achieve this if peaceful measures proved futile, although no time limit was set on these 'peaceful measures'. Hence France backed the UN decision to disarm Saddam's regime via the inspection, detection and destruction of any WMDs; indeed, French representatives played a central role in drafting UNSC Resolution 1441. But crucially, from a French perspective, this decision did not refer to regime change. So once the Bush administration decided, in mid-January 2003, to invade Iraq regardless of the verdict from the UN's WMD inspectors, the French leadership had no choice but to vehemently oppose the American position. The view from Paris was that it was essential that this American unilateralism based on the concept of pre-emptive action be countered by further recourse to the UNSC, where France was obviously a major player and where it could lay claim to elevated global standing. For François Heisbourg, 'being a permanent member of the UNSC gives France its global position, therefore the French fight has always been to put the UNSC in the center of the picture and keep it there. That is more important than whether or not there is a war'.[55]

As Bush's determination to pursue the military option seemingly strengthened, Chirac called for an intensification of the WMD inspections,[56] and in this he had quite widespread international support. A note here is that the inspectors were not saying they could not get the job done; they just needed more time. Nevertheless, Thierry de Montbrial noted that there was by this time an, albeit quiet, recognition in Paris that the American-led military deployment was prompting the Saddam regime to engage in a real disarmament process.[57] Meanwhile, as the UK and US sought a new UNSC resolution designed to give military action wider legitimacy, France made it clear that it would deploy its veto.[58] Chirac's team was interpreting British and American efforts as seeking a vote to go to war, and this made their initiative totally unacceptable. In this, noted Elizabeth Pond, Chirac was emboldened by the uncharacteristically vocal, belligerent and unilateral opposition to American policy coming out of Berlin.[59] John Gaffney, for one, noted that 'France spoke in diplomatic terms almost as the US' equal', and that the French diplomatic attitude, discursively at least, featured 'a kind of imagined parity' between France and the US.[60] Indeed, French representatives were actually portraying the Franco-German opposition to US actions as a common European view and thereby antagonizing feelings in London, Madrid and elsewhere.[61]

Domestically, meanwhile, support for Chirac's stance came from across the political spectrum: the whole Left, the Greens, parts of the governing *Union pour un Mouvement Populaire* (UMP) (but not the party's Atlanticist wing), the National Front; this was mirrored in the media and popular opinion (there was a 70 per cent approval rating for France's veto).[62] That said, there were some prominent dissenting voices, notably the foreign affairs commentator Dominique Moïsi, the humanitarian aid expert and founder of *Médecins Sans Frontières* (and now French Foreign Minister) Bernard Kouchner and the UMP's main international expert, Pierre Lellouche.[63] According to Dominique de Villepin, meanwhile, from London there were references to complete intransigence in Paris and from Washington there were claims that the French 'were poisoning the diplomatic bloodstream'.[64] Regardless of whether or not the French position was correct in terms of international law, Frédéric Bozo observed that the threat, or the tabling, of the veto would be interpreted in Washington as a French denial of America's right to self-defense and protection of its vital interests.[65] Once the military operation was underway, French diplomacy went quite quiet, apart from calling for a swift end to the campaign and for the lead role in the post-war reconstruction to be given to the UN. In addition, after the 21 March special EU summit in Brussels, Chirac did declare that America and its coalition partners had 'strayed' from international legality with the launch of the war.[66] Nevertheless, French airspace remained open to American and British military aircraft. Elsewhere, although still rejecting any direct participation in the occupation of Iraq, French representatives were swiftly making concerted efforts to promote improved Franco-American relations. De Villepin, for example, pointed to his country's 'unwavering solidarity' with the US straight after 9/11 and to the countries' shared values[67]; the French, after all, consider themselves to be America's oldest ally.

Conclusion and Future Prospects

At first glance, the 2003 Iraq crisis had served to further sideline the UN in terms of global security management (NATO had previously bypassed the organization so as to launch its military campaign in Kosovo and Serbia in 1999), had provided a further graphic illustration of the fragility of the EU as an international actor (13 out of the soon-to-be EU25 supported the American action) and had caused a major rift in Franco-American relations the likes of which had not been seen since the great NATO crisis of 1966. (Indeed, it could be argued that this was the first time that France and the US stood on opposite sides of a major security crisis since Suez in 1956.) French ambitions for the global security order seemed to be in tatters. Indeed, French actions at the UN during the 2003 crisis may actually have served to deter the US from turning to the UN/UNSC when faced with a similar scenario in the future. But to explain away this rift as the result of simply another French attempt to demonstrate the ability to pursue a diplomatic path independent of the US, to underline continued French significance in world affairs, is too simplistic.

True, French foreign policy was driven by concerns to convince the world that France matters and is a global player, but also on this occasion there was the belief that the Americans had simply got it wrong. Pond, for example, refers to Justin Vaisse's observation that the French approach was anti-Bush, not anti-American.[68]

In addition to a central role for the UN, French global strategic ambitions rest on the ability of the Europeans to project power effectively. But, noted Keane, to do this there at least needs to be a political consensus about what you are planning. For this, there first needs to be a common coherent foreign policy backed by a common defense culture.[69] Anand Menon, meanwhile, noted in 2000 that there was no real consensus on what form ESDP should take,[70] and this is largely still the case today. There is no agreement about ESDP's geographic scope or whether priority should be placed on the 'soft' or 'hard' end of the Petersberg Tasks spectrum. France, unsurprisingly, appears to have the broadest interpretation. That said, some observers noted that the French position on an autonomous ESDP was gaining support among Brussels-based elites and other EU leaders and that the transatlantic rift was being deliberately inflated as a result; this was referred to as 'Euro-Gaullism'.[71] As regards the Atlantic Alliance, meanwhile, Guillaume Parmentier argued that, since the Kosovo campaign, NATO had been perceived as too American by many European leaders and as too multilateral by many of their American counterparts.[72]

Prior to the 2003 Iraq crisis, it is clear that American leaders were reassured by the British commitment to the furtherance of ESDP within a NATO context, but equally they had been alarmed by statements aspiring to a form of operational autonomy for the Europeans that emanated in particular from the French leadership.[73] Alain Joxe, for one, wrote that this crisis demonstrated the necessity of a European global strategy that was different to that of the United States.[74] But such a unified alternative strategy was surely made even more elusive by the EU's 2004 and 2007 enlargements that brought in several new 'atlanticist' members openly disposed to supporting the US on the world stage. Nevertheless, as noted by Leo Michel, the French *White Book on Defense and National Security*, published in June 2008, predicted a reduced American capacity to shape global affairs and a shift in American focus away from the European space.[75]

From 2009, French and American forces have been cooperating in both Kosovo and Afghanistan. And there has been significant collaboration in areas such as intelligence, counterterrorism and civil emergency response, not to mention France's reintegration into NATO's integrated military structures, 12 years after Chirac's similar but ultimately aborted initiative, as highlighted at the start of this chapter. Unlike some observers, Michel does not see the latter as simply a concession to the US. Rather, he sees tangible benefits emerging for the EU and the future capability of ESDP.[76] Certainly, there has not been the major political or popular outcry across France that some might have expected. Meanwhile, Bruno Tertrais highlighted the noticeable impact of Nicolas Sarkozy's arrival at the Elysée in May 2007, with the ensuing period of extraordinary Franco-American cooperation on strategic questions.[77] Bozo relates that once in office, Sarkozy made no effort to conceal his desire to re-establish close relations with the US, as indeed Chirac himself had been trying to do from 2004, and to finally draw a line under the traumatic tensions of 2003 and their fall-out.[78] The formalization of France's 'return' to NATO, as announced at Strasbourg in April 2009, was clearly a symbolic representation of this new intent but does not automatically rule out tensions in the future, even with Barack Obama residing at the White House. French strategic objectives based on the *grandes lignes* remain, and so it is more than likely that France will make, at some point, even more tactical adaptations in order to attain them.

6 Germany

From Civilian Power to International Actor

Gale A. Mattox

Introduction

The European security landscape changed dramatically with the end of the Cold War, but perhaps as dramatic or even more dramatic have been the changes over the past several years since the tragic events of 9/11.[1] The longer-term consequences of the two events are only now truly evident in the shifts—often quite significant shifts—in the perception of individual countries of their national security identities and impact on the future role of the European Union (EU) and the transatlantic community. There is additionally a perceptible generational change occurring that reinforces and may be expected to propel change in the security paradigm of the past generation. In particular, rising elites perceive their futures within the broader European space and project their activities into the international arenas with an assertiveness that has not previously been the case. The rising new leadership on the continent, most recently in the UK, France and Germany as well as in other countries, reflects this change. Their views of their roles are clearly a departure from their predecessors'. These changes have been reflected in transatlantic relations and may be expected to be even more profound as the Obama administration fully develops its foreign and security policy agenda.

This chapter will focus on the shifts that have occurred in Germany and the impact of these shifts. First, has there been change as a result of an emerging generation raised in a unified, considerably more diverse post-Cold War Germany and more comfortable with a national identity? Second, how has the political and security landscape been transformed, and with what impact? What are Germany's threats, and how do they align with those of the United States? Third, what have been those changes and how have they been reflected in German views of Germany's security role? Finally, how have the changes to Germany as a state and as a European, transatlantic, and international actor affected the European security paradigm and US-European security?

Perceptions of a New Generation

Christian Democrat Chancellor Angela Merkel has throughout her career been underestimated.[2] A protégé of Chancellor Helmut Kohl, she was thought to be finished in politics when allegations of Kohl's involvement in the scandal involving the Elf Corporation and Christian Democratic Union (CDU) party finances broke.[3] Her willingness to speak out on the moral reprehensibility of the deeds saved both the party and her. As the jostling for 2005 CDU chancellor candidacy began, she was thought not to have the stature to win a national campaign, not to mention an intra-party fight to be named the CDU candidate. Again the pundits were proved wrong. As the Christian Democratic/Christian Social Union (CDU/CSU) chancellor candidate, she won by a mere 1% margin, so thin that in the immediate aftermath, Social Democratic Party (SPD) Chancellor Schroeder underestimated her with a blustery attempt to seize the chancellorship on election night. As she has done so often in the past, she asserted her leadership, became the first East German—and first female—chancellor of Germany and assumed the helm of the somewhat tenuous Grand Coalition in 2005. Not an auspicious start to the chancellorship and certainly lacking in flourishes, but true to her low-key, meticulous approach.

For this reason, her success on the international stage should not have been surprising. It came as a result of both her sharp and pragmatic, if understated, political instincts and the emergent role of Germany on a number of international fronts. Not only were her EU presidency and the EU summit in the first half of 2007 more successful than even her supporters had prophesied, but also her role as host of the G-8 conference, which was held in June 2007, demonstrated a confident and assured country under her direction as chancellor—a result of her leadership, but also reflecting the confidence of Germany as a state finally more comfortable with its national identity. As Chancellor Merkel has articulated and represented Germany's emergence from the strictures of its post-World War II history, a second component of Germany's change has come from a sense of its national identity, at once within the European Union/North Atlantic Treaty Organization (NATO)/Organization for Security and Cooperation in Europe (OSCE)/G-8/G-20, but also as a state prepared to pursue its interests and identity, preferably within multilateral organizations but also on its own, as necessary. This change in Germany represents more than just having its first East German leader—it is a new confidence in its identity more generally.

For decades there has been talk of the 'normalization' of Germany—that is, the evolution of Germany as a nation state in its domestic role and, even more so, in its role as a state actor on the global scene. This is occurring, albeit only in fits and starts and with a not-surprising German *angst* as it happens. It will, however, be for the historians to determine whether the expression of German 'selfhood', as evidenced by the flying of German flags and public pride exhibited during the World Cup, will eventually translate into a new and significant milestone or whether it was merely a public articulation of a growing sense of self that reflected a role Germany had already begun to take in the political and security sphere. This latter would appear to be the case. The process of German identity—some call maturation—is less one of surging forward and more one of gradual evolution—at times two steps forward and one step back.[4] Germany has remained at once cautious in any active military deployments abroad while also increasing its international diplomatic activity and broadening its peace-keeping role.

Changing Political and Security Landscape

Germany's evolution has occurred within the parameters of a changing political and security landscape. The fall of the Berlin Wall in November 1989 brought about the unification of the country; less recognized is that it also changed the status and broader context under which the country had operated since 1945. On September 12, 1990, the Second World War allies—the United States, Russia, France and Britain—signed the Four Power Agreement, conveying final full sovereignty on the country.[5] On October 3, a month later, the two states unified as one country, less than a year after the fall of the Berlin Wall. As negotiated at the time of their inception, the European Union and NATO both recognized the newly unified Germany as a full member, as did other European and international organizations.[6]

But not only had the internal character of Germany altered, the security paradigm of the previous 40 years had changed as well. Just two years after unification the Soviet Union disintegrated, the direct threat of the Cold War had ceased, and the Cold War institution of NATO and other European institutions had begun to transform to meet the new challenges. Defining the threat and reconfiguring Cold War institutions to meet that threat, if any, was itself a challenge. The transatlantic allies were more than ready for a 'peace dividend'; for their part, the former communist societies were anxious to join the transatlantic community of free markets and democratic governance. Not as sanguine about Russia, these emerging democracies quickly made their desire to join the EU and NATO known. While US President George H. W. Bush discussed 'stability' as an objective of security in Europe, European members of NATO cut defense budgets and focused on deeper EU integration (while also reaching out to Sweden, Finland and Austria), including in the 1992 Maastricht Treaty agreeing to a Common Foreign and Security Policy (CFSP),which included a European Security and Defense Policy (ESDP).

The 1990s witnessed an increasing divergence between the US and other European allies in their perception of the threat, with differences between the US and Germany as well as other European allies. While the US assumed the role of the lone superpower, the Germans focused on domestic issues, particularly unification of the two Germanies, which cost the country roughly $10,000 annually for every man, woman and child. But the Balkan wars could no longer be ignored. The Europeans had not resolved the unrest to their south as Belgium Prime Minister Poos had assured President Bush they would do. The conflicts in the Balkans led to German involvement with UN peacekeeping in Bosnia, followed by deployment of the German Tornados in Kosovo, with Germany participating in a conflict for the first time in the post-World War II era. During the 1999 Kosovo conflict, the gap that had arisen between the US and the European allies in perception of the threat became perceptible. with glaring differences in military readiness, technology and capabilities.

What can be expected of Germany, and what factors may result in Germany's assuming a role equal to other major international actors? There are four complementary processes in the German evolution as a state actor since 1945 and during the Cold War decades. While Germany became a substantial economic power and a growing political power, the end of the Cold War enabled Berlin to assume a more prominent role in the security arena as well.[7]

This has required, first, a self-perception which was prompted by unification; second, recognition as a European power, which has accorded it an influence in the EU equal to or exceeding that of France; third, a sense of greater equality in its relationship with the United States, as witnessed by its resistance to join the Iraq coalition while at the same time consciously choosing to lead the NATO ISAF force in Afghanistan in 2003; and, fourth, a quest to assume a greater international role through United Nations permanent Security Council membership with all the attendant responsibilities, including an increasing role in non-combat contingencies such as peacekeeping and humanitarian relief but also, albeit reluctantly, in combat operations as necessary.

German Evolution as a State Actor

While unification was clearly the major turning point for Germany as a state actor, the 2006 World Cup sparked a public perception of Germany as a nation in a way that was previously not possible. In Berlin, as all over Germany, in 2006 German flags fluttered along all major arteries into the city during the games. This sign of pride in the country (and in German athletic prowess on the soccer field, which led to third place overall) was the healthy sign of a country with confidence; a country that had not shed its past, but was also determined to move beyond the self-hatred that came with that past. It represented a change in generations to a younger generation that can acknowledge the past, but feels that nearly sixty years of democracy represents a commitment that cannot be denied and an acceptance of their German identity. The outdoor cafes in even the smallest German village with their flags and outdoor large screen TVs manifested the pride. That reaction exceeded the normal enthusiasm for an athletic event and became a metaphor for Germany itself, a Germany proud of its accomplishments. For any other country, this would not be exceptional or unusual. For Germany, it was both, even though on the day after the competition was over, the flags came down and life returned to its everyday routine. On the next occasion, the flags may well return, but again not in a threatening mode but rather in recognition of a normal relationship between citizen and country. The sense of finality—not in leaving history behind—but in moving to the next phase of its development as a state—is accepted broadly and appears to have been internalized.

The impact of this new sense of self has yet to emerge again after summer 2006, but the development has deeper roots than enthusiasm for soccer. The election of 2005 had already signaled a willingness to accept a new conception of Germany and, in essence, a greater German international role. The election of a woman, and even a woman from East Germany, who in every respect does not fit the 'mold' of a German chancellor, was clearly a departure from the familiar. Without the confident sense of self sparked by unification, would such an election have been possible?

Chancellor Angela Merkel has a strong personality, but one willing to negotiate and forge cross-political agreements to achieve reform. She is the daughter of a Lutheran minister who emigrated to the East with his family in 1955 soon after his daughter's birth in Hamburg. She grew up in the East German Protestant Church but did not join the opposition that the church later spawned. She studied physics and the sciences and worked for a period as the spokesperson for the Academy of Sciences as well as for East German Governor Lothar de Maiziere at the foreign minister level two-plus-four talks in Moscow in September 1990. One observer has described her thus: "This is remarkable, because here is a protestant, divorced, Northern German woman from the East who leads a catholic, male dominated, family oriented, predominantly Southern German party."[8] For Germans, she exemplifies the reach to the new, the unique, for society.

Chancellor Merkel's assertive, yet reasonable, demeanor mirrors Germany's growth as a state actor—assertive yet open for consensus. This Germany has been determined not to be labeled and instead follows the dictates of its own conscience. A manifestation of this new Germany as a state actor is its refusal either to be pushed into Iraq or to shun responsibilities in the Balkans and Afghanistan. Its development is by no means complete, but there is a clear sense of comfort with its identity as a state actor in the European and international arena, as well as in its transatlantic relations.

This change in Germany's identity has evolved from a 'culture of restraint', as the only NATO state with a standing army not to participate in combat operations during the Gulf War in 1990/91 (Japan [$10B] and Germany [$6.6B] funded the allied participation in the Gulf War), to the Bundeswehr's providing medical assistance for Cambodia in 1992/93, to deploying in the Balkans in 1995. This last, which signaled the German sense of identity as an equal state actor, was based on a Constitutional Court ruling on July 12, 1994, that German forces could operate outside of German territory with the majority consent of the German parliament. Previous to 1994, the German armed forces had been guided by Article 24, para 2 of the Basic Law: "with a view to maintaining peace, the Federation may enter into a system of mutual collective security; in doing so it shall consent to such limitations upon its sovereign powers as will bring about and secure a lasting peace in Europe and among the nations of the world."[9] They also saw themselves restrained by Article 87a of the Basic Law, which stated that "apart from defense, the armed forces may be used only to the extent explicitly permitted by this constitution," or under NATO Article 5, which restricted NATO to defend against attacks on member states.[10] The Constitutional Court decisions made German deployments possible in the Balkans and in Afghanistan.

The impact of the Constitutional Court decision that permitted German forces—approved by the German parliament and often termed a Parliamentary Party—to participate in contingents led by the UN, NATO or the EU (called Western European Union at the time), was significant. To this point, the Germans had pursued what has been termed a 'civilian power paradigm', and the public had been comfortable with it.[11] But this concept of the state as strictly a civilian power had become increasingly untenable for a such substantial economic and geopolitical state actor as Germany. For the country not to participate with its allies in the post-Cold War environment as a fully active and responsible partner no longer fit the perception of Germany's appropriate role, a role strongly transatlantic and evolving in its European security identity.[12] Not only was Germany in fall 1995 a full participant in the Dayton negotiations over the future of Bosnia-Herzegovina, but the Constitutional Court decision permitted Germany to contribute nearly 4,000 troops to the NATO peacekeeping force. The Bundestag vote was 543 (of 656) in favor of the Implementation Force (IFOR) deployment, in the first vote after the 1994 court ruling.[13] Since that time, the parliament has supported a number of deployments from Kosovo to Afghanistan, a clear shift from the civilian power paradigm. At the same time that German perception of its responsibilities as a state actor has widened, the public and government have maintained restraint as well, declining, for instance, to join the US and many of its allies in overthrowing Saddam Hussein in 2003. Similarly, in Afghanistan Germany has at times exercised restraint (e.g., in caveats attached to German forces in Afghanistan) while at the same time contributing the third largest force to the NATO force there.

Germany's Evolution as a European Actor

Over the decades since the end of World War II, and particularly with the signing in 1957 of the Rome Treaty, Germany has looked to Europe to establish its legitimacy. This has evolved from being accepted as a member of the European Economic Community (EEC) to becoming a growing economic power within the European Community (EC) to acting as a natural leader with France in much of the decision-making for Europe. Germany's EU membership reinforced the important role Germany assumed as a civilian power and an economic force within Europe, made clear in the role it played in the financial crisis over Greece debt.[14] Its non-threatening role within the confines of this growing institution was, first, as an economic actor on the international markets and, second, as a political force on a wide range of issues affecting Europe.[15] Working together with France, Germany was able to legitimize itself through the medium of Europe.

The jury is still out on the EU after EU voters rejected its constitution and accepted the less ambitious Lisbon Agreement. Furthermore, the EU has named a President and High Representative for security and defense, roles which do not appear to take the EU in new directions immediately but hold the potential to do so in the future. The European defense force has cautiously assumed more roles. Since the 2005 election and with full German involvement, the EU has completed a Macedonian mission (albeit without a German parliamentary debate as a peacekeeping responsibility), increased the Kosovo mission, and taken on additional responsibilities in Bosnia as the United States trimmed down its role.[16] In early 2004, the Germans joined the British and French in laying out a formal "battlegroup concept" for 1,500 personnel to be deployed in 15 days, particularly for use in support of a UN mission. The German battlegroup contribution to the European force has been one of the larger commitments, with the country taking the lead in a few and contributing to several other battlegroups over the next several years, even as the battlegroups have not yet been deployed.[17] In addition, the Germans have participated in other EU efforts, for instance, after March 2006 as part of EUSEC in the Democratic Republic of Congo supporting the reform of its security sector.[18] In the *Financial Times* Hugh Williamson commented in late 2004 that "gone are the days when German Chancellors practiced only softspoken, cheque book diplomacy."[19] In contrast to Germany's decision not to put boots on the ground in Iraq, these missions are largely peacekeeping and essentially non-threatening—they enable Germany to assume international responsibilities without direct combat.

Another issue on which the Germans have attempted to make their mark is in the area of energy security, one of the central issues confronting Europe and the US and one where the relationship with Russia is particularly important, providing Germany with one-third of its energy supplies. Having cut a deal with Russia to bypass Poland and other countries with a direct natural gas pipeline through the Baltic Sea, Germany has now been confronted with a Russia willing to cut off vital energy supplies, for instance, in the case of Ukraine and Belarus. Energy security is a critical challenge to continental security and vitally important to resource-dependent Germany. Chancellor Merkel has expended tremendous effort—albeit to date futile efforts—through the EU trying to assure an extension of the Russia-EU Cooperation Partnership Agreement.[20] As Constanze Stelzenmueller has argued recently, Berlin's policymakers' insistence on labeling German relations with Russia a "strategic partnership" poses the question of whether Germany will be able and willing to use its considerable political resources to change Russia's behavior and to stand up to Moscow when necessary."[21]

Furthermore, Russia poses an even more complicated challenge, as Germany has interests that are at once state-to-state, within the European framework, and as a member of the transatlantic community. As Russia's largest single trading partner, Germany has attempted to pursue a stable relationship with Russia, if not as friendly under Chancellor Merkel and Foreign Minister Steinmeier as it was under Schroeder. In 2008, Georgia exemplified the often-difficult nature of the relations—first, with Germany along with France and others refusing to offer a Membership Action Plan (MAP) to Georgia and Ukraine during the 2008 NATO Bucharest summit in the face of Russian objections (and in contrast to the US position); and second, with the splintered European reaction to the Russian confrontation in South Ossetia in the summer of 2008. In the latter instance, while the initial official German reaction was mild, this reaction changed with the further advance of Russian forces. and by the time of the Sochi-Medvedev/Merkel meeting, Merkel spoke out in favor Georgia's right to NATO membership.[22]

One element that is hard to assess is the continued long-term direction of the French-German relationship, particularly as it affects the long-standing and traditional leadership of the two countries in the EU. The 2007 election of President Sarkozy made this assessment more difficult. There is no question that in the past, France and Germany had been the motor behind the EU. Any major initiative had traditionally required French and/or German support, preferably both. The political weight of the two was substantial and, in addition, the economic support of the Germans for the European Union for many years far exceeded any equitable monetary distribution. Quite simply, Bonn/ now Berlin sought its acceptance into the democratic community through a number of channels, including prominently, the European Union. With Germany embedded in the EU as well as other institutions, the fear of a German resurgence had been soothed in the post-World War II era.

In more recent years, Germany has continued to wrap its domestic and foreign policy within the EU mantle. This has been particularly necessary with the increase in its size from moderately larger than Britain or France in the past to significantly larger than either of those countries with the unification of East and West Germany (totaling 80 million plus).

Since 2005 Chancellor Merkel has maintained an active EU role for Germany, but with greater caution than has been true in the past, particularly over the EU constitutional issue. Also, her own personality is clearly tilted toward the United States, in a way that was not true of her predecessor. But she recognizes the importance of the multilateral comfort the EU affords. Note that she traveled to Paris on her inauguration day—within hours of assuming the chancellorship! She next chose to travel to Brussels to visit the EU and NATO, and to London. She then flew to Washington with, by the way, Russia quite a distant destination in comparison. She made the interesting decision at that point to make visits to Warsaw and Jerusalem, including a visit with the outgoing leadership of the Palestinian Liberation Organization (PLO) in Ramallah.

The Berlin-Paris duo continues to function in many areas of EU policy, but the willingness of the Germans to carry the financial burden in these tight economic times has greatly reduced. A degree of skepticism is further indication of the German's growing reluctance to 'carry' weaker EU states, as it has in the past, Merkel's remarks with respect to EU membership of Turkey has been one example of Germany's caution. She has been outspokenly in opposition to full membership, indicating an unwillingness to underwrite the costs of Turkish economic shortfalls as the EU has in the past with new members, and has advocated a 'privileged' member status for Turkey for the foreseeable future. Finally, there has been growing skepticism about the ability of Europe to reflect German interests, with German court decisions reflecting caution with respect to European defense and other areas. *Financial Times* editorialist John Thornhill has pointed out that "Germany's postwar Bonn consensus that projected the country's national dreams on to Europe has shattered." He cites Jan Techau of the German Council on Foreign Relations as commenting that "Germans have lost faith in their ersatz religion of Europe ... Nobody would now automatically say that what is good for Europe is good for Germany." For Thornhill, "Germany is simply behaving like other big member states."[23] This move away from the expectation that Europe will become increasingly federalist means that Germany will have to pursue its own interests as a state, a further indication of its evolving role and a complicating factor for transatlantic relations.

Germany as a Transatlantic Actor

If Chancellor Merkel appeared more comfortable with President George W. Bush than her predecessor Schroeder, this did not translate in every instance into blind acquiescence on issues.[24] She clearly recognized that the German public moved in its sentiments during the Bush administration. The perception of national identity discussed above manifested itself in a more critical view of the United States, particularly in light of the conflict in Iraq. Despite the 200,000 who lit candles on September 12, 2001, in solidarity with the American people after 9/11 at the Brandenburg Gate and despite Germany's joining the NATO force in Afghanistan against terrorism, the public became disaffected with the United States in large part over Iraq, but also over the Kyoto Agreement on greenhouse gases, the US' nonparticipation in the treaty on land minds and other issues. The chancellor could not ignore this shift, which crossed German party lines.[25]

While the relationship became a friendly one, with Chancellor Merkel visiting President Bush and he in turn visiting the home town of the chancellor, state relations between Merkel and Bush appeared to be far more in the realm of 'normal' than during the Kohl administration, when Germany routinely accepted US decisions—particularly at the official level—without major dissent. A striking example of this was during the 1980s, when at the same time that there were massive demonstrations over the deployment of intermediate range nuclear (INF) weapons, Chancellor Schmidt supported the deployments and the government fell over the issue. There was eventually public acceptance, particularly in light of later arms control negotiations.[26] German

Atlanticism strongly marked characterized the post-World War II era; in the post-Cold War era, the Atlantic partnership has remained strong, but both a European and international role based on German interests have increasingly supplemented it.[27]

On taking office in 2005, Merkel made clear that she would not override the Schroeder refusal to join the coalition in Iraq. Even in her home town, when hosting the US president, Chancellor Merkel confronted demonstrations by her fellow townspeople protesting the conflict in Iraq. The contrast between Bush's visit and visits by earlier US presidents was striking. It was within this political landscape that, leaving all possible personal sentiments between the two leaders aside, she had to navigate her coalition government.[28]

For this reason, Chancellor Merkel surprised a number of her constituents on her first visit after her 2005 election to Washington—positively surprised them, according to polls. Even before leaving Germany, she called on the United States to close down the Guantanamo installation where the United States was holding suspected al Qaeda terrorists. She repeated this admonition directly to the president in their formal meeting in Washington. In response, he acknowledged her concern and her right to comment but, in essence, made clear that he begged to differ. The trip proved highly successful, but Merkel's refusal to defer to the president on this issue, while not unusual for most countries, was at the very least unusual for the Germans and a clear sign of an increased German assertiveness.

The US-German relationship has evolved over the years and, one could say, matured. But the magnitude of the evolution probably became most noticeable after the Iraq crisis, followed by the Teuven "chocolate summit" in which Germany, France and Belgium and Luxembourg asserted European defense efforts. The impact of the disagreement over the appropriate action with respect to Iraq was tremendous, but many viewed it also as partly due to the stark difference between the Social Democrat Gerhard Schroeder and the conservative Republican George W. Bush. As it became evident that the new conservative Christian Democrat Merkel would not always agree with the US, the divergence in approach and, in many respects, philosophy between the two countries was hard to deny.

The Chancellor Merkel's relationship with President Obama continues to evolve, but it is clearly one that builds on a foundation of greater equality as partners. The popularity of then-candidate Obama on his July 2008 visit to Berlin and the astounding audience of 200,000 who heard his speech there illustrate the enthusiasm of the German public for Obama. Surely the expectations for him have outstripped what any one president could deliver. Already, at the Victory Angel, candidate Obama foreshadowed his expectations as well—his appeal for more support in Afghanistan was heard but it was not greeted with the cheers that his remarks on multilateralism and other commentary drew. There was no doubt that tough negotiations were ahead as the US shifted its focus from Iraq to Afghanistan. But the groundwork for more cooperation even in Afghanistan was laid.

The NATO missile defense discussions have been instructive. While the Germans have accepted the value of missile defense in the face of growing evidence of an Iranian threat to Europe, initially the lack of consultations with all the allies caused frictions within the alliance. Once consultations on the need for radar in the Czech Republic, with missiles in Poland, occurred in NATO, and the decision could be widely vetted and agreed, the Germans accepted this decision. They also accepted President Obama's 2009 revision to engage in a sea-based response to the anticipated Iranian threat. The need to discuss and consult in a timely manner has long been a problem in the alliance. With the increasingly higher level of activity within NATO, as well as within the EU, coordination becomes particularly critical.

Even as the Berlin-Washington relationship has evolved, the priority Chancellor Merkel places on NATO is impressive and represents a move away from the leanings of her predecessor. In her remarks at the 2006 Wehrkunde (Munich Security Conference) two months after she assumed office, the chancellor made the following points about NATO: it is central to consultation on conflicts and threats on a global scale; it represents the key decision-making institution for political and military action; and its discussions must involve issues that are not exclusively European issues, but include the Middle East and Iran. She furthermore declared that for NATO the European Security and Defense Policy (ESDP/now CESDP) is an opportunity, not a challenge.[29] In other words, she reiterated that NATO is an essential foundation for Germany but added that the US must understand ESDP as an important complement.

Germany will continue as a strong transatlantic partner to the United States and, in a different way from Britain, a "special partner" to the United States. The depth of that special relationship has diminished with the advent of a new German leadership in Berlin that did not experience the World War II or even receive aid from the US-sponsored Marshall Plan (in the case of Angela Merkel), prompting a different frame of reference.[30] But this viewpoint is not limited to the chancellor. Even the traditionally more American-oriented Parliamentary State Secretary Christian Schmidt has commented that "our American friends should accept that Europe is becoming a more mature and equal partner of the United States. That is nothing to worry about; on the contrary, we are following similar interests, sometimes in different ways and with dissimilar means, but we always pull on the same side of the rope." He went on to call for a transatlantic relationship and a European security identity that are "fully compatible with one another."[31]

The US-German relationship will in the future be based on mutual values, strategic interests and strong economic and political ties as well as common threats. But while Germany will continue to see NATO as its primary security guarantee, and likewise the partnership with the United States through that alliance's lens and through a strong bilateral relationship as elements in its security, Berlin will inevitably have to find a balance with the emerging responsibilities of the EU in security and defense. For the foreseeable future, EU interests will focus on those challenges beyond the capacity of NATO—domestic catastrophes such as floods, fires and peacekeeping/modest intervention in areas as Africa, particularly countries with strong ties to Europe. This balancing will require careful and close consultations.

This will mean that the US-German relationship will not be as automatic as one could argue was the case in the past, with large numbers of American forces stationed in Germany and a dependence on the United States in a wide range of areas. As Germany asserts its national identity and emerges as a 'normal' power with strategic interests not bound to the World War II memories that spawned its identity as a "civilian power," US expectations have likewise increased about German contributions. It will no longer be enough for Germany to fund a joint effort rather than send forces (as was the case in the 1990/91 Gulf War) or stand on the sidelines during a NATO conflict. While the Germans recognize this and, in fact, were out front on the NATO declaration of Article 5 on September 12, 2001, and in assuming responsibilities in Afghanistan already in early 2002, Germany's modest defense budget (which nevertheless is sixth largest in the world) and use of caveats in its Afghan mission have created tensions with the Americans. So as the Germans assume a more "normal" posture in their relationship with the United States, tensions will be unavoidable and both countries' focus is required for the relationship to remain close.

Germany as an International Actor

Since the election of Chancellor Merkel, the international role of Germany has been quietly stabilizing and attempting to find its appropriate equilibrium. This has continued into the second Merkel administration, after the 2009 election resulted in a change to a CDU/CSU/FDP coalition resulting in a Free Democratic Party (FDP) Vice Chancellor and Foreign Minister Westerwelle and Christian Social Union (CSU) Defense Minister Zu Guttenberg. Germany has avoided over-committing its forces and has been steadfast but cautious in those missions on which it has cautiously decided to embark. During the Bush Administration the shift in public opinion to a more critical stance toward the United States and traditional German policies had, in a sense, put the government out in front of the population in its more positive approach; making international forays requested by the US posed high political risks for the government. This is expected to moderate under the popular Obama administration.

On the cautious side, Chancellor Merkel explicitly and repeatedly stated her intention not to send German troops to Iraq—no German boots on the ground in Baghdad. The reluctance to send forces was coupled with a willingness to assist in training Iraqi police and army personnel either in Germany or outside of Iraqi borders. This position remained constant from the Schroeder to the Merkel administration.[32] Even Germany's announcement in 2004 that it would not participate in the agreement by NATO to open a modest training center in Iraq found support from Chancellor Merkel, and there has been continued resistance to participation with the coalition in Iraq.

But this caution in the case of Iraq does not reflect and, in fact, is contrary to the general acceptance by both the previous and current government of an enhanced role for Germany in support of European stability in the Balkans and in addressing the threat of terrorism in Afghanistan. In the Balkans, German participation has increased as the United States gradually reduced its presence in the region to meet its needs in Iraq and elsewhere. Not only are there German forces in Bosnia-Herzegovina (since 2004/EUFOR) and Kosovo (since 1999 KFOR), but the Germans also have had a presence as part of the European force in Macedonia (2002/3 Operation Concordia). In the case of Kosovo, in 1999 opposition to a first-ever German participation in a conflict since 1945 was stopped in its tracks by the unlikely Green coalition partner Foreign Minister Joschka Fischer, whose party had opposed NATO until it entered the Schroeder government. Minister Fischer argued that Germany of all countries could not refuse to assist when there was clear evidence of genocide. As a result, dedicated Tornados flew in Kosovo. Germany's presence in the Balkans is political as well as military and includes substantial development assistance; it is, in essence, primarily peacekeeping. Parliament has repeatedly approved the stationing of forces there with the support of both coalitions over the past decade.[33]

A more striking and assertive move has been the German presence in Afghanistan. While the Americans' initial decision in fall 2001 not to involve NATO forces per se against the Taliban caused consternation among the European allies, Germany's commitment to the War on Terror was demonstrated with a Bundestag vote in November 2001, posing a risk to the Schroeder government in a deployment of troops to Afghanistan. But Defense Minister Struck made the telling comment with respect to Afghanistan that German defense begins at the Hindu Kush. In February–August 2003, the Germans joined the Dutch in assuming leadership of the International Security Assistance Force (ISAF) forces. In August 2003 NATO assumed overall leadership of ISAF and the German Parliament—as required by the 1994 decision—since that time has approved over 4,500 troops, with approximately 500 more approved after the Obama 'surge' announced at the end of 2009, in addition to an increase in development aid. While this is less than the U.S. may have desired, nevertheless it is an increase during the financial crisis. The 2009 election was an interesting example of German support for the NATO mission in Afghanistan and the commitment to the U.S. global war on terror that has underpinned the German force, despite a skeptical public. There was an elite CDU/CSU/SPD governing consensus on the need to contribute forces in Afghanistan as well as support from the opposition FDP that replaced the SPD—i.e., all the mainstay parties, with only Die Linke (Left Party) opposed-and thus the German mandate was extended from late 2008 for a full year rather than the usual six months, to avoid Afghanistan becoming an issue in the election. The government's commitment faced persistent public opposition to German forces in Afghanistan. During the election campaign, al Qaeda also attempted intimidation tactics in the media, warning of the consequences of continued German presence in Afghanistan. In addition, a night-time airstrike in the German northern district of Afghanistan that killed civilians prompted the chancellor to address parliament on the issue for the first time on Afghanistan. Despite the pressure of public opinion, the airstrike appears to have had little impact as an election issue (but concern later in the public), and the German Afghan mission received a further mandate after the September 27 election and the formation of the new CDU/CSU/ FDP government, which continued Germany's commitment of approximately 4,500 troops.

Beginning in November 2001, there have been a number of debates and votes in parliament on German military deployments to territory outside of that defined during the Cold War as the Euro-Atlantic area of operations. While there have been dissenting votes, by and large support for German military operations 'out of area' has been cross-party. These and subsequent votes fall under the 1994 Constitutional Court ruling that requires majority parliamentary approval for the use of Bundeswehr troops. But there is increasingly support for demonstrating Germany's commitment in the international arena to stability and security. For example, although it declined for historical reasons to put boots on the ground in the Lebanon/Israeli confrontation, Germany did send frigates to assist in the UN force in Lebanon in the summer of 2006 as part of UNIFIL; there they remain off the coast preventing arms smuggling, monitoring the ceasefire, and undertaking mine clearance.[34]

While the Iraq conflict brought large numbers of the German public into the streets to demonstrate against the United States, the other activities of the German forces have not encountered tremendous opposition. German chemical warfare specialists stationed in Kuwait in case chemical weapons stockpiles were found during the Iraq conflict and German frigates off the Horn of Africa did not elicit public concern in 2003 and the German military, in part, remain as part of Operation Enduring Freedom (OEF) to secure sea lines of communication, stop transport of drugs and weapons, which assists international terrorism and the newer threat from piracy. A quiet sense of German responsibility internationally first found expression during the 1999 Kosovo conflict and has continued in the Afghanistan deployment as well as in anti-piracy operations. But the willingness of the Germans to deploy Post-Conflict Reconstruction Teams (PRTs) to Afghanistan and support the third largest force in the country has its limits; it refused at the same time to lift caveats on those forces that do not permit deployment to the south, where they are needed, creating friction with the US and allies, who are forced to bear the burden on the Pakistan border.

A clear sign of Germany's desire to assume responsibilities in the international arena is certainly the quest for a permanent UN Security Council seat,

All Ongoing Deployments as of 1 January 2009

2007	Sudan/UNAMID
2006	Lebanon/UNIFIL
	Democratic Republic of Congo/EUSEC RD Congo
2005	Sudan/UNMIS
2004	Bosnia-Herzegovina
	Ethiopia and Eritrea/UNMEE
2002	Afghanistan/UNAMA
	Horn of Africa/OEF
	Afghanistan/ISAF
2001	Mediterranean OAE
1999	Kosovo/KFOR
1994	Georgia/UNOMIG

Listed (selected) chronologically by End Date

7/2006–11/2006	Democratic Republic of Congo/EUFOR RD Congo
2004	AMIS disaster relief (Darfur)
3/2003–12/2003	Macedonia/Operation Concordia
2/2002–7/2003	Kuwait/OEF
2002	Elbe Flood Relief
1997	Oder Flood Disaster
12/1995–12/1996	Former Yugoslavia/IFOR
8/1991–9/1996	Iraq/UNSCOM
8/1994–12/1994	Rwanda/UNAMIR
5/1992–11/1993	Cambodia/UNTAC
1960	Earthquake in Morocco

FIGURE 6.1 Selected Bundeswehr Missions. Information taken from German Government (Bundesregierung)/German Military (Bundeswehr) website: http://www.bundesregierung.de/content/EN/Artikel/Auslandseinsaetsze-der-bundeswehr. The Bundeswehr has deployed 130 missions since its inception.

a request that the US has not welcomed, countering that the issue needs a broader discussion. During the Schroeder administration, German UN Ambassador Gunter Pleuger actively worked for a UN Security Council (UNSC) seat in New York and did the same later from his position in the Foreign Ministry. With the failure of a broader UN reform, the German efforts have taken a lower priority, but the goal of taking a seat at the table as a permanent member with veto powers remains on Germany's agenda. The accompanying discussion of the responsibilities which would attach to a permanent UNSC member revealed a serious commitment, but the limitations of German active participation beyond peacekeeping, development activities, etc. belie the yet-unresolved contradictions in a country moving from a forty-year stance as a civilian power to one ready to assume the responsibilities of a major power.

There are signs as well for a healthy future, despite the shifting German roles. While deployments of German forces in and outside Europe have stabilized since 1994 and the government and public appear to have absorbed the impact of this effort, Germany on the international level has become increasingly active in diplomatic efforts. Particularly in crisis/conflict management and peacekeeping, so-called 'soft power', their efforts have increased to the advantage of the transatlantic alliance. In the negotiations on the future of Kosovo, the Germans have played an active, even leadership, role and presumably will participate in any longer-term settlement.[35] In the European arena, EU efforts—including German—in crisis management in Europe have also taken the burden off of the transatlantic agenda generally.

The German role at NATO with respect to Afghanistan was reinforced in the summer of 2008 by a visit of then-Foreign Minister Steinmeier to Afghanistan, where he committed Germany to the stabilization and reconstruction of the country, an area of German strength. At the same time, the German impact in the Balkans has been substantial and the German presence has been effective—as part of an EU or UN mission. While it is at a standstill for the present, German participation in negotiating the 'roadmap' for the Middle East toward a settlement in the Israeli/Palestinian conflict has been equal to that of the other major EU actors.

Significant also has been the German diplomatic role in the effort to stem the development of Iran's nuclear capabilities.[36] Note that the determination of all three EU actors—Germany, UK and France—has been predicated on nonmilitary action to the extent possible. Immediately before the 2005 election, Chancellor Schroeder "called on the United States to leave 'the military option off the table.'"[37] The American threat of military action was rejected in the early stages of the tension over the nuclear issue, albeit never ruled out entirely for reasons of deterrence. It is the United States that adopted the more cautious option in negotiations, not the other way around. The German role in the 'discussions' with Iran has been constructive and has been in coordination with the other European allies as well as the US. It has built on the low-level but sustaining relationship that Germany has maintained over the years with the Iranians. This relationship has not been available to the Americans since 1979 and the German role has proved beneficial for the negotiations by the EU-3 and the US.

As NATO increasingly assumes a global role, Germany's history of working through multilateral institutions will also mean that Germany will become more involved internationally. This would be a quite natural development even for Chancellor Merkel, given her remarks at Wehrkunde in 2006. Not comfortable to strike out alone, Germany prefers to work within the framework of multilateral institutions. The evolution of NATO suggested in an article by Ivo Daalder and James Goldgeier may not occur as they intimated, but certainly their thesis that NATO has already 'gone global,' in the limited sense of 'out of area', is based on a realistic assessment of NATO today.[38] Germany will remain a part of that NATO, but only within its self-established confines.

In *International Peacekeeping*, Maren Tomforde cites sociologists including David Segal, Charles Moskos and Morris Janowitz who "describe soldiers' roles in UN missions as that of constabularies." But Tomforde concludes that "German soldiers' self-perception is even less robust than that. Due to " . . . Rules of Engagement, and very limited opportunities to practice law enforcement, many soldiers see their roles rather as aid volunteers and 'helpers in uniform' . . . these new tasks and roles mostly contradict traditional tasks of combat and the exertion of physical violence in conflict."[39]

Germany has found a new sense of national identity that is manifested not only in unification, but also in its contributions to ISAF in Afghanistan with troops, aerial support and leadership, and in its role in the negotiations with Iran and in the Balkans. In all these instances, the Germans have taken an equal role and assumed the corresponding responsibilities. But all of these undertakings remain within the broader context of multilateral institutions. As Anne-Marie LeGloannec concludes in her analysis of Germany's power, one cannot speak of increased German power.[40] But there has been an increase in involvement by Germany in relationships with its allies, in the European Union and NATO as well as negotiations within the United Nations, the International Atomic Energy Agency and other bodies.

In the areas considered above, under Chancellor Merkel the relationship between Germany and the United States has notably improved, and it is unlikely to return to the more traditional subservience of Berlin to Washington.

Germany's role as a European power is long established and assuming the 2007 EU presidency permitted Germany to take a prominent leadership role in that institution—particularly on the issues of energy security and the European Security and Defense Policy (ESDP). As co-host with France of NATO's 60th anniversary celebration in April 2009, Germany signaled its role as a stalwart ally in NATO, participating substantially in Afghanistan but not abandoning the caveats that demonstrate its historical hesitation over the use of force.

But as the 2006 Lebanon crisis revealed, there will continue to be regions and countries where Germany's comfort level for intervention, even as peacekeepers, is low. While supporting the efforts of the UN, the Germans opted not to participate in the Lebanon ground force due to its history and a reluctance to take on a potentially confrontational role with traditional allies like Israel. While sending a naval unit to secure the coast and two C-160 Transall transport planes, the chancellor ruled out "the deployment of German police and combat troops."[41] This would, in any case, require parliamentary majority approval in any conflict situation. But despite such exceptions, Germany's contribution to peacekeeping has steadily risen, including assistance in the Pacific and Indian Oceans after the 2004 tsunami. The Germans appear to have little reluctance to be involved in crisis management either in Europe through ESDP/CESDP or internationally through the United Nations, and the requirement for a parliamentary vote does not pertain in such instances.[42]

Conclusions

What then is the bottom line for Germany since the assumption of the chancellorship by Angela Merkel and the German display of national identity during the World Cup? The answer is that, surprisingly, there has been only gradual change at best and, in essence, there has been no major deviation from the cautious military forays into the international arena made by Merkel's predecessors. Under Chancellor Merkel, there has been an increase in diplomatic involvement and in the use of the military in peacekeeping. This trend may be expected to continue: a willingness to deploy militarily, but with great caution, while at the same time an acceptance of a larger diplomatic, conflict management and peacekeeping role for Germany. That said, the distance that Germany has traveled—from unification to a cautious stance with respect to the 1990/1 Gulf War under the Kohl administration to the Constitutional Court's 1994 decision to the involvement of Germany in the 1999 Kosovo conflict, when Germany, as noted by Chancellor Schroeder, became a "normal" state—is substantial. But there remain a number of potentially contentious issues for transatlantic relations:

First, despite the atlanticist focus of Chancellor Merkel, German policy is increasingly grounded in national interests, which, unlike in the Cold War, are not always and necessarily identical with those of the US. The fact that the Bundestag extended Afghanistan deployments beyond the usual six months in the 2009 elections demonstrated the high stakes for the CDU/CSU/SPD Grand Coalition government, with the chancellor and foreign minister challenging each other in national elections for the chancellorship. Each party attempted to stake out their positions for an election year that proved highly polarizing, including Germany's relations with the United States and with Russia. In the election an atlanticist focus clearly continued, but again there was divergence from it at points, particularly with respect to foreign policy, with the FDP insisting on the inclusion in the coalition agreement of an intention to remove all nuclear weapons from German soil that may prove uncontroversial, but at the time was not U.S. declared policy and continues to be a topic of discussion both bilaterally and within NATO.[43]

Second, but related to the first point, the German public has been opposed to the direction American policy has taken at least from the beginning of the discussion of the Iraq conflict. By deploying troops to the Horn of Africa, to Kuwait and in the Balkans, the Schroeder government was as far forward in 2003—maybe even beyond German opinion had the public focused on the nearly 10,000 forces deployed outside of Germany at one point—as it could possibly be. After the 2005 election, the CDU/CSU/SPD government took a similarly cautious position on Iraq deployments, and such caution has continued as well in the CDU/CSU/FDP administration..

Third, the German government has increased its commitment to Afghanistan only gradually, albeit that commitment is the third largest of NATO European members and has been increased with the necessary consent of the Bundestag, most notably in spring 2010 in response to the Obama surge. The incident in Kunduz in fall 2009 with the use of firepower and subsequent civilian deaths has precipitated more discussion by the chancellor, including a speech on the German Afghanistan mission by Merkel to the Parliament in April 2010. The casualties in Afghanistan (second only to the UK in terms of European casualties among the coalition partners) and any deterioration of the conflict can be expected to take their toll on the public and public support. The German commitment has come with caveats that, contrary to US pressure, can be expected to remain, with corresponding friction in transatlantic relations more generally.

Fourth, the Germans have had a forward-leaning policy on UN Security Council membership, although pressure for it slowed, even stopped, as a result of a stalemate in the United Nations itself on the broader membership reform issue. The United States did not support the German position, not with respect to Germany per se, as much as a difference in the US approach to reform more generally. The issue remains on the back burner for German politicians.

Fifth, while rejecting military deployments (Iraq) without public support, the Germans have accepted crisis management and peacekeeping as legitimate responsibilities (as in the Balkans), either as part of a transatlantic NATO deployment (preferably with a UN resolution) or an EU deployment (as in the Democratic Republic of Congo and Macedonia). As the EU increases its role in crisis management, there may be increasing strain on German forces for deployments sought by NATO, that could potentially put further strain on the transatlantic relationship.

Sixth, because of domestic pressures due to unification, the worldwide financial crisis and other demands on the budget, German defense budgets have been held below 1.5% and these strictures have the potential to cause friction despite the German public's (and elite) attraction to President Obama.[44] All areas of the military budget and acquisitions have been affected.[45] In fact, since the financial crisis has strained the domestic economies of all members of the transatlantic alliance, it will doubtless affect forces and resources for joint endeavors. The enduring burden-sharing disputes within the alliance will not go away and can be expected to increase, and perhaps even intensify.

On the day before Chancellor Merkel's 2005 inauguration, Wolfgang Munchau commented that " . . . a new style of foreign policy may still achieve something. But it would be a mistake to expect too much of Germany's new chancellor."[46] While Germany is retreating from its traditional vision of the civilian power paradigm, it is also not venturing outside its traditional multilateral parameters. Driven by not only financial considerations but also a German tradition of caution, Chancellor Merkel has, and may be expected to continue, a limited approach to the use of German power and its military force, but, as noted by Rainer Baumann, that will not rule out growth and change in non-defense operations.[47] This is evident in ongoing dialogue with

Iran, with Israel and Palestinian leaders, in the wide-range of peacekeeping operations in which Germany has participated, and even in the training, but not with troops, it has undertaken in Iraq.

What will this mean for the European security paradigm? It will mean an assertive chancellor not just under Merkel, but most likely continuing for the longer term with consequences for the German role as a European and NATO partner. Close US-German relations will persist, but with the Germans moving increasingly into responsible roles and taking positions that do not necessarily mirror those of the US. Internationally, Germany will continue to involve its parliament in the issue of deployments, but with an increasing willingness to play a role in the international arena, including, but not limited to, crisis management, humanitarian cases, and military assistance. In short, Germany's changes in its perception of its national identity will challenge the existing roles it has played in the postwar era, as a European actor, an international actor, and in the transatlantic alliance.

7   Turkey and the US

A Transatlantic Future?

Bill Park[1]

Introduction

Towards the end of the Bush presidency, Pew Global Attitudes Project findings suggested that only 12% of Turks view the US favorably, fewer than the number favoring Saudi Arabia, Iran or Pakistan, thereby identifying Turks as the most anti-American population of those polled.[2] Indeed, Turkish anti-Americanism emerged as a threat to Turkish-US relations in its own right, and much of it can be traced back to the invasion of Iraq in 2003 and events in Iraq since.[3] An intensified Turkish nationalism[4] frequently combines with an emotionally charged approach to the US[5] to inflate the negative impact of any Turkish-US policy difference. As former US ambassador to Turkey Mark Parris expressed it, the Bush administration left US relations with Turkey 'worse than he found them'.[6] This was despite the attempt in the second Bush term to redress the 'deferred maintenance'[7] from which US-Turkish relations had been suffering since the mutual misunderstandings and the mishandling of policies (by both sides) that accompanied the US-led invasion of Iraq in March 2003.[8]

The efforts to improve the relationship were not without substance. In July 2006 Secretary of State Condoleezza Rice and then Turkish Foreign Minister Abdullah Gul initiated the 'Shared Vision and Structured Dialogue to Advance the Turkish-American Strategic Partnership', referring to the shared ideals and objectives of the two allies and instituting regular bilateral meetings to ensure cooperation.[9] In December 2005 a new US ambassador to Turkey, Ross Wilson, occupied the 'empty chair' in Ankara that had been vacated bitterly by Eric Edelman in March 2005. Numerous delegations visited in both directions, and many of the US 'neo-conservatives' who had been most bitter at Turkey's March 2003 'failure' to support US military planning and were inclined to accuse Turkey's ruling Justice and Development Party (Adalet ve Kalkinma Partisi, or AKP) of 'Islamization'—or even 'Islamofascism'—lost influence or had left office.[10] Efforts to factor differences over Iraq out of the relationship in an effort to compartmentalize issues met with some success. The bureaucracies in both capitals focused on pragmatic cooperation and on rebuilding relationships that had been allowed to atrophy.[11]

More significantly, at a 5 November 2007 meeting between Turkish Prime Minister Tayyip Erdogan and President George W. Bush in Washington, the US agreed to provide Turkey with 'actionable intelligence' on the Kurdish Workers Party's (Partiya Karkari Kurdistan, or PKK) movements and bases in northern Iraq and to permit cross-border Turkish military operations against the estimated 3000–4000 separatist fighters holed up there, who were held responsible for continuing attacks on Turkish territory. At the meeting, Bush referred to the PKK as 'a common enemy' of both the US and Turkey. The improvement in the atmosphere of Turkish-US relations in the wake of this agreement was remarkable. President Gul's trip to Washington in January 2008 was heralded in both the US and Turkey as a new 'honeymoon' between the two NATO allies.

Turkish F-16s began their US-sanctioned bombing campaign against PKK targets in northern Iraq on 16 December 2007. The initial bombing raids were followed on 21 February by a surprise, and surprisingly short, eight-day ground troop incursion.[12] The incursion was abruptly terminated in the immediate aftermath of US warnings that the operation should be brought to an early close; it was just a day after the Turkish military authorities had insisted the mission would last for as long as deemed necessary. This turn of events produced some quite scathing comment from the usually pro-military Kemalist opposition parties, who said that the campaign had been prematurely aborted due to US pressure, an allegation denied by the Turkish General Staff (TGS) and government.[13] Nevertheless, in Turkish political comment it became *de rigueur* to refer to the role of US pressure in the termination of the ground force attack as if it were an established fact. Much of Turkey's initial flood of goodwill towards the US subsequently evaporated, and suspicion of US Kurdish policy persists. An opinion survey published in August 2009 by the Ankara-based International Strategic Research Organization found that the public still regarded the US as the biggest threat to Turkey.[14]

Thus it was vital that the Obama administration got off to a good start with respect to Turkey and built upon the improved relationship in the wake of the November 2007 agreement. The appointment of Hillary Clinton as secretary of state, and her successful visit to Turkey in March 2009, indeed suggested that the Clintonites had returned, hinting at what perhaps had been the warmest era in Turkish-US relations. During her visit, Secretary Clinton called for an end to the isolation of northern Cyprus. Obama himself chose Turkey as his first bilateral visit (other than to Canada) in April. In his address to the National Assembly, he spoke of Turkey as a 'critical ally' and strongly supported Turkey's EU accession. He also insisted that the US was not at war with Islam, a point reiterated in his Cairo address in June, when he called for 'a new beginning between the US and Muslims around the world'. He has spoken of the need for a two-state solution to the Israeli-Palestinian problem, and spoken out against Israeli settlement on the West Bank.[15] He clearly believes the Iraq war to have been a mistake, calling it a 'war of choice' that divided the US itself, and pledged to terminate the US combat mission in Iraq by 31 August 2010, and that he intends to honor the US-Iraq security pact by withdrawing all U.S. troops by the end of 2011.

The wider atmospherics too appear favourable. Obama has already adopted a more multilateralist approach to diplomacy than that associated with his predecessor. The Obama team favors engagement with its adversaries, and to that end has already made overtures to Iran, in particular, and to Russia. It has also shown itself to be more ready to consult with its allies, and to be ready to commit the US to institutionalized approaches to global problems. Washington's cooperation with the UN and with bodies such as the International Criminal Court (ICC) is predicted to expand, and the administration has indicated its willingness to adopt the Kyoto Protocol. Obama himself appears to exhibit greater cultural sensitivity, a disinclination to think or speak in moralistic tones, and an aversion to ideological absolutes. There will likely be less talk of a Greater Middle East. In his person, policies and presentation, he offers a much-needed global 'rebranding' of the US, which makes demonization of the US more difficult than has latterly been the case.[16] Foreign Minister Ahmet Davutoglu's June 2009 visit to the US appeared to go well, and the Turkish Defense Secretary Vecdi Gonul declared the Turkish-US relationship to be better than it had ever been since the AKP came to power.

Yet because ill feeling has persisted, and Turkey's internal and external circumstances have been transformed, it is possible that the foundations upon which the half-century-old relationship was constructed may have shifted too dramatically to permit its resurrection along familiar lines. This shift need not be an unwelcome development. As one analyst has expressed it, the damage inflicted on Turkish-US relations by differences over Iraq may have induced in both sides 'a more realistic perception' of the relationship's limitations.[17] If this is so, what kind of relationship with Turkey might the US's post-Bush administrations expect to achieve in today's much-altered regional and global security environment? In exploring this question, it might first be instructive to re-examine the relationship's past Cold War foundations. The chapter will then consider how the end of the Cold War shook these foundations, how the regional foreign policy initiatives of the AKP government and the domestic political and social shifts that are associated with the AKP have raised further questions about the basis of Turkish-US relations in the post-Cold War era, before it goes on to consider options and prospects for Turkey's future transatlantic relationships.

Cold War Relations

Washington's approach to Turkey in the Cold War was underpinned by the imperatives of containment. Geostrategically, Turkey's location on the Soviet Union's southern flank, when added to the country's proximity to the oil-rich and conflict-strewn Middle East, ensured Turkey's salience in American strategic calculation. For Turkey, too, the Cold War value of the relationship with Washington was paramount. Suspicion of Soviet intentions ran deeply in Turkey, and the country's reliance on US financial and military assistance was profound. Encouraging and enabling the US to commit to Turkey's defense constituted a cornerstone of Turkey's security outlook.[18]

Furthermore Ankara was aware that 'its friendships in the world (did) not run deep'.[19] With the founding of the republic in 1923 Turkey largely turned its back on the Middle East. This stance, combined with Turkey's determined secularism and (from 1952) NATO membership, limited Ankara's capacity to function as a 'bridge' to the wider Middle East region,[20] a fact often overlooked in Washington. Additionally, west Europeans—then as now—sometimes failed to reciprocate the Turkish elite's attachment to their country's European 'destiny'. Some initially opposed Turkey's NATO membership, and the British initially thought Turkey would be more suitably incorporated into a Middle Eastern regional alliance. Europeans also did not initially envisage Turkey as a member of the Council of Europe, established in 1949.[21] Thus, current doubts about Turkey's European essence are far from new. Indeed, during the Cold War the Turkish Republic was seen as largely peripheral to the core dynamics of European, Middle Eastern, Caucasian or Balkan politics. In this context, the US offered Ankara a rare and constant friendship, and NATO a foothold in an otherwise sometimes discouraging Europe.

Yet their bilateral relationship was never conflict-free. Turkey's strategic location meant that its importance to the United States was primarily a function of US objectives in Turkey's neighboring regions. The Bush administration's approach to Turkey followed this pattern. Differences were especially evident in Turkey's neighborhood, where it felt its core national interests were engaged—notably, over Greece, Cyprus and the Middle East. These differences led to the 'Johnson letter' of 1964, which warned Turkey that it might not receive the sympathy of its allies in the event of a confrontation with the Soviet Union over Cyprus. According to one US official, after this the Ankara-Washington relationship 'never really recovered the initial closeness',[22] with the arms embargo and closure of US facilities during the 1970s, and with Turkey's flirtation with both Moscow and with neutralism. There were serious tensions between the two countries over Turkey's domestic opium production,[23] and Ankara repeatedly restricted US access to Incirlik Air Base and other facilities whenever Middle Eastern crises broke out.[24]

In short, during the Cold War more expectation was placed on the relationship, and more exaggerated rhetoric expended on it, than regional realities sometimes enabled it to bear. Furthermore, Greek and Armenian lobbying in the US occasionally soured the atmosphere, and augmented congressional concerns about Turkey's human rights record. Overall, areas of agreement between Washington and Ankara during the Cold War were quite narrow, though intensely important, and the areas of divergence wide. The relationship had a hard center, but its outer layers were flaky. Furthermore, US advocates of Turkey did not match their inclination to stress the country's geopolitical significance with an interest in the 'black box' of Turkey's domestic political, economic and social evolution, nor with much regard for Turkey's regional dilemmas. Location has been what mattered.[25]

Without Containment

The Cold War's end and the demise of the Soviet threat were bound to shift the foundations of the Turkish-US relationship. US assessments of Turkey's geostrategic value now would derive from its proximity to the energy resources and trouble spots of the Middle East and the Persian Gulf. Furthermore, Turkey came to be seen as instrumental in Washington's dual containment of two of Turkey's troublesome neighbors, Iraq and Iran. With the exception of Turkish President Turgut Ozal's domestically isolated stance in support of the US-led effort against Iraq in 1990–1991—largely in order to prove Turkey's continuing salience to US geostrategic considerations[26]—Turkey has been generally unhappy with the role allotted it. During the 1990s, Turkey's predicament—in hosting coalition operations ('Safe Haven' and 'Northern Watch') that enabled the Kurds to break free from Baghdad's grip whilst simultaneously opposing Kurdish autonomy in both Iraq and Turkey—was a painful one. It intensified both Ankara's mistrust of US policies towards Kurdish self-determination—which were presumed to be favorably disposed—and its frustration at Turkey's strategic dependence on an American ally that was seemingly indifferent to Turkey's most profound security sensitivities.[27] Turkey's non-compliance with American wishes in 2003 reflected this dissatisfaction. Furthermore, US military aid to Turkey, which had declined throughout the 1990s, and the still substantial but reduced Turkish military dependence on the US put the relationship now on a more commercial basis.

The US itself became less 'transatlantic' in its post-Cold War strategic focus, a tendency intensified by the Bush administration's unilateralist inclinations. Perhaps of more enduring significance was the fact that the geostrategic transformation that accompanied the Cold War's demise profoundly altered Ankara's geopolitical circumstances and its diplomatic options. To Turkey's north, states such as Georgia, Azerbaijan and Ukraine sought Turkey's friendship as a bridge to the west and an alternative to the Russian shadow. The same was true of post-communist Bulgaria, Romania and Albania. In Central Asia, Turks found that a resource-rich Turkic world had suddenly opened up to them, seemingly offering economic opportunity as well as political alliance and cultural brotherhood. All in all, the post-Cold War world appeared to offer Turkey far greater scope for regional dynamism and diplomatic diversification than it had ever before enjoyed in its history.[28] The US has been supportive of Ankara's cultivation of post-Soviet neighbors and of its multilateral regional initiatives such as the Black Sea Economic Cooperation (BSEC), which engaged with former Soviet bloc states. The US hoped that Turkey could offer a secular alternative to the Iranian model of Islamic radicalism in Central Asia, a political and economic counter to lingering Russian influence throughout the post-Soviet space,[29] and an alternative to Iran and Russia as the outlet of choice for Azerbaijani and Central Asian energy supplies. The governments of the US and Turkey have pursued closely aligned policies throughout the former Soviet south, and worked jointly towards getting the Baku-Tbilisi-Ceyhan oil pipeline project off the ground.[30]

Indeed, there have been numerous bright points in US-Turkish relations since the end of the Cold War. Their diplomatic approaches to the crises that accompanied the Yugoslav breakup were broadly convergent, and Turkey contributed both to the UN Protection Force (UNPROFOR) and to the NATO Implementation/Stabilization Force (IFOR/SFOR) in Bosnia. Turkey has twice taken command of the International Stabilisation Force for Afghanistan (ISAF), established in the aftermath of the overthrow of the Taliban regime,[31] and has also made a significant contribution to UN Operations in Somalia (UNOSOM). Intelligence cooperation in the post-9/11 'war on terror' has been close, and Washington values Ankara's extant military and intelligence relationship with Israel. The US sponsored the IMF's rescue plan for the Turkish economy after its 2000/2001 collapse, and has strongly supported Turkey's EU accession aspirations. These additional 'sinews' to the relationship are not without significance, and more could yet be added.

A paradox of the post-Cold War period has been that it has encouraged the EU to ponder a 'deepening' of its integration in ways that have had a mixed impact on Turkey's accession quest and have muddled Turkey's place in Euro-Atlantic relations more broadly. Although negotiations for Turkey's EU accession commenced in October 2005, they have been fraught and accession looks some way off. In addition to the Cyprus issue, existential doubts in Europe about Turkey's European character, and Turkey's failure to meet the requirements of the Copenhagen and other criteria, the formal context of Turkey's security relationship with the EU has been contested. The 'deepening' of the EU that has been associated with the post-Cold War era has had as one of its manifestations an endeavor to create a Common European Security and Defence Policy (CESDP). As Turkey is not a EU member, this implies its exclusion, and as such Ankara has regarded the policy as threatening both to its direct regional security interests and to its full participation in western security arrangements.

Specifically, Turkey fears that the EU, which includes Greece and Cyprus, could arrive at security policies detrimental to Turkey's interests. In its quest for reassurance, Ankara's weapon was to withhold its acquiescence in the so-called 'Berlin plus' agreement, which would enable EU access to NATO assets in EU-led operations. An EU-Turkey agreement on the issue was finally signed in March 2003, but the issue remains somewhat unresolved in practical terms, as the terms of Cypriot contributions to EU-led operations in particular continue to be contested by Ankara. Turkey's confrontational negotiating style lost it much sympathy in Europe's capitals, and it has slowed both the development of CESDP and of NATO-EU institutional cooperation. To this degree, Turkey's position in the Euro-Atlantic alliance now appears problematic. Hitherto, this wrangling has caused little more than irritation in Washington, but the longer-term ramifications for the Atlantic alliance generally could be acute.

The AKP and Turkey's Foreign Relations

Turkey's foreign policy agenda has been overburdened since the end of the Cold War. The opening up of the Caucasus, Central Asia and the Balkan region has intensified Turkey's porosity to and involvement in events beyond its borders. The related and growing significance of energy in regional and global politics and Turkey's emergence as an energy hub have similarly contributed to Turkey's exposure to external developments. The EU accession process and the domestic reform program it has inspired, the Cyprus question, the ramifications of 9/11 and Iraq can be added to the range of issues that have jostled for the attention of Ankara's policy makers, and they continue to do so. The multi-focused foreign policy that Turkey has been obliged to pursue has in and of itself produced a collateral de-emphasis on the US relationship.[32]

Related to these post-Cold War shifts, but especially notably since the AKP came to power in 2002, Ankara has also adopted a more consensus-seeking and engaged diplomatic approach, particularly towards its Middle Eastern neighborhood and the wider Islamic world, in contrast to the Kemalist Republic's regional isolationism and indifference towards its own Islamic heritage.[33] Sometimes this shift is said to be at the expense of or in place of Ankara's more familiar western policy alignment.[34] However, as Erdogan has expressed it, 'We don't have the luxury of remaining insensitive to the problems in our neighborhood . . . because of our geographic location, our history, our civilization and our national interests'.[35] The ideas of Turkey's current foreign minister and former foreign policy advisor to the prime minister, Professor Ahmet Davutoglu, are central to an understanding of this new approach,[36] although he has also insisted that Turkey's post-Cold War circumstances ensure that Turkey's more multi-directed and engaged policy will outlive both him and the AKP government that he serves.[37]

Derived from an appreciation of Turkey's complex geography, history and identity, Davutoglu promotes a proactive and multi-dimensional foreign policy aiming to create 'strategic depth' in the country's foreign policy and a lessening of the perceived over-dependence on Turkey's western alignments. He rejects the notion that Turkey is or should be a bridge between regions, but instead idealizes Turkey as a country that is central rather than peripheral to the diversity of regions with which it overlaps. Davutoglu stresses the 'soft power' regional impact of Turkey's democracy, the aspiration to pursue a 'zero problem policy' towards Turkey's many neighbors, and the virtues of multi-dimensional diplomacy. None of this implies a rejection of Turkey's western orientation, but it does imply a less exclusive emphasis on it and hints that Turkey might be a less pliable regional ally to the US.

Turkey has accordingly exhibited a readiness to grapple with some of the region's more intractable political problems, often by using a 'soft power' approach not traditionally associated with Turkey's Middle East diplomacy.[38] In addition to the ruling AKP's clumsily handled January 2006 invitation to the Palestinian Hamas leader Khaled Mashaal to visit Turkey, which aroused considerable US anger, can be cited the emergence of Ankara as a mediator in talks between Israel and Syria, a role that took shape during the first half of 2008 and derived from Turkey's having relationships with both parties,[39] although since Prime Minister Erdogan's January 2009 outburst in Davos, Ankara's relations with Israel have withered while those with Syria have continued to blossom. There is also the Ankara Forum, established by business groups from Turkey, Israel and the Palestinian Authority at Turkey's initiative in April 2005, which has as its flagship project the re-opening of the Eraz Industrial Zone in Gaza under Turkish management.[40] Turkey is contributing 1000 Turkish troops to the UNSCR 1710—mandated UNIFIL mission in southern Lebanon, albeit on condition that they are confined to humanitarian rather than disarmament tasks. Gul seems to have been instrumental in persuading Damascus to hand over the suspect in the assassination of former Lebanese Prime Minister Rafik Hariri and in bridging differences between the various Lebanese factions during that country's governmental crisis in May 2008.[41] As Obama took office, Iran even seemed inclined to take up Ankara's offer to mediate between Washington and Tehran,[42] and Turkey's relationships with Gulf Cooperation Council (GCC) states have also intensified.[43]

The US-led invasion of Iraq intensified incentives for Ankara to more actively engage with its neighbors. The most unambiguous manifestation of this new direction is the 'desecuritization' of Turkey's relations with Syria and Iran, Washington's two regional *bête noirs.*[44] The dramatic relaxation of the relationship with Damascus dates back to Syria's 1998 expulsion of PKK leader Abdullah Ocalan and the closure of PKK bases in Syrian-controlled Bekaa valley in Lebanon, in the face of considerable pressure from Ankara.[45] The improvement in Turkish-Syrian relations has gathered pace remarkably since the AKP came to power, however, and is not unrelated to their shared suspicion of the aspirations of Iraqi Kurds. Turkish officials have even favorably contrasted Syrian cooperation with Turkey over the PKK with that offered by Washington.[46] President Bashar Assad paid the first ever visit to Turkey by a Syrian head of state in January 2004; it was reciprocated in February 2005 when Turkish President Necemet Sezer pushed ahead with his state trip to Damascus, notwithstanding evident American displeasure. The two countries have negotiated a range of economic, cultural, security and military agreements. Ankara, though attentive to the intensification of US pressure on Damascus for its alleged support of terrorism in both Palestine and Iraq and for its close involvement in Lebanese affairs, remains committed to friendship with its neighbor. Syria appears no less committed, and Arab reports have even identified a Syrian effort to create a Turkey-Syria-Iran regional bloc.[47]

Ankara's approach to Tehran, although wary, has also more closely resembled Europe's intermittent policy of engagement with Iran than it has Washington's more confrontational approach. Turkey has signed gas-purchasing and resource-development agreements with Tehran that have sat uneasily with Washington's preference for Iran's containment.[48] Turkish and Iranian security forces have cooperated especially closely in northern Iraq, and at the eleventh meeting of their High Security Commission in February 2006 the two neighbors renewed their counter-terrorism security pact, aimed at the PKK in northern Iraq, even as the tension over Iran's WMD program was intensifying.[49] Turkish political and military figures have spoken out against any militarization of Iran's nuclear programme, but Ankara has strongly opposed a military approach to the problem. Indeed, the Iranian nuclear program could yet provide an interesting test of US-Turkish relations. On the other hand, should the Obama administration's attempt to engage with Iran meet with some success, Washington's frustration with Ankara's cultivation of Tehran might dissipate.

Turkey's more accommodating approach to its regional relationships could prove diplomatically beneficial to the US. Ankara could be instrumental in facilitating Israeli-Palestinian contact, in weaning Syria away from its somewhat defensive, often unhelpfully meddlesome, and economically autarchic relationship with much of the outside world, and in reducing tension between Damascus and Tel Aviv. The same logic applies to Iran. For Turkey to play this role, however, whilst simultaneously preserving its relationship with the US, will require Washington to allow Ankara some slack in the conduct of its regional foreign policy, and to appreciate that Turkey's indirect contribution to broader US aims in the region might not be best served by a fully compliant Turkish ally.[50]

Turkey's expanded diplomatic engagement extends beyond the Middle East, of course. Thus, as Washington's relationship with Moscow dipped, Ankara's appeared to strengthen, based on trade and energy and the shared preference that regional confrontations be avoided. It has also been argued that 'Turkey and Russia are frustrated that the United States does not consider their interests in its forays into their neighborhoods . . . The Turkish-Russian relationship . . . is founded on a sense of exclusion by the United States, not mutual interest'.[51] If so, then this could perhaps offer a clue to the kind of foreign policy Turkey could pursue in the event of a sustained loosening of its transatlantic ties. As an example of the complementarity of their regionally-based security perspectives, Ankara and Moscow found themselves on the same side in resisting the expansion into the Black Sea of NATO's naval counter-terrorism task force, Operation Active Endeavour.[52] In its place, Turkey initiated the Black Sea Harmony task force, open to littoral states only, including Russia.

The August 2008 Georgian crisis demonstrated in a number of respects the potential pitfalls of Ankara's 'strategic depth' approach, however, and the risks to Turkey's Atlanticist connections. Turkey had cultivated Tbilisi, too, with regard to the Baku-Tbilisi-Ceyhan pipeline, trade relations, military training, and diplomatic sponsorship—for example, Turkey championed

Georgia's 'intensified dialogue' with NATO and its membership aspirations. However, as Georgia reeled in the face of a Russian onslaught, Ankara now felt obliged to sit on the fence. Moscow's assertiveness in the Caucasus also indicated the limits of Ankara's sway in the region, and the extent to which both its aspiration to enhance its energy transportation role and its longing for regional tranquillity are at Moscow's mercy. Furthermore, Ankara's nervousness concerning the escalatory potential of the Georgian crisis, and its jealous guardianship of the responsibilities allocated to Turkey by the 1936 Montreux Convention, illustrated the region's post-Cold War political complexities. Ankara restricted the nature and level of the US naval presence in the Black Sea during the crisis, in accordance both with Moscow's preferences and the Convention.[53] Given the accession to NATO of Bulgaria and Romania, and the NATO aspirations of Georgia and Ukraine, Turkey now finds itself walking a tightrope with respect to the Black Sea and its NATO obligations as a result of Russian assertiveness.

A Regional 'Model'?

Turkey's predicament as an 'echo chamber'[54] for conflicts in its environment was made manifest by the post-9/11 'war on terror' and its associated hint at 'civilizational' conflict. These developments are compromising for Turkey, an Islamic society with 'western' leanings. In response, Ankara has helped initiate a 'civilizational' dialogue, for example by organising and hosting a EU/Organisation of Islamic Conference (OIC) inter-civilizational conference in February 2002 and by co-sponsoring with Spain an 'Alliance of Civilizations' initiative under UN auspices.[55] Turkey emerged as a key partner in the Democracy Assistance Dialogue established during the 2004 G-8 summit in the US. Washington's enduring inclination to hold Turkey up as a model for other Islamic states to emulate was strengthened in the context of the Bush administration's aspiration to democratize the Middle East as a means of stabilizing it,[56] and Turkey's AKP government has been keen to contribute to the debate over Islam and modernization.

Indeed, both as foreign minister and president, Abdullah Gul—whilst at all times insistent that any reforms must emanate from within the region and not be imposed from outside—repeatedly expressed sympathy for the broad contents of the Bush administration's so-called 'Greater Middle East Initiative' and has insisted on the need for regional transformation.[57] Gul first outlined what he has dubbed 'the Turkish vision' for the Middle East region at the Islamic foreign ministers' conference in Tehran in May 2003, where he argued that the Muslim world needed 'to determine the issues and shortcomings that continue to hamper our progress', and that it needed to put its own house in order.[58] In an interview with the *International Herald Tribune* towards the end of 2003, he asserted that 'Turkey is living proof that a Muslim society can be governed in a democratic, accountable and transparent manner in accordance with European norms . . . Turkey testifies to the fact that European values indeed transcend geography, religion and cultures'.[59] Gul has also argued that, due to its unique cross-cultural nature and its broad experience of multilateral and regional diplomacy, Turkey is well placed to mobilize 'the dynamics of multilateral regional cooperation in the Middle East'.[60]

The AKP government's support for regional reform hints at the scope for placing the US-Turkish relationship on a new footing, one more rooted in a 'soft' security approach, derived from a shared commitment to regional democratization, rather than in 'hard' security cooperation. An AKP-led and diplomatically energetic Turkey can plausibly present itself as offering a more palatable model of progress for this troubled region. Indeed, that Turkey is widely perceived in the region as having put some distance between itself and Washington probably enhances its appeal. Turkey's western links can be a hindrance as well as a help in its regional relationships,[61] an observation that Washington might do well to ponder.

Domestic Changes

Turkey is in the throes of a major domestic transformation, and should it continue on its present trajectory this could provide an additional challenge to the traditional shape of Turkish-US relations. Turkey's EU accession process has provided much, though not all, of the impetus behind these changes and, if it is to be successful (a big if, perhaps), will continue to do so.[62] At least during its first term the AKP government demonstrated its readiness to introduce far-reaching political, social and economic reforms in order to align the country with EU norms. More generally, the intellectual life of the country, its media, educational system, pressure groups of all kinds and the judiciary are being progressively, if erratically, freed from state control and supervision. Minorities such as Chechens, Azeris and Bosnians and other sectors of society, such as the media and the cultural, business, economic, women's, human rights, conservationist, and environmental lobbies, have all acquired a higher political and social profile in Turkish domestic politics. The emergence of the AKP, and the Welfare and Virtue parties that preceded it, conceivably demonstrates the fact that Islam has been 'normalised' as a political force, to the point that Islam is now arguably the predominant feature of Turkey's political and social landscape.[63]

The AKP's relative successes in office—in economic management, EU relations, regional diplomacy, and domestic reform—have reinforced the challenge to the old order. The mere fact that the Ergenekon investigation into the activities of Turkey's so-called 'deep state' has been able to take place at all is ample testimony to the strength of this challenge.[64] As a consequence of Turkey's enhanced pluralism, policy outcomes will be more influenced by the free play of debate and sectional interest, and by civil society and public opinion. The institutions of the state, and the Kemalist elite that straddles the key ministries, the military leadership, the secular political parties, academia, the media, and the judiciary, seem less able to monopolise the country's foreign policy agenda and processes than formerly, and this change is enabling shifts in the content of Turkey's external policies. This more complex interplay also means that Turkey's external policies could well become more variable and less predictable.[65]

The Turkish military is greatly affected by these changes, and this is sure to affect Turkish-US relations. Notwithstanding the reproach to the quality of Turkish democracy that their deep involvement in Turkey's domestic politics offers, the military's political involvement has ensured both a degree of domestic order and a degree of continuity in foreign and security policy.[66] Furthermore, the Turkish-US relationship has hitherto been in no small measure a military-to-military one, and the TGS has been thoroughly committed to the alliance with the US despite occasional difficulties. Furthermore, the military-to-military relationship, combined with the efforts of Turkey's Kemalist foreign ministry bureaucrats and the fragility of Turkey's elected governments, injected an element of bureaucratic inertia and continuity into Turkish-US state-to-state relationships.[67]

Based on present trends, the capacity of the TGS to offer Washington an effective conduit to Turkish policy will erode. EU pressure has led to a reform of Turkey's National Security Council (NSC) in order to moderate the military's dominance of it. Pressure for greater civilian oversight of Turkey's armed forces, by both parliament and a civilian defence ministry, continues.

Military representation on state courts and on the educational board has been terminated. These and other institutional and legal changes in themselves do not and cannot fully align Turkish civil-military relationships with those more commonly found in Europe, but the process of EU accession itself creates an incentive for the military to step back from the political arena.[68] Indeed the commitment of many in the military—though not all—to Turkey's EU vocation is sincere.[69] Yet the TGS remains robust in its defense of the Kemalist faith and even of the military's domestic political role, and this approach could cause friction with both the AKP government and Turkey's allies, perhaps including an Obama-led US administration.[70]

What Kind of Future?

Given the shifts, differences and developments outlined above, perhaps the best that can be hoped for in the short term is that Turkish-US relations can be maintained at a low but reasonably calm plateau. The atmospherics remain troubled, however. For the Democrats, Turkey's illiberal tendencies, anti-Americanism, and the 'Armenian genocide' issue are always lying in wait for an opportunity to derail the relationship. This was demonstrated by Ankara's decision to withdraw its ambassador to Washington in the wake of the March 2010 vote by the House of Representatives' Foreign Affairs Committee calling on the US to recognize the 'Armenian genocide'. Obama's statement on Armenian Remembrance Day on 24 April 2009, in which he used the Armenian term for the genocide, *Meds Yeghern*,[71] and his reference in his address to the Turkish National Assembly to 'the terrible events of 1915', suggests he has not altered his mind on the issue. On the other hand, the opening up—at last—of an internal Turkish debate on the Armenian past, and the current thaw in Ankara's relationship with its Armenian neighbor, might encourage Americans to once again put the 'genocide' issue on the back-burner—at least until it becomes clear that the thaw with Yerevan is not bearing fruit.[72] On the Turkish side, Turkish society and elite circles of all political persuasions now appear to harbor an instinctive coolness towards the US, and an inclination towards a diplomatically unhelpful emotional, and intensely nationalistic, response to many of the issues that make up the US-Turkish relationship.[73] In addition, the weakening of the Pentagon's trust of Ankara in the wake of the Iraq debacle could turn out to be an enduring development in US-Turkish relations. Much depends on the fortunes of Turkey's EU accession process, over which the US has little control, and on the quality of transatlantic relations more broadly, which are expected to improve post-Bush.

The Iraq issue, too, has the potential to derail US-Turkish relations.[74] Of course, Ankara and Washington do share a commitment to and interest in Iraq's territorial integrity, political stability and economic recovery, and Turkey has worked hard to persuade Iraq's Sunni factions to engage with the new Iraq.[75] However, Ankara remains committed to minimum autonomy for the Iraqi Kurds, who in turn are intent on maximum autonomy. Turks recognise the scope for events to escape control. Thus, there is nervousness in Ankara at the implications of the US troop pullout,[76] although Turkish assistance in the logistical aspects of the withdrawal looks assured. Turkish policy has also helpfully shifted towards economic and political cooperation with and accommodation to the KRG,[77] and the Turkish economic presence in the KRG zone is considerable. Turkey's domestic 'democratic' or 'Kurdish opening', announced amidst much controversy in August 2009, might both impress Washington and further enable Ankara's relations with the KRG to progress. It is interesting, though, that the opposition in Turkey accused the government of pandering to the dictates of the US in launching the policy.[78] However, Kurdish ambitions and Turkish preferences will need to be manoeuvred towards greater alignment than hitherto. Turkey might more easily acclimatise to the reality of the KRG, if it were not for the issue of oil-rich Kirkuk and the surrounding areas, which the KRG seeks to incorporate.[79] The issue remains unresolved and very tense, and is currently waiting on UN efforts to devise a power-sharing formula which it hopes will satisfy all parties and negate the requirement for a divisive referendum.[80] Washington has adopted a somewhat low-key stance with regard to the looming crisis over Kirkuk's future. Turkish-US relations remain highly vulnerable to any Kurdish lack of restraint or to a wider collapse of the Iraqi state, and Washington might be impelled to intervene in the event of a crisis.

More generally, although Turkey's future is strewn with obstacles, the country's economic development and democratization and changes in its broader geopolitical context may have unleashed enduring forces for structural change that will not easily be denied. It is therefore reasonably safe to assume that the Turkey with which Washington will be obliged to deal in the future will be quite different from the country with which it built such a close security relationship during the Cold War. In future, Washington might be advised to look into and cultivate a little better Turkey's social, political and economic black box, as US-Turkish relations will be less purely state-to-state than hitherto. Persuading Ankara will become a more arduous and less certain enterprise, and Washington must not take Turkey's compliance for granted. In short, and as expressed by a former Turkish ambassador to the US, it could now be that 'neither country is indispensable to the other'.[81]

Turkey's utility to the US might now hinge primarily on its stability and democratization in a troubled and often hostile region—in other words, on 'soft' rather than 'hard' attributes. It is a higher US strategic interest that these qualities be encouraged and entrenched. Additionally, Turkey's 'failure' as a westernized state or its 'loss' to the US would constitute a seriously unwelcome development. In the long term, the avoidance of such outcomes will be best served by Turkey's progressive 'democratization', even though that is likely both to be a rocky road and to bring inconvenience to the US. Furthermore, in its external policies Turkey's 'soft power' attributes, whether through economic relations, endeavors to nurture more cooperative diplomatic approaches to its region's problems, or via its potential as a 'model' or 'source of inspiration' for alternative forms of domestic political, social and economic development in the Islamic world, now represent the most constructive contribution Turkey might make to a world compatible with US and broader western interests. The details might not always be to Washington's liking, and Ankara might continue to exhibit an irritating criticism towards US policies. But the costs to Washington might pale in comparison with the rewards that an influential, constructive and regionally integrated Turkey might bring.

Turkey's inclination has been to regionalize issues that Washington's involvement unavoidably internationalizes. Overlaps of interest, perspective and policy in US-Turkish relations are frequent, but they are also increasingly context-dependent, conditional and, to a degree, disconnected from each other. Furthermore, such policy convergence as emerges will be balanced by issues where there is little direct overlap of interest, perspective, or policy, and sometimes profound disagreement. There are divergences that are as or more serious than those that afflicted US-Turkish relations during the Cold War, and convergences that create less bonding than did the glue of Cold War containment. Overall, Washington's, and Ankara's, deeper long-term interests might best be served by a loosening of their strategic ties, and by a greater American willingness to allow Turkey to grow and evolve in its own way. In the meantime, and for all Obama's good intentions, there is certainly scope for specific policy differences to emerge between the two allies, for the Obama administration's more general approach to global issues to unsettle Turkey, and for Turkish political and social atmospherics to unsettle and frustrate the US.

8 The Transatlantic Relationship

Poland and the United States

Anna Zielińska

Introduction

Once Poland gained its full independence, a process that started in the 1980s and continued into the 1990s, it formed an alliance with the United States and NATO for geopolitical purposes. Poles saw their security as being guaranteed against Russian domination in this new political-military partnership. At the same time, Poland applied to the EU for membership, initially with the aim of promoting economic development rather than political and military co-operation. The close relationship between Poland and the United States was built on a cultural, historical and strategic background. As early as the eighteenth century, Poles fleeing their partitioned homeland fought under George Washington in the American War of Independence. In 1918 President Woodrow Wilson proposed the reconstruction of Poland in point 13 of his famous Fourteen Points speech to the Congress of the United States.[1] The Treaty of Versailles led to the existence of Poland as an independent entity for the first time in over 100 years; this situation lasted between 1918 and 1939. In September 1939, after Germany invaded Poland, Poland was divided between Hitler's Germany and Stalin's Soviet Union. As the Second World War headed towards an end, the 'Big Three' (US, United Kingdom and Soviet Union) agreed at the Yalta Conference to place Poland in the Soviet Union's sphere of influence.

During the Cold War era, Poles were grateful for the broadcasts of the Voice of America, interpreting them as proof of American support for the nation, now under domination once again. In the 1980s the anti-Soviet stance of

the Reagan administration gave opposition leaders and the Solidarity movement that had developed in Poland new energy and fostered the belief that the
Western world would support changes in their country.

Changes finally came in 1989, when Poland regained sovereignty for the
first time in 50 years and once again joined the Western world. It became a
member of NATO and the EU and for many years was a true Atlanticist; in
parts of Europe this security policy was perceived as obsessively pro-American and much less geared towards European interests. For this reason, for
many years Polish politicians believed that the best place to develop European
capabilities in defense policy was within NATO.

Since the beginning of the twenty-first century, however, much has
changed. In the security field Poland transformed itself from 'security consumer' to 'security provider' for third nations through the commitment of
Polish soldiers to foreign missions. The close relationship between Poland
and the United States has also evolved. Today Poland expects more from the
partnership than it did formerly; and, to Poland's increasing disappointment,
a growing stagnation can be detected in the relations between the two countries. The upcoming years will show how close Poland and the US will remain.

Milestones in Poland's Contemporary History—NATO Membership

Poland is regarded as the United States' closest ally in Central and Eastern
Europe. It gained a leading position in the eyes of the Western world early on
by being a role model because of its peaceful democratic transformations of
1989 (as a consequence of the Round Table Agreements) and its subsequent
economic reforms, despite having been under the domination of the Soviet
Union's Communist regime for almost 50 years. In this period, Poland once
again became part of the Western world and wished to be an active partner.
This couldn't be done, however, without the support of other democratic
states. The United States has undoubtedly been Poland's closest ally and pro-
moter in world affairs. What is more, the United States became Poland's security guarantor—the kind of powerful supporter for which Poland longed
throughout its turbulent history since the late eighteenth century.[2]

Poland's history and geographical position mean that the country still retains the fear of being marginalized. Therefore, from the time it gained its
freedom from Soviet domination it began looking for strong structures of co-

operation and collective guarantees to prevent being excluded or abandoned ever again.[3] It tried to detach itself from the periphery of Europe and become an active part of the ongoing geopolitical game. Therefore, in the early 1990s Poland applied for accession to NATO and the European Union (EU): the former alliance offering hard political and military security guarantees and the use of force if necessary, the latter being an alliance of 'close neighbors'— European states which supported peace and prosperity on the continent.

Poland achieved one of its primary goals on 12 March 1999 when it joined NATO. The Polish government identified NATO as the zone of common interests in which it could live safely by becoming a consumer of the security offered by the alliance. On this occasion Bronislaw Geremek, then the minister of foreign affairs, said:

> This ceremony is truly a unique event in the history of my country. For over two hundred years, when foreign leaders put their signatures under documents concerning Poland, disasters were sure to follow. Today, I am to witness Poland's friends sign a document which is a source of joy, pride and hope for me and my compatriots.[4]

Minister Geremek was referring to the partitioning of Poland in the eighteenth century, the Ribbentrop-Molotov Pact of 1939 and the Yalta Agreement of 1945, each of which decided Poland's geopolitical position and the country's future without the presence of Polish officials or any reference to Polish leaders.[5] Therefore, joining NATO was a moment of great historical significance for Poland; strong relations both with NATO and the US were crucial to offsetting the continuing fear of Russian domination in the region, which Poland felt could be balanced only by having the support and military strength of NATO. To this day, NATO membership remains the main pillar of Polish security policy, and through the commitments of Article 5 it is also the main security guarantor.[6] Membership in NATO is also strongly supported by public opinion in Poland. Surveys conducted on the 10th anniversary of accession to NATO in 2009 showed that 80% of Poles surveyed support the country's membership in this organization.[7] Despite this support some analysts have argued that Poland must also develop alternative ways of protecting itself as a country, since the commitment based on Article 5, and therefore the real scale of American solidarity with and support of Poland, will vary, depending on whether Poland does or does not continue to be perceived as a true partner for American interests in the geopolitical arena.[8]

After half a century of Russian domination the new Polish government was confronted with difficult choices. The United States opened an Agency for International Development (USAID) office in Warsaw and conducted several projects. Support was aimed first at debt-restructuring and bank privatization, second at stimulating the private sector at the firm or company level, mainly by providing training, and third at building a competitive, market-oriented financial sector. The third would be highlighted by increasing liberalization and investment in the banking sector, as well as encouraging effective, responsive, and accountable local government. Thanks to American support, by 1999 four major structural reforms had been finalized, in the fields of public administration, health, education, and pensions—all of which have been supported by USAID. The agency also assisted in collaboration with other US government agencies in order to improve other areas of concern—including environmental protection (Environmental Protection Agency), redeployment of redundant Silesian coal miners (Department of Labor), modernization of the criminal justice system (Department of Justice), and assistance in tax administration (Department of the Treasury).[9]

Another Milestone—Becoming a Member of the European Union

After joining NATO, Poland's second goal was reached five years later when on 1 May 2004 Poland became a member of the European Union. Membership in the two organizations fulfilled the Polish aspiration of "returning to Europe" and becoming a world player freed from its historical bonds with Russia. Five years after accession, Poland took note of the positive effects of membership in the EU. In February 2009, 75% of Poles surveyed supported Poland's membership in the EU, which is a direct response to the benefits of accession. They include, among others: freedom of movement (Poland joined the Schengen area on 21 December 2007 which lifted controls on the land borders between Poland and other EU member states, making border crossing easier and more accessible), the opportunity for legal employment and education in other member states, improvements in the domestic labour market, and substantial economic development and growth.

Financial transfers from the EU have also been an important factor in Poland's economic growth, amounting to 26.5 billion Euros between 1 May 2004 and 31 December 2008.[10] At the same time, Poland paid only 12.5 billion Euros in contributions to the EU budget; thus there was a positive balance of financial flows with the EU at a level of 14 billion Euros after 5 years of membership. Furthermore, between 2004 and 2006, Poland availed itself of approximately 12 billion Euros from the EU's Cohesion Fund Policy (allocated to projects in the area of transport infrastructure, environmental protection, support to small and medium enterprises and occupational activation of the unemployed). In the years 2007–2013 approximately 68 billion Euros are scheduled to be committed to Poland.[11]

Apart from the social and economic benefits, Poland has become an active player in the EU's Common Foreign and Security Policy (CFSP) and the European Security and Defence Policy (ESDP). Poland has also continued its strong support for cooperation with NATO in collaboration with an informal group of other EU countries within the EU Council (including the United Kingdom, the Netherlands and Denmark). It has also joined the group that promotes a more assertive EU position towards Russia (along with the United Kingdom, Sweden, Lithuania, Latvia, Estonia and the Czech Republic). Poland has also been an active participant in enhancing the EU's dialogue with the United States. The strategic discussions on the future of EU-US cooperation (initiated in Avignon in 2008) have contributed to broadening and substantiating the political agenda of cooperation with the new US administration.[12]

Becoming a member of the European Union at first seemed to create a new situation for the Polish government. It was confronted with the competing needs of Washington and Brussels, and, whenever a conflict arose, each time having to decide which side to choose. It was torn between competing visions of Atlanticism whilst still being a core member of the EU. Current policies, however, show that Poland is no longer caught between the European Union and the United States, but rather Poland is *in* the European Union and *in an alliance with* the United States.[13]

Some analysts show considerable skepticism about the relative ambiguity of Poland's foreign policy. They say that since full independence in 1989 Poland has had close political and military relations with the United States and NATO as a security guarantor against the threat of Russia, whilst treating the European Union as a structure for economic integration, essential for its further development. At the same time the EU hasn't been perceived as a forum for political and military integration due to the relatively weak development of its foreign and security policy.[14] However, this situation has changed and therefore the European Union should consider how Poland can assert a role that reflects its potential as one of the largest member states, one that has a foreign policy of its own which involves being an active partner in *both* NATO and the European defence.

The European Security and Defense Policy—An Alternative to NATO?

Poland's accession to the EU and its becoming part of the European Security and Defense Policy expanded the country's security cooperation, which until that time had been based upon the strategic partnership with the United States and membership in NATO. At first Poland was skeptical about the development of a separate European defense capability, seeing this as a potential threat to NATO's position in Europe. However, the government's position has begun to change, and Poland is currently building defense capacities within ESDP, which it no longer regards as a competitor to NATO's (in reality America's) presence in Europe. Poland also has emphasized its belief in the need for further co-operation and co-ordination between NATO and the EU.

As part of this change in the first half of 2010 Poland, together with Germany, Slovakia and Lithuania, became the 'framework state' (that is, coordinator of the preparation process and of the possible operational use of the unit) of one of the EU's two ready Battle Groups. Furthermore, in 2006 Poland declared its commitment, together with Germany and France, to the establishment of the 'Weimar Group' in 2013, as well as to the establishment of the 'Vysegrad Group' with the Czech Republic, Slovakia and Hungary in 2015. Poland has also actively participated in the EU's military and civil operations.[15]

Poland's active presence in the EU and NATO missions shows that it has evolved from being a 'security consumer' into a 'security provider' for third nations by the commitment of Polish soldiers to foreign missions. The table shows the commitment to EU, NATO and UN missions in 2009.

Poland as a Regional Leader

The idea of Poland being the regional leader was promoted by the US on a few occasions. Joining NATO was perceived as a vital step in Poland's return to the role of a globally significant power, and since then Poland was declared to be America's favorite partner in the East.[17] The US administration wanted Poland

2009—Missions with Polish soldiers and military employees[16]

Mission	Country	Number of Soldiers
ISAF International Security Assistance Force (Polish Task Force in Ghazni)	Afghanistan	2000
UNIFIL United Nations Interim Force in Lebanon	Lebanon	500
UNDOF United Nations Disengagement Observer Force	Syria	470
EUFOR TCHAD/RCA\UN Mission (an EU mission through March 2009)	Chad and the Central African Republic	330
KFOR NATO Kosovo Force	Kosovo	300
EUFOR ALTHEA European Union Forces	Bosnia and Herzegovina	200
EUMM European Union Monitoring Mission	Georgia	20
NTM-I NATO Training Mission— Iraq	Iraq	20

to change its role from 'student' to 'teacher' in NATO, in order to show other Central and Eastern European states how to successfully 'return to Europe'.[18] Therefore, it was in Poland that President George W. Bush announced in 2001 America's support for the second wave of NATO enlargement (which Poland had strongly promoted) and described Poland as a 'bridge and good example' for its neighbors.[19] A further manifestation of the closeness of the two states dates from December 2002, when the US Congress granted an unprecedented financial package in the form of a $3.8 billion loan to Poland (to be repaid over 15 years) in order to purchase 48 F-16 aircrafts from Lockheed Martin.[20] The loan was undoubtedly a confirmation of the close relations between the two countries.[21] It was noticeable that the purchase was for American aircraft instead of European (the two other companies competing were Rafale from France and Gripen, a British-Swedish consortium), and this was an essential step in developing the strategic partnership between the two countries.

In 2003 Poland contributed 2,500 troops to the conventional phase of the war in Iraq and subsequently led a multinational division (MND(C)), which formed part of the stabilization force. The division was responsible for creating the grounds for Iraqi central and local administration, providing security to the civilian population and coalition army as well as training the Iraqi army and police.[22] Polish support in this endeavour undoubtedly had an influence on future relations with the European Union.[23] In January 2003, Poland was one of eight European countries (the others were the Czech Republic, Denmark, Hungary, Italy, Portugal, Spain and the United Kingdom), which declared in the "Letter by the Eight" their support of the US stance on Iraq.[24] The letter was criticized by the then-president of the European Commission, Romano Prodi, who said that such actions diminished the work being conducted by European diplomats and the European Commission in an effort to peacefully solve the crisis.[25] Since Poland was scheduled to formally join the EU some 15 months later, this perceived lack of support for a more independent European line looked potentially troublesome, especially when the French president, Jacques Chirac, called the letter infantile and dangerous, and added: 'They missed a great opportunity to shut up'. The Polish administration did not leave the comment unanswered. Deputy Foreign Minister Adam Rotfeld replied: 'France has a right to its opinion and Poland has the right to decide what is good for it. France should respect that'.[26] Polish political parties supported the government's decision to send troops to Iraq, and there were no mass anti-war demonstrations held, such as were common in many other European states, including Great Britain.[27]

It is essential to analyze why Poland engaged in Iraq. It was not the case that Poland perceived the mission in the context of the so-called War on Terrorism, nor did it engage because of the supposed possession by Iraq of weapons of mass destruction (WMD). Poland was not threatened by terrorists, its relations with Arab countries were good and the argument of WMD possession was infrequently present in the national debate. In fact, other factors were at play. Historical ties might have played a minor part. In the 1970s and 1980s, Polish companies had operated in Iraq. However, the relative size of the economic relationship prevented it from being a major influence on the Polish government's decision. Instead, the most decisive factor was the need to demonstrate Polish loyalty towards the US and its commitment to being a model ally as a quid pro quo for the Article 5 guarantee that the United States was effectively providing. Poland was, therefore, ready to join any American or NATO action to strengthen the transatlantic bond.[28] Both factors have a background in Poland's history—its betrayal by the allies at the beginning of World War II, which has influenced Poland's view of the USA as its security guarantor. Moreover, after its release from the Soviet Union's sphere of influence, successive governments have supported the fight for democracy and human rights protection in oppressed states as a matter of principle.[29] Based on their own experience, it was natural for Poles to believe that Iraqis wanted to free themselves from Saddam Hussein's domination and for that to become the core Polish mission in this situation. It is noteworthy that when the final Polish troops were withdrawn from Iraq in October 2008, the withdrawal was accompanied by comments and criticism that the Polish policy had been led by the fear that the US might abandon Europe, the implication being that therefore Poland felt obliged to support all American actions, in order to insure that the USA would not do this.[30]

However, having supported the US, Poland gradually began to change its policy. Since it was soon to join the EU, there were real fears about the inequality of power within the community. In particular, the Polish government had the impression that the EU foreign and security agenda was dominated by two states—France and Germany—that had opposed the war in Iraq, and Poland's open Atlanticism threatened Polish hopes of shaping new EU-US relations. Poland's experiences with stabilization in Iraq proved frustrating. Once there were causalities and no visible profit from the engagement, support from politicians and the public for the mission weakened. Poles also expected that after showing so much support to the US, they would be able to travel to the US without visas and that Polish companies would be involved in the reconstruction of Iraq. Neither of these hopes was realized—the visa policy remained as before the war,[31] and only a few Polish companies have been involved in the reconstruction programs. As Poland did not experience much in return for its engagement, the subsequent erosion in Polish Atlanticism weakened the political consensus about this policy. As a result the Polish government chose to get closer to its other ally, the European Union, which until this moment had always been placed in second position. Poland's attitude towards the EU Common Foreign and Security Policy (CFSP) and the European Security and Defense Policy (ESDP) began to change, and Poland became more 'pro-European' than 'pro-American'.[32]

By 2007 Polish-American relations were dominated by the Bush administration's proposal that Poland join the American Ballistic Missile Defense

(BMD) program.[33] But in 2009 the new administration decided that 'the new American administration is not ready yet to fulfill all assumptions from the signed agreement, that is why we do not have the missile defence shield'.[34] When discussions about the mission shield started, many centered on the necessity of placing part of the missile defense shield in Poland (the other part of the system was to be deployed in the Czech Republic). Some held the opinion that it would guarantee Poland's long-term security by linking the country closely to the US (which therefore could not afford to be indifferent to Polish security). However, at the same time, the US plans were negatively perceived in Russia, which began to treat the plan of placing missiles in Poland as a potential threat against itself, not Iran. This led to tensions in relations between Poland and Russia; Russia reacted by placing a battery of S-300 rockets in Belarus, only 150 km from the Polish border, as a reaction to the arrival of F-16s for the Polish air force.[35] As a consequence, Poland argued with Washington about what form of compensation the US would provide to offset the risk connected to deploying part of the missile defense shield on Polish territory. Minister of Foreign Affairs Radoslaw Sikorski said:

> One must take into account that the shield installation in Poland will become the target of any potential adversary of the United States, as well as of terrorist activities. What is more the Russian position on all this and its perception is very negative. And we have the right to demand that any potential acts of retaliation against Poland will be neutralized by an appropriate American offer.[36]

The public's support towards placing a component of the missile defense shield in Poland has also dramatically decreased. In December 2005 the level of support stood at 50%, whilst by March 2009 it was only 29%.[37]

In August 2008 both states signed a declaration confirming their strategic cooperation and cooperation on missile defence.[38] On the basis of this declaration the US agreed to deploy a US Army Patriot air and missile defense battery in Poland (potentially in 2009), with the US establishing a permanent garrison to support the Patriot battery by 2012. This would mark the first permanent deployment of US forces to territory of the former Warsaw Pact. By the summer of 2009, both administrations were still negotiating the status of American soldiers on Polish territory and the timing of placing the Patriot battery in Poland. The minister of national defense stated that he expected the American administration to fulfill its declaration in 2009 or 2010, and by that time to place at least one Patriot battery in Poland.[39] Then, suddenly, on 17

September 2009 President Barack Obama announced that the US would with-draw from its previous plans of placing the missile defense systems in Poland and the Czech Republic. This decision provoked diverse reactions in Poland. Opponents of the original plan declared it was a good day for Poland; others saw it as a change in relations between Poland and the US, adding that for the first time in 20 years, Washington was publicly diminishing the role of Cen-tral Europe in order to gain better relations with Russia.[40] Irrespective of the view taken, the date of the announcement was undiplomatic in the extreme: the Obama administration announcement was made on the 70th anniversary of the USSR's invasion of Poland.

Instead, the US has decided to invest in a four-phase system protecting Europe and the US. In the first phase (until 2011), at least three Aegis ships were to be placed on the Mediterranean Sea with Standard Missile 3 (SM-3) interceptors. By 2015, a more advanced interceptor and additional sensors are to be placed in Europe in order to protect the continent. This phase will include land-based SM-3s in southern Europe, in addition to their sea-based locations. In phase 3 (by 2018), a second land-based SM-3 will be located in northern Europe together with a new generation of SM-3 missiles, which will be allocated in order to protect the US from medium- and intermediate-range threats. These changes would extend coverage to all NATO allies in Europe. Finally, phase 4 (by 2020) would provide protection to the US from a potential Intercontinental Ballistic Missile launched from the Middle East, by upgrad-ing the SM-3s.[41]

Despite the change, Poland was promised that the US would fulfill its ob-ligation to place the Patriot battery on Polish territory. The missiles would be armed and equipped with systems that would allow them to form part of an integrated Polish air defense network. The first Patriots will arrive in Poland by the end of May 2010 and will be based in Morag in north-east Poland. Un-til 2012 the Patriots will be in Poland periodically and may be transferred to Germany or other NATO partners. After 2012 they will stay in Poland perma-nently. The Patriot battery will be accompanied by American soldiers, who will be based in Morag according to the Status of Forces Agreement (SOFA) from February 2010.[42]

The Polish Spécialité—the Eastern Policy:
Another Zone for Transatlantic Relations?

The Eastern Partnership initiative is one of Poland's largest successes within the CFSP. Poland and Sweden proposed a partnership with countries neighboring the EU in the East that would formally become part of the European Neighborhood Policy (ENP). During the Prague Summit on 7 May 2009, the European Union signed the Eastern Partnership declaration with six countries (Armenia, Azerbaijan, Belarus, Georgia, Moldova and Ukraine). At first, due to the general reluctance of EU member states to increase funds devoted to the ENP, the Polish-Swedish financing proposal was limited to resources available within the ENP. However, in March 2009 the Eastern Partnership received the promise of an additional 600 million Euros for the years 2010–2013 from the European Commission in its Communication on the Eastern Partnership in order to fulfill all agreed projects. The ENP foresees deep and comprehensive free trade agreements, visa facilitations, promotion of democracy and good governance, as well as social cooperation programmes (such as student exchange programmes) with EU member states. Creating a 'ring of friends' has, for many years, been one of the main goals of Polish foreign policy. Poland would like the United States to support the EU's Eastern Partnership as an alternative to Russian attempts at rebuilding their old zone of influence; however, it emphasizes that the policy's aim is supporting transformations in Eastern Europe, not isolating Russia.[43]

The strong sense of 'community of destinies' with countries in the region goes hand in hand with Poland's desire in its foreign policy to exercise political leadership in the region drawing on its knowledge of Eastern Europe vis-à-vis NATO and the EU, among others. For the past six years of membership in the EU, Poland has also been part of transatlantic negotiations on maintaining US support to Eastern European states in transition.[44]

The Polish mission as the EU's and the US's link to the East is noticeable in its relations with Ukraine, which has become a very important element in Polish foreign policy. Strong attempts have been made to anchoring Ukraine in the West by helping it join the World Trade Organization (WTO), the EU and NATO. The continuation of this effort could be observed during the events of the 'Orange Revolution' in November and December 2004 in Ukraine, where opposition leaders fought for democracy and loosening of Ukraine's 'dependency' upon Russia. These attempts are so close to Polish hearts that the Polish president, Aleksander Kwasniewski, was one of the main mediators for Ukraine, whilst the Polish members of the European Parliament (MEP) encouraged an act of support for democratic reforms in Ukraine—both through substantial resolutions and symbolically, by asking MEPs to wear orange scarves as a sign of solidarity. Poland has shown itself to be a 'good specialist' on Eastern European affairs, with the result that it has promoted itself as an active regional player (supporting reforms in Belarus, after Ukraine) with a specific *niche* that could become the specialty of Poland within the EU.

Poland's support for democratic reforms in countries to the East led to a conflict of interest between it and Russia, which treated all the above actions, and later the Eastern Partnership, as interventions in its 'zone of influence'. Shortly after the 'Orange Revolution', a worsening in bilateral relations was evident when Russia withdrew from an agreement to build a gas pipeline (Yamal 2) to run through Poland to Germany and other Western European states. More recently in May 2009, during the final negotiations regarding the Eastern Partnership at the Prague EU Summit, when Belarus was invited to be one of the signatories, Russian officials expressed their dismay.

Linked to this has been the Polish-American-Ukrainian Cooperation Initiative (PAUCI), which was established to facilitate Poland's sharing with Ukraine its 'best practices' on how to reach a liberal and market-oriented democracy. Thanks to Polish expertise, American money was directed towards Ukrainian needs. Since 2005, this initiative has been transformed into the Polish-Ukrainian Cooperation Foundation, and its current mission is to build and develop Ukraine's closer integration with the European Union and NATO. The initiative has also a regional benefit, with Ukraine able to pass on the knowledge it has obtained to other states in the post-Soviet area, including Belarus and Moldova.[45]

The above examples show that Poland has an important role to play to the East vis-à-vis the European Union. Its pivotal role can and should be a bridge between the EU and its eastern neighbors. Nevertheless, there still remains a place for American cooperation in this part of the world if Washington has the will to do it. In the future Washington might also serve a similar role for Russia, which still has an uneasy relationship with Poland.

The Polish Security Culture—Historical Foundations

In order to understand the Polish foreign policy and its relations with allies and neighboring states more fully, we need to look at the country's security culture.[46] In Poland's case, its security culture is undoubtedly based on its geopolitical position. Located between two traditionally expansionary powers—Germany and Russia (until 1991, the Soviet Union)—it has been an unfortunate victim throughout its history. Polish security culture began to emerge when Poland lost its status as a sovereign entity in the eighteenth century. The Polish-Lithuanian Commonwealth, once the largest polity in Europe, was then successfully divided between the neighboring states of Prussia, Russia and Austria three times between 1772 and 1795. As a consequence, the Polish state was erased from the map until 1918. Nevertheless, a strong Polish identity had developed in the previous centuries, and it continued to develop during those times through such mechanisms as underground Polish schools that sought to preserve the Polish language, which the occupying powers had officially forbidden.

In November 1918, after the surrender of Germany, the Second Republic of Poland was proclaimed. The country was positioned between an unstable German state and a post-revolutionary Soviet Union. Therefore, the principal aims of the new Polish leadership became first to defend the Polish borders against any external threat from its neighbors and second to protect the independence of the newly proclaimed Polish state. This position was extremely important for Polish citizens, as subsequent events often proved, unfortunately, during the country's later history.[47] Polish foreign policy therefore concentrated on overcoming the 'geopolitical trap' by building alliances with the Western Powers. Doing so proved only partially successful: whilst the United Kingdom and France entered the Second World War following the German invasion of Poland, they ultimately were unable to prevent Poland returning to the Russian sphere of influence at the end of the war. This experience is also key to understanding Poland's security culture. Poland felt abandoned by its guarantors of security—the United Kingdom and France. The size and persistence of the Polish resistance against the Nazi-Soviet assaults in September 1939, and later throughout the war, proved that a powerful commitment to Polish independence was one of the foundational values of the Polish security culture. Poland's experience in the Second World War, and in particular the Warsaw Uprising of 1944, undermined the Poles' conviction that they were capable of protecting Poland's borders and defending its nation. Their feeling of abandonment and betrayal strongly influenced Poland's future perception of the world.

One further event influenced the Polish security culture—the Yalta Agreement. At Yalta, the Big Three of Churchill, Roosevelt and Stalin decided to move Poland to the west—the Curzon Line was to become Poland's new eastern border, with the rivers Oder and Neisse becoming the western frontier. This agreement was contrary to the Atlantic Charter of 1941, which stated that border changes would not be made without the consent of the respective state involved. What is more, the Big Three intervened also into the shape of the Polish government, favoring a Communist-controlled provisional government.[48] This decision led to 44 years of Russian influence and a Communist regime, which only began to change in 1989. Poland's security culture under Communism is important because of the role of the strong émigré circles abroad and a democratic opposition in Poland. Poland's Communist government took the position that an alliance of Poland with the Soviet Union and an acceptance of limited sovereignty were the only options, and that Poland should be grateful to the Soviet Union for 'liberating' the country from the Germans. The Communists portrayed themselves as nationalists who accepted limited sovereignty as the only solution for Polish existence, inasmuch as the state was still being threatened by German expansionism (as West Germany refused to recognize the new Polish border) and was therefore dependent on Soviet guarantees.

Immediately after the events of 1989, Polish politicians knew all too well that they could decide little on the subject of international affairs and that while creating their own foreign policy they should follow the trends of western democratic states. This situation was entirely due to the political, economic and social problems that the new Poland inherited. The Polish political elite, well aware of the lessons of its history, felt that these points should strongly influence their future foreign and security policies. One of their main goals became building a strong and stable state which could return to its true position—characterized as 'the return to Europe'. This meant Poland must reach for and join in the common values and goals of Western European states and cut itself off from its artificial partnership with the Soviet Union.

The consequence of Poland's particular history can be seen in the decisions of successive Polish governments since 1989, who have only agreed to 'hard' security guarantees; the Third Republic of Poland built upon its position as a good ally to achieve better cooperation with its new Western partners and the United States. In the 1990s it was already safe to say that the Third Polish Republic was surrounded mostly by friends. Its main aim was to 'return to its true place'—the Western world—and this was the reason for applying both to the EU and to NATO. After the accession in 1999 to NATO and in 2004 to the EU, Poland opened a new chapter in its foreign policy. For the first time in over 200 years geopolitics would play a different role. Poland became the bridge between the West and the East, becoming the ambassador of Eastern European states in the EU.[49]

After 1989, Poland visibly identified its security with the United States and NATO as guarantees of military force and strong leadership. It feared that the creation of a political union in the European sphere of security would weaken the position of the US in the old world and would resurrect strong rivalries between European states.[50] However, in subsequent years Poland found its place both in NATO and in the EU. Joining the EU in 2004 as one of its largest member states, Poland was recognized as an important strategic actor with a large armed force and wide-ranging capabilities. More states perceived it as both an active partner in policy formation and a contributor to peacekeeping missions beyond European borders and to US-led operations in Afghanistan and Iraq. Poland became a supporter of the Common Foreign and Security Policy and the European Security and Defense Policy and sought to improve European capabilities in security matters due to the fact that it saw a role for itself within these structures.

History has undoubtedly influenced Polish politics and the security culture still determines the state's reactions to international affairs. The Polish fight for independence has led to an emphasis on the protection of the weak and a readiness to fight 'for our freedom and yours'.[51] This is a key element in the 'Polish way of thinking'. The legacy of the Solidarno (Solidarity) anti-communism movement has also influenced its future reactions: Poland has become known for its solidarity with nations fighting for their independence and for its support of peace-keeping missions, even if there is no clear legal basis for action.[52]

As a consequence of this, Polish governments have come to differentiate the various international organizations. They hold NATO and the EU in higher regard than the UN and OSCE, essentially because the former are more credible security actors. They are also seen as more effective in making decisions and engaging in common actions, whilst the latter are viewed more as discussion forums.

As a member state of the European Union, Poland no longer fears Germany. However, the situation with its second historical adversary is very different. It remains deeply troubled by Russia, which is perceived by its neighbors as a partner that tends to change agreements unilaterally according to its own needs. Therefore Poland, like Sweden and Finland, perceives its security relations with Russia through a different prism than that of many other EU member states. If a situation arose in which Russia broke all the recognized agreements or rules and diplomatic negotiations seemed incapable of bringing about a satisfactory compromise or outcome, Poland would most probably resort to force. The 2007 National Security Strategy of the Republic of Poland clearly underlines all the above points and mentions that it correlates with the European security strategy and NATO's strategic concept.[53]

The Future of Transatlantic Relations

Poland's emphasis on the political and military dimensions of transatlantic relations is gradually weakening and decreasing in importance. However, Poland treats the United States with a large dose of "inborn" fondness. In 1993, 62% of Poles surveyed declared that they like the Americans; in December of 2008 the percentage had decreased to 47%,[54] which is still relatively positive. However, the feeling that the US had abandoned Poland and other states in the region could be observed in July 2009, when 22 current and former leaders of Central and Eastern European countries wrote an open letter to Barack Obama's administration (including two former presidents of Poland—Lech Walesa and Aleksander Kwasniewski—as well as former Polish minister of foreign affairs Adam Rotfeld and former defense minister Janusz Onyszkiewicz). In their letter they emphasized the key position of the United States in the region since the Cold War, even stating that without help from Washington it is doubtful that the countries would be where they are, both in NATO and in the EU. The signatories expressed their regret that 'Central and Eastern European countries are no longer at the heart of the American foreign policy',[55] and said that little new was being done to preserve their historically good relations with the US. Furthermore, they addressed threats to NATO's credibility and voiced their uncertainty of the alliance's reaction to potential crises in member states. They also said that countries from the region would be unable to engage in NATO's missions abroad without being able to assure local public opinion that the country's security concerns were being addressed in the alliance. (Their main concerns currently were energy security and mitigating their dependency on Russia in this matter, and addressing fears of Russia's behaving in a revisionist manner.)

The Central and Eastern European countries strongly believe in the transatlantic alliance and await definite actions from Barack Obama's administration confirming their commitment to it. Poland, as the regional leader, expects clearer indications of solidarity from the United States and greater understanding for the concerns of the region. For these reasons, therefore, strong regret was voiced that on his way to Moscow, President Obama did not visit Warsaw or Kiev. Doing so would have been a signal that the US treats Central and Eastern Europe seriously and would not agree to any expansionist attempts by Russia such as those seen in August of 2008 in Georgia. The change in US plans for missile defense installations in Poland and the Czech Republic raised doubts about the US guarantee, they continued, and President Obama should urgently rethink how to reassure the Central and Eastern European states that the US would once again commit to the region, especially with the European Union taking a more and more important position in all of the states. Poland for one hoped that its accession to the EU would strengthen the strategic cooperation between Europe and America. Instead, the previous few years had shown that contacts with Brussels were easier and more fruitful than with Washington.

Conclusions

At this point in history, EU membership continues to be very important for Poland for many reasons—political, economical, military and social. One may discuss whether the EU is not more important in various strategic and political areas than it is emotionally close or friendly; nevertheless, at the moment Poland's strategic political relations with the US and military relations with NATO do seem to be weaker or more questionable than in the past, and stronger EU relations and reliance upon membership in the EU seems to be a better bet for Poland.

Poland has been more supportive towards the development of ESDP, which it regards as the way to prevent the re-nationalization of security in Europe and thus stave off a resurgence of rivalries and old enmities among the nations of the region. It is also of the opinion that NATO and ESDP should complement one another rather than compete with each other. NATO could be responsible for hard security matters, whilst the ESDP could be a tool used by the EU to take actions in different world crises. Nevertheless, the Polish government emphasizes that NATO, as the main security guarantee in the Transatlantic area, should be the place for consulting on American and European goals and also the forum for deciding the means by which they will be reached. There are positive expectations that the Obama administration will seriously take into account its allies' interests, whilst Europe wants to be and should be an equal and fully valued partner of the United States. However, the alliance needs to adapt to new challenges by discussing and defining new strategic concepts relevant to the new political situation in Eastern Europe. Poland supports the balance in NATO between the alliance's basic function of collective defense related to Article 5 and the need for capability development in out-of-area operations. NATO needs to transform itself in order to increase its political and military credibility.

That Poland's Atlanticism cannot survive in the present form without making significant adjustments became clear when its sovereignty and security were fragile. Today, after the US decision to abandon the missile defence shield in Poland, both administrations must think about how to restore good relations and renew trust between the countries. Currently, Europeanist and Atlanticist policies are competing with each other. The US should not squander the large dose of the "inborn" fondness that Poles have towards Americans, because by doing so they may lose one of America's staunchest allies in Europe.

9 Russian Views on the Future of Transatlantic Relations

Alex Marshall

RUSSIAN VIEWS ON 'TRANSATLANTIC' RELATIONS (WHICH I shall characterize here as the three-way dialogue between Russia, Europe and America, though even that characterization implicitly implies a more overarching uniformity to Russian-European relations than is in fact the case) have traditionally been overshadowed by the bilateral relationship between Russia and America. Consequently, whilst this chapter will certainly consider the broader aspects of Russian views along this wider foreign policy vector, it begins with an examination of the current Russian-American relationship, not least because, during the latter half of 2008, that relationship itself appeared to be reaching a new post-Cold War nadir. It will then go on to examine Russian strategic culture, which has become notably more complex and nuanced since the first hesitant adoption of a 'human security' agenda in the Gorbachev era, to the point where today demographic security and environmental security are standard touchstones in successive drafts of the Russian Foreign Policy Concept (even whilst conventional military reform also remains an ostensible main priority). Here I will also consider the ambiguous relationship of Russia to Europe, where the concept of the 'transatlantic community' itself is also in flux due to overly rapid NATO and EU expansion, publicly unpopular expeditionary wars in Central Asia and the Middle East, and the American financial crisis of 2008, which left China as one of the few remaining centres of continuing global economic growth in 2009.[1] In the final section I will then consider whether the global financial crisis and its particularly heavy impact on the Russian domestic economy are likely to alter Russian approaches to the West, in the light of recent statements by American Vice President Joe Biden.[2]

Russia as a Transatlantic Actor

Russian-American relations emerged out of the shadow of the Cold War, during which time the United States and the Soviet Union had for the majority of the period since 1948 seen each other as implacable ideological enemies—the 'empire of liberty' versus the 'empire of justice'.[3] Characteristic of that earlier period of mutual hostility was the fact that relatively isolated moments of cooperation—for example, the activities of the American Relief Association (ARA) of 1921–23 in providing famine relief to the Soviet Union, or the personal ties forged by the American entrepreneur Armand Hammer with Lenin's new government, remained exactly that, isolated moments, which failed to cultivate any broader mutual cultural understanding, or help span the broader ideological gulf more significantly. With Marxism-Leninism effectively creating a 'dual' foreign policy of peaceful coexistence (the mission of the Soviet Foreign Ministry or, as it was initially known, the *Narkomindel*, for much of its existence) running in parallel with a utopian belief in socialist revolution and wars of 'national liberation' (embodied by the Comintern up until 1943, and the International Department of the CPSU thereafter), Soviet security policy for the majority of the Cold War overall remained locked into a heavily ideologized Leninist version of Clausewitz's most famous dictum— that 'war is the continuation of politics by classes and governments through forceful and coercive means.'[4] The decline of 'actually existing socialism' itself, however, after 1970—a stagnation accelerated by the immense expenditures, and associated internal infrastructural decay, imposed by the very military defensive measures related to this world view (expenditures which assumed the grotesque scale that they did partly as a direct consequence of the very notion of irreconcilable political differences with bourgeois capitalist states)—also inserted growing confusion and complexity into Soviet security doctrine after 1984. General-Secretary Mikhail Gorbachev's more general diplomatic 'peace offensive' after 1987 was married to doctrinal military innovations orientated around a rediscovery of the Soviet military theorists of the 1920s, alongside the emerging concept of 'defensive sufficiency', but few of these trends had been played out, or assumed any firm doctrinal shape or coherence, before the far broader collapse of Communist governments across the whole of Eastern Europe during 1989. This largely unforeseen development simultaneously also effectively destroyed the Warsaw Pact, the major multinational security organisation anchoring Soviet military strategy in Europe since 1955, thereby pulling the rug out from under the whole of Soviet security policy.[5]

With the collapse of communism as the dominant political ideology, and the subsequent breakup of the Soviet Union itself into sovereign nation states, the Russian-American relationship post-1991 then passed through two clearly definable successive waves of hope and recrimination. The mutual benefits achieved by both sides through joint nuclear weapons reduction programs were soon followed by Russian anger regarding NATO intervention over Kosovo in 1999. Thereafter, the fresh hopes sparked after 9/11 over joint cooperation to topple the Taliban regime in Afghanistan were rapidly followed by Russian resentment over the American-backed 'colour revolutions' in Georgia, Ukraine and Kyrgyzstan from the end of 2003 onwards.[6] The Georgia crisis of August 2008, however, marked a fundamentally deeper breakdown in trust between the two sides beyond simply 'agreeing to disagree', whilst also witnessing for the first time since 1991 a brief but significant escalation in real military tension, with bellicose rhetoric on both sides and American warships anchored off the Georgian coast. In December that same year, one Russian analyst summarised the watershed in Russian attitudes towards the United States by suggesting that the following three conclusions were now being widely drawn by his fellow analysts:

First, the United States is hopeless; nothing can be explained to it; and it will resort to any lie for its own interests.

Second, the United States is deliberately arming Russia's neighbours that are unfriendly to it in order to be able to put more pressure on Russia.

And third, it is impossible to come to terms with the U.S.[7]

Against that gradually emerging analytical backdrop, in November 2008, in what many interpreted as a diplomatic tit-for-tat rebuff to American interference in Russia's own 'backyard', Russian President Dmitri Medvedev toured Venezuela and Cuba, under the official remit of expanding trade contacts, defense ties and energy co-operation with both states. This visit, however, was also framed against a background of growing arms sales, the arrival of a Russian naval task force in Latin America which had stopped off in Libya en route, and the landing of Russian strategic nuclear bombers on Venezuelan airfields just weeks beforehand.[8] The presidential grand tour, which included visits to Brazil and Peru, was made, according to Medvedev himself, to underline a 'serious geopolitical decision—we *will* develop relations with Latin America and the Caribbean basin'. However, it also partly reciprocated an earlier 2007 trip by Venezuelan President Hugo Chavez to Moscow, during which time the latter had urged Russians to commemorate Lenin's ideas, and revive the general world-wide campaign against hegemonic 'imperialism'.[9] Many American and European commentators might therefore be forgiven for believing, under these circumstances, that the ending of both the Cold War itself, and the ideological conflict associated with it, had been but a pleasant day-dream.

With the re-election of Daniel Ortega to the post of Nicaraguan president in 2006, in conjunction with Vietnam veteran and Republican presidential candidate John McCain's consistent verbal targeting of Russia throughout 2008, voters on both sides of the Atlantic might in fact assume that Russian-American relations were trapped in a particularly ugly time warp from around the early 1980s. One American commentator in this context even compared President Medvedev's 2008 call for a revisiting of European collective security agreements to Soviet diplomatic efforts of the mid-1970s, out of which the Helsinki Final Act had emerged. In response, he urged that America take up rather than neglect the challenge, and again use it to pen in and roll back ('push back') the uncultured Russian bear.[10]

Rhetoric aside, however, the world *has* changed since 1991, in radical ways; Russian foreign policy therefore needs to be understood less as a complete return to the immediate Soviet past, and more as a national response to the universally felt conditions of modern globalisation. In this context, President Putin himself during his term in office underlined the fact that he 'regards globalisation, primarily in the form of international economic integration, as a powerful and irresistible force', whilst also emphasising that 'isolation from the world economy is a recipe for underdevelopment'.[11]

In the analytical paradigm that follows, therefore, I shall treat Russian security doctrine and Russian foreign policy alike as an ongoing work in progress, with the emphasis on transition rather than stagnation or relapse. Whilst geopolitics may after all dictate that many aspects of contemporary Russian security policy carry a distinctively Soviet physical and even intellectual legacy (amongst the most notable of them being the retention of a large nuclear deterrent, and a dedication to maintaining a million-strong regular army, even in the face of epic demographic and recruitment problems), the presence of legacy attitudes and strategic postures should not be confused with the assumption that nothing fundamental has changed. Russian foreign and security policy in this sense *does* reflect broader shifts in the international arena, which in turn compel any analysis of Russian attitudes to attempt to go beyond simplistic declarations that 'Russia is back'.

The post-1991 world order was founded *intellectually* on the premise that the absence of competing major ideologies would lead to the absence or sharp reduction of all sources of tension between states; democracy and commerce would flourish, and international political life would become both safer and much more boring as a direct consequence. The post-1991 global geopolitical reality, however, has seen the systemic decay and irrelevance of this initial intellectual premise become increasingly apparent, given the rise in energy (in)security, the relatively recently demonstrated ability of non-state actors to deliver strategic effects, the collapse of the globally imposed model of American free-market capitalism in 2008 under the sheer weight of its own multiple internal contradictions, and the more general and irrevocable slide towards a future 'multi-polar' world order.[12]

Before considering this broader international context, one must also take into account the domestic scene in attempting to analyse Russian views of the transatlantic community. Because Russian foreign policy is so rarely put in its domestic context, and because that domestic context itself is in turn so often misinterpreted or even misrepresented, Western views of Russia are often confused, and Russian views of the Transatlantic West prone to bouts of extreme irritation as a result. Outgoing President Putin's opening comment to *Time* magazine in 2007, that he was tired of Russians being presented as 'a little bit savage . . . or [as if] they just climbed down from the trees', captured the latter mood with typical brusque clarity.[13] Furthermore, nothing could be more damning or revealing of the mediocrity of most recent Western analysis of contemporary Russia (much of which incidentally remains curiously removed from any analysis of the broader global scene, or even of the writings of Russian counterparts in the Russian-language equivalents of journals like *Foreign Affairs*) than the sombre fact that the analyses of Western Cold War dinosaurs are again topping the West's best-seller lists.[14]

Russian Strategic Culture

The creation of any strategy or coherent foreign policy in any country is the result of an interaction between official and unofficial organs of power, inherited traditions, geography, and various 'agents of influence'. Russia after the Soviet collapse remained both a federal, multi-ethnic state, and one of the largest and most natural resource-rich countries on earth. Vladimir Putin also inherited from Boris Yeltsin a firmly presidential system of power, Russian parliamentary democracy having never fully recovered from the bombardment of the White House in Moscow by troops acting under Yeltsin's orders in 1993. Putin then at one and the same time both accelerated this trend towards centralization during his own term in office, fostering the establishment of a nationwide 'party of power' (*Edinaia Rossiia*, or 'United Russia') under conditions of 'managed democracy', and simultaneously created an interesting constitutional dilemma—the appearance of the oft-cited 'tandem' or 'diarchy' in Russian decision making, upon taking up the post of prime minister following completion of his second presidential term in 2008.

At the same time, however, the broader strategic context also obviously remains crucial—Russia is *not* a member of NATO or a member of the EU, but she *is* playing a role again in a number of old and new strategic forums, amongst them the United Nations Security Council (UNSC); the G-8 and G-20; the Collective Security Treaty Organisation (CSTO, comprising Russia, Belarus, Armenia, Kazakhstan, Uzbekistan, Tajikistan and Kyrgyzstan); the Shanghai Cooperation Organisation (SCO, comprising Russia, China, Uzbekistan, Tajikistan, Kazakhstan and Kyrgyzstan); the Eurasian Economic Community (EEC); and the more loosely aligned BRIC states (Brazil, Russia, India and China) of rapidly developing economies. This institutional context provides Russia with a complex and interwoven set of global and regional priorities, encompassing both 'hard power' and 'soft power' security issues. One significant aspect of President Medvedev's recent trip to Brazil, for example, was the reaching of an agreement waiving visa requirements for citizens of both states travelling between the two countries on short trips.[15] One level of engagement for the Russian Federation regarding current events in Afghanistan, meanwhile, has been an initiative to establish a joint SCO-CSTO anti-narcotics belt around Afghanistan, accompanied by the opening of a spacious new Russian embassy in Kabul.[16]

One might therefore very easily analyse the changing shape of Russian foreign policy purely by examining the similarities and differences between the three key foreign policy documents produced since 1991, namely the Russian Foreign Policy Concepts of 1993, 2000 and 2008.[17] Such an analysis would be adequate, but far from sufficient, however, just as an analysis of Washington policymaking would be, were the latter to be limited entirely to summarising the legal framework of the US Constitution. Such an analysis, in the case of Washington, would pass over in silence the position and role of NATO in American strategy, the significance of any president's personality and that of his immediate entourage, and even the 35, 000-some lobbyists and special interest groups who attempt, often by offering substantial financial donations, to influence national and even international policy.[18]

In short, a bare-bone textual analysis of this type applied to *any* state would contain important lacunae such as, for example, in the case under discussion here, the undeniable role of Russian public opinion, which contributed to President Putin's sky-high popularity ratings in repeated polls during his two terms in office. President Putin enjoyed substantial domestic support between 2000 and 2008 due to the perception that he was both a modernizer and a 'conviction politician'—one who had, moreover, been demonstrably successful in rebuilding stability within the Russian Federation and the former Soviet space. The irony throughout, however, has been that a revival of national pride and economic strength in Russia has been received less than enthusiastically by her immediate neighbours in the Transatlantic community:

> When foreign-based commentators and academics celebrate Yeltsin's Russia, which was worth a paltry $200bn and suffered international humiliation, while denouncing Putin's Russia, which has a GDP of $1.3 trillion and has regained global stature, most Russians detect not just incomprehension but ill-will.[19]

In this connection, Robert Kagan, in a typically provocative piece, argued relatively recently that Russian politics and public opinion were now effectively on a conceptual collision course with the EU. Given that the EU represents a postmodern security organisation, one in which 'Europe's nightmares are the 1930s, Russia's nightmares are the 1990s', Kagan suggested that this situation would lead to an inevitable conflict between 'a 21st century entity and a [nationalist] 19th century power.'[20] However, this chapter argues that such an analysis is not only inaccurate in certain important respects, (assuming for example that Russian policy remains unengaged with complex security problems such as drug trafficking and trans-national terrorism in a globalizing age) but quite clearly self-serving. If, after all (in a variation of Kagan's classic argument), 'Russians are from Mars, and Europeans are from Venus' then, by implication, given the surprising durability of such a Hobbesian universe, Europeans would ultimately have to continue relying upon American power in the long term—Americans luckily happening to also be 'from Mars'—in order to check the Russian bear.[21] However, this chapter will argue that, in certain respects, matters have already moved on too far for such a classic Cold War-style balance of power to be recreated—not least because the coherence of any notion of a common 'transatlantic community' is gone forever, and cannot be imminently or easily recreated.

The inability to recreate an essentially Cold War version of stability appears to be the result of twin trends interacting simultaneously, but (to-date) with an alarming lack of coordination or harmonious synergy. In the first place, NATO—without much deeper thought about rationale or concern about longer-term consequences—has continued to expand, and is now engaged in ongoing discussions to accept two states well within Russia's traditional sphere of influence, Georgia and the Ukraine. In addition to fulfilling ongoing NATO commitments in Afghanistan, the possibility of a 'global NATO', complemented by a 'League of Democracies' bypassing the United Nations, was also being promoted in certain Western political circles during 2008.

Secondly, however, Russia has unquestionably and simultaneously also revived as a regional economic hegemon, and is poised to unleash a major modernization drive, one which not only appears destined to bring about a much-needed overhaul of the state's infrastructural capacity, but also (given a scheduled $140 billion increase in federal budget allocations for 2009–11 for the procurement of over 400 new weapon types) could potentially revive conventional Russia's military capability substantially, rendering her a far more potent regional actor than she has been for many years.[22] Amongst the new procurement programs being discussed are plans to acquire 3,000 new armoured vehicles, upgrade and repair an additional 5,000 tanks and armoured personnel carriers, acquire 60 Iskander missile complexes and 1, 000 aircraft and helicopters, and bring online five new nuclear submarines.[23] Russia's corresponding re-engagement with her periphery, meanwhile, has also been not so much classically geopolitical as geo-economic, and the fact that Russia and the EU are now economically heavily interdependent, and appear destined in the short to medium term at least to remain so, renders any possibility of a

Cold War-style return to physical walls, ideological divisions, and economic autarchy utterly remote.[24]

The revival of Russia, in short, is no longer necessarily predominantly a transatlantic concern or existential ideological threat, so much as something that Europe itself will simply have to eventually recognise, deal with, and accommodate, whether by following the lead of de Gaulle's old vision of a 'Europe between the Atlantic and the Urals', or by reviving some variation of ex-Soviet President Gorbachev's call for a 'Common European Home'.[25] How this will then change Europe, or dilute the transatlantic relationship (which certainly cannot continue unaltered for much longer along its present strategic trajectory anyway, given broader phenomena such as the haemorrhaging of political willpower for the NATO effort in Afghanistan, or the 2008 global financial crisis which began in the United States), becomes a subject for debate beyond the remit of this chapter.

Against this background of an economic and potentially also a military revival, shaped both by more complex security threats and by the territorial sensation of a rapidly encroaching NATO, understanding Russia's attitude to the transatlantic relationship requires a degree of reorientation from the post-1945 analytical assumptions that are still relatively commonplace in, for example, a politically conservative country like the United Kingdom. Nowhere in the 1993, 2000 or 2008 Russian Foreign Policy Concepts, for example, is the notion of a 'transatlantic relationship'—i.e., the intellectual conceit of a coherent 'community of values and interests', as still popularly understood and espoused in some parts of Western Europe—engaged with or even mentioned.[26] Nor is there any clear hierarchy of 'special relationships' implied in the Russian Foreign Policy Concept, beyond a consistently expressed desire to secure, first and foremost, good neighborly relations around Russia's immediate borders. In the words of Dmitri Trenin in 2006, 'having left the Western orbit, Russia is [now] working to create its own solar system'.[27] By way of contrast, as late as 2008, the UK National Security Strategy, even whilst openly acknowledging that the international landscape since the end of the Cold War had been fundamentally 'transformed', still dogmatically took refuge in references to liberal 'core values', labelled the United States 'our most important bilateral relationship', and invoked the EU largely as an afterthought.[28] Within each revision of the Russian Foreign Policy Concept, on the other hand, a growing emphasis has come to be placed over time on globalization and multi-polarity, implying the *transcendence* of the transatlantic concept still implicit in UK thinking.

On the one hand, of course, such a distinction might reflect no more than Russia's traditionally prickly relationship with the whole intellectual concept of 'the West', with President Putin during his first term in office emphasising that Russia was culturally and economically part of Europe, but institutionally and politically distinct—pursuing, in Dmitri Trenin's words, integration *with*, as opposed to *within*, the European Union.[29] Such ambiguities reflect the fact that both Russia's foreign policy and her security policy continue to exhibit strong, undeniable underlying traits of an ongoing identity crisis, one not resolved by the famous debates between 'Atlanticists' and 'Eurasianists' during the 1990s.[30] In this context, there might in fact be seen to be two Wests in Russian thinking: the 'far West' of the United States and the 'near West' of the EU.

The 'near West' and the 'far West' may form the Euro-Atlantic community, but the 'near West' and the post-Soviet space create 'greater Europe'.[31]

The ambiguity of Russian elite attitudes in this regard, however, would also appear to mirror popular sentiment, with more than two-thirds of Russians surveyed in one recent opinion poll identifying the future of the state with the Commonwealth of Independent States (CIS) rather than with Europe; for the Russian government itself of course these are commitments which are concretely embodied in the security architecture of the CSTO, created in 2003.[32] Under this remit, Russian defensive commitments to Armenia, for example, provide Russia with a degree of leverage in that country's territorial dispute with neighbouring Azerbaijan over Nagorno-Karabakh that would otherwise be denied to her almost overnight. Were the Russian commitment removed, Armenian national security would be substantially affected, not least since Armenia has been deliberately bypassed by Western-orientated strategic energy pipelines in the region, and therefore lacks the capacity of Azerbaijan to divert profits from oil sales rapidly into a conventional military build-up. The recent Georgian conflict, therefore, merely highlighted traditional Russian sensitivity towards its security commitments in the region, with President Medvedev underlining the fact that Russia would remain the 'guarantor' of security in the Caucasus, in accordance with the conviction that they 'never have and never will be passive observers in the region'.[33] One might also argue further, though, that the evolution of the Russian Foreign Policy Concept pragmatically reflects a recognition that the very notion of a common transatlantic 'community of values and interests' itself has simply become outdated, in the face of newly emerging challenges and opportunities.

The imminent collapse of the whole Western notion of a globally applicable and inherently universal moral and economic order, in the wake of the end of the Cold War, which ironically appeared to herald its triumph, was after all being prognosticated by the English political theorist John Gray as long ago as 1994.[34]

The initial 1993 Russian Foreign Policy Concept on its own marked a clear break with the immediate past, underlining that 'national interests' rather than 'international class interests' were now the key determinants of Russian foreign policy, but otherwise it did markedly little else, being mainly a clearly recognisable stopgap document, focused primarily on internal economic reform, border stability, and the attempt to defend the rights of the 25 million Russians who suddenly found themselves living 'abroad' after the collapse of the Soviet Union. The only clue to the future direction of Russian foreign policy in any substantial sense was the already-present insistence upon the need to strengthen a 'unified military strategic space' in the newly founded CIS.[35]

The Foreign Policy Concept that followed in 2000 was both more developed, and highly pragmatic, emphasising above all the need 'to achieve firm and prestigious positions in the world community, most fully consistent with the interests of the Russian Federation as a great power, as one of the most influential centres of the modern world, and [as is furthermore] necessary for the growth of [her own] political, economic, intellectual and spiritual potential'. This was then further articulated in a concrete desire to seek a 'multipolar system of international relations', whilst also noting increasing regional and sub-regional integration, and emphasizing Russia's own stance of 'consistency and predictability [founded upon] mutually advantageous pragmatism'. The United Nations was highlighted as the guarantor of the new world order: 'attempts to introduce into international parlance such concepts as "humanitarian intervention" and "limited sovereignty" in order to justify unilateral power actions bypassing the U.N. Security Council are not acceptable.' Furthermore, the document also highlighted that 'NATO's present-day political and military guidelines do not coincide with the security interests of the Russian Federation, and occasionally directly contradict them. This primarily concerns the provisions of NATO's new strategic concept, which does not exclude the conduct of use-of-force operations outside of the zone of application of the Washington Treaty without the sanction of the UN Security Council. Russia retains her negative attitude towards the expansion of NATO.'[36]

The 2008 Foreign Policy Concept represents, as one might expect, a fur-

ther development and maturation of the views and concerns that had begun
to be expressed in the 2000 document. Emphasis upon a 'socially oriented
market economy' reflected the development of the concept of 'sovereign democracy' in Russia, in which the leading political elites have come to see preservation of the existing social consensus, alongside the fostering of a patriotic
business-orientated middle class, as critical to the overall integrity of the state
itself. Equally revealing, however, was the emphasis on 'overcoming . . . the
resource-based economy and [transitioning] to [one of] innovation', reflective of the more general Russian desire to become a top-five world economy
by 2020,[37] alongside the emphasis laid upon improving the 'demographic situation'—demographic security having moved steadily up the list of Russian
security priorities during President Putin's own two terms in office. Also bitterly noted in passing was 'the reaction to the prospect of the loss by the historic West of its monopoly in global processes, [which] finds its expression, in
particular, in the continued political and psychological policy of "containing"
Russia, including the use of a selective approach to history for those purposes,
[primarily] regard[ing] World War Two and the postwar period'.[38] The revised concept reiterated that 'Russia maintains its negative attitude towards
the expansion of NATO, notably to[wards] the plans [for] admitting Ukraine
and Georgia to membership in the alliance, as well as [towards] bringing
NATO military infrastructure closer to the Russian borders, which violates
the principle of equal security, leads to new dividing lines in Europe, and runs
counter to the [need to increase] the effectiveness of joint work [to meet the]
real challenges of our time'. Above all else, though, the new foreign policy
concept underlined that Russia for her own part saw herself as ready to 'go
global', with the prospect of revitalised partnerships or trade agreements with
Turkey, Egypt, Algeria, Iran, Saudi Arabia, Syria, Libya, India and Pakistan
now also openly mentioned for the first time—the rhetorical transcendence
of the very notion of a transatlantic community incarnate.[39]

Perceptions, Capabilities, Doubts: Back to the West?

Critical to debate about Russia's revival and the manner in which it will affect her attitudes along the transatlantic vector of her foreign policy is an assessment of the economic and cultural aspects associated with this revival.
Much criticism in the West has been levelled at the manner in which Russia's
revival under Putin has actually been managed and executed in practice—

the nationalization of former oligarch-owned economic assets, a perceived crackdown on media freedoms, the repression of dissidents, and an increasing emphasis on recreating a centralized state power vertical in the wake of the Beslan school siege of 2004. A distinct sub-theme of this criticism has been concern over how stable, transparent and predictable this revised state structure and the broader economic boom actually are.

Russia's decision to cut off gas to the Ukraine in 2006 and 2009 undermined the European faith in Russia as a dependable energy provider, and thereby revived fears over European 'energy security'; in particular it restoked European interest in further diversifying sources of energy supply via the long-planned, American-backed, but potentially commercially unviable Nabucco gas pipeline project. Russian energy companies' external-orientated investment strategies in both Europe and Africa have also periodically been heavily criticised in some circles, both for occurring to the detriment of vital internal infrastructural and environmental investment, and for potentially revisiting the 'resource curse' of pursuing a form of economic growth that was too narrowly based and market-fluctuation dependent—the very error which earlier doomed the Soviet Union.

Finally, of course, the 2008 military intervention in South Ossetia by Russian Federal forces was portrayed by its critics in the West as an 'act of aggression' against a NATO-leaning democracy, despite the almost immediate abundance of physical evidence on the ground of Georgian responsibility for initiating hostilities, via a wholly indiscriminate use of force.[40] With the global financial crisis of 2008, meanwhile, Western commentators were also emphasizing apparent cracks in the Russian decision-making edifice, including what appeared to be open policy disagreements between Medvedev and Putin, whilst at the same time highlighting growing social unrest, particularly over protectionist measures to raise import tariffs on autos in the Far East, as signs of a potential growing regional fault line in the post-2000 'social contract' between state and society. Whilst Russia possesses the world's third largest supply of foreign reserves, and therefore is in a better position than most to ride out the global financial downturn, her efforts to stabilise the rouble also led to an immediate $210bn drain on her foreign exchange reserves, against a background of double-digit inflation. This turn of events led some commentators to remark that 'the west may soon be worrying again about [Russia's] weaknesses rather than its strengths.'[41] In July 2009 US Vice-President Joe Biden neatly encapsulated the essence of much of this criticism by remarking that Russia's 'withering' economy and demographic difficulties gave the United States and the 'West' in general a far stronger negotiating hand than many realized, adding that Russia would be simply compelled over time to further loosen its grip on countries in its immediate geopolitical or-bit whilst also accepting a diminished global role. Biden's comments proved extraordinarily controversial, however, coming as they did in the wake of the Obama administration's attempted strategic 'reset' of relations with Moscow, and were met by an almost immediate and entirely predictable riposte from both the Russian Foreign Ministry and domestic media.[42]

It would appear dangerous at present to assume that economic and demo-graphic challenges will inevitably lead to a downward, less ambitious revision of Russian security and foreign policies. Whilst Russia unquestionably faces formidable obstacles in implementing her ambitious internal modernization program, not least crippling levels of corruption, a still-bloated bureaucracy, concern over the rule of law and consequent periodic capital flight, together with shortages of skilled labour for many of her largest infrastructure proj-ects, there is little evidence as yet to suggest that the threat to Russia's recovery in both the regional and international arenas will prove terminal, or that a relapse to the financial torpor of the 1990s is imminent. Shifts in the broader global economy to a large extent will determine whether the Russian econ-omy faces a 'lost decade' (recovering only to 2008 levels of income and growth by 2014), or whether the 'Russia 2020' economic program has in fact only been delayed by a year or two.[43] Macro-economic analysis to date has led many economists to instead assess the major Russian fundamentals as sound, and, with a recovery in the international oil and metals market widely predicted in an era of 'peak oil', some see Russia as a country that could *potentially* yet emerge as 'one of the few islands of growth left in the global economy by the end of 2009'.[44]

Barring a cataclysmic unforeseen collapse, one can therefore also predicate that Russian views of the transatlantic vector in her foreign policy will also remain broadly unchanged, with cultural anti-Americanism running parallel with increasing investment, consultation, trade talks and technological inter-changes with the EU. The spirit of 'mutually advantageous pragmatism', first expressed in the 2000 Russian Foreign Policy Concept, has after all remained the guiding force behind the recently signed agreement in April 2010 between presidents Obama and Medvedev to jointly reduce the size of their respective nuclear arsenals. However at the same time, Russia's commitment to helping evolve a genuinely multi-polar world, one transcending trans-atlanticism, also remains embodied in her revealed proposals for a new European security architecture, which initially proposed the incorporation of China as a consultative partner, and also strives to attain an 'equal partnership' between NATO and the CSTO.[45] Russian relations with the EU do contain an underlying degree of tension, however, though not necessarily for the *realpolitik* reasons of Russians-as-Martians invoked by Kagan. The EU's failure to institute a joint consultative body paralleling the Russia-NATO Council has generated a degree of irritation, which was then exacerbated by tensions over the chairmanship of the Organisation for Security and Cooperation in Europe (OSCE) and its performance in election monitoring. The EU's divided front after 2009 in adopting a Polish-sponsored 'Eastern Partnership'—that explicitly excluded Russia, on the one hand, but still ran in parallel with the French-backed 'Mediterranean Union' project initiated in 2007—also reflected strategic incoherence on the part of the EU and further irritated Russia.[46] Plainly, Europe will have to choose in future between being a major actor on the Mediterranean rim or a major actor in the Transcaucasus and Central Asia; it has neither the economic strength nor the political will to do both, and will have to take account of Russian interests at some level. Nonetheless, the Russian tendency to evolve in a direction dubbed by some 'European but not Western' does not mean that every security issue will invariably be reduced to a zero-sum game, since behind the headlines the Russian business class will still continue to look predominantly to invest in the West.

Whilst in the United States the incoming Obama administration still appears to have a narrow window of opportunity to improve bilateral relations again, given recent announcements to change the deployment of a U.S. anti-ballistic missile shield in Europe in response to the threatened—but now temporarily suspended—Russian counter-deployment of short range ballistic missiles in Kaliningrad, rebuilding a more lasting strategic relationship will also have to accommodate broader global shifts and trends. One of the more encouraging aspects to emerge out of both the Georgian crisis of 2008 and the 2009 Ukrainian gas crisis was the willingness of the EU to act as a negotiator and interlocutor. However there are also deep tensions between EU policy as currently configured, and current U.S. and NATO policy, and both stand urgently in need of review and amendment. It has aptly been pointed out that 'if for the United States the post-Soviet space is a theatre, for the EU it is a neighbourhood.'[47] Before a Russian revival looked to be in prospect, there were grounds for arguing that these two attitudes were complementary; as noted correctly by Kagan however (though with some erroneous reasoning), there is now an increasing body of evidence since at least 2004 to suggest that the era of complementarity is ending. For whilst Kagan is correct to note the increasing challenge to the EU's post-modern security paradigm created by Russian revival, there is also very little evidence to support the idea that either NATO or notions of a coherent 'transatlantic community' need only a little further tweaking in order for balance and solidarity to be restored, penning in the 'Russian bear' in the process. Instead, in a global economy that seems destined to be dominated by China, Europe faces the new challenge of having to become a pragmatic rather than an idealistic or values-based actor, one which will just have to learn to live in a multipolar world.

If one cannot therefore immediately envision the resolution of a European security crisis without resort to the implicit backup of Kagan's American 'Martians', then there is also nothing written in stone to suggest this will always be the case. The Russian nuclear shield offers a potential level of protection for Europe as well, Russia remains the key to helping unlock the Iranian nuclear issue, and the ongoing slowdown in most developed European economies will render access to and dialogue with geographically neighbouring (and rapidly developing) markets increasingly critical for overall macroeconomic stability, not least given the also recently demonstrated constraints and limitations of the Euro in terms of generating a flexible and effective monetary policy across 27 states. With Germany now the key player in European measures to maintain stability in light of the proposed bail-out package to Greece in 2010, it should be noted that German-Russian relations in particular look set to remain and indeed become increasingly important, with the two countries historically since 1991 sharing an attitude of understanding and mutual trust that has been striking.

The ultimate outcome of all of this will most likely resemble neither a utopian postmodern security paradigm nor a return to the messy Hobbesian European great power universe of the eighteenth century. Instead, what will probably emerge is a hybrid system, reflective more broadly of a modern, interconnected, but nonetheless multipolar age. It will, in short, be messy and highly ambiguous, much as the content of both Russian foreign policy and cultural identity currently is. Prophecy in international affairs is, of course, a notoriously inexact science. In 1980, one of the CIA's leading Soviet foreign policy analysts predicted that by the 1990s, 'the U.S. will have ceased to be a great power and will be struggling to hold itself together as a viable nation. The Soviet Union will [by then] be approaching hegemony over most of the world.'[48] But if one cannot currently envisage the resolution of a dispute in Europe without the participation and oversight of American representatives, there is nonetheless nothing to say that this will remain the case in, say, twenty, thirty or fifty years time. For Russia, meanwhile, it appears likely that the new rationale underlying her foreign policy—the rhetorical transcendence of the very notion of transatlanticism, combined at the practical level with an expectation of equal cooperation with the West and a demand for respect of her national interests—will prove enduring.

10 Transatlantic Relations

A View from Ukraine

Deborah Sanders[1]

Introduction

Since the 'Orange Revolution' at the end of 2004, Ukraine's foreign policy prioritized Euro-Atlantic integration.[2] The former president, Viktor Yush-chenko, stated that his main goal was to secure Ukraine's membership in the EU and NATO and, at least in the early months of his presidency, the prospects of membership in both organisations appeared bright.[3] With the election this year of a new Ukrainian president, Viktor Yanukovych, Ukraine continues to pursue a foreign policy that prioritises Europe and good relations with the US, but has moved decisively away from actively pursuing NATO membership. In a recent visit to Brussels President Yanukovych highlighted the elements of continuity in Ukraine's foreign policy by signaling his intent to secure Ukraine's membership of the EU and signed an association agreement to build closer trade, political and social links between the EU and Ukraine. In April of this year Yanukovych also highlighted the importance of strengthening good relations with the US when he agreed at the Nuclear Security Summit in Washington to renounce the nation's stockpile of highly enriched uranium and reaffirmed his government's commitment to the 2008 US-Ukraine Charter on Strategic Partnership. Yanukovych has, however, explicitly rejected Ukraine's former foreign policy goal of securing NATO membership. Yanukovych has instead pledged to continue cooperation with NATO while pursuing non-bloc status aimed at improving and strengthening relations with Ukraine's largest and most powerful neighbour, the Russian

Federation. Despite the adoption of a more nuanced Euro-Atlantic foreign policy by the new president, the success of Ukraine's attempt to build good relations with Europe, the US and the Russian Federation will continue to be affected by domestic political factors. In particular, Ukraine will continue to face endemic political instability as well as deep divisions between the Ukrainian political parties as to the pace and shape of Ukraine's Euro-Atlantic ambitions.

This chapter will begin by exploring how political instability and infighting have damaged Ukraine's Euro-Atlantic goals and will continue to affect and shape Ukraine's foreign policy. The second part of this chapter will then consider how Ukraine's previous foreign policy goal of Euro-Atlantic integration has shaped security policy—in particular, Ukraine's participation in regional organisation, its military transformation and its commitment to regional and international peacekeeping operations. The third part of this chapter will examine Ukraine's relationship with the US before offering an assessment of Ukraine's Euro-Atlantic ambitions.

Domestic Political Instability in Ukraine and Its Impact on Foreign Policy

During his presidency Viktor Yushchenko failed to establish a stable and effective working government or coalition able to implement his domestic or foreign policy agenda. This has not only hampered Ukraine's Euro-Atlantic ambitions but also damaged the development of a coherent and effective foreign policy to achieve this objective. The unworkable nature of the semi-presidential, semi-parliamentary political system in Ukraine combined with President Yushchenko's inability either to work with the leader of the two main parties or to build a working coalition in parliament has ensured that Ukraine made very little progress after the Orange Revolution in securing either NATO or EU membership. As will be discussed later, political infighting has also delayed the introduction and effective funding of NATO and EU awareness campaigns which would help build public support for Ukraine's foreign policy goals.

After Prime Minister Yulia Tymoshenko and President Yushchenko proved unable and unwilling to work together during the first few months after the Orange Revolution, the former was sacked by the latter and parliamentary elections were held in March 2006, forcing Ukraine into its first political crisis. Nevertheless, as a result of international goodwill towards Ukraine's democratic revolution, Ukraine appeared to be making progress in advancing its foreign policy goal of Euro-Atlantic integration. Four months after the inauguration of the new president in 2005, Ukraine was offered an 'intensified dialogue on membership' at the NATO Foreign Ministers meeting in Vilnius.[4] It was widely assumed that Ukraine would be offered a Membership Action Plan (MAP) in 2006 and would be invited to join NATO at the 2008 Summit in Bucharest. However, these early signs of foreign policy progress were to be thwarted by domestic political developments in Kiev. By the end of 2005 the Orange parliamentary coalition made up of President Yushchenko's Our Ukraine Party and Tymoshenko's party, the Tymoshenko Bloc, had splintered with bitter recriminations, and Ukraine was left without a working government for five months.

To further complicate matters, a package of political reform was adopted in January 2006 wherein Ukraine would move towards a parliamentary as opposed to a presidential system of government. The new prime minister (PM), who would form a cabinet to run the government, would no longer be appointed by the president but instead be drawn from the political party that won the most seats in the Ukrainian parliament, the Rada. These constitutional changes have unfortunately not produced a stable democracy in Ukraine.[5] In March 2006, Ukraine held parliamentary elections, which, due to these constitutional changes, would also decide the appointment of the next prime minister and cabinet. In the parliamentary election the Party of the Regions, the party of Viktor Yanukovych, Yushchenko's discredited rival in the October 2004 presidential elections, formed the so-called Anti-Crisis Coalition with the Socialist Party and the Communist Party. With a majority in the Rada, Yanukovych eventually became prime minister.[6] His appointment took many months to negotiate, leaving Ukraine without an effective government and revealing division between the parties as to the pace and shape of Ukraine's Euro-Atlantic integration.

Political instability in Kiev has also hampered Ukraine's aspirations to join the European Union, despite there being a consensus across Ukraine's political elite about the importance of this goal. In an attempt to secure EU membership during 2006 and into 2007, political and diplomatic contacts with the EU were stepped up. Ukraine's president had a number of meetings with top EU officials and PM Yanukovych led Ukraine's delegation at a meeting of the Ukraine-EU Cooperation Council.[7] In Brussels in September 2006, PM Yanukovych spelled out his government's commitment to EU membership, stating that Ukraine would continue to pursue EU membership and would push ahead with the reforms necessary to establish a free trade zone with the EU.[8] Despite these attempts to strengthen relations with the EU, the question of Ukraine's membership continues to hinge on progress in consolidating its democracy and domestic reform. The EU sees internal political instability as one of the main impediments to membership. EU leaders, the European Commission and the European Parliament have expressed concern about political developments in Ukraine.[9] Political competition between the three main parties over who controls government and the parliament, as well as changes in the constitutional framework, have created instability and also hampered the implementation of necessary reforms laid out in the EU Action Plan. In particular, Ukraine has struggled to develop an independent judiciary, has had little success in fighting corruption, has been slow to make socio-economic reforms, and has made little progress in improving public health.[10] In light of these problems, the German Chancellor Angela Merkel, speaking towards the end of 2006, stressed that Ukraine was not yet ready for EU membership,[11] a sentiment she expressed again eighteen months later in light of the continuing political crisis in Ukraine.[12] Political instability will continue to be a major impediment to President Yanukovych's stated goal of joining the EU. Although Yanukovych has built a slim majority in the Ukrainian Rada, this is an inherently unstable coalition of three parties and independent MPs drawn primarily from its Orange competitors—former PM Tymoshenko's party and former president Yushchenko's alliance. It is unlikely to be a robust coalition able to support and approve the tough reforms required to either stabilize the Ukrainian economy or engage in the radical reforms required for EU membership. Further exacerbating these problems, Yanukovych has also packed his cabinet with close allies rather than attempting to build a government based on consensus and able to implement the broad and difficult reforms required by the EU.

Political instability and infighting have also damaged Ukraine's future membership of NATO as they revealed key differences amongst the political elites about the pace and shape of possible membership. In 2006, PM Yanukovych declared that his government would suspend negotiations on NATO membership. Citing public opposition as the need to do so, he went on to suggest that while he was not turning his back on the West, he believed that Ukraine should instead act as a 'reliable bridge between the European Union and Russia'.[13] During a visit to Brussels in September 2006, he stated that

Ukraine was not yet ready to implement a NATO Membership Action Plan (MAP), something the president and his government had been working solidly towards since the beginning of 2005.[14] Yanukovych stated that in his view membership should be delayed and, rather than sign a MAP, Ukraine should focus instead on deepening its partnership with the alliance.[15]

As well as perhaps altering the pace and shape of Ukraine's Euro-Atlantic ambitions, a power struggle between PM Yanukovych and the president hampered the development and implementation of Ukraine's foreign policy during 2006. Not only was Yanukovych responsible for the resignation of Ukraine's pro-Western foreign minister, Boris Tarasyuk, but the power struggle between PM and president hampered the effective working of the Ukrainian Ministry of Foreign Affairs. For four months, it paralysed the Ministry of Foreign Affairs: embassies were not funded, its accounts were blocked and a number of overseas visits were postponed.[16] In his resignation speech, Foreign Minister Tarasyuk claimed that the protracted standoff with the Yanukovych's government he had been engaged in had made it impossible for him to perform his role.[17] Amendments to the Ukrainian constitution had created overlapping powers between the PM and president, and it was unclear just who was responsible for the development of foreign policy. This battle over the control of foreign policy broke out when the Ukrainian Rada voted to remove Foreign Minister Tarasyuk, following a request by PM Yanukovych. This action was rejected by President Yushchenko, who continued to support Tarasyuk, whom he had appointed. However, PM Yanukovych then barred Tarasyuk from attending cabinet sessions despite President Yushchenko's claims that the Rada had exceeded its authority.[18]

In April 2007, when it proved impossible for him to work with Prime Minister Yanukovych, President Yushchenko dissolved parliament. In September 2007 parliamentary elections took place again.[19] Yulia Tymoshenko was eventually appointed prime minister at the end of 2007, after her party and the pro-presidential party, Our Ukraine—People's Self Defence Union, gained a small majority in the Rada.[20] However, protracted and difficult negotiations between the two party leaders again left Ukraine without an effective working government for many months. At the beginning of 2008, however, it appeared that Ukraine's Euro-Atlantic foreign policy objectives were back on course after a bumpy start. In an interview in January 2008, President Yushchenko optimistically stated that 'Ukrainian authorities for the first time are in a situation where the president, the prime minister and the speaker of the parliament are all openly proposing a pro-west path and Euro-Atlantic coordination.'[21] Nevertheless, despite his optimism about the key political players' commitment to Euro-Atlantic integration, the president proved unable and unwilling to work with his new PM, and by the end of 2008 Ukraine was again facing a political crisis. Relations between the PM and the president were precarious throughout 2008 and 2009, with the president continually criticising and attempting to distance himself from PM Tymoshenko in preparation for the presidential elections in 2010. As part of this campaign of undermining Tymoshenko, the head of the Presidential Secretariat, Viktor Baloha, engaged in a relentless campaign of criticising PM Tymoshenko.[22] By the late summer of 2008 relations had broken down, with President Yushchenko accusing the PM of treason for failing to publicly criticize the Russian intervention in Georgia and for blocking a parliamentary motion to condemn Russia's aggression. These allegations, combined with an attempt by the PM to pass legislation diluting presidential authority, contributed to the collapse of the government coalition in early October.

PM Tymoshenko has struggled to build a working coalition within the Rada after President Yushchenko's party, Our Ukraine, withdrew from the coalition. In December 2008 the PM built a working majority in the parliament by combining her party, the Lytvyn Bloc and the majority of the formerly pro-Yushchenko Our Ukraine People's Self Defence Caucus. The Communist Party has remained outside the alliance, but has backed the coalition in several important parliamentary votes. In November 2008 Ukraine negotiated an IMF loan to bail out its banks, and in January the following year Gazprom stopped the supply of Russian gas to Ukraine, forcing the PM into protracted and difficult negotiations with Moscow.[23]

Ukraine's ongoing political instability was cited as one of the main reasons it was offered an Annual National Plan (ANP) instead of a MAP at the NATO ministerial meeting in December 2008, despite Kiev's expectations that Ukraine would be invited to join the alliance in 2008. Earlier that year, the prime minister, the president and the speaker of the Ukrainian Parliament had all signed a letter requesting a MAP for Ukraine in 2008 and expectations were high. At least on the surface, it appeared that Ukraine was making progress in its Euro-Atlantic ambitions during 2008. At the Bucharest Summit in April 2008, the final NATO communiqué not only welcomed Ukraine's Euro-Atlantic ambitions but more importantly agreed that Ukraine would become a member of NATO. It made clear that NATO members supported Ukraine's application for MAP and would begin a period of intensive engagement to begin this process.[24] However, this communiqué hid deep divisions within the transatlantic community over future enlargement of NATO. The US, Canada, the UK and most of the Central and East European member states supported MAPs for both Ukraine and Georgia. France, Germany, Italy, Spain, Greece and Norway expressed reservations and opposed offering Ukraine a MAP at Bucharest.

In Ukraine the major political parties have expressed differences as to the pace and shape of Ukraine's Euro-Atlantic integration, but in addition, domestic opposition to NATO membership, in particular, remains high and is a cause for concern amongst some European states. The lack of public support for NATO membership has been one of the main arguments used by France and Germany to argue against offering Ukraine a MAP.[25] Surveys in Ukraine consistently show that the majority of the Ukrainian people are opposed to NATO membership, but support did increase by ten points to 31% in early September 2008, after the Russian intervention in Georgia.[26] The Ukrainian public remain skeptical and are ill-informed about NATO.[27] Public opinion polls have shown that stereotypes formed during the Cold War still shape many Ukrainians' views of NATO; NATO is perceived to be an aggressive military bloc that provokes conflicts. The public are also concerned about the financial and political costs of joining NATO.[28] Many Ukrainians also fear that NATO membership will damage relations with Ukraine's largest neighbour, the Russian Federation.

In parts of Ukraine, notably the Crimea, there is also a tendency to confuse NATO with the US. In a sign not only of the strength of domestic opposition to Ukraine's NATO membership but also confusion about NATO's objectives and its relationship to the US, residents in Feodosiya in the Crimea blockaded a port in 2006 to protest what they saw as an attempt by NATO to establish a naval base in the Black Sea.[29] Displaying anti-NATO slogans, residents picketed the port hampering the ability of US Marines to begin preparations for a forthcoming US-Ukrainian naval exercise. In another sign of the lack of public understanding about NATO, the Ukrainian defence minister was forced to deny media reports that the crew of the US ship were planning on building a NATO base near Feodosiya.[30] In a sign of the depth of public opposition in the Crimea to what was perceived as a NATO operation and Ukraine's future membership of NATO, the day after the arrival of a US ship to begin preparations for the bilateral military exercise, the Feodosiya town council declared the town a 'NATO-free area'.[31] This proclamation was followed a week later by the adoption by the Crimean parliament of a statement declaring the peninsula a 'NATO-free territory'.[32]

Early in 2008 at a rally in Simferopol in the Crimea, demonstrators again signaled their opposition to Ukraine's membership of NATO.[33] A poll conducted in the Crimea in December found that almost 70% of residents believed that Ukraine's foreign policy priority should be relations with Russia, rather than with Europe.[34] In light of the strong public opposition to and misunderstanding about NATO, the Ukrainian government has been heavily criticised by the Ukrainian Constitutional Court for failing to inform the public and gain popular support for its plans to join NATO.[35]

In 2008 the Ukrainian government not only allocated insufficient funds for a NATO awareness campaign but also failed to implement an effective campaign. Early in 2008, signaling the government's cognizance of the scale of the problem, the Ukrainian foreign minister called for a 'quiet and fair' information campaign about the advantages of NATO membership that would address Ukrainians' concerns about the financial costs and concern about the aggressive tendencies of NATO.[36] It has been estimated, however, that the Ukrainian government has spent only a third of the rather small state budget allocated to improving domestic understanding of the role of NATO.[37] These failures might prove a serious mistake in light of the recent ruling by the Ukrainian Constitutional Court on the necessity for Ukraine to hold a nationwide referendum on future membership in NATO.[38]

Polls suggest that the Ukrainian people are more supportive of Ukraine's European ambitions, however, than they are of NATO membership. A poll conducted by the Razumkov Centre in June 2007 found that more than half of Ukrainian citizens supported the idea of Ukraine's accession to the EU.[39] A poll conducted towards the end of 2008 by the US Agency for International Development (USAID) suggested that this figure has not changed significantly. It also indicated that membership of the EU is seen as providing economic benefits and, unlike NATO membership, does not run the risk of antagonising the Russian Federation.[40] In recognition of the low level of public knowledge and understanding of the EU and what membership would mean for Ukraine, the Ukrainian cabinet approved a European information strategy. The program's objectives are to raise public awareness about European integration and create a stable pro-European majority within Ukrainian society.[41] However, this program lacks detail and funding has been low. The

Ukrainian government's European information strategy has put too much emphasis on the need to explain government policy to the Ukrainian people, and not enough on how and why the EU exists and, more importantly, what advantages membership would offer Ukraine. Its budget in 2007, which was approximately one tenth of the amount spent by the Polish Government on public awareness in 2004, is simply too small to have much of an impact on Ukraine's public opinion.[42] These issue will have to be addressed by the new Yanukovych government if it is to inform and prepare the Ukrainian people for future EU membership.

European concern about the ongoing political instability and the absence of an effective European public awareness campaign in Ukraine was evident at the launch by the European Commission of the Eastern Partnership Plan in December 2008.[43] This plan, aimed at political and economic integration of six of the former Soviet states, is a clear signal that EU membership is still a long way off for Ukraine. More importantly, this plan also shows that the EU still views Ukraine in the same light as its less developed neighbours Belarus, Moldova, Georgia, Armenia and Azerbaijan.

Ukraine's foreign policy objectives vis-à-vis Euro-Atlantic integration have also been hampered by two interconnected factors: Ukraine's difficult relationship with the Russian Federation and divisions within the transatlantic alliance. These divisions are most notably over relations with Russia, especially in the aftermath of its intervention in Georgia. After the Orange Revolution brought to power a pro-Western president committed to EU and NATO integration, relations between Russia and Ukraine deteriorated. Sensitive to the need to maintain good relations, President Yushchenko made his first formal state visit after his inauguration to Russia in early 2005. Despite early signs that relations between these two states were improving, the Ukrainian government's attempts to secure NATO membership have been vociferously opposed in Moscow, and relations have soured. Moscow has viewed Ukraine's membership in NATO as a threat. In April 2008, President Vladimir Putin stated that 'the appearance on our borders of a powerful military bloc will be taken in Russia as a direct threat to the security of our country'.[44] In a joint press conference with President Yushchenko, President Putin stated that if NATO or the US deployed military installations in Ukraine, Russia could target its missile systems at Ukraine.[45] Relations have also been strained in light of calls by the Ukrainian government for negotiations over the removal of Russia's Black Sea Fleet (BSF) from its naval base in Sevastopol when its lease expires in 2017. The Ukrainian president damaged relations further by suggesting that restrictions should be placed on the movement of the Russian BSF, in light of its blockade of Georgian ports and its use in landing Russian military forces during the summer conflict. The Ukrainian government also accused Russia of fermenting separatism within Crimea and distributing Russian passports, and charged Russian intelligence with attempting to hire Ukrainian reservists for operations in Georgia.[46]

Relations hit another low point when, in early January 2009, Gazprom, the Russian national gas company, announced that it had cut off supplies of gas to Ukraine. Gas negotiations have also been hampered by domestic political instability and infighting in Ukraine. Prime Minister Tymoshenko, who is responsible for negotiating a deal, has been thwarted in her attempts by the president, who cancelled Tymoshenko's trip to Moscow at short notice. As Ukrainian pipelines carry almost 80% of Russian gas supplies to Europe, the disruption to supply had a devastating effect on many European states. In response to this crisis a European-brokered deal resulted in the resumption of gas supplies through Ukraine to Europe.

Changes in Russia's strategic environment—including the expansion of NATO to include former Soviet bloc countries such as the Baltic States, US plans to position new missile defence systems in Poland and the Czech Republic and Kosovo's declaration of independence—have all affected relations between Moscow and the transatlantic community. Sensitive about antagonizing the Russian Federation further, key European states have attempted to slow down Ukraine's accession to NATO, despite Washington's strong support for it. Just before the April 2008 summit, President Bush stated that he firmly believed that Ukraine should be given a MAP.[47] At the NATO summit in Bucharest, Germany and France blocked attempts by the US and some newer NATO members to give Ukraine and Georgia MAPs amidst fears that doing so could jeopardise relations with the Russian Federation. In an interview about enlargement, the Germany's foreign minister, Frank-Walter Steinmeier, said that after Russia's anger over Kosovo's independence 'we could see no convincing reason to create more tension'.[48] Eight months later at the NATO meeting in Brussels in December, the same group of countries again opposed US attempts to extend a MAP to Ukraine, in light of Russia's intervention in Georgia. Many European states have adopted a more cautious position towards the Russian Federation that includes, in effect, calling for a pause in NATO's enlargement plans. In an early sign of this change, the German Chancellor Angela Merkel told a meeting of the Atlantic Treaty Association that NATO's signal to Russia should be one of outreach and cooperation, and that neither Georgia nor Ukraine would be ready to join NATO in the foreseeable future.[49]

Relations between Russia and Ukraine improved dramatically, however, with the election of Viktor Yanukovych in February 2010. One of his key foreign policy objectives has been to strengthen and build relations with the Russian Federation. A recent example of this new policy towards Russia has been the announcement of a plan to extend the lease of the Russian Black Sea Fleet in Sevastopol to 2042. As part of this agreement the Ukrainian government has also secured significant discounts on the price it pays for Russian natural gas, easing pressure on the struggling Ukrainian economy. In an early sign that the Ukrainian government will continue to advance its national interests and attempt to balance between Europe and Russia, Yanukovych has indicated that he would not join the customs union with Russia, Belarus and Kazakhstan but would instead seek a free trade agreement with the European Union.

Security Policy and Security Sector Reform

As we have seen, Ukraine's main foreign policy priority has been Euro-Atlantic integration, and as such its security policy has been developed over the last few years to achieve this objective. Despite the slight shift in emphasis in Ukraine's foreign policy its security policy is unlikely to change over the next few years. Ukraine's security policy is to 'support peace and stability at the regional and global levels' by remaining an active supporter of peaceful resolution of conflicts, peacekeeping activities, and cooperating in the defence and security sphere with regional and international organisations.[50] In order to achieve these objectives, the government has pursued an active regional policy aimed at developing cooperation within the Organisation for Democracy and Economic Development, or what used to be called GUAM (consisting of Georgia, Ukraine, Azerbaijan and Moldova) and the Black Sea Economic Cooperation Organisation. A few months into his presidency, Yushchenko signaled his willingness to increase Ukraine's involvement in regional cooperation by reactivating GUAM, with the aim of developing it into a full-fledged international organisation. GUAM emerged in the mid-1990s as a political, economic and strategic alliance designed to strengthen the independence and sovereignty of Georgia, Ukraine, Azerbaijan and Moldova. When Uzbekistan joined in 1999 GUAM became GUUAM, but Uzbekistan suspended its membership in 2001 and finally, after the Andijan massacres, withdrew altogether in 2005. In 2006, as part of the Ukrainian government's attempt to revitalize the organization, it was renamed the Organisation for Democracy and Economic Development (ODED) at a summit meeting in Kiev. Signaling that the organisation was deepening its cooperation, the members agreed to set up a group of anti-terrorism experts and exchange information in an attempt to combat organised crime in the region. A further sign that the organisation was evolving was the setting up of an ODED General Secretariat in Kiev in February 2009.[51] At the earlier summit in Baku the ODED appeared to be firmly established as a significant regional organization, with representatives from Lithuania, Poland, Romania, Bulgaria, Estonia, Latvian, US, Japan, OSCE, BSEC, UNESCO all attending.

For Ukraine, GUAM membership served to promote Ukraine's democratic transformation, enhance its regional security and facilitate European integration. It also had the added benefit of allowing Ukraine to move away from the Russian-dominated and -controlled Commonwealth of Independent States (CIS). The CIS was set up in 1991 by Russia, Ukraine and Belarus after the collapse of the USSR. Since then, its membership has expanded to include the five Central Asian republics of Armenia, Azerbaijan, Moldova and Georgia. Subsequently, the Ukrainian government signaled that its membership in this organization was merely a formality by refusing to sign its treaty on collective security and economic union. In recent years the Russian government has been critical of the ODED, seeing it as a challenge to the CIS, particularly in light of attempts to create collective peacekeeping forces for possible deployment to South Ossetia and Transnistria. Despite attempts by Ukraine to develop the ODED into a regional organisation able to address security concerns, recent events have revealed the lack of commitment of key members—including Ukraine. In 2007 the Moldovan president failed to attend the ODED summit in Baku, and instead flew to Moscow to try and find a bilateral solution to the conflict in Transnistria. In addition, the ODED has failed to develop the security structures and peacekeeping forces envisaged three years ago. In an indication that the Ukrainian political crisis has also affected the development of the ODED, the Ukrainian Rada has yet to ratify the organization's statute.

Another organization that Ukraine played an important role in attempting to develop is the Organisation of Black Sea Economic Cooperation (BSEC). Established in 1992 on the initiative of Turkey's President Turgut Ozal, BSEC is made up of 12 states in the region: Bulgaria, Georgia, Romania, Russia, Turkey, Ukraine, Albania, Armenia, Azerbaijan, Greece, Moldova and Serbia. Due to political conflict and mistrust amongst its members, BSEC has evolved primarily into a regional economic rather than a security or political organisation.[52] In 2001 Ukraine's foreign minister, Anatoliy Zlenko, emphasized the 'great importance of regional organizations like BSEC' in promoting regional ties with neighbouring states and the interests of Ukraine at the regional and international level.[53] Six months after the inauguration of President Yushchenko, at the 25th session of the BSEC Parliamentary Assembly the Speaker of the Rada, Voldymyr Lytvyn, signaled the new government's commitment to revitalizing and strengthening cooperation with BSEC.[54] President Yushchenko also spelled out the link between Ukraine's membership in BSEC and its Euro-Atlantic integration. He stated: 'I consider the Organization of the Black Sea Economic Cooperation a promising instrument for developing partnership among its Member-States and establishing a meaningful dialogue with the EU and other international structures'.[55]

Grigory Perepelytsia, an advisor to the Ukrainian government, has argued that Ukraine's membership and participation in BSEC would allow it to develop its economy to EU standards and thereby facilitate membership.[56] At the BSEC Summit in Istanbul in June 2007, members, including Ukraine, reinforced their commitment to enhancing trade and energy cooperation and upgrading transport links.[57] As chair of the BSEC, Ukraine hosted a meeting of BSEC transport ministers in Odessa 2008 to develop a comprehensive transport and railway system amongst member states. However, in April 2008 there were signs that BSEC might be running into problems, with ten countries sending low-ranking officials rather than their foreign ministers to the 18th foreign ministers' meeting in Kiev. In recognition of the extent of the difficulties facing BSEC in developing regional cooperation, the meeting approved the introduction of a fast-track process, which effectively enables some members to opt out of unpopular or controversial BSEC policies.[58]

A second aspect of Ukraine's security policy has been its attempt to build an effective and efficient military able to contribute to international and Euro-Atlantic security and thereby facilitate its foreign policy objectives.[59] Following many years of military downsizing and political and financial neglect, the Orange Revolution provided the political impetus necessary to kick-start radical military reform in Ukraine.[60] The nature of the revolution, which ushered in a democratically elected pro-Western government that actively sought Euro-Atlantic integration, added a new impetus to military reform. For President Yushchenko, military reform, which included the adoption of dominant western values and concepts, would create a virtuous circle by not only helping to facilitate foreign policy goals but in addition developing an effective and efficient fighting force in Ukraine. It would allow Ukraine to build a military that would reflect and uphold its democratic values, which would ultimately support its Euro-Atlantic integration and signal its commitment to membership in NATO and the EU. By subscribing to the same set of military values, aspirations and standards as NATO members, the Ukrainian government believed it would move swiftly towards Euro-Atlantic integration.

Recognizing the need for radical reform in how it structures and organizes its military, Ukraine will move from a conscript to a fully professional standing force. The last year for conscription in Ukraine will be 2010, and a year later Ukraine plans to have an all-volunteer force. Ukraine has also introduced a new military structure in an attempt to develop flexible and versatile forces able to operate across a range of high intensity operations including peacekeeping, counter-terrorism and emergency relief. For Ukraine, active participation in peacekeeping operations is a crucial element of its security policy. To facilitate this objective, the government has radically re-structured its armed forces into three functional divisions: the Joint Rapid Reaction Force (JRRF), the Main Defence Force, and Strategic Reserves. The JRRF, which is responsible for peacekeeping operations, will be the most powerful part of Ukraine's fighting forces, and its prioritisation in terms of funding and equipment reflects the government's emphasis on developing peacekeeping forces able to contribute to regional and international security.[61]

As part of its commitment to Euro-Atlantic security, Ukraine has consistently demonstrated its commitment to peacekeeping through its active involvement in NATO and UN led operations. Currently, Ukraine is contributing to peacekeeping operations in neighbouring Moldova and UN missions in Congo, Georgia, Liberia and Sudan.[62] Ukraine has also co-operated with NATO in maintaining peace and stability in the Euro-Atlantic area. In the Balkans Ukraine contributed an infantry battalion, a mechanized infantry battalion and a helicopter squadron to the NATO-led peacekeeping forces in Bosnia and Herzegovina, and it currently has 183 service personnel in Kosovo.[63] Ukraine has been an active participant in Operation Active Endeavour, NATO's maritime operations in the Mediterranean. It also has military personnel engaged in the ISAF mission in Afghanistan. Ukraine has also been engaged in discussions with the chairman of the EU Military Commission on ways in which it can contribute to the EU's European Security and Defence Policy.[64] These discussions included Ukraine's provision of an airmobile battalion, a marine battalion, emergency response units, medical evacuation aircraft, landing ships, military police and combat divers. Ukraine is also likely to provide tactical helicopters for EU operations in Chad, as the operation is desperately short of airlift. The chief of the general staff of the Ukrainian Armed Forces has also recently been discussing Ukraine's involvement in the NATO Response Force.[65]

Ukraine's peacekeeping operations, like its Euro-Atlantic foreign policy objectives, have not always been well supported by the Ukrainian people. In 2003, during the first phase of the US-led invasion of Iraq, then-President Leonid Kuchma authorized the deployment of a chemical and biological decontamination unit to Kuwait; this was followed by the deployment of 1,600 Ukrainian peacekeeping troops to the Polish-controlled sector of Iraq. The US-led invasion of Iraq was unpopular in Ukraine, and there has been little support either in parliament or amongst the Ukrainian people for the deployment of Ukrainian peacekeepers into these theatres. The death of eight Ukrainian soldiers in Iraq in January 2005 in an explosion led to calls by the Ukrainian parliament for the immediate withdrawal of forces.[66] The parliament also called on the president to withdraw the Ukrainian peacekeepers.[67] In light of domestic opposition, Ukrainian forces withdrew from Iraq at the end of 2005.

Ukraine's ambitious military reform package could be derailed by years of underfunding and the current economic crisis in Ukraine, however. Over the past few years Ukraine has struggled to finance its military transformation. In early 2006, the Ukrainian parliament approved a significant increase in the defence budget for 2006 from 1.36% of gross domestic product to 1.74%. This signified recognition of the need to increase defence funding if Ukraine was to engage in the radical military transformation that would enable Ukraine to build an effective military.[68] The direct link between defence spending and successful military reform was spelled out by the commander-in-chief of the Ukrainian armed forces, Serhiy Kyrychenko, who stated that 2 to 3% of GDP would have to be spent on the armed forces between 2008 and 2011 in order to achieve the goals laid out in the reform package in 2006.[69] In recognition of the need to further increase the defence budget in order to reform successfully, the president pledged to spend 2% of GDP on defence in 2007; in 2008 Prime Minister Tymoshenko promised to allocate between 2.5 and 3% of GDP a year, which amounts to between US$3 billion and 6 billion.[70]

Even if the government does increase the defence budget to 3% of GDP, there is no guarantee that this would be enough to finance radical change. The costs of moving from a conscript to a professional standing army are enormous. In order to attract and retain personnel, particularly combat personnel, according to former Defence Minister Grytsenko, the government would need to raise military salaries by about 40%.[71] Highlighting the problem of pay, Grytsenko added that military personnel leave the service not because they do not want to serve, but simply because they cannot provide for their families.[72] The Ukrainian president has pledged to increase military wages three-fold and increase military pensions by 70% in order to redress this problem of recruiting and retaining a voluntary military.[73] President Yushchenko estimated that the total cost of transition to a professional military in 2010 would be about 1.4 billion US dollars.[74]

Indicating that Ukrainian government clearly recognised the need to invest in military reform, Defence Minister Yurii Yekhanurov said in 2008 that Ukraine's defence budget for 2009 would be almost US$5.1 billion.[75] In November 2008, however, 'due to the financial crisis' in Ukraine, Yekhanurov stated that the defence budget would be cut by half. In the draft of the 2009 budget this reduction was confirmed, with defence allocated slightly less than half the requested US$5.1 billion. Ukraine has been very badly hit by the economic downturn, and the defence budget is likely to be further squeezed. In November 2008, GDP shrank by more than 14% from the previous year and industrial production fell by half. The Ukrainian currency also plummeted in response to the country's declining economic prospects and financial difficulties. In November 2008, Ukraine agreed a US$16.4 billion package with the IMF to revive the banking sector and ensure it could service its large external debt.[76]

Ukraine's Relationship with the United States

From 2005 on, the Bush administration played a decisive role in encouraging Ukraine's democracy and its Euro-Atlantic ambitions. In an early sign of good relations, just months after his inauguration, President Yushchenko visited Washington to hold meetings with President Bush and was also given the rare opportunity to address a joint session of Congress. Not only did the Bush administration regard Ukraine as 'a model for the region of democratic transition', but also, and more importantly, it saw Ukraine's successful democratic and military transformation as important to US national interests in the Black Sea and beyond.[77] US engagement with Ukraine was part of the Bush Administration's policy of encouraging democratization around the world. US interests in the Black Sea are focused on advancing democratic and market reforms.[78] For the US, the Orange Revolution in Ukraine and the Rose Revolution in Georgia created the opportunity to consolidate democracy in the former Soviet Union.

Under the Bush administration, US engagement with Ukraine was also shaped by its foreign and security policy of 'extended homeland defence' and countering the reach of terrorists and proliferators in many regions including the Black Sea.[79] The 9/11 terrorist attacks on the US altered the broad outlines of US foreign policy, moving the need to address specific challenges such as counter-terrorism and the fight against the proliferation of weapons of mass destruction to the top of the agenda.[80] US interests in the Black Sea area—energy transit, security, counterterrorism, proliferation of weapons of mass destruction (WMD), and the traffic in drugs, weapons, and people—therefore took on particular significance after 9/11.[81] The US increasingly recognized the Black Sea region as a strategically important, but inherently unstable, region facing many diverse security challenges from drug smuggling to human trafficking to providing safe havens for terrorist and organised crime networks.[82]

The presence of 'frozen conflicts' and weak states neighboring Ukraine provide an ideal environment in which criminals and terrorists can operate. The term 'frozen conflicts' has been used to identify a series of separatist conflicts in the post-Soviet region that, after a period of fighting and often brutal ethnic cleansing in the late 1980s and early 1990s, created a belt of internationally unrecognized but de facto states from Transnistria in Moldova to Abkhazia and South Ossetia in Georgia to Nagorno Karabakh in Azerbaijan. These de facto states constitute entities which operate outside of international law, often with unaccountable governments providing safe havens for organized crime and potential terrorist groups. Abkhazia has been described by Georgian analyst Irakli Menagarishvili as a 'criminal enclave' which provides 'safe havens for illegal dealing in arms, narcotics and smuggling.[83] Organized crime groups, benefiting from the lawless republics and weak governments in the wider Black Sea, engage in smuggling and manufacturing drugs, selling and smuggling illegal weapons and nuclear material, and human trafficking. A high level of corruption amongst border guards has made Ukraine, in particular, a soft target for drug smuggling in the Black Sea. In 2007 the US Department of Justice reported that 'of the 1,500 roads connecting Ukraine with its contiguous states in the north, east and southeast, only 98 have customs facilities'.[84] In a sign of the severity of the drug smuggling problem, the Ukrainian Security Service confiscated 460 kilos of heroin worth $32 million in just six months in 2008—more than the total amount of heroin seized in Ukraine in the previous 15 years. The Black Sea has also become a favorite transit zone for human trafficking—a business estimated to be worth $12 billion in 2007.[85] To address these security concerns, the US has invested heavily in Ukraine's democratic and military transformation. For 2009 the administration requested a total of $86.48 million in aid for Ukraine. A significant proportion of this aid was spent on preparations for presidential elections in 2010 and improving local government, and some was spent on military training and assistance.

Signaling its strong commitment to transformation in Kiev, the Bush administration was also critical of Russian foreign policy towards Ukraine and Eurasia. In 2006 Vice-President Richard Cheney characterized Russia's energy policy towards countries like Ukraine as 'blackmail' and 'intimidation'.[86] More recently, the US criticized Russia's intervention in Georgia, claiming that Moscow's actions raised serious questions about its intentions in the region and jeopardised relations with the US and Europe. In a visit to Kiev in September 2008, Cheney not only reiterated US support of Ukraine's membership in NATO but also made clear that Moscow did not have a veto.[87] In a sign of its ongoing commitment to Ukraine, in mid-December 2008 the then-secretary of state, Condoleezza Rice, and Ukraine's foreign minister, Voldymyr Ohyzko, signed a security charter that established areas of co-operation and re-emphasized US commitment to Ukraine's NATO membership. Rice stated that the US 'supports Ukraine's integration into the Euro-Atlantic structures' and added that 'the declaration at Bucharest which foresees that Ukraine will be a member of NATO when it can meet those standards is very much at the centre of our policy'.[88] The charter encompassed broad areas of cooperation, including political, cultural, economic development and defence. In response to Ukrainian concerns about

Russia's intervention in Georgia, it also pledged US support for Ukraine's sovereignty, independence and territorial integrity.[89]

Despite his commitment to 'reset' relations with the Russian Federation, President Obama has not radically altered US policy towards Ukraine. The Obama administration continued, up until the election of a new Ukrainian president, to support Ukraine's stated foreign policy of goal of Euro-Atlantic integration. Preoccupied with domestic and major international problems, President Obama, unlike President Bush, has adopted a more balanced and less confrontational approach to relations between Ukraine and the Russian Federation. In an early sign of the attempt by the new US administration to balance its interests in strengthening relations with both Russia and Ukraine, two weeks after the US president visited Moscow for talks with President Medvedev, Vice President Joe Biden visited Kiev. During this visit Biden assured President Yushchenko that the US would continue to support Ukraine's attempt to secure membership in NATO. With the election of a new Ukrainian president, President Obama has reaffirmed his commitment to Ukraine in a bilateral meeting held on the margins of the Nuclear Security Summit in April this year. At this meeting the two leaders concluded a landmark deal in which Ukraine will eliminate its stocks of highly enriched uranium over the next two years. In addition, the two leaders signaled their commitment to build upon the US-Ukraine Charter on Strategic Partnership signed in 2008 by former presidents Yushchenko and Bush, suggesting that relations were back on track.

Conclusion

This chapter has argued that domestic political instability in Ukraine has hampered Ukraine's Euro-Atlantic ambitions in two ways: first by halting the development of an effective foreign policy in Ukraine; and second by stopping the implementation of a much-needed NATO and EU Awareness information campaign aimed at the Ukrainian public. Political instability in Ukraine was also successfully exploited by key members of the transatlantic community, such as Germany and France, to forestall Kiev's earlier foreign policy goals of securing membership in NATO. The actions of key European states to slow down future enlargement of NATO, in the face of strong support by Washington for Ukrainian future membership, suggest that there are deep divisions within the Euro-Atlantic alliance as to the future architecture of European security. Events in the summer of 2008 and immediately after the Russian-Georgian conflict revealed that these deep divisions can, at least in part, be traced to differences in opinion over policy towards the Russian Federation. The prospects for future Euro-Atlantic integration for Ukraine will therefore ultimately hinge on Ukraine being perceived as a stable democratic state, improving its relations with Russia and, most important of all, continuing US support for its Euro-Atlantic foreign policy.

11 Georgia and the Transatlantic Relationship

The New Kid on the Block

Tracey C. German

Introduction

In January 2009 Georgia and the United States signed a strategic accord, deepening American cooperation with the South Caucasian state and strengthening the latter's ties with the West. Relations between the two countries were already strong, but the strategic partnership accord serves to underline the importance that Washington has placed on its ties with westward-leaning states in the former Soviet bloc.[1] The Georgian-US relationship only came into existence in the 1990s, with Georgia's independence from the Soviet Union. Georgia is a relatively new actor on the transatlantic stage, but it has already proved itself to be a keen supporter of US policy and is eager to establish itself as a valuable member of the Euro-Atlantic community. It is the most pro-Western of the three South Caucasus states,[2] and, since independence in 1991, it has sought to maintain an autonomous and pragmatic foreign policy that removes it from the Russian sphere of influence, an objective that dominates policy-making in all areas. Following the 2003 'Rose Revolution', President Mikhel Saakashvili's government has been even more inclined to seek the active engagement of external actors such as the US, NATO, the EU and the Organization for Security and Cooperation in Europe (OSCE), and has consistently sought to demonstrate its desire to integrate with the West.[3]

This desire for integration into the Euro-Atlantic community is a key priority for Georgia's foreign and security policy-makers, but has provoked fundamental rifts both between Washington and its European allies and between

Washington and Moscow. The US has made its support for Georgia's NATO aspirations clear, stating that the country is part of the Euro-Atlantic community and a 'beacon of liberty' for the wider Caucasus region.[4] However, this has upset Moscow, which is unhappy with its southern neighbor's European leanings and rewarding relationship with Washington. Although Russia remains both the key economic and military power in the South Caucasus, the US has identified the area as a foreign policy priority, precipitating continued clashes of interest in an already unstable region as Moscow attempts to counterbalance growing American (and European) involvement within its traditional sphere of influence.

In 2008 Sergei Lavrov, the Russian foreign minister, accused Washington of 'infiltrating the post-Soviet space ever more actively: Ukraine and Georgia are graphic examples' and warned that if either country becomes a NATO member-state there will be a 'substantial negative geopolitical shift'.[5] In his view 'NATO's incomprehensible, unwarranted expansion' is dividing Europe. Whilst he has stressed that Moscow 'is interested in partnership' with Western organisations such as NATO and the EU, there was a recent tendency, in his opinion, to build 'a bloc . . . against Russia'.[6] Consequently, much of Georgia's policy-making, both domestic and foreign, is governed by its generally negative relationship with Moscow and the tensions resulting from its Euro-Atlantic orientation. Its strong ties with the US are a clear effort to rid itself of Russian hegemony.

The key strategic location of the South Caucasus, squeezed between the Black and Caspian Seas, Iran, Russia and Turkey, make it an area of increasing significance in the contemporary security environment. It constitutes a vital land bridge between Asia and Europe, physically linking the Caspian Sea region and Central Asia with the Black Sea and Western Europe. Nevertheless, there was a relative lack of Western interest in the South Caucasus region during the initial post-Soviet era. The area only began to grow in importance to the US and the West during the mid-1990s, when it was identified as both a source of and key transit route for hydrocarbons from the Caspian Sea. Speaking before the US House of Representatives' Armed Services Committee in 2008, the commander of the US European Command, General Craddock, clearly enunciated the significance of both Georgia and the wider Caucasus region for the Euro-Atlantic community:

> The Caucasus' geostrategic location makes the region an important area for the US and its Allies. Caucasus nations actively support [Operation] IRAQI FREE-

DOM and ISAF. They provide alternative hydrocarbon sources from the Caspian Sea and alternative routes of access to Central Asian hydrocarbon reserves. It is an important region for European energy diversification.[7]

The international significance of this former Soviet state in the South Caucasus increased greatly in the wake of September 11, 2001, and the initiation of the global war on terror. Already on the map thanks to its position on a key transit route for oil and gas from the Caspian region, the country's alleged links with international terrorism propelled it further into the spotlight. In 2003 former NATO Secretary-General Lord Robertson described the Caucasus region as an 'area of crucial importance to [NATO's] common security. In facing the threats of terrorism, proliferation and regional instability the countries of the Caucasus are front-line states. They are also important partners in finding common solutions to these deadly challenges.'[8] The European Parliament's 2004 Gahrton report also recognised its growing importance, stating that 'due to its geographical location, the South Caucasus can play an increased role in strengthening international security; whereas if it is instead left out of the evolving networks of interdependence and co-operation, the susceptibility of the South Caucasus states to the danger of export of instability from neighbouring regions would increase'.[9]

This chapter will examine Georgia's efforts to establish itself within the Euro-Atlantic community, focusing on how both internal political changes and external influences have had an impact on its strategic direction. What are the drivers of Georgia's aspirations for closer integration with the US and Western security structures such as NATO and the EU? How do its security interests intersect with those of the Euro-Atlantic area? And what does the future hold for Georgia's international relations in the wake of its military conflict with Russia in August 2008?

Developing Statehood: Capabilities and Challenges

Georgia became the first Soviet republic to vote for a non-communist government when it elected nationalist Zviad Gamsakhurdia to head the Supreme Soviet in 1990, as the USSR was slowly unravelling against the backdrop of Mikhail Gorbachev's reformist policies. The renewed upsurge of Georgian nationalism during the *glasnost* era increased inter-ethnic tensions within the Soviet republic, as manifold national groups were permitted free expression throughout the USSR and the manipulation of ethnic affiliation became a key dynamic in political life. Separatist tensions were reignited, heralding a period of instability and internal conflict within Georgia, as the Soviet Union finally disintegrated in 1991 and new independent states emerged.[10] During the early post-Soviet period, Georgia can best be characterised as a weak state, whose newly established statehood was extremely fragile, threatened by numerous factors including internal conflict between the center and the separatist regions of Abkhazia and South Ossetia, Russian pressure, pervasive corruption and a lack of effective central power. Struggling with the impact of the dual political and economic transformation, inter-ethnic strife and challenges to its internal and external sovereignty, the Georgian state teetered on the brink of failure during the 1990s. Nevertheless, President Eduard Shevardnadze kept it from total collapse.[11] The end of the twentieth century witnessed significant developments in Georgia's strategic orientation, as the country sought to partially rid itself of Moscow's domination and become more westward-looking, gaining membership of the Council of Europe and driving forward the controversial Baku-Tbilisi-Ceyhan pipeline project, a US-backed plan to export Caspian oil without transiting Russian territory.

Georgia's domestic political scene has tended to be dominated by charismatic individuals with an emphasis on personalities rather than policies. A multi-party democracy, it was established as a presidential republic with the adoption of a new constitution in 1995 and parliament is relatively weak.[12] During the 1990s Shevardnadze dominated Georgian politics, providing much-needed stability, but also provoking accusations of cronyism and corruption, which were ultimately his undoing. The bloodless 'Rose Revolution' of November 2003,[13] which saw the dramatic departure of Shevardnadze, affirmed Georgian statehood and was a defining moment in the country's democratic development, with the non-violent transfer of political power. Mikhel Saakashvili swept to power on the back of the peaceful uprising, and his inauguration in 2004 cemented Georgia's move away from the Russian sphere of influence, strengthening an increasingly close relationship with Washington.

Saakashvili has come to dominate Georgian politics in much the same way that his predecessor did, and his personality determines much of the country's policy-direction. A US-educated lawyer, he was first elected to parliament in 1995 and has consistently campaigned against corruption and cronyism.[14] Buoyed by his political success in both the presidential and parliamentary elections held in early 2004, Saakashvili vowed to tackle many of the country's seemingly intractable problems, notably crime, widespread corruption, cronyism, economic stagnation and separatism. He made significant headway on some issues, tackling corruption at the grassroots level, but there are still many challenges to Georgian security, particularly the secessionist territories. Reflecting Saakashvili's international experience, a large proportion of the ruling political elite in Georgia is Western-educated and has a clear understanding of the crucial role of the media and public relations. A significant characteristic of Saakashvili's government is its relative youthfulness. There has been and continues to be a preponderance of young ministers, many under the age of 40, suggesting the leadership's desire to visibly distance itself from any connection with the previous Shevardnadze regime.[15] These young politicians with substantial experience of the West have, to a large extent, been driving Georgia's Euro-Atlantic orientation.

External influences have a significant impact on Georgian domestic politics, particularly the threat from their northern neighbor, Russia. During periods when the perceived threat intensifies, the Georgian population tends to unite behind the government: the Russian military intervention in August 2008 boosted Saakashvili's waning popular support. There is very little opposition to the country's Western alignment and referendums on the issue of NATO membership demonstrate consistently high levels of support for accession, even amongst opposition groups.[16] The majority of the population support closer ties with both the US and the Euro-Atlantic community, revealing the depth of concern there is about the Russian 'threat'. Moscow is often blamed for the country's ills, from supporting the secessionist regions to inciting political unrest.[17] NATO membership is viewed by many Georgians as the country's 'only chance of surviving' in the face of an increasingly assertive Russia, whilst relations with the US will help it to 'preserve independence'.

Over the past decade the US has also had a considerable influence on the direction of Georgian domestic politics, supporting democratic reform. In the run-up to the 2003 parliamentary elections, former US Secretary of State James Baker was instrumental in resolving a confrontation between the Shevardnadze administration and leading opposition parties.[18] Furthermore, then US Secretary of State Colin Powell is reported to have played a key role in defusing the crisis during the Rose Revolution, encouraging Shevardnadze to take actions that would ensure a peaceful transition of power. The consolidation and advancement of democratic reforms have been a significant focus of US assistance to Georgia. During 2008, over US$13 million was allocated to governance programs that were intended to improve government capacity, transparency, accountability and decentralization, advance the rule of law and strengthen civil society.[19] US support for democratic reform in the South Caucasus ties in with its desire to promote democracy across the globe: post-Cold War American foreign policy has been driven by a belief that promoting the spread of democracy will also promote global peace and security.[20] Whilst Washington has generally been supportive of Georgian reform efforts, it also acknowledges that there is still a long way to go in terms of advancing democratic and judicial change.[21]

Charting a Western Course

In the decade that followed Georgian independence in 1991, little progress was made in terms of the country's security policy direction and security sector reform. David Darchiashvili believes that the most prominent characteristics of the Georgian security sector prior to 2003 were a 'diversity of agencies, lack of coordination between them, lack of clarity in . . . security policy, including the absence of a national security concept.' He goes on to criticize the 'complete confusion' between military and civil roles prior to 2003, as well as the existence of military and paramilitary formations that were completely independent of central government control.[22] The principal obstacle to both security sector reform and the development of a national security concept was the lack of clear and coherent strategic direction. Torn between seeking greater integration with the West and not wanting to rile Moscow, the Shevardnadze government refrained from publishing any official document that outlined Georgia's security direction. Nevertheless, despite this cautious stance, Georgia was the first country in the South Caucasus to articulate its desire to join the NATO alliance, expressing its membership aspirations in 2000, and it became an official aspirant at the Prague Summit held in November 2002.

Saakashvili's inauguration in 2004 hastened Georgia's move away from the Russian sphere of influence, and there has been a raft of official publications delineating Georgian security strategy and orientation since he became president. The National Security Concept, adopted in 2005, was presented as a 'keystone' document that outlined fundamental values and interests, set the principal directions of national security policy and would serve as the basis for all subsequent strategies and plans. It describes democracy and liberty as 'Georgian traditional values', together with independence, the rule of law, prosperity, peace and security, stating that 'Georgia, as an integral part of the

European political, economic and cultural area, whose fundamental national values are rooted in European values and traditions, aspires to achieve full-fledged integration into Europe's political, economic and security systems. Georgia aspires to return to its European tradition and remain an integral part of Europe'.[23]

The notion of Georgia 'returning' to Europe is a common one in Georgian political and popular discourse, reflecting the belief of many in the country that they are 'European'. In his inauguration speech in 2004, Saakashvili stated that 'not only are we old Europeans, but we are ancient Europeans'.[24] This view has been encouraged by many in Washington. Speaking in Tbilisi in 2007, US Assistant Secretary of State for European and Eurasian Affairs Daniel Fried declared that not only was Georgia 'in Europe' in geographical, cultural, political and historical terms, but that it was part of the Euro-Atlantic community: 'Georgians are a part of the transatlantic world, and therefore institutions of the transatlantic world should be open to Georgia as much as to any other European country'.[25]

However, this belief is not shared by all European allies, reflecting, to some extent, the situation in the 1950s over Turkey's application for NATO membership.[26] Whilst Washington is lobbying strongly for Georgian accession, there are doubts amongst some Western European allies about the country's ability to contribute to security in the transatlantic area, and Georgia's potential membership has become a divisive issue between the US and European pillars of NATO.

Georgia's ambitions for European and Euro-Atlantic integration are reflected in the fact that its principal strategic partners (Turkey, Ukraine and the US) lie predominantly to the west of the country, with the notable exception of neighboring Azerbaijan. The government is seeking to establish a stable democracy in Georgia and develop a prosperous economy under a Euro-Atlantic security umbrella. It has ambitions of acting as an example for other countries in the South Caucasus, as well as across the wider former Soviet space. Speaking at the 2002 NATO summit in Prague, then-president Shevardnadze underlined the significance attached to Georgia's engagement with NATO and expressed the country's understanding of the need to promote 'Euro-Atlantic values' in the region.[27] Georgia has a strategic long-term relationship with Ukraine 'based on both countries' belonging to Europe and the Euro Atlantic space, and on their shared commitment to establishing democratic values in all aspects of state and social life'.[28] The two countries have close ties and share a common goal of achieving NATO and EU integration. Georgia has always viewed itself as European in orientation and believes that it is in the process of 'returning' to Europe. This conviction has been reinforced by Russia's lack of interest in providing security and stability—over the years it has shown itself to be far more concerned with destabilizing its southern neighbour in order to thwart its western ambitions.

Georgia views NATO membership as key to its national security and Article 5 of the Washington Treaty is a key driver of this desire for membership. The country's National Military Strategy makes it clear that a shift from the principle of territorial defense to one of collective defense is a cornerstone of Georgian defense policy. Without security guarantees from a third party, there is a fear that the state is not strong enough to survive in the face of an increasingly assertive Russia. According to the 2007 Strategic Defense Review the 'need for collective defence is underscored by Georgia's inability to put significant resources against a variety of internal and external threats, some originating from significantly more powerful sources.'[29]

The Strategic Defense Review, approved in late 2007, was the culmination of a comprehensive analysis of Georgia's armed forces, which was conducted after the publication of the National Security Concept. Taking the range of threats to Georgian national security—political, economic, military and informational—that had been outlined in a Threat Assessment Document, the SDR addressed those threats that military forces could respond to (see Table 1 below).[30] Interestingly, although the National Security Concept identified violations of territorial integrity and a renewal of separatist conflict as major threats, the SDR concluded that 'the probability of direct large scale military aggression against Georgia for the foreseeable future is relatively low; however, the potential consequences from direct aggression, should it occur, are severe'.[31]

The military conflict with Russia in August 2008 undermined Georgian military doctrine, proving its planning assumptions to be wrong. The armed forces had been training for military operations other than war (MOOTW) rather than for conventional military operations against a state actor, perhaps persuaded that, in the 21st century, there was little threat of a large-scale conventional war. Although the Georgian armed forces have undergone a major overhaul since the Soviet era, including a transition to NATO standards, an increase in civilian control and democratic accountability, the 2008 conflict revealed there is still much work to be done, particularly at brigade level. The

TABLE 11.1 Threat Category and Risk Assessment

Threat Category	Likelihood	Likelihood Trend	Warning & Preparation Time	Impact on Vital Interests
Large-scale military intervention	Very low	Decrease	Very long	Catastrophic
Conflict in Breakaway Region(s)	High	Increase	Short	Moderate
Conflict Spillover from North Caucasus	Low	Increase	Long	Moderate
Conflict Spillover from South Caucasus	Very low	Increase	Long	Moderate
International Terrorism	High	Increase	Short	Moderate

Table from the Strategic Defence Review, p. 76.

lack of strategic planning and decision-making, as well as the government's lack of systems for crisis management, attracted considerable criticism.[32]

There are currently two important directions in Georgia's military reform: upgrading equipment in order to modernize the armed forces and revisiting the planned response to immediate threats. In addition to improving its ability to provide for its own security, modernization should increase Georgia's capacity to contribute to international security efforts and assert itself as a fully functioning state actor on the world stage. An important element of the National Military Strategy (NMS), signed by Saakashvili in 2005, was the desire for Georgia to contribute to the international security environment. The NMS stressed the benefits that would be gained from participation in coalition operations, as well as the need for the armed forces to conduct joint planning and operations. Thus, there has been a significant and deliberate shift in Georgia's security strategy, away from a large number of armed forces configured for territorial defence to smaller, better-equipped forces that have focused on MOOTW, including international stabilisation efforts. However, the assistance that the military received from the US and NATO ultimately undermined the country's security: since it prepared the armed forces for peacekeeping operations, rather than territorial defence, Georgia was vulnerable to the Russian incursion in August 2008.

The Georgian Dragon and the Russian Bear

Georgia's security concerns have been dominated by Russia since independence in 1991. Many of the major threats to Georgian security are driven by Moscow, from the country's long-running disputes with its separatist territories of Abkhazia and South Ossetia, to economic security, to energy dependence, to spillover from Russia's volatile North Caucasus region. Challenges to Georgia's national security were outlined in the 2005 National Security Concept, which defined security in its broadest sense, from military intervention to environmental issues and social challenges such as the degradation of healthcare and education. Principal threats noted by the concept included:

Violations of territorial integrity

Renewal of hostilities in separatist regions

International terrorism

Smuggling and organised crime

Corruption and ineffective governance

Economic and social challenges

Energy dependence

Environmental challenges[33]

Georgia's secessionist regions represent one of the most serious threats to the security and stability of the multi-ethnic country, a threat exacerbated by Russia's backing the separatist territories. Following wars of independence in South Ossetia and Abkhazia in the early 1990s, both have existed as *de facto* independent states for over a decade. From the beginning of his presidency, Saakashvili has made the restoration of Georgia's territorial integrity a priority, expressing his wish to consolidate the country by resolving the enduring conflicts with the two secessionist regions. Saakashvili's desire to resolve the protracted secessionist conflicts in Abkhazia and South Ossetia has become symbolic of his vigorous approach to tackling Georgia's more intractable problems. The disputes have not only fractured the country and contributed to continued internal instability, they have also exacerbated its relations with Moscow. It has been several years since he came to power, but the disputes are still unresolved and the parties remain locked in stalemate. The unresolved conflicts mean that over 15 per cent of Georgian territory is outside the control of the central authorities; this has led to the displacement of around 260,000 people, as well as providing a fertile ground for the smuggling of weapons, narcotics and people.[34] These conflicts also undermine regional stability, not just because of the threat of a renewal of fighting, but because they have created security vacuums that are outside of government control, providing ideal conditions for transnational security challenges such as terrorism, organised crime and illegal trafficking to flourish.

Saakashvili's desire to consolidate Georgia's territorial integrity has pushed the country towards renewed conflict with Russia, which not only has peacekeeping contingents in the two regions but also provides support for the separatists. Since 1991 the hand of its powerful northern neighbor has been visible in all of Georgia's separatist conflicts, as Moscow seeks to maintain political leverage over the South Caucasian state, and Tbilisi has frequently accused Russia of seeking to undermine Georgian sovereignty by supporting separatist provinces. The Georgian leader presciently warned that in the event of large-scale armed conflict erupting in South Ossetia, it would be an issue of bilateral Georgian-Russian relations, not merely an internal conflict. Speaking in September 2005, Saakashvili declared that there is "no Ossetian problem in Georgia," but "a problem in Georgian-Russian relations with respect to certain territories."[35] Efforts to restore central Georgian control over South Ossetia in August 2008 triggered a Russian military invasion, jeopardizing security across the unstable Caucasus region. Russia's military intervention demonstrated that apparently domestic separatist disputes have serious ramifications for the international community and relations between states. Tbilisi has lost control of its separatist regions and now has not only Russian troops on its territory but also an international monitoring mission, led by the EU, that is mandated to cover all of Georgia.

Russia remains the key economic power in the country, further undermining Georgia's security. Many important Georgian enterprises are in the hands of Russian investors, including critical infrastructure such as mobile telephone communications and energy. Furthermore, until late 2008 Georgia was heavily dependent upon imported Russian gas and consequently at the mercy of Moscow's mood. The Kremlin has shown an increasing willingness to utilise its energy resources as a political weapon and has wielded the energy weapon several times in its spats with the Georgian government over the years. Gas supplies have frequently been cut off during the winter months as political tensions spill over, forcing Tbilisi to seek increased supplies from neighbouring Azerbaijan. Until 2006 Russia was also one of the principal markets for Georgian products, particularly wine and mineral water, two of the country's most famous exports. In 2006 Moscow imposed a ban on Georgian wine exports, mineral water and other foodstuffs, claiming that they were contaminated and did not meet Russian health standards, allegations that were strenuously denied by Georgia. This unilateral action had a serious impact on the Georgian economy; in 2005 Georgian wine exports to Russia totalled US$63 million, whilst exports of mineral water amounted to US$23.6 million.[36]

Georgia has also suffered spillover from the instability in Russia's North Caucasus region. It is the only foreign country bordering Chechnya, and from the outset of the second military operation there in 1999, Russia accused its southern neighbor of harbouring Chechen rebels and foreign Islamist mercenaries, as well as supporting the transit of arms and mercenaries across its territory into Chechnya.[37] Over 7,000 Chechen refugees crossed the border into Georgia and were concentrated in the northern Akhmeta district, which was already home to a large ethnic Chechen-Kist population (that has lived on Georgian territory for centuries), particularly in the Pankisi Gorge adjacent to Russia. The 40–mile long gorge became a notorious center of crime, no longer under the control of the Georgian authorities, and Russia argued that the lawlessness of the area provided rebel fighters with an ideal base in which to regroup and rearm before returning across the border to continue their battle.[38]

The situation in Pankisi Gorge demonstrated the weakness of the Georgian state at that time and triggered direct US involvement in the country. American intelligence services reportedly registered a mobile telephone call in the immediate aftermath of the September 11 terror attacks from Afghanistan to the Pankisi Gorge, allegedly to Abu Hapsi, a Mujahideen commander and associate of Osama Bin Laden.[39] A key lesson of September 11, 2001, for the US government was that countries must not be allowed to become breeding grounds for extremism and terrorism and that the US must engage to promote long-term stability and prevent a security vacuum. Speaking in 2003 about US engagement in Central Asia and the Caucasus, the State Department's Assistant Secretary for European and Eurasian Affairs, Elizabeth Jones, said that the US 'disengagement from Afghanistan in the 1980s taught us a harsh lesson, one that we do not want to repeat in other countries. We learned that we must engage the region's governments and people to promote long-term stability and prevent a security vacuum that provides opportunities for extremism and external intervention. This is particularly true in Georgia, Uzbekistan, Kyrgyzstan and Tajikistan, where terrorist groups have threatened our national interest.[40] Consequently, US engagement with Georgia, particularly since 2001, has deepened, driven by a desire to assist the development of a stable country in an unstable region that is capable of tackling its own problems and that can act as a 'beacon of liberty' for the wider Caucasus area, a vital energy transit corridor and a key partner in the war on terror.

A Growing Alliance? Georgian-US Relations

The close relationship between the US and Georgia is most obviously manifest on the main route into Tbilisi from the international airport. Renamed President George W. Bush Street in honor of the US leader's triumphant visit in 2005, the street sign is accompanied by a large picture of the smiling American president. Sitting on Russia's southern flank, astride a vital transit route for Caspian hydrocarbons heading for international markets, Georgia has witnessed a veritable flood of assistance from the US: financial support for Georgia totals over US$1 billion, making Georgians the second biggest *per capita* recipients of American aid after the Israelis.[41]

US support for Georgia has focused on the promotion of democratic transformation, part of wider efforts to support the development of democracy around the world, together with assistance in security sector reform. The largest financial commitment has been made to security and law enforcement efforts with the goal of assisting the development of a secure, stable country that is able to protect its own borders and assist in the war on terror. US officials have described Georgia as a 'strong partner in the Global War on Terror'.[42] Prior to September 11, 2001, the possibility of a formal American military commitment to the former Soviet states in the Caspian region was assumed to be remote, and the region was not considered to be of vital strategic importance to the US. However, this changed dramatically with the terror attacks against New York and Washington, as discussed above. The Pankisi Gorge situation, however, graphically illustrated the weakness of the Georgian state and, in response to a request for assistance from Shevardnadze in October 2001, the US decided to provide military assistance in order to prevent the situation there further undermining both the security of Georgia and stability in the wider Caucasus region.

A US$64 million 'Train and Equip' (GTEP) programme began in May 2002 to train Georgian troops in anti-terrorist techniques and to assist in bringing the lawless Pankisi Gorge region under control. Reflecting a similar American-run training programme in the Philippines, GTEP was initiated to help the country address security threats and 'enhance the capability of selected Georgian military units to provide security and stability to the citizens of Georgia and the region'.[43] In particular, the programme was intended to train four combat infantry battalions (three army units and one unit from the Georgian National Guard) and one mechanised company to defend Georgia against potential terrorist threats in the gorge. GTEP also provided for the permanent transfer of military equipment to Georgia, including communications equipment, small arms, uniforms, fuel, and construction material. However, the Americans emphasised that any such equipment was to be provided for the four battalions and one company only for the duration of their training and that it was not intended to be a rearmament programme for the entire Georgian army.

In 2003 the Georgian parliament ratified the December 2002 military cooperation agreement with the US, granting US military personnel visa-free entry, exemption from criminal prosecution, and permission to carry weapons when off-duty. The US was also granted overfly rights and the unimpeded deployment of military hardware in the country. This agreement boosted tensions with Russia, as it put US military personnel on a par with the diplomatic corps—which was far more than was granted to Russian troops based in Georgia.

GTEP ended in April 2004, but was followed by a 15-month, US$64 million 'Sustainment and Stability Operations Programme' (GSSOP) launched in 2005 to train four battalions of troops, partly to support US-led coalition operations. A five-phased train-and-equip programme, GSSOP focused on enhancing the capabilities of the Georgian armed forces to meet their deployment obligations in support of coalition stability efforts. According to US military representatives, GSSOP fostered interoperability and also made Georgia 'a viable candidate for NATO accession'.[44]

These military training programmes were conducted in conjunction with the 'Georgia Border Security and Law Enforcement' (GBSLE) assistance program. Together, they were intended to help this US 'ally in the Global War on Terror' become a 'strong and stable nation', improving stability across the Caucasus region and preventing the area from becoming a safe haven for terrorists.[45] GBSLE is the largest single US-funded program in Georgia and has helped the country to secure its borders since the departure of Russian border guards in 1998. It has been boosted by the introduction of the 'Export Control and Related Border Security' (EXBS) assistance program; combined, the two programs are intended to help the border-guard, coast-guard, customs and other security forces become more effective in the protection of Georgia's land and sea borders.[46]

In return for assistance with the reform of its armed forces in line with NATO standards, Georgia has become a staunch supporter of US foreign policy; it was vocal, for instance, in its support for the war in Iraq, and has provided troops for NATO- and US-led operations in the Balkans and Afghanistan. The first Georgian peacekeeping platoon was deployed in the Balkans in 1999. Since then, the level of troops participating in international peacekeeping and stabilization missions has increased dramatically. At the end of 2008 there were 2,000 troops from the First Infantry Brigade deployed in Iraq and it has offered forces for Afghanistan. According to US officials, Georgia is the 'number one OIF [Operation Iraqi Freedom] coalition contributor per capita and second only to the United Kingdom in terms of total troops'.[47] This reflects the country's desire to be a fully functioning actor on the global stage: an important element of the National Military Strategy (NMS), signed by Saakashvili in 2005, was the desire for Georgia to contribute to the international security environment. The NMS stressed the benefits that would be gained from participation in coalition operations, including the opportunity to acquire practical experience and demonstrate willingness to cooperate with both NATO and individual countries. Thus, the US military assistance programmes have not only reinforced Georgia's security as an independent state, they have also helped it achieve the key strategic objective of contributing to the international security environment, whilst Washington has gained a loyal ally willing to contribute troops to coalition operations in Iraq and Afghanistan.

However, the US needs to balance its relations with Tbilisi against those with Russia. Moscow is understandably uncomfortable about the US military presence in its traditional sphere of influence, as well as the prospect of Georgia's becoming a member of the NATO military alliance, and is concerned that the new leadership may endeavor to accelerate Georgia's membership in

Western alliances such as NATO and the EU. As a result, it has been seeking to re-assert its waning influence by means of political posturing and sabre-rattling. Although to a certain extent it has viewed the presence of the US military as justification for its claims that it has been fighting international terrorism in Chechnya, it is also concerned about American intentions in the longer term.[48]

A prevalent view amongst many Georgians is that the Russian military intervention in South Ossetia in 2008 was intended to 'punish' Georgia for its Euro-Atlantic aspirations. Certainly the conflict revealed a significant level of misunderstanding between Washington and Tbilisi over their expectations of the bilateral relationship. Tbilisi clearly overestimated the level of support it could anticipate from Washington, which was very slow in reacting to the conflict. Apparently distracted by the opening of the Beijing Olympics, President Bush took over a week to publicly condemn Russian action as an 'invasion', although once he did, he slammed the violation of Georgia's territorial integrity. The military action pushed Georgia further towards the Euro-Atlantic community and hardened Washington's position towards Moscow. In the weeks following the conflict, the US reiterated its support for Georgia's territorial integrity and outlined three key objectives it would pursue in its relations with Tbilisi: '1) support Georgia; 2) blunt Russia's strategic objectives of dismembering Georgia and undermining the Southern Energy Corridor; and 3) bolster our friends and partners in the broader region.'[49] As part of this, Washington pledged US$1 billion in support of Georgia's economic recovery and humanitarian needs, whilst a team from the US Defense Department arrived in Tbilisi to assess the country's 'legitimate' defense needs and develop the necessary response. The 2009 US-Georgia Charter on Strategic Partnership underscored Washington's continuing support for the Saakashvili government and made it clear that the Obama administration would not be altering this course. Emphasising that US-Georgia cooperation is based on 'shared values and common interests', the accord stressed that 'deepening Georgia's integration into Euro-Atlantic institutions is a mutual priority', and that therefore there would be a 'program of enhanced security cooperation intended to increase Georgian capabilities and to strengthen Georgia's candidacy for NATO membership'.[50]

NATO and the EU

The US is a keen advocate of Georgia's accession to NATO. Georgia was the first country in the South Caucasus to articulate its desire to join the NATO alliance, expressing its membership aspirations in 2000, and it became an official aspirant at the Prague summit, held in November 2002. As its relations with Russia deteriorated over the Pankisi Gorge issue in 2001, then-President Shevardnadze sought to accelerate Georgia's membership of NATO, and a special government commission was instructed to prepare a program on integration into the organization in the political, economic and military spheres. This desire to join the western military alliance was underlined in Tbilisi in December 2002 by a parade of the first battalion of Georgian troops to be trained in anti-terrorist techniques by the US. Speaking at the parade, Shevardnadze stated that 'Georgia has pledged to modernize its army to meet the criteria needed to join NATO, and that is the path we have chosen. The Commando battalion of the Georgian armed forces . . . will form the basis of our future professional army.'[51]

Georgia views NATO membership as key to its national security. The country's National Military Strategy makes it clear that a shift from the principle of territorial defence to one of collective defence is a cornerstone of Georgian defence policy. According to the National Security Strategy, NATO membership would 'not only endow Georgia with an unprecedented degree of military and political security, but would allow it to contribute to strengthening the security of Europe, particularly the Black Sea region.'[52] However, its accession to NATO is complicated by the long-running secessionist conflicts with Abkhazia and South Ossetia. As peaceful conflict resolution is a core NATO value, the political settlement of its separatist disputes is key to Georgia's membership hopes.

Georgia's relations with NATO have been rewarding, and the country has benefited from cooperation with the alliance, particularly within the area of security sector reform. The 2004 Istanbul summit placed special emphasis on the importance of the military alliance's relations with the South Caucasus, appointing a special representative and liaison officer. NATO's assistance to the region is focused on boosting stability in order to foster a better environment for conflict resolution, primarily by helping the states of the South Caucasus to establish institutions that are better able to deal with the varied security challenges each country faces. Since 1994 Georgia has been a member of NATO's

Partnership for Peace program (PfP), the alliance's principal vehicle for deepening its engagement in the South Caucasus, and participates in the Euro-Atlantic Partnership Council (EAPC), which affords it the opportunity to hold political discussions and receive assistance on political and security issues. It also participates in the Planning and Review Process (PARP), which aims to ensure interoperability between NATO members and partner countries.

Georgia deepened its relationship with NATO in October 2004 with the conclusion of an Individual Partnership Action Plan (IPAP), which outlined a specific program for reform considered vital for development into a stable democracy, encompassing both civilian and military issues. Considerable progress was made implementing this and, as a result, in September 2006 NATO made the decision to commence Intensified Dialogue with Tbilisi, which raised hopes that Georgia was one step closer to accession. However, potential Georgian membership in the military alliance has proved to be a divisive issue, both between member-states and between NATO and Russia.

Possible future NATO accession for Georgia and Ukraine has driven a wedge between the European and US pillars of an alliance that is still recovering from the deep rift over the 2003 invasion of Iraq. The friction has highlighted questions about the fundamental nature of the alliance, and whether there are limits to enlargement, in spite of Article 10 and the 'open door' policy. France and Germany led the opposition (which included Italy and Spain) to Georgia and Ukraine being offered MAPs at the 2008 Bucharest summit, arguing that the alliance should be focusing its efforts on existing operations in Afghanistan rather than enlarging still further. There is concern that the addition of new members will transform the alliance from one concerned primarily with military matters to one concerned more with political issues, akin to the EU. Ultimately, a final decision on MAP was deferred, although the summit's final statement did stress that Georgia and Ukraine 'will become members of NATO'.[53] The tensions over Georgia and Ukraine have not only undermined NATO's fragile cohesion, but have also highlighted the divergence between the European and US approach. European member-states are more likely to be directly affected by the negative impact of any decision to enlarge, as they are far more dependent upon Russia, particularly in terms of energy. There is concern that, contrary to the aims of the alliance, accession for former Soviet states will actually undermine security in the Euro-Atlantic area rather than strengthen it.

As with the US, the role of NATO is complicated by its relations with Russia and the need for it to maintain transparent relations. Moscow was angered by the declaration at NATO's Bucharest summit in April 2008 that Georgia and Ukraine were likely to become members of the military alliance at some unspecified point in the future, and the Kremlin subsequently increased its cooperation with Georgia's separatist territories and unilaterally bolstered the number of troops deployed in Abkhazia.[54] At first glance, the events of August 2008 appear to have been successful for Moscow. Not only did it demonstrate the lengths it was prepared to go to in order to protect its 'citizens', the military action also acted as a warning shot to other former Soviet states, such as Ukraine, and also to the West, that it will not stand by and let countries in what it considers to be its strategic sphere of influence integrate more closely with the West. NATO has subsequently made it clear that it is not going to withdraw, establishing the NATO-Georgia Commission, whilst the EU has also indicated that it intends to intensify its cooperation with former Soviet states, rather than reduce it. However, Georgian membership in either organization remains a distant dream in the wake of August 2008—possibly more remote now than at any time since the 2003 Rose Revolution.

In spite of its close relationship with the US, Georgia feels that it has much in common with European nations and, as discussed above, is seeking a 're-turn to Europe'. The country has ambitious aspirations for its relationship with the EU and what the organization could and should be doing to support it. In particular, prior to August 2008, it hoped that the EU would provide it with greater political support in its strained relations with Russia and the resolution of its separatist disputes. The EU has gradually been deepening its engagement with Georgia and the wider South Caucasus, reflecting a grow-ing recognition of the region's significance for European security. Deepening EU engagement with the three countries of the South Caucasus was demon-strated by the appointment of the European Union's special representative (EUSR) for the region in 2003 and the inclusion of the three states in the Euro-pean neighbourhood policy (ENP). The relationship between Tbilisi and the EU acquired considerable momentum after Saakashvili's accession to power. EU financial aid to the country increased significantly post-2003, and in 2004 the European Commission utilized its Rapid Reaction Mechanism (RRM) to support Georgia's democratization, providing ¤4.65 million. However, this aid is being driven by a desire to boost stability on its periphery and, despite Georgian accession aspirations, the organisation is unlikely to dangle the membership carrot.

The EU, under the leadership of French President Nicolas Sarkozy, was instrumental in achieving a ceasefire between Russia and Georgia in August 2008. It presented a united front in September 2008, strongly condemning Russia's 'disproportionate reaction' in Georgia and postponing negotiations on a new partnership agreement until all Russian troops were withdrawn.[55] The organization now has an autonomous civilian monitoring mission in Georgia, mandated to monitor the implementation of the ceasefire agreements and contribute to the stabilisation and normalisation of the situation in areas affected by the conflict. The EU-led deployment is much more acceptable to Russia than any similar NATO-led force, which would have represented too great a threat to Moscow in what it has traditionally perceived as its own strategic backyard.

The Future of Transatlantic Relations

Georgia is a relatively young state that is still finding its feet within the international community. Since independence, its development and policy direction have been consistently influenced by the pervasive Russian shadow, and Tbilisi has deliberately courted the West, particularly the US, which is a keen advocate of Georgia's NATO membership, in an attempt to counterbalance Moscow's influence. Occupying a key strategic location between Europe, the former Soviet Union and the Middle East, Tbilisi is keen to protect its political autonomy from the influence of its powerful northern neighbor. Consequently, it is dependent on its Western alignments; relations with its immediate neighbours in the Caucasus region are less well developed. Whilst Tbilisi has ambitious aspirations regarding further integration into the Euro-Atlantic community, these ambitions may well be dashed as Western European allies seek to safeguard their relationship with Russia. The Russian factor remains a key influence on both Georgian policy-making and how US and other western states deal with Georgia. The events of 2008 provided a wake-up call for Tbilisi, demonstrating the true extent of US (and European) support. Misperception and misunderstanding appear to dominate: Georgia (wrongly) believed that the main focus of Western support was securing its deeper integration into the Euro-Atlantic community, whilst in actual fact the principal objective of such assistance has been the development of a stable, autonomous country that is capable of tackling its own security problems.

In the wake of the crisis in international relations following the controversial operation in Iraq in 2003, the Bush administration sought to shore up its relationship with new allies in the pivotal Caucasus and Caspian region. US officials at the time made it clear that the Bush administration had no plans to disengage from the South Caucasus region, reaffirming its commitment 'in the strongest terms . . . , as a stable and prosperous Central Asia and the Caucasus will mean a more secure world for the American people and a more prosperous future for the people of the region'.[56] A symbiotic relationship subsequently developed between the two: the US gained a compliant ally in an area of vital geostrategic and economic importance, whilst Georgia has benefited from considerable amounts of aid, be it financial, military or political. However, Georgia cannot rely upon a future US commitment to Georgia, particularly its assistance within the framework of the Global War on Terror. Although the 2009 US-Georgia Charter on Strategic Partnership reiterated Washington's continuing support for the Saakashvili government, there are signs that the Obama administration may take a less assertive approach towards Georgia's accession to NATO in an attempt to revitalise its relationship with Moscow.

Conclusions

Reflections on the Future of Transatlantic Relations
Andrew M. Dorman and Joyce P. Kaufman

IT IS CLEAR FROM THE PRECEDING CHAPTERS THAT TRANS-
atlantic relations will continue to play a significant part in world
affairs. It would be entirely conventional to argue that the economic downturn, the change in leadership throughout the major states and the ongoing
war on terrorism, as manifested in ongoing conflicts in Iraq and Afghanistan,
mean that this is a pivotal or turning point in transatlantic relations. It is not
that this is *not* the case, but it is not our intention in this conclusion to do so.
Rather, we would suggest that a significant number of trends and events are
running in parallel at present; these might, in time, show this to be a turning point for a host of reasons. One thing is for certain-these relations run
deep and are surprisingly strong, as Wallace Thies' book *Why NATO Endures*
demonstrates.[1] It is our intention to avoid suggesting an 'End of History' moment, as Francis Fukuyama suggested in 1989,[2] and instead to argue that it
is too early to say that this is necessarily a decisive point in the evolution of
transatlantic relations. Rather, what the various national case studies have
highlighted is a series of common elements that will not only influence future
developments in transatlantic relations but also provide us with important
insights into the international system as a whole.

First, transatlantic relations are, at one level, deeply personal. It is clear
that individuals play an important part, be they Chancellor Angela Merkel of
Germany or President Viktor Yushchenko of the Ukraine. Whilst all the individual leaders are influenced by the structural determinants around them,

such as alliance commitments, they are also individuals with particular agendas. Moreover, the role of personality does not depend on a state's size or its particular political leaning, but the role of agency, understated within neo-realist and neo-liberalist literature, is significant.[3] In other words, in the traditional debate about free will-the extent to which we are products of our environment versus the extent we are able to determine our future-these chapters suggest that within international relations the role of environment has been significantly understated. This is an important challenge to traditional assumptions of structural determinism within international relations.

It is not that structures, be they the international system itself, parliamentary systems, alliances or whatever, do not have a part to play. Instead, what these chapter show is that a combination of *both* structure and agency is what leads to policy development and implementation. There is, therefore, a need to redress the relative assumptions of balance within the structure and agency to acknowledge that this is a symbiotic relationship. This also has implications for the realist camp, which tends to focus so much on the national interest, power politics and the pursuit of national security often at the expense of the individual policy-maker. However, this conclusion is not just applicable to the neo-realists but spans the theoretical discourse within international relations as a whole.

Second, in many of the states there is a division in outlook between the political elite and the society which they represent. As the more traditional security dynamic typified by the Cold War has waned, the political elites have tended to recognize that changing definitions of security have caused their respective states to focus on new security challenges. In contrast, their electorates have taken longer to recognize these changes. For example, President Sarkozy's decision that France should rejoin NATO's integrated military structure has been far less controversial outside France than it is in France. Similarly, Ukrainian public opinion about NATO is at odds with a significant part of the political establishment. The same is true in Britain regarding NATO's Afghanistan involvement, with the political elite remaining in favour of it whilst the general population has swung against Britain's participation. There is, therefore, a time lag between the views of the political elite and those of the wider society, which has led to friction and misunderstanding that have affected domestic elections. Thus, political leaders need to reflect on how they engage with the civil populace and how to move it on from its current perceptions to a new understanding that might better reflect changing political and strategic realities. However, a danger may arise when leaders believe that they have an understanding that the public lacks, and then embroil their countries in wars that are not popularly supported, for example. Many have argued that this was the case with Tony Blair and the 2003 Iraq War, a commitment which ultimately undermined his popularity at home and remains an area of controversy within Britain.[4]

Third, and linked to the second point, is the question of identity. During the Cold War both sides were able to identify the other as the principal security threat, and this brought groups of states together to form NATO and the Warsaw Treaty Organization. This factor is most evident in the case of Poland, which has sought to 'rejoin' the West since the end of the Cold War. The absence of a shared or common threat has led to too much unravelling of the previous transatlantic consensus.[5] When Robert Kagan suggested that 'Americans are from Mars and Europeans are from Venus',[6] his statement contained an element of truth that many found uncomfortable. In referencing Hobbes and Kant, Kagan failed to accept that whilst this picture might have been true for a particular moment in time, the difference was not inevitably permanent and events might prove the reverse. If Americans and Europeans were separating because of a lack of a common threat, then presumably the re-emergence of such a threat would drive them back together. Moreover, Kagan's collective use of 'Europeans' was a generalization too far. As the case studies in this book have shown, there are wide-scale differences among the various European states. De Gaulle would probably have referred to the Anglo-Saxon world and the civilized world. This point ties back to the first point, specifically the way in which the change in European and North American leaders is having a profound impact on transatlantic relations.

Fourth, the armed forces are an important domestic actor in all the states studied. Whilst in many respects Turkey is probably the most overt case, with the military seeing themselves as the custodians of the Atatürk legacy, in the other states they equally play a role. The United Kingdom, for example, has seen public opinion turn markedly in favor of its armed forces, as evidenced by the support for returning units, even though at the same time opinion has remained hostile both to the wars in Iraq and Afghanistan. Similarly, in the case of the United States, in contrast to the war in Vietnam—where public hostility toward the war was manifested in hostility towards the troops—currently there is support for the troops on the ground in Iraq and Afghanistan amidst questioning of the policy decisions. Furthermore, some of the architects of parts of those conflicts, such as David Petraeus, generally are held in high regard and have become important actors in policy-making.[7] This situation is nothing new, as the interaction of Winston Churchill with various elements of the British military establishment showed, but it is often under acknowledged. [8]

Fifth, clearly a rebalancing of power is occurring at the moment, which the financial meltdown is further complicating. The current economic instability may well bring to fruition such a change in the balance of power far earlier than would have been the case otherwise. The likes of John Mearsheimer have consistently argued that Europe would ultimately want to counter-balance the United States and also counter-balance themselves. In many ways the period since the end of the Cold War has been a period of unprecedented stability and peace, which was unlikely to remain given Europe's history. As the chapter on Russia highlights, it has also been a period in which the Russian voice was unusually quiet. The recent Russian military action in Georgia and pipeline politics with the Ukraine and the rest of Europe are actually closer to the norm of European politics and the exam question is probably not 'why are we witnessing a resurgent Russia?' but rather 'why was Russia so quiet for so long?' Furthermore, if we are witnessing a period of structural rebalancing within the international system, then there are likely to be quite profound changes to the relative balance of power between states and within states. Conversely, redefining the balance of power within and among the transatlantic countries may lead to a significant rebalance internationally.

Sixth, it is also readily apparent that there is no agreed definition of "transatlantic relations." Different elements are often used in reference to the term, such as geographic, cultural, historical, bilateral, US-focused, institutional and religious. But even within individual states, the definition of transatlanticism changes over time and is largely dependent on context. Are we talking about some form of geographical or philosophical bloc? Or are we talking about a community that does something or a community that has something done to it? There is clearly some debate. Depending on the answer to the range of questions implicit in these various perspectives, the future direction and composition of such a bloc vary. Perhaps the quietest player within this debate has been the Canadians, with many states defining transatlantic relations as those solely with the United States. Yet, the Canadian role is significant, and it appears to have been forgotten, for two reasons. Firstly, it is dwarfed by its neighbor to the south and thus the two countries tend to be seen as one and the same. Secondly, the withdrawal of Canadian land and air units from Germany since the end of the Cold War has resulted in a loss of visibility in Europe and enabled the Canadian government itself to partially withdraw from engagement in NATO in particular and with Europe more generally. However, the significant commitment of Canadian troops to NATO's mission in Afghanistan and the disproportionate casualties that they have suffered have partially reawakened the Canadian voice. Added to this has been the shift towards the English-speaking world's becoming the default partnership of choice for the Bush administration, which has given the Canadians a vehicle to have their voice heard.

Seventh, transatlantic relations are being engaged, in a variety of fora simultaneously. Both the European Union and NATO play an extremely important role for all the member nations, albeit for differing reasons, and interest groupings vary between them. For example, within NATO the Americans, Canadians, British, Dutch, Danes and Poles tend to work closely together and generally share similar views. Likewise, Germany, France, Luxembourg and Belgium form another grouping, which tends most likely to be at odds with the US grouping. Yet when it comes to trade, the division tends to be between the EU and the NAFTA countries. These divisions would be relatively straightforward, except there are a number of areas where the defense (NATO) and economic (EU) factors come into conflict with one another. Defense procurement remains a highly contentious issue and is the one area where there has not been a political coming together.

Eighth, there are real differences over security. All have generally agreed that one of their principal security challenges is terrorism, although they define it differently. For example, whilst the US is looking at al-Qaeda and the threat it poses, the United Kingdom is looking at a mix of domestic (Northern Ireland) and international (al Qaeda) terrorism, and Turkey defines terrorism as the Kurds. These differences in outlook have significant policy implications with, for example, the US viewing the Kurds as an issue being largely determined by the future of Iraq, whilst Turkey views the Kurds as a direct challenge to the Turkish state. Moreover, immediate security challenges are often being felt differently. Thus, in Europe Russia's pipeline politics had a rapid effect as gas supplies were reduced or switched off completely, whilst in North America there was no issue. This is leading to differences in approach to the issue of energy security: to Europe it is a critical component of the concept of security, while it seems to be less so for the United States. This is true in spite of US dependence on foreign oil, which carries with it other security challenges.

It would be impossible to look at the issue of security without bringing in the question of Afghanistan. Just as Iraq seemed to divide the transatlantic countries, in many ways Afghanistan united them, at least initially. While there have been issues surrounding which countries will continue to send troops—and how many—there was little discussion of the rationale behind the conflict in the wake of 9/11. The question facing these countries now is whether they can maintain that unity as they struggle to determine next steps both within Afghanistan, and as allies in general.

Ninth, Afghanistan remains the elephant in the room. There are clearly many differences of view between the various capitals over the appropriate strategy and the ultimate goals of the NATO mission. President Obama's troop surge was accompanied by further calls for the remainder of NATO to increase its commitment of personnel to the conflict.[9] These are likely to be largely ignored as the other partners seek to limit their exposure. Nevertheless, if ultimately NATO's war in Afghanistan fails, it is highly likely that it will bring the partners back together, as Kosovo did a decade earlier. The central importance of NATO remains, especially as the European ESDP alternative appears to have fallen by the wayside.

Tenth, Afghanistan has once again exposed the differences in capability amongst NATO's military forces. In our Introduction, we highlighted the debate that occurred on both sides of the Atlantic about the future role of armed forces and whether there is a difference between the United States and Europe (where Canada fit seemed to have been ignored). Tony Blair's division between those that do war-fighting and peacekeeping and those that do just the latter now seems to have a little more resonance.[10] The Canadian and Dutch decisions to pull their forces out of the south of Afghanistan in the future and the question marks that have been raised over the British military may now have confirmed that Rumsfeld was right, albeit a little ahead of his time. The test of this will be what will happen if NATO is confronted by defeat.

Finally, lurking in the background but becoming more prominent, the economic downturn remains an issue whose impact is still to be fully felt. The failings of the banking sector, and the respective national responses to them, have highlighted differing philosophical approaches. This was made clear in the discussions surrounding the G20 summit in London in April 2009, where arriving at a common approach to solving the problem proved to be problematic. Tied to the economic issue are the varying degrees to which countries have been affected domestically by the economic downturn, and how each has chosen to respond domestically. Here, there is a direct relationship between the domestic and international policies, with one affecting and reinforcing the other. Especially at a time of economic downturn, countries have had to make policy choices that resulted in reassigning priorities which, in turn, could come at the expense of broader international relationships (i.e., cases of "guns versus butter").

Despite the range of issues that seem to divide the countries included in this volume, it also seems safe to conclude that transatlantic relations in the various forms they take are likely to remain important for some time to come. All of the cases underline the importance of the relationships that exist between and among these countries, and also demonstrate how interwoven their economic and security policies are. Despite much questioning about the wisdom of these relationships, few countries have indicated any willingness to break them. And, in fact, France's decision to rejoin the NATO military structure stands as further proof of the importance that this alliance continues to have. Similarly, the desire of countries such as Georgia and Ukraine to join both the EU and NATO also speaks to the role that countries see these organizations playing internationally, as well as supporting the calculation that there are more benefits to be derived from being part of them than remaining outside.

What is also safe to assert is that their way forward is not altogether clear, and history tells us there will be a number of twists and turns in the journey ahead. But we cannot doubt that the transatlantic journey will continue.

Glossary

ACT	Allied Command Transformation
AKP	Adalet ve Kalkinma Partisi
ANP	Annual National Plan
ARA	American Relief Association
Bn	Billion
BQ	Bloc Québecois
BRIC	Brazil, Russia, India and China
BSEC	Black Sea Economic Community
BSF	Black Sea Fleet
CA	Comprehensive Approach
CESDP	Common European Security and Defence Policy
CSSS	Center for European Security Studies
CF	Canadian Forces
CESDP	Common European Security and Defence Policy
CFDS	Canada First Defence Strategy
CFSP	Common Foreign and Security Policy
CIS	Commonwealth of Independent States
COMISAF	Commander International Security Assistance Force
CPSU	Communist Party of the Soviet Union
CRS	Congressional Research Service
CSTO	Collective Security Treaty Organisation
EAPC	Euro-Atlantic Partnership Council

EEC	Eurasian Economic Community
ENP	European Neighbourhood Policy
ESDI	European Security and Defence Identity
ESDP	European Security and Defence Policy
EU	European Union
EUSR	EU Special Representative
EXBS	Export Control and Related Border Security assistance program
FDI	Foreign Direct Investment
G-7	Group of Seven industrialized nations
GBSLE	Georgia Border Security and Law Enforcement assistance program
GCC	Gulf Cooperation Council
GDP	Gross Domestic Product
GSSOP	Georgia Sustainment and Stability Operations Program
GTEP	Georgia Train and Equip Program
GUAM	Georgia, Ukraine, Azerbaijan and Moldova
GUUAM	Georgia, Ukraine, Uzbekistan, Azerbaijan and Moldova
ICC	International Criminal Court
IFOR	Implementation Force
IMF	International Monetary Fund
IPAP	Individual Partnership Action Plan
IPS	International Policy Statement
ISAF	International Security Assistance Force
JRRF	Joint Rapid Reaction Force
JSCSC	Joint Services Command and Staff College
KRG	Kurdistan Regional Government
MAP	Membership Action Plan
MoD	Ministry of Defence
MOOTW	Military Operations Other than War
NAFTA	North American Free Trade Agreement
NATO	North Atlantic Treaty Organization
NDP	New Democratic Party
NDS	National Defense Strategy
NMS	National Military Strategy
NSS	National Security Strategy
NORAD	North American Aerospace Defense Command

NSC	National Security Council
ODED	Organization for Democracy and Economic Development
OIC	Organisation of Islamic Conference
OSCE	Organization for Security and Co-operation in Europe
PARP	Planning and Review Process
PCC	Prague Capabilities Commitment
PfP	Partnership for Peace program
PKK	Partiya Karkari Kurdistan
PM	Prime Minister
QDR	Quadrennial Defense Review
SALIS	Strategic Airlift Interim Solution
SCO	Shanghai Cooperation Organisation
SDI	Strategic Defense Initiative
TGS	Turkish General Staff
UAV	Unmanned Aerial Vehicle
UK	United Kingdom
UMP	Union pour un Mouvement Populaire
UN	United Nations
UNESCO	United Nations Educational, Scientific and Cultural Organization
UNIFIL	United Nations Interim Force in Lebanon
UNPROFOR	United Nations Protection Force
UNSC	United Nations Security Council
UNSCR	United Nations Security Council Resolution
US	United States
USSR	Union of Soviet Socialist Republics
WEU	Western European Union
WMD	Weapons of Mass Destruction

Notes

Introduction

1. Edward N Luttwak, "Toward post-heroic warfare," *Foreign Affairs*, May/June 1995, pp. 109–22.

2. Robert Kagan, *Of Paradise and Power: American and Europe in the New World Order*, (New York: Alfred A Knopf, 2003), pp. 1–2.

3. "Secretary Rumsfeld briefs at the Foreign Press Center," Pentagon, Washington, DC, 22 January 2003, http://www.defenselink.mil/transcripts/transcript.aspx?transcriptid=1330, accessed 12 January 2009.

4. Tony Blair, "Our nation's future—defence," speech delivered on HMS *Albion*, 12 January 2007, http://www.number10.gov.uk/Page10735, accessed 12 January 2009.

5. Michael Evans & David Charter, "Barack Obama fails to win NATO troops he wants for Afghanistan," *Times Online*, 4 April 2009, http://www.timesonline.co.uk/tol/news/world/us_and_americas/article6032342.ece, accessed 9 November 2009.

6. See Geoffrey Lee Williams, *NATO and the Transatlantic Alliance in the 21st Century*, (Basingstoke: Palgrave Macmillan, 2001).

7. For North Atlantic Treaty, see NATO website at http://www.nato.int/cps/en/natolive/official_texts_17120.htm, accessed 18 April 2009; see also Gustav Schmidt, *A History of NATO: The First Fifty Years*, 3 vols., (Basingstoke: Palgrave, 2001); William H Park, *Defending the West: A History of NATO*, (Brighton: Wheatsheaf Books Ltd, 1986); Wallace J Thies, *Why NATO Endures*, (New York: Cambridge University Press, 2009).

8. See http://www.icasualties.org/OEF/Nationality.aspx, accessed 9 November 2009.

9. The Contact Group was created in April 1994 and included representatives from

the United States, Germany, the United Kingdom, France and Russia. Italy was added to the group in 1996.

10. Article 2, "The North Atlantic Treaty."

11. "Statement by the North Atlantic Council', *Press Release (2001)124*, 12 September 2001, http://www.nato.int/docu/pr/2001/p01–124e.htm, accessed 13 January 2009.

12. See Alyson K Bailes, 'The EU and a 'better world': what role for the European Security and Defence Policy?', *International Affairs*, vol. 84, no. 1, January 2008, pp. 115–130; Christopher Reynolds, 'Military capability development in the ESDP: Towards effective governance?', *Contemporary Security Policy*, vol. 28, no. 2, 2007, pp. 357–83; Anthony King, 'The Future of the European Security and Defence Policy', *Contemporary Security Policy*, vol. 26, no. 1, 2005, pp. 44–61; Elke Krahmann, 'Regulating private military companies: What role for the EU?', *Contemporary Security Policy*, vol. 26, no. 1, 2005, pp. 103–125; F Heisbourg, 'Europe's strategic ambitions: the limits of ambiguity', *Survival*, vol. 42, no. 2, 2000, pp. 5–15; C Kupchan, 'In defence of European defence; an American perspective', *Survival*, vol. 42, no. 2, 2000, pp. 16–32; J Howorth, 'Britain, France and the European Defence Initiative', *Survival*, vol. 42, no. 2, 2000, pp. 33–55; Mark Webber, Stuart Croft, Jolyon Howorth, Terry Terriff & Elke Krahmann, 'The governance of European security', *Review of International Studies*, vol. 30, no. 1, January 2004, pp. 3–26; Jeff Huysmans, 'Shape-shifting NATO: humanitarian action and the Kosovo refugee crisis', *Review of International Studies*, vol. 28, no. 3, July 2002, pp. 599–618; Paul Cornish and Geoffrey Edwards, 'Beyond the EU/NATO dichotomy: The beginnings of a European strategic culture', *International Affairs*, vol. 77, no. 3, July 2001, pp. 587–603; Jolyion Howorth, 'France, Britain and the Euro-Atlantic crisis', *Survival*, vol. 45, no. 4, 2003, pp. 173–92.

13. See Andrew Dorman, Joyce P Kaufman & Craig Stone, 'Australia, Britain, Canada, the USA and the ABCA relationship', in *Handbook of Defence Politics,* ed. Isaiah Wilson III and James J F Forest, (London: Routledge, 2008), pp. 227–40.

14. Dana H. Allin, Gilles Andreani, Philippe Errerea and Gary Samore, "Repairing the damage: Possibilities and limits of transatlantic consensus," Adelphi Paper 389 (Oxford: Routledge, 2007), p. 9.

15. See, for example, Hans J Morgenthau, *Politics Among Nations: The Struggle for Power and Peace,* (New York: Alfred A Knopf, 1953).

16. Helmut Schmidt, "The 1977 Alastair Buchan Memorial Lecture," published in *Survival*, Jan/Feb 1978, accessed on-line December 21, 2008.

17. "President Truman's address before a joint session of Congress, March 12, 1947," available at http://avalon.law.yale.edu/20th_century/trudoc.asp, accessed December 22, 2008.

18. Idem.

19. "The North Atlantic Treaty."

20. "The machinery of NATO," in *NATO Handbook* (Brussels: NATO Office of International and Press, 1995), p. 93.

21. Joyce P. Kaufman, *NATO and the Former Yugoslavia: Crisis, Conflict and the Atlantic Alliance,* (Lanham, MD: Rowman & Littlefield Publishers, Inc, 2002), pp. 8–9.

Also see David N. Schwartz, *NATO's Nuclear Dilemmas*, (Washington, DC: Brookings Institution, 1983); and Leon V. Sigal, *Nuclear Forces in Europe: Enduring Dilemmas, Present Prospects*, (Washington, DC: Brookings Institution, 1984). Although these last two sources are relatively old, they provide a comprehensive history of the alliance during these periods of crisis.

22. Among the most detailed of the histories and discussion surrounding NATO enlargement see James Goldgeier, *Not Whether but When: The U.S. Decision to Enlarge NATO*, (Washington, DC: Brookings Institution Press, 1999).

23. Kaufman, *NATO and the Former Yugoslavia*, p. 33.

24. Michael Mandelbaum, *The Dawn of Peace in Europe*, (New York: Twentieth Century Fund Press, 1996), p. 64.

25. NATO Press Release, "Statement by the North Atlantic Council," 12 September 2001, http://www.NATO.int/docu/pr/2001/p01–124e.htm, accessed March 2, 2009.

26. "NATO-EU: A Strategic Partnership," http://www.nato.int/issues/nato-eu/index.html, accessed 2 March 2009.

27. "EU-NATO Declaration on ESDP," 16 December 2002, http://www.nato.int/cps/en/SID-2D72C454–EF183FBD/natolive/official_texts_19544.htm, accessed 18 April 2009.

Chapter 1

1. Michael Cox, "Martians and Venutians in the New World Order," *International Affairs*, vol. 79, n. 3 (2003), p. 524.

2. The literal translation is "the weak (*minor*) capitulates before the strong (*major*)." But its broad sense is that when there is a significant challenge, smaller problems disappear.

3. See, for example, David Hastings Dunn, "European Security and Defence Policy in the American Policy Debate: Counterbalancing America or Rebalancing NATO," *Defence Studies*, vol.1, no.1 (Spring 2001), pp. 146–55, quote from p. 146.

4. On the question of conflicting attitudes toward security and military issues in the US and Western Europe, it is useful to remember that, as the Pew Research Center has estimated, "Americans are more likely than Western Europeans to believe in the necessity of sometimes using force to deal with global threats." Conversely, "Americans are much more comfortable with the idea of military preemption—the use of force against potentially threatening countries who have not attacked—than are Western Europeans" Andrew Kohut, *Anti-Americanism: Causes and Characteristics*, http://pewglobal.org/.

5. The exercise of power by states toward each other is called "power politics" or "realpolitik." For Mearsheimer, a Germany not checked by American power could become aggressive again and lead to war in Europe. John Mearsheimer, "Back to the Future: Instability in Europe After the Cold War," *International Security*, vol. 15, no. 1 (Summer, 1990).

6. Jeffrey Anderson, G. John Ikenberry, and Thomas Risse, *The End of the West? Crisis and Change in the Atlantic Order* (Ithaca, NY: Cornell University Press, 2008).

7. The disagreement over Iraq prompted consensus on the hypothesis that, with the end of the Cold War, the basis for transatlantic relations was eroding. Perhaps the most famous argument for this position has been made by Robert Kagan in his 2002 article, "Paradise and Power," *Policy Review* (June and July 2002), an argument that was later expanded into the book *Of Paradise and Power: America and Europe in the New World Order* (New York: Alfred A. Knopf, 2003). Robert Kagan, "One Year After: A Grand Strategy for the West?" *Survival*, vol. 44, no. 4 (Winter 2002–03), pp.135–156.

See also Francis Fukuyama, "The West May Be Cracking," *International Herald Tribune*, August 9, 2002, p. 4, in which he talks about deep differences between the US and Europe. Charles Krauthammer, "Reimagining NATO," *Washington Post*, May 24, 2002, argues that NATO is dead; see also Josef Joffe, "The Alliance Is Dead: Long Live the New Alliance," *New York Times*, September 29, 2002. Joffe asserts that the anti-Soviet alliance is dead and has been replaced by one "that allows the United States to pick and choose." Following the Iraq crisis, others envisaged the crisis as the cause of transatlantic political differences. Tony Judt, for example, argued that "we are witnessing the dissolution of an international system." See Tony Judt, "The Way We Live Now," *New York Review of Books*, March 27, 2003, vol. 50, no. 5, p. 6. Former Secretary of State Henry Kissinger wrote that "if the existing trend in transatlantic relations continues, the international system will be fundamentally altered" (quoted in Philip Gordon and Jeremy Shapiro. *Allies at War: America, Europe, and the Crisis over Iraq* [New York: McGraw-Hill, 2004], p. 4). See also Charles Kupchan, who stated that the US and Europe were headed toward "geopolitical rivalry." He makes this argument in *The End of the American Era: U.S. Foreign Policy and the Geopolitics of the Twenty-First Century* (New York: Knopf, 2002) and in "The Alliance Lies in the Rubble," *Financial Times*, April 10, 2003; see also William Wallace and Christopher Phillips, "Reassessing the Special Relationship," *International Affairs*, vol. 85, no. 2 (March 2009), pp. 263–284.

8. For more current references on US and European relations, see Francis Fukuyama, "The West May Be Cracking Europe and America," *International Herald Tribune*, 9 August 2002, pp. 4–10; John Leech, *Whole and Free: NATO, EU Enlargement and Transatlantic Relations* (Federal Trust for Education & Research, 2002); Philip H. Gordon, "Bridging the Atlantic Divide," *Foreign Affairs*, (Jan.–Feb. 2003), vol. 82, no. 1, p. 70; James B. Steinberg, "An Elective Partnership: Salvaging Transatlantic Relations," *Survival*, (June, 2003), vol. 45, no. 2, p. 113; Christopher Layne and Thomas Jefferson, "America as European Hegemon," *The National Interest* (Summer 2003), vol. 13, no. 72, pp. 17–30; Ivo H. Daalder, "The End of Atlanticism," *Survival* (June 2003), vol. 45, no. 2, p. 147; Hall Gardner, *NATO and the European Union: New World, New Europe, New Threats* (Burlington, VT: Ashgate Publishing, 2004); Gordon and Shapiro, *Allies at War*; Jaap de Hoop Scheffer, "New Trans-Atlantic Unity," in *NATO's Nations and Partners for Peace* (2004), pp. 20–24; William Wallace, "Broken Bridges," *The World Today* (Dec. 2004), vol. 60, no. 12, pp. 13–16; Daniel Hamilton and Daniel

Sheldon, *Conflict and Cooperation in Transatlantic Relations* (Baltimore, MD: Johns Hopkins University Press, 2004); Tod Lindberg, "We: A Community in Agreement on Fundamentals," *Policy Review* (Dec. 2004–Jan. 2005), no. 128, pp. 3–19; Elizabeth Pond, *Friendly Fire: The Near-Death of the Transatlantic Alliance* (European Union Studies Association, 2004); Werner Weidenfeld, *From Alliance to Coalitions: The Future of Transatlantic Relations* (Bertelsmann Foundation Publishers, 2004); E. A. Turpen, "Free World: America, Europe, and the Surprising Future of the West," *Choice* (June 2005), vol. 42, no. 10, p. 1895; Ivo Daalder, *Crescent of Crisis : U.S.-European Strategy for the Greater Middle East* (Brookings Institution Press, 2006); Matthew Evangelista, *Partners or Rivals?: European-American Relations After Iraq* (V & P Publishing, 2005); Vittorio Emanuele Parsi, *The Inevitable Alliance: Europe and the United States Beyond Iraq* (New York: Palgrave Macmillan, 2006); Massimo D'Alema, "Diplomacy Al Dente," *Wall Street Journal*, 14 June 2006, p. 14; Pierangelo Isernia and Philip P. Everts, "European Public Opinion on Security Issues," *European Security* vol. 15, no. 4 (Dec. 2006), p. 451; Thomas Ilgen, *Hard Power, Soft Power, and the Future of Transatlantic Relations* (Burlington, VT: Ashgate, 2006); Jeremy Poulter, "NATO as a Security Organization: Implications for the Future Role and Survival of the Alliance," RUSI Journal, vol. 151, no. 3 (2006) pp. 58–62; Andrew A. Michta, "Transatlantic Troubles," *The National Interest* (Nov.–Dec. 2006), pp. 62–67; Ryan C. Hendrickson, "The Miscalculation of NATO's Death," *Parameters*, vol. 37, no. 1 (Spring 2007), pp. 98–115; Daniel Dombey, "Transatlantic Climate Shift," *Financial Times*, 4 June 2007, p. 2; Richard Haass, "The Atlantic Becomes a Little Wider," *Financial Times*, 19 December 2007, p. 2; Lance Smith, "Is the Transatlantic Relationship Still Important?," *Vital Speeches of the Day* (June 2007), vol. 73, no. 6, pp. 249–252.

9. See Chris Brown, *Understanding International Relations*, 2d ed. (Basingstoke: Palgrave, 2001).

10. For a balance-of-power explanation of international relations see the canonical neo-realist work of Kenneth Waltz, *Theory of International Politics* (Redding, MA: Addison-Wesley, 1979); see also Stephen Walt, *The Origins of Alliances* (Ithaca, NY: Cornell University Press, 1987); and John Mearsheimer, *The Tragedy of Great Power Politics* (New York: Norton, 2001). It is worth noticing the distinction between neo-realists and "classical" realists. While the former stress that the international system is made of great powers, each seeking to survive, the latter group, including scholars such as Hans Morgenthau, emphasize that states, like human beings, have an innate longing to control others, which leads them to conflicts. See Hans Morgenthau, *Politics Among Nations: The Struggle for Power and Peace* (New York: McGraw Hill, 1993. For neo-liberals who emphasize the role of international institutions through which concerted action can be achieved, see Robert Keohane, *After Hegemony: Cooperation and Discord in the World Political Economy* (Princeton, NJ: Princeton University Press, 1984); and Robert Keohane and Lisa Martin, "The Promise of Institutionalist Theory," *International Security*, vol. 20, no. 1 (Summer 1995), pp. 39–51. On regimes as a set of principles, norms, rules and decision-making procedures that regulate states' behavior, see Robert Keohane and Joseph Nye, *Power and Interdependence*, 3rd ed. (New

York: Longman, 2001). This book was published in its first edition in 1977. On regimes see also Hedley Bull, who argues that institutions help states' adherence to rules. See Hedley Bull, *The Anarchical Society: A Study of Order in World Politics* (New York: Columbia University Press, 1977). It is also important to mention that there is a debate in the study of international relations in the US between neo-realism and liberal institutionalism. Such debate is presented in David A. Baldwin, ed., *Neorealism and Neoliberalism* (New York: Columbia University Press, 1993). It is important to note that constructivists, with their focus on the role of norms, identity and culture in world politics, challenge the dominance of neo-realism and neo-liberalism in the field of international relations by offering alternative understandings of key topics such as the prospects for change in world politics, the relationship between identity and interest, the meaning of balance of power and of anarchy. See Nicholas Onuf, *World of Our Making: Rules and Rule in Social Theory and International Relations* (Columbia: University of South Carolina Press, 1989); Peter J. Katzenstein, ed., *The Culture of National Security: Norms and Identity in World Politics* (New York: Columbia University Press, 1996); and Yosef Lapid and Friedrich V. Kratochwil, eds., *The Return of Culture and Identity in IR Theory* (Boulder, CO: Lynne Rienner, 1996). Alexander Wendt, "Anarchy Is What States Make of It: The Social Construction of Power Politics," *International Organization*, vol. 46, no.2 (Spring 2002), pp. 391–425.

11. Mearsheimer, "Back to the Future," p. 52; Harries, "The Collapse of 'The West,'" p. 42; Kupchan, "Reviving the West," p. 3; Walt, "The Ties that Fray," *The National Interest* (Winter 1998–1999), p. 4.

12. See John Mearsheimer, "The False Promise of International Institutions," *International Security*, vol. 19, no. 3, pp. 5–58; and Waltz, *Theory of International Politics*.

13. See Waltz, *Theory of International Politics*; and Mearsheimer, *The Tragedy of Great Power Politics*.

14. Stephen Walt, "The Precarious Partnership: America and Europe in a New Era." In *Atlantic Security: Contending Visions*, edited by Charles Kupchan (New York: Council on Foreign Relations, 1998), p. 8.

15. This theory claims that states will seek to balance the power of threatening states. The most rigorous account of balance of power theory can be found in Waltz, *Theory of International Politics*. Walt refined such an argument by focusing on the role of threats, rather than power alone, in stimulating balancing behavior. See Walt, *The Origins of Alliances*.

16. Kenneth Waltz, *Theory of International Politics*; and Walt, *The Origins of Alliances*.

17. Joseph Grieco, "Anarchy and the Limits of Cooperation: A Realist Critique of the Newest Liberal Institutionalism," *International Organization*, vol. 42, no. 3, pp. 485–507.

18. A more detailed account of these arguments is offered in the following pages. Figure 2 is a graphic synthesis of their understanding of what kept the United States and Europe together during the Cold War. My synthesis was inductively constructed through theorists' arguments addressing the future of transatlantic relations. To give

quotations in the text would constitute redundancy; thus, sensible to parsimony, I will provide the sources from which the arguments were extrapolated, and the graph will illustrate the arguments.

19. A bipolar system contains two great rival states or alliance blocs. The "polarity" of an international power distribution is the number of independent centers of power in the system. The Cold War period was characterized by two great rivals: the US and the USSR, or NATO and the Warsaw Pact. The US-Soviet competition seemed to provide stability in the system. Some, however, argue that peace is best preserved by multi-polarity (i.e., five or six centers of power, where states are not grouped into alliances.

20. Mearsheimer, "Back to the Future," p. 52.

21. Mearsheimer, "Back to the Future," p. 5.

22. Mearsheimer, "Back to the Future," p. 52.

23. Mearsheimer, "Back to the Future," p. 18.

24. Mearsheimer, "The Future of the American Pacifier," *Foreign Affairs,* vol. 80, no. 5, (Sept.–Oct. 2001), pp. 46–61.

25. Walt, "The Ties that Fray," p. 4.

26. The argument Walt makes is that the US needed Europe to be economically strong so that it could contribute to the US economic prosperity, and that strengthened the transatlantic alliance. See Walt, "The Ties that Fray," p. 6.

27. For neo-realists, trade should serve power. Because power is relative, trade is desirable only when the distribution of benefits favors one's own state over rivals. See Joseph Grieco, *Cooperation among Nations: Europe, American and Non-Tariff Barriers to Trade* (Ithaca, NY: Cornell University Press, 1990); Joanne Gowa, *Allies Adversaries, and International Trade* (Princeton, NJ: Princeton University Press, 1993).

28. Walt, "The Ties that Fray," p. 6.

29. In "The Ties that Fray," after rejecting the argument that cultural and ethnic ties brought Europe and America together, Walt argues that to the extent that such ties reinforced American interests in Europe, their success is diminishing in the post-Cold War era because, he states, figures like Dean Acheson, Dwight Eisenhower, Paul Nitze and John Foster Dulles are no longer making foreign policy decisions and have been succeeded by a new generation with "different memories." He contends that watching *Saving Private Ryan* is no substitute for having lived through the real thing." The lack of a direct experience with World War II is, in Walt's opinion, reason to be pessimistic about the future of the transatlantic alliance. He concludes by saying that even if the new generations might recognize the importance of transatlantic cooperation, "it will never kindle the reflexive emotional response that it did for their parents and grandparents." What is significant about such an argument is that while he makes a neo-realist argument in the article, with the classical assumptions about power balancing and threat, in the last part, when he discusses "generational change, he does not look at the international system or at the state, but rather at the socio-cultural level" (Walt, "The Ties that Fray," p. 8).

30. Walt, "The Ties that Fray," p. 8.

31. Among many, see Kagan and Nye works cited above.

32. Kagan, cited above.

33. In order to increase their influence, states can use power capabilities in different ways. Joseph Nye makes a significant distinction between "hard" and "soft" power. "Hard power" is the method of exercising power directly, through coercion and reward. "Soft power" is influence through attraction and ideology to shape states' preferences. Joseph S. Nye, *Soft Power: The Means to Success in World Politics* (New York: Public Affairs, 2004).

34. Kagan, "America's Crisis of Legitimacy," *Foreign Affairs,* vol. 83, no. 2 (2004), p. 71.

35. This is power as *capability.*

36. Ronald D. Asmus and Kenneth M. Pollack, "The New Transatlantic Project," *Policy Review,* vol. 115 (Oct.–Nov. 2002), p. 5.

37. Ivo H. Daalder, "The End of Atlanticism," in *Beyond Paradise and Power: Europe, America, and the Future of a Troubled Partnership*, ed. Lindberg, Tod (New York: Routledge, 2005), p. 42.

38. For the neo-liberals' approach to post-Cold War transatlantic relations, see James Elles, "Towards a New Transatlantic Relationship," *European Business Journal,* vol. 5, no. 3, pp. 34–41. John Duffield, "NATO's Functions after the Cold War," *Political Science Quarterly,* vol. 109, no. 5, pp. 763–787. Robert Blackwill, *The Future of Transatlantic Relations* (Council For Foreign Relations Press, 1999). Daniel Deudney and John Ikenberry, "The Logic of the West," *World Policy Journal,* vol. 10, no. 4 (Winter, 1993), pp. 17–25. Nye, "The US and Europe." Robert McCalla, "NATO's Persistence After the Cold War," *International Organization* (Summer 1996), pp. 445–475. Anthony Blinken, "The False Crisis over the Atlantic," *Foreign Affairs* (May–June 2001), pp. 35–48. Ivo Daalder, "Europe: Rebalancing the U.S.-European Relationship," *The Brookings Institution* (Summer 1999), p. 22–25.

39. Elles, "Towards a New Transatlantic Relationship", p. 36. Elles claims that "the US has learned that its resources are finite and that the defense of its own legitimate interest, as in the Gulf war, has to be conducted in partnership with others." In this sense Europe is America's "natural" partner because of its economic and military capacity. The logic behind his argument is that they are partners because the US and Europe are committed to democratic institutions and market economy. Elles, "Towards a New Transatlantic Relationship, p. 36.

40. Duffield, "NATO's Functions After the Cold War," p. 766.

41. Blackwill, *The Future of Transatlantic Relations,* p. 10.

42. Nye, "The US and Europe," p. 54.

43. Karl W. Deutsch et al., *Political Community and North Atlantic Area: International organization in the Light of Historical Experience* (Princeton, N. J.: Princeton University Press, 1968).

44. Elles, "Towards a New Transatlantic Relationship," p. 36.

45. Deudney and Ikenberry, "The Logic of the West," p. 18.

46. Deudney and Ikenberry, "The Logic of the West," p. 18.

47. Nye, "The US and Europe," pp. 54–55.

48. Nye, "The US and Europe," p. 55.

49. Anthony J. Blinken, "The False Crisis Over the Atlantic," *Foreign Affairs*, vol. 80, no. 3 (May–June 2001), p. 36.

50. Mark Landler and David E. Sanger, "World Leaders Pledge $1.1.Trillion for Crisis," *New York Times*, 2 April 2009, p. A1.

51. Deudney and Ikenberry, "The Logic of the West," p. 19.

52. International regimes are a set of norms, rules, institutions and decision-making procedures that govern actors' behavior in an issue-area. See Robert O. Keohane and Joseph S. Nye, *Power and Interdependence: World Politics in Transition*, 3rd ed. (New York: Addison-Wesley Longman, 2001); and Stephen D. Krasner, ed., *International Regimes* (Ithaca, NY: Cornell University Press, 1983).

53. Elles, "Towards a New Transatlantic Relationship," p. 41.

54. Elles, "Towards a New Transatlantic Relationship," p. 35.

55. Charles Kupchan, "Rethinking Europe," *The National Interest*, vol. 56 (Summer 1999), p. 78.

56. Nye, "The US and Europe," p. 55.

57. Blinken, "The False Crisis over the Atlantic," p. 3.

58. Blinken, "The False Crisis over the Atlantic," p. 3.

59. Tod Lindberg, "We: A Community in Agreement on Fundamentals," *Policy Review*, no. 128 (Dec. 2004–Jan. 2005), pp. 3–19; and Tod Lindberg, "The Atlanticist Community," pp. 215–235, in *Beyond Paradise and Power: Europe, America, and the Future of a Troubled Partnership*, ed. Tod Lindberg (New York: Routledge, 2005).

60. On the justification of the use of force against another state on humanitarian grounds without explicit Security Council authorization, as well as on the question whether violence can serve humanitarian purposes, see Nicholas J. Wheeler, *Saving Strangers* (Oxford: Oxford University Press, 2000).

61. The terms "norm" and "value" here are used interchangeably as a set of rules to which states adhere to intentionally or unintentionally and which defines their identity.

62. Elles, "Towards a New Transatlantic Relationship"; Duffield, "NATO's Functions after the Cold War"; Robert Blackwill, *The Future of Transatlantic Relations*; Deudney and Ikenberry, "The Logic of the West"; Nye, "The US and Europe"; McCalla, "NATO's Persistence After the Cold War"; Anthony Blinken, "The False Crisis over the Atlantic."

63. In this sense the ICC case shows cultural and identity variation.

64. Ted Hopf, "The Promise of Constructivism in International Relations Theory," *International Security*, vol. 23, no. 1 (Summer 1998), p. 172.

65. Ted Hopf, "The Promise of Constructivism in International Relations Theory," *International Security*, vol. 23, no. 1 (Summer 1998), p. 173.

66. Ted Hopf, "The Promise of Constructivism in International Relations Theory," *International Security*, vol. 23, no. 1 (Summer 1998), p. 173. See also Ronald L.

Jepperson, Alexander Wendt and Peter J. Katzenstein, "Norms, Identity and Culture in National Security," in Katzenstein, *The Culture of National Security*.

67. By "constitutive practices" I mean the practices or praxis that constitute the actor and determine the actor's politics as understood by constructivists. See Hopf, "The Promise of Constructivism in International Relations Theory," pp. 176ff. See also Katzenstein, *The Culture of National Security*.

68. The term "intersubjective" is used by Hopf, in "The Promise of Constructivism in International Relations Theory," pp. 173ff.

69. Ted Hopf, "The Promise of Constructivism in International Relations Theory," *International Security*, vol. 23, no. 1 (Summer 1998), pp. 175–176. Many constructivist works have shown how identities set policy preferences. Many of these works can be found in Katzenstein, *The Culture of National Security*. Some examples from Katzenstein are: Martha Finnemore, "Constructing Norms of Humanitarian Intervention," pp. 153–185; Robert Herman, "Identity, Norms and National Security: The Soviet Foreign Policy Revolution and the End of the Cold War," pp. 271–316; and Thomas Berger, "Norms, Identity, and National Security in Germany and Japan," pp. 317–356.

70. This term, of Greek origin, means *action*. In Marxist terminology, praxis refers both to the relationships between production and labor which constitute the social structure and to the transforming action that the revolution is supposed to exercise on those relationships. Marx and Engels argued that we need to explain the formation of ideas through the "material praxis." See Karl Marx and Friedrich Engels, *The German Ideology* (1845). In customary international law, the norms that regulate the behavior of *all* states are praxis-based. The term praxis refers to the behavior of states. States, by believing that their behavior is norm-based, repeat such behavior (praxis), and in so doing they establish new norms that are not written but are nonetheless believed to be legitimate and therefore to be obeyed by all. See Karol Wolfke, *Custom in Present International Law*, 2nd rev. ed. (Dordrecht: Martinus Nijhoff Publishers, 1994); and Benedetto Conforti, *Diritto Internazionale* (Napoli: Editoriale Scientifica, 1997). In international relations, Martha Finnemore seems to be the closest to this understanding of the meaning of praxis when she analyzes change in the normative context that shapes states' behavior. See Finnemore, "Constructing Norms of Humanitarian Intervention," pp. 153–185. In common parlance, praxis means practice as opposed to theory. My conceptualization of praxis follows in the footsteps of constructivist theorists such as Hopf, for whom "meaningful behavior, or action, is possible only within an intersubjective social context." As he further explains, "Actors develop their relations with, and understandings of, others through the media of norms and practices." See Hopf, "The Promise of Constructivism in International Relations Theory," pp. 173ff. In the present study, the term *praxis*, most simply defined, means reciprocal interaction of actors in the social context of world politics, and it is conceived as a causative force determining politics.

71. For an analysis of the distinction between action and behavior, see Charles Taylor, "Interpretation and the Sciences of Man," in *Interpretative Social Science: A*

Second Look, ed. Paul Rabinow and William M. Sullivan (Berkeley: University of California Press, 1987), pp. 33–81.

Chapter 2

1. The views expressed in this chapter are those of the author and do not necessarily reflect those of the Department of National Defence or the Government of Canada.

2. The leader of the Liberal Party, former Harvard University professor Michael Ignatieff, is on record as supporting Canada's mission in Afghanistan.

3. Doug Saunders, "Canada-EU trade proposal rivals scope of NAFTA," *Globe and Mail,* 18 September 2008, A6.

4. Stormy-Annika Mildner, "Junior partner Canada," *International Journal,* vol. 63, no. 3 (Summer 2008), 658.

5. Saunders, ibid.

6. The North Atlantic Treaty http://www.nato.int/docu/basictxt/treaty.htm, accessed 14 March 2009.

7. Foreign Affairs Canada, http://www.international.gc.ca/ministers-ministres/Cannon_Albania-Albanie_Croatia-Croatie.aspx?lang=eng, accessed 4 March 2009.

8. For a list of capability areas, see http://www.nato.int/issues/prague_capabilities_commitment/index.html, accessed 4 March 2009.

9. In 2007 Canada began taking delivery of four Boeing C-17 strategic transport aircraft, which will obviate the need to recommit to SALIS after 2012.

10. Kerry Longhurst, "The concept of strategic culture," in G. Kummel and A. Prufert, eds., *Military Sociology* (Baden-Baden: Nomos Verlagsgesellschaft, 2000), 301.

11. The International Commission on Intervention and State Sovereignty (ICISS) was established by Canada at the September 2000 UN Millennium Summit. Its controversial signature project, *The Responsibility to Protect,* specified that intervention could be diplomatic, economic, or legal rather than just military. ICISS, *The Responsibility to Protect* (Ottawa: International Development Research Centre, 2001), xi.

12. Eugene Lang, "Canadians fool themselves about modern peacekeeping," *The Toronto Star,* 14 January 2009, 12.

13. Longhurst, ibid.

14. *Canada's International Policy Statement: A Role of Pride and Influence in the World (Defence)* (Ottawa: Government of Canada, 2005), 24.

15. Ibid.

16. Ibid.

17. *Canada First Defence Strategy* (Ottawa: Government of Canada, 2008), 12. Both the CFDS and the IPS are available at www.forces.gc.ca, accessed 4 March 2009.

18. Ibid., 1.

19. Ibid., 9.

20. While serving as president of the Canadian Institute of Strategic Studies, the author noted that the IPS was almost crowded out of the media spotlight by the death of Pope John Paul II in April 2005.

21. D. W. Middlemiss and J. J. Sokolsky, *Canadian Defence: Decisions and Determinants* (Toronto: Harcourt Brace, 1989), 115.

22. Ibid., 116.

23. Angus Reid Strategies, "Canadians question Afghanistan mission, but Alberta bucks the trend," http://www.angusreidstrategies.com/polls-analysis/opinion-polls/canadians-question-afghanistan-mission-alberta-bucks-trend 4. According to the December 2008 poll, 67 per cent of Quebecers favoured a withdrawal before 2011, versus 53 per cent of Canadians overall.

24. Jean-Sébastien Rioux, *Two Solitudes: Quebecers' Attitudes Regarding Canadian Security and Defence Policy* (Calgary: Canadian Defence and Foreign Affairs Institute, 2005), 3.

25. Ibid., 22.

26. Middlemiss and Sokolsky, *Canadian Defence,* 117. The authors describe this as the result of "a latent anti-Americanism and moral rectitude in the Canadian body politic."

27. Joseph T. Jockel, *Canada and International Peacekeeping* (Toronto: Canadian Institute of Strategic Studies, 1994), 13.

28. Ibid. Jockel observes that, until the 1990s, were any Canadian government to turn down a UN request, "it would have had to brave substantial criticism at home."

29. "Comprehensive political guidance—endorsed by the heads of state and government," 29 November 2006, Riga, http://www.nato.int/docu/basictxt/b061129e.htm, accessed 14 March 2009.

30. See *International Policy Statement (Defence),* 5; and *Canada First Defence Strategy,* 6.

31. For a comprehensive list of capability acquisitions, see Alexander Moens, "Afghanistan and the revolution in Canadian foreign policy," *International Journal* vol. 63, no. 3 (Summer 2008), 572–573.

32. Walter Dorn and Michael Varey, "Fatally flawed: The rise and demise of the 'three block war' concept," *International Journal,* vol. 63, no. 4 (Autumn 2008), 977–978.

33. Canadian Coalition to End Global Poverty, "Canada's whole-of-government approach in Afghanistan: Implications on development and peacebuilding," November 2007. www.ccic.ca/e/docs/002_humanitarian_2007–12_ccic_submission.pdf, accessed 4 March 2009.

34. General Hillier responded to public angst over the ISAF mission saying that the Canadian Forces were not social workers in uniform.

35. The *Presidential Directive to Establish US Policy in the Arctic Region* also cites strategic concerns such as the need for missile defence and early warning, counter-terrorism, and projecting sea power through the region. See http://www.america.gov/st/texttrans-english/2009/January/20090112161521eaifas0.2872126.html&distid=ucs.

36. In 2006, Prime Minister Harper "surprised and annoyed" EU leaders by cancelling a planned summit for fear of being criticized for eschewing the Kyoto accord.

See S. Ganzle and S. Retzlaff, "So, the European Union is 50 . . . " *International Journal* vol. 63, no. 3 (Summer 2008), 633.

37. As the number one supplier of energy to the US, Canada has begun to express concerns that the Obama Administration may stop purchasing oil gleaned from the Alberta tar sands because the extraction process is energy-intensive and, according to some, environmentally unsound. See "A sticky end for the tar sands," *The Economist,* 17 January 2009, 40.

38. Petra Dalata-Kreutzkamp, "Energy security and climate change," *International Journal* vol. 63, no. 3 (Summer 2008), 677.

39. "The European Union and the Arctic Region" outlined three goals: environmental protection, responsible resource development, and enhanced multilateral governance. http://europa.eu/rapid/pressReleasesAction.do?reference=IP/08/1750&form at=HTML&aged=0&language=EN&guiLanguage=en.

40. See David Pugliese's *Defence Watch,* 25 January 2009. http://communities. canada.com/ottawacitizen/blogs/defencewatch/default.aspx?PageIndex=3, accessed 4 March 2009.

41. Members include Canada, Denmark (including Greenland and the Faroe Islands), Russia, Iceland, Norway, Finland, Sweden, and the United States. It has accorded "permanent participant" status to indigenous groups from each country. The EU announced in its 2008 communiqué that it would seek observer status.

42. Nevertheless, some analysts predict the gradual marginalization of NORAD as a result of (a) Canada's decision in 2005 to eschew participation in the US ballistic missile defence system, and (b) the establishment of US Northern Command (NORTHCOM) and its Canadian counterpart, Canada Command (CANCOM). These strategic-level entities will partner with civilian authorities to address what some consider the most likely threats to public safety—terrorism and natural or man-made disasters.

43. "Germany can do more," *Der Spiegel* (online), 26 March 2008. http://www. spiegel.de/international/world/0,1518,543480,00.html, accessed 4 March 2009.

44. "Realism in Afghanistan," *National Post,* 3 March 2009. http://www.nationalpost.com/news/world/afghanistan/story.html?id=1346367, accessed 4 March 2009.

45. See Thomas Walkom, "If we can't win, why stay in Afghanistan?" *Toronto Star,* 4 March 2009. http://www.thestar.com/comment/article/595966, accessed 4 March 2009.

46. See Rioux, *Two Solitudes,* 9–14, for an analysis of the public impact of local media versus that of nationally syndicated dailies.

47. Angus Reid Strategies, 8.

48. Derek Burney, "Where do we show resolve, if not Kandahar?" *The Globe and Mail,* 13 February 2008, http://www.theglobeandmail.com/servlet/story/RT-GAM.20080213.wwcoburney13/BNStory/Front/ accessed 4 March 2009. See also the report of *The Independent Panel on Canada's Future Role in Afghanistan,* http://dsp-psd.pwgsc.gc.ca/collection_2008/dfait-maeci/FR5–20–1–2008E.pdf, accessed 4 March 2009.

49. Douglas Bland, "The Afghan mission has taught our politicians a lesson," *The Globe and Mail*, 27 November 2008. http://www.theglobeandmail.com/servlet/story/ RTGAM.20081126.wcoafghan27/BNStory/International/, accessed 4 March 2009.

50. David Rudd, *Canada and the Post-Atlantic World*, Strategic Datalink, no. 127 (Toronto: Canadian International Council, 2005).

51. Oliver Moore, "Canadians have 'obligation' to step in," *The Globe and Mail*, 1 December 2008. http://www.theglobeandmail.com/servlet/story/LAC.20081201. POLL01/TPStory/?query=Douglas+Bland, accessed 4 March 2009.

52. http://www.defense-aerospace.com/article-view/release/101739/iiss-publishes-military-balance-2009.html, accessed 4 March 2009.

53. "A new alliance with Europe?" *National Review*, 8 April 2009. http://article. nationalreview.com/?q=M2U2ZGIwZmRhODc5OGU2OWNhYjc3NGI5NWYwNDY xZmQ=, accessed 4 March 2009.

54. Debra Black, "Ambassador lauds Canadian soldiers," *Toronto Star*, 25 November 2008. http://www.thestar.com/printArticle/542835 accessed 4 March 2009.

55. Sven Biscop, *Permanent Structured Cooperation and the Future of ESDP*, Egmont Paper, no. 20 (Gent: Academia Press, 2008). www.egmontinstitute.be/paperegm/ep20.pdf.

56. Randy Boswell, "NATO cautions against division over Arctic," *Ottawa Citizen*, 30 January 2009. http://www.ottawacitizen.com/news/NATO+cautions+agains t+division+over+Arctic/1233655/story.html, accessed 4 March 2009. Russia's ambassador to NATO, Dmitri Rogozin, strongly objected to any possible NATO role in the Arctic. See "There is nothing for NATO to do in the Arctic-Rogozin," *ITAR-TASS News Agency*, 28 March 2009.

57. For an examination of the arguments for/against a territorial versus expeditionary stance, see Timo Noetzel and Benjamin Schreer, "Does a multi-tier NATO matter?" *International Affairs*, vol. 85, no. 2 (2009), 211–226.

58. John Ibbitson, "As Obama bestrides the world stage, Canada has nothing to say," *The Globe and Mail*, 4 February 2009. http://www.theglobeandmail.com/servlet/story/LAC.20090204.COIBBI04/TPStory/?query=John+Ibbitson accessed 4 March 2009.

59. www.transatlantictrends.org/trends/doc/2008_English_Key.pdf, accessed 4 March 2009.

60. Paul Hockenos, "Is the EU better for Obama than NATO?" *Der Spiegel*, 9 March 2009. http://www.spiegel.de/international/europe/0,1518,612105,00.html, accessed 14 March 2009.

Chapter 3

1. See "COMISAF Initial Assessment (Unclassified)," http://www.washington-post.com/wp-dyn/content/article/2009/09/21/AR2009092100110_pf.html.

2. "Remarks by the President at the Veterans of Foreign Wars Convention," Au-

gust 17, 2009, http://www.whitehouse.gov/the_press_office/Remarks-by-the-President-at-the-Veterans-of-Foreign-Wars-convention/.

3. See "Agreement Between the United States of American and the Republic of Iraq on the Withdrawal of United States Forces from Iraq and the Organization of Their Activities During Their Temporary Presence in Iraq," http://www.mnf-iraq.com/images/CGs_Messages/security_agreement.pdf.

4. Alan Cullison and Matthew Rosenberg, "Taliban Attacks Kill U.S., Afghan Troops," *Wall Street Journal*, September 14, 2009, A9.

5. For example, a headline in the *Wall Street Journal* read: "U.S. Missile U-Turn Roils Allies," *Wall Street Journal*, September 18, 2009.

6. Philip H. Gordon, "The End of the Bush Revolution," *Foreign Affairs*, vol. 85, no. 4 (July–Aug. 2006), 84.

7. Zbigniew Brzezinski, "An Agenda for NATO," *Foreign Affairs*, vol. 88, no. 5 (Sept.–Oct. 2009), 14–15.

8. "Barack Obama's Inaugural Address," prepared text as provided by the Presidential Inaugural Committee, http://www.iht.com/bin/printfirendly.php?id=19532874, accessed January 20, 2009.

9. See Joseph S. Nye, Jr., *The Paradox of American Power: Why the World's Only Superpower Can't Go It Alone* (New York: Oxford University Press, 2002).

10. See, for example, Dana H. Allin, Gilles Andreani, Philippe Errerea and Gary Samore, "Repairing the Damage: Possibilities and Limits of Transatlantic Consensus," *Adelphi Paper*, no. 389 (Oxford: Routledge, 2007). Also see Robert Kagan, *Of Paradise and Power: America and Europe in the New World Order* (New York: Alfred A. Knopf, 2003).

11. "Obama's Speech in Berlin," July 24, 2008, http://www.nytimes.com/2008/07/24/us/politics/24text-obama.html?_r=1&adxnnl=1&pagewanted=print&adxnnlx=1253552671–MPe91L8yEYoHouyjEUs8rg. Emphasis added.

12. Richard Wilke, "Obamamania Abroad: The Candidate Can Expect a Warm Welcome in Europe, Not So In the Middle East," July 16, 2008, http://pewresearch.org/pubs/900/obama-trip-abroad.

13. The Pew Global Attitudes Project, "Confidence in Obama Lifts U.S. Image Around World," July 23, 2009, www.pewglobal.org.

14. Condoleezza Rice, "Promoting the National Interest," *Foreign Affairs*, vol. 79, no. 1 (Jan.–Feb. 2000), 45.

15. Ibid., 53.

16. Ibid., 54.

17. Ibid., 62.

18. "Statement by the North Atlantic Council," September 12, 2001, http://www.nato/int/docu/pr/2001/p01–124e.htm, accessed March 30, 2009.

19. Lord Robertson, "NATO After September 11," Speech to the Pilgrims of the United States, New York, January 31, 2002, http: nato.int/docu/speech/2002/s020131a.htm, accessed March 30, 2009.

20. A few months later, in April 2003, those three nations were joined by Lux-

embourg in a "mini-summit" to discuss European defense cooperation. According to Rebecca Moore, "the meeting was widely interpreted as an effort to construct a counterweight to the United States and, ultimately, to undermine NATO." Rebecca Moore, *NATO's New Mission: Projecting Stability in a Post-Cold War World* (Westport, CT: Praeger Security International, 2007), 97.

21. Ibid., 95.

22. Pew Global Attitudes Project, "Global Public Opinion in the Bush Years (2001–2008)," available at http://wglobal.org/reports/pdf/263/pdf.

23. "Transatlantic Trends 2006," available at http://foreignaffairs.house.gov/110/gle032207A.pdf, accessed December 23, 2008.

24. Ibid., 5.

25. Ibid., 4.

26. Pew Global Attitudes Project, "Global Public Opinion in the Bush Years (2001–2008), 1.

27. Sean Loughlin, "House Cafeterias Change Names for 'French' Fries and 'French' Toast," http://www.cnn.com/2003/ALLPOLITICS/03/11/sprj.irq.fries/.

28. Pew Global Attitudes Project, "America's Image Slips, But Allies Share Concerns over Iran, Hamas," available at http://pewglobal.org/reports/pdf/252.pdf.

29. Pew Global Attitudes Project, "Confidence in Obama Lifts U.S. Image Around World," 5.

30. "President Obama and the Obama Administration," http://www.pollingreport.com/obama_ad.htm.

31. Jennifer Agiesta and Jon Cohen, "Public Opinion in U.S. Turns Against Afghan War," http://www.washingtonpost.com/wp-dyn/content/article/2009/08/19/AR2009081903066.html.

32. Sixty-seven British citizens were killed in the attacks. Tom Leonard, "US Remember 9/11 as UK Response Is Muted," http://www.telegraph.co.uk/news/world-news/1562830/US-remembers-911-as-UK-response-is-muted.html.

33. Alan Cowell, "A Nation Challenged: Britain; Blair Declares the Airstrikes Are an Act of Self-Defense," *New York Times*, October 8, 2001, http://query.nytimes.com/gst/fullpage.html?res=9F00E2DF103CF93BA35753C1A9679C8B63&sec= . . .

34. Elaine Sciolini and Steven Lee Myers, "A Nation Challenged: Coalition; Bush Says 'Time Is Running Out': U.S. Plans to Act Largely Alone," *New York Times*, October 7, 2001, http://query.nytimes.com/gst/fullpage.html?res=9404E3DF133CF934A3575 3C1A9679C8B63&sec=. . . .

35. "ISAF History," www.nato.int/isaf/topics/history/index.html, accessed August 26, 2008.

36. Paul Gallis, "NATO in Afghanistan: A Test of the Transatlantic Alliance," CRS Report for Congress, May 6, 2008, order core RL 33627, 1.

37. "NATO in Afghanistan," www.nato.int/issues/Afghanistan/, accessed August 26, 2008.

38. Casualty numbers can be found at iCasualties.org/OEF/DeathsByYear.aspx,

accessed December 25, 2008. Also see "Mounting Casualties in Afghanistan Spur Concern," *Wall Street Journal*, July 13, 2009, A7.

39. Gallis, "NATO in Afghanistan," 5.

40. Ibid., 10.

41. Ibid., 17.

42. Gallis notes that in 2002, 62% of Canadians polled supported sending Canadian forces to Afghanistan which had dropped to 52% in April 2007. Presumably, with an increase in Canadian deaths in 2008, that number will have fallen still further. Ibid., 19.

43. Karen DeYoung, "Allies Feel Strain of Afghan War: Troop Levels Among Issues Dividing U.S., NATO Countries, *Washington Post*, January 15, 2008, A1.

44. See, for example, ibid. See also Cullison and Rosenberg, "Taliban Attacks Kill U.S., Afghan Troops," and "Mounting Casualties in Afghanistan Spur Concern."

45. DeYoung, "Allies Feel Strain of Afghan War," A1.

46. Ibid.

47. *Department of Defense National Defense Strategy*, 1, www.defenselink.mil/news/2008%20national%20defense%20strategy/pdf, issued June 2008, accessed December 24, 2008.

48. "Revitalizing National Defense: Making America More Secure by Transforming Our Military," www.whitehouse.gov/infocus/defense.

49. "Foreword," *Quadrennial Defense Review Report*, www.comw.org/qdr/gdr2001.pdf, issued September 30, 2001.

50. "Preface," *Quadrennial Defense Review Report*, www.defenselink.mil/qdr/report/Report20060203.pdf, issued, February 6, 2006, v, accessed December 24, 2008.

51. Ibid., ix.

52. See "The National Security Strategy of the United States of America," www.whitehouse.gov/nsc.nss/2006/nss2006.pdf, issued March 2006, accessed December 24, 2008.

53. "Foreword," *Department of Defense National Defense Strategy*.

54. It is instructive to note that this particular section of "The National Security Strategy of the United States of America" is found under the broader heading of "Develop Agendas for Cooperative Action with the Other Main Centers of Global Power," which is number 4, following "The Western Hemisphere, Africa and the Middle East."

55. "The National Security Strategy of the United States of America," 38.

56. *Department of Defense National Defense Strategy*, 15.

57. Marc Champion and Peter Spiegel, "U.S. Missile U-Turn Roils Allies," *Wall Street Journal*, September 18, 2009.

58. Ibid.

59. Philip H. Gordon, *Winning the Right War: The Path to Security for America and the World* (New York: Times Books, 2007), 96.

60. Steven Lee Myers, "Question of Bush's Legacy Lingers over His Farewell Visits to European Capitals," *New York Times*, June 14, 2008, A8.

61. Quoted in ibid.

62. Quoted in ibid.

63. Gordon, *Winning the Right War*, 97.

64. Ibid.

65. "Transatlantic Trends 2006," 3.

66. Barack Obama, "Renewing American Leadership," *Foreign Affairs* (July–Aug. 2007), 5, http://foreignaffairs.org/20070701faessay86401/barack-obama/renewing-american-leadership.html., accessed December 23, 2008.

67. "Full Script of Obama's Speech," July 24, 2008, Berlin, Germany, http://edition.cnn.com/2008/POLITICS/07/24.obama.words/ accessed August 1, 2008.

68. Ibid.

69. Gerald F. Seib, "Capital Journal: U.S. Woes Open Door for China," *Wall Street Journal*, December 23, 2008, A2.

70. Just prior to the summit, Doyle McManus, writing in the *Los Angeles Times*, noted the differences between the United States and many of the European countries as to the best way to address the economic crisis. Furthermore, he also noted that there are divisions among the European countries, as well as within the United States, as the president has to contend with a Congress and domestic public that have raised questions about the stimulus package. See Doyle McManus, "It'll Be Uphill at the Summit," *Los Angeles Times*, March 29, 2009, A31.

Chapter 4

1. The analysis, opinions and conclusions expressed or implied in this paper are those of the author and do not necessarily represent the views of the Joint Services Command & Staff College, the United Kingdom's Ministry of Defence or any other government agency.

2. See Winston Churchill, *A History of the English-Speaking Peoples*, 4 vols, (London: Cassell, 1956–8); Andrew Roberts, *A History of the English-Speaking Peoples Since 1900*, (London: Phoenix Paperback, 2007).

3. See Paul Kennedy, *Rise and Fall of the Great Powers: Economic Change and Military Conflict from 1500 to 2000*, (London: Fontana Books, 1989).

4. Michael Portillo, 'We're not top dog . . . but we don't have to be a poodle', *Sunday Times*, 3 December 2006, p. 19.

5. Tony Blair, 'Britain's role in Europe', *Speech to the European Research Institute*, Birmingham, UK, 23 November 2001.

6. See John Dumbrell, *A Special Relationship: Anglo-American relations from the Cold War to Iraq*, (Basingstoke: Palgrave Macmillan, 2006); John Baylis, *Anglo-American Defence Relations, 1939–84*, 2nd ed, (London: Macmillan Press Ltd, 1984); Andrew Gamble, *Between Europe and America: the Future of British Politics*, (Basingstoke: Palgrave Macmillan, 2006); Ritchie Ovendale, *Anglo-American Relations in the Twentieth Century*, (Basingstoke: Macmillan Press Ltd, 1998); Geoffrey Lee Williams and Barkley Jared Jones, *NATO and the Transatlantic Alliance in the Twenty-first Century: The Twenty Year Crisis*, (Basingstoke: Palgrave, 2001).

7. John Dumbrell, 'The US-UK special relationship: Taking the 21st century temperature', *British Journal of Politics and International Relations*, vol. 11, no. 1, February 2009, pp. 64–78, quote is from p. 65.

8. See Andrew Dorman, Joyce P Kaufman, and Craig Stone, 'Australia, Britain, Canada, the US and the ABCA relationship', in *Handbook of Defence Politics: International and Comparative Perspectives*, ed. Isaiah Wilson III and James J F Forest, (London: Routledge, 2008).

9. See http://www.abca-armies.org/Default.aspx?AspxAutoDetectCookieSupport=1, accessed 30 March 2009.

10. Sam Coates, David Robertson and David Charter, 'More strikes loom in foreign workers row', *The Times*, 2 February 2009, p. 3.

11. See Michael Howard, *The Continental Commitment: The Dilemma of British Defence Policy in the Era of Two World Wars*, (London: Temple Smith, 1972); Basil Liddell Hart, *The British Way in Warfare*, (London: Penguin, 1942); C J Bartlett, *Defence and Diplomacy: Britain and the Great Powers, 1815–1914*, (Manchester: Manchester University Press, 1993); Michael Heehan, *The Balance of Power: History and Theory*, (London: Routledge, 1996); Richard Little, *The Balance of Power in International Relations: Metaphors, Myths and Models*, (Cambridge: Cambridge University Press, 2007).

12. See William Park, *Defending the West: A History of NATO*, (Brighton: Wheatsheaf Books Ltd, 1986); Andrew Dorman and Adrian Treacher, *European Security: An Introduction to Security Issues in post-Cold War Europe*, (Aldershot: Dartmouth Publishing Co. Ltd, 1995).

13. Michael Portillo, 'We're not top dog . . . but we don't have to be a poodle', *Sunday Times*, 3 December 2006, p. 19.

14. 'US/UK relations still special', *Sky News Online*, 3 February 2009, http://uk.news.yahoo.com/5/20090203/twl-us-uk-relations-still-special-3fd0ae9.html, accessed 3 February 2009.

15. Hillary Rodham Clinton, 'Issues facing the United Kingdom, the United States and the world: Remarks with British Foreign Secretary David Miliband after their meeting', 3 February, http://www.state.gov/secretary/rm/2009a/02/115902.htm, accessed 5 February 2009.

16. Richard Beeston, 'Race against time for Brown', *The Times*, 6 February 2009, p.4.

17. Andrew Sparrow et al., 'Special relationship as strong as ever, Obama tells Brown', *The Guardian Online*, 3 March 2009, http://www.guardian.co.uk/politics/2009/mar/03/obama-brown-special-relationship, accessed 30 March 2009.

18. Anthony Seldon, *Major: A Political Life*, (London: Weidenfeld & Nicolson, 1997), p. 353.

19. Alastair Campbell, *The Blair Years: Extracts from the Alastair Campbell Diaries*, (London: Random House Group Ltd, 2007), p. 485.

20. Glenn Kessler, 'Blair and Bush are duo even in descent', *Washington Post*, 26 May 2006, http://www.washingtonpost.com/wp-dyn/content/article/2006/05/25/AR2006052501918.html, accessed 6 February 2009.

21. Michael Portillo, 'We're not top dog . . . but we don't have to be a poodle', *Sunday Times*, 3 December 2006, p. 19.

22. 'Does Brown pose a risk to the 'special relationship'?', *Daily Telegraph*, 14 July 2007, http://www.telegraph.co.uk/news/main.jhtml?view=BLOGDETAIL&grid=F 11&blog=yourview&xml=/news/2007/07/14/view14.xml; George Bush and Gordon Brown, Press Conference, Camp David, 30 July 2007, http://www.number10.gov.uk/output/Page12765.asp.

23. Jonathan Freedland, 'More bulldog than poodle, Brown has signalled a new special relationship', *The Guardian Unlimited*, 1 August 2007, http://www.guardian.co.uk/commentisfree/story/0,,2138973,00.html.

24. 'Mr Brown goes to Washington: Britain's standing has declined in America. The Prime Minister must reverse this', *The Times*, 17 April 2008, p. 16; Simon Jenkins, 'All quiet on the leadership front as our troops die in faraway lands', *Sunday Times*, 7 October 2007, p. 16.

25. Greg Hurst, 'Brown attempts to mend fences with Bush and vows US is most important ally', *The Times*, 12 November 2007, p. 2.

26. 'US commander thanks UK for contribution to Iraq and Afghanistan', *MOD Press Release*, 6 February 2009, http://www.mod.uk/DefenceInternet/DefenceNews/DefencePolicyAndBusiness/UsCommanderThanksUkForContributionToIraqAndAfghanistan.htm, accessed 7 February 2009.

27. See Peter R Mansoor, 'The British Army and the Lessons of the Iraq War', *British Army Review*, no. 147, Summer 2009, pp. 11–15; Daniel Marston, '"Smug and Complacent?" Operation Telic: The Need for Critical Analysis', *British Army Review*, no. 147, Summer 2009, pp. 16–23; Anthony King, 'Beyond the crisis: Critical requirements for successful military transformation', *British Army Review*, no. 147, Summer 2009, pp. 24–28.

28. Daniel Finkelstein, 'If this is a triumph, I'd hate to see a disaster', *Times Online*, 15 October 2008, http://www.timesonline.co.uk/tol/comment/columnists/daniel_finkelstein/article4944288.ece, accessed 30 March 2009.

29. Jonathan Oliver et al., 'Brown gambles on spin at summit', *Sunday Times*, 29 March 2009, pp. 12–13.

30. 'Muslim protest at Luton Army parade was 'upsetting', says senior officer', *Daily Telegraph Online*, 11 March 2009, http://www.telegraph.co.uk/news/newstopics/politics/defence/4972211/Muslim-protest-at-Luton-Army-parade-was-upsetting-says-senior-officer.html, accessed 30 March 2009.

31. Michael Portillo, 'We're not top dog . . . but we don't have to be a poodle', *Sunday Times*, 3 December 2006, p. 19.

32. John Dumbrell, *A Special Relationship: Anglo-American Relations from the Cold War to Iraq*, (Basingstoke: Palgrave Macmillan, 2006), p. 168; see also Walter Russell Mead, *God and Gold: Britain, America and the Making of the Modern World*, (London: Atlantic Books, 2007); Alex Danchev, *On Specialness: Essays in Anglo-American Relations*, (London: Macmillan Press Ltd, 1988); John Dickie, *'Special' No More: An-*

glo-American Relations: Rhetoric and Reality, (London: Weidenfeld & Nicolson, 1994); David Dimbleby and David Reynolds, *An Ocean Apart*, (London: BBC Books, 1988)

33. J. T. Richelson and D Ball, *The Ties that Bind: Intelligence Cooperation between the UKUSA Countries*, (London: Unwin Hyman, 1990), p. 301, quoted in John Dumbrell, *A Special Relationship: Anglo-American Relations from the Cold War to Iraq*, (Basingstoke: Palgrave Macmillan, 2006), p.169.

34. Christopher Meyer, *DC Confidential*, (London: Weidenfeld & Nicolson, 2005), p. 188.

35. See *Butler Report*, http://www.archive2.official-documents.co.uk/document/deps/hc/hc898/898.pdf accessed 30 march 2009.

36. Richard Ford and Francis Elliott, 'US threatens to stop sharing intelligence if 'torture' of British detainee is revealed', *The Times*, 5 February 2009, p. 5.

37. See John Simpson, *The Independent Nuclear State: The United States, Britain and the Military Atom*, 2nd ed, (London: Macmillan Press Ltd, 1986).

38. See Richard Moore, 'British nuclear warhead design 1958–66: How much American help?', *Defence Studies*, vol. 4, no. 2, Summer 2004, pp. 207–28.

39. See 'RUSI interview with General David Richards', *The RUSI Journal*, vol. 152, no. 2, April 2007, pp. 24–32, p. 24.

40. Brigadier Nigel Aylwin-Foster, 'Changing the Army for Counterinsurgency Operations', *Military Review*, November-December 2005, pp. 2–15.

41. See Warren Chin, 'Why did it all go wrong? Reassessing British counterinsurgency in Iraq', *Strategic Studies Quarterly*, vol. 2, no. 4, Winter 2008, pp. 119–37.

42. Paul Cornish, 'The US and Counterinsurgency', *International Affairs*, vol. 85, no. 1, January 2009, pp. 61–79; Thomas E Ricks, *The Gamble: General Petraeus and the Untold Story of the American Surge in Iraq, 2006–8*, (London: Allen Lane, 2009); Peter R Mansoor, *Baghdad at Sunrise: A Brigade Commander's War in Iraq*, (New Haven, CT: Yale University Press, 2008).

43. Warren Chin, 'Why did it all go wrong? Reassessing British counterinsurgency in Iraq', *Strategic Studies Quarterly*, vol. 2, no. 4, Winter 2008, pp. 119–37; Peter R. Mansoor, 'The British army and the lessons of the Iraq war', *British Army Review*, no. 147, Summer 2009, pp. 11–15; Daniel Marston, '"Smug and complacent?" Operation Telic: The need for critical analysis', *British Army Review*, no. 147, Summer 2009, pp. 16–23; Anthony King, 'Beyond the crisis: Critical requirements for successful military transformation', *British Army Review*, no. 147, Summer 2009, pp. 24–28.

44. Simon Jenkins, 'All quiet on the leadership front as our troops die in faraway lands', *Sunday Times*, 7 October 2007, p. 16.

45. See Paul Cornish and Andrew Dorman, 'Blair's wars and Brown's budgets: From Strategic Defence Review to strategic delay in less than a decade', *International Affairs*, vol. 85, no. 2, March 2009, pp. 247–61.

46. See *BAE Systems Annual Accounts 2007*, p. 100, available at http://production.investis.com/annualreport07/siteware/pdf/segmental_analysis.pdf accessed 31 March 2009.

47. Alan Sharman, 'Sealing the 'special relationship',' *Jane's Defence Weekly*, 28 September 2005, p. 29.

48. Lord Drayson, Minutes of evidence, 19 December 2006, House of Commons Defence Committee, 'Sixth report: The defence industrial strategy: Update', *HC. 177*, session 2006–7, (London: TSO, 2007), pp. evidence 15–16, http://www.publications. parliament.uk/pa/cm200607/cmselect/cmdfence/177/177.pdf, accessed 9 February 2009.

49. 'Papers dominated by Northern Rock', *BBC Online*, 18 February 2008, http:// news.bbc.co.uk/1/hi/uk/7250053.stm, accessed 9 February 2009.

50. Daniel Finkelstein, 'If this is a triumph, I'd hate to see a disaster', *Times On-line*, 15 October 2008, http://www.timesonline.co.uk/tol/comment/columnists/daniel_finkelstein/article4944288.ece, accessed 30 March 2009.

51. See John Baylis, *Anglo-American Defence Relations 1939–84: The Special Relationship*, (London: Macmillan Press Ltd, 2d ed 1984; 1st ed 1981); Tim Dunne, "When the shooting starts': Atlanticism in British security strategy', *International Affairs*, vol. 80, no. 5, October 2004, pp. 893–909.

52. S J Croft and P Williams, 'The United Kingdom', in *Security Without Nuclear Weapons? Different Perspectives on National Security*, ed Regina Cowen Karp, (Oxford: Oxford University Press, 1991), p. 147; see also Michael Dockrill, *British Defence Policy since 1945*, (Oxford: Basil Blackwell Ltd, 1988); William Jackson, *Britain's Defence Dilemma: An Inside View*, (London: B T Batsford Ltd, 1990); John Baylis (ed), *Britain's Defence Policy in a Changing World*, (London: Croom Helm Ltd, 1977); Ritchie Ovendale, *British Defence Policy since 1945*, (Manchester: Manchester University Press, 1994); Stuart Croft (ed), *British Security Policy: The Thatcher Years and the End of the Cold War*, (London: Harper Collins Academic, 1991); Peter Byrd (ed), *British Defence Policy: Thatcher and Beyond*, (Hemel Hempstead: Philip Allen, 1991); Malcolm McIntosh, *Managing Britain's Defence*, (London: Macmillan Academic & Professional Ltd, 1990).

53. See Paul Cornish, *British Military Planning for the Defence of Germany, 1945–50*, (Basingstoke: Macmillan Press Ltd, 1996); Christoph Bluth, *Britain, Germany and Western Nuclear Strategy*, (Oxford: Oxford University Press, 1995), pp. 10–30; 'Statement relating to defence, 1948,' *Cm 7,327*, (London: HMSO, 1948), reprinted in *Brassey's Naval Annual*, ed Rear Admiral H. G. Thursfield, (London: William Clowes & Sons Ltd, 1948).

54. John Baylis, 'British nuclear doctrine: The 'Moscow criteria' and the Polaris Improvement Programme' *Contemporary British History*, vol. 19, no. 1, Spring 2005, pp. 53–65; Andrew Dorman, *Defence under Thatcher*, (Basingstoke: Palgrave Macmillan, 2002), p. 44.

55. 'Statement relating to defence, 1948,' *Cm 7,327*, (London: HMSO, 1948), reprinted in *Brassey's Naval Annual*, ed Rear Admiral H. G. Thursfield, (London: William Clowes & Sons Ltd, 1948), p. 528.

56. 'The future of the United Kingdom's nuclear deterrent', *Cm.6,994*, (London:

TSO, 2006), http://www.mod.uk/NR/rdonlyres/AC00DD79–76D6–4FE3–91A1–6A56B03C092F/0/DefenceWhitePaper2006_Cm6994.pdf, accessed 9 November 2009.

57. See Sir Lawrence Freedman, *The Official History of the Falklands Campaign*, 2 vols, (London: Routledge 2005) (vol 1: *Origins*, vol 2: *War and Diplomacy*).

58. John Kampfner, *Blair's Wars*, (London: Free Press, 2003).

59. Geoffrey Wheatcroft, *Yo, Blair!* (London: Politico's Publishing, 2007), p. 55.

60. See Tony Blair, 'Doctrine of the international community', speech given at Chicago, IL, 24 April 1999, http://www.pbs.org/newshour/bb/international/jan-june99/blair_doctrine4–23.html, accessed 18 November 2008.

61. 'British troops start work in East Timor', *BBC Online*, 20 September 1999, http://news.bbc.co.uk/1/hi/uk/452208.stm, accessed 15 March 2008.

62. Tony Blair, 'Our nation's future', speech made at Plymouth, 12 January 2007, http://www.number10.gov.uk/output/Page10735.asp, accessed 5 December 2007.

63. 'SDR: A new chapter', (London: TSO, 2002), http://www.mod.uk/NR/rdonlyres/79542E9C-1104–4AFA-9A4D-8520F35C5C93/0/sdr_a_new_chapter_cm5566_vol1.pdf and http://www.mod.uk/NR/rdonlyres/DD89DBE6–CEAA-4995–9E01–52EF6D19FC73/0/sdr_a_new_chapter_cm5566_vol2.pdf accessed 22 March 2008.

64. http://interactive.cabinetoffice.gov.uk/documents/security/national_security_strategy.pdf, accessed 21 March 2008.

65. Ann M Fitz-Gerald, 'A UK national security strategy: institutional and cultural challenges', *Defence Studies*, vol. 8, no. 1, March 2008, pp. 4–25, p. 4.

66. http://www.number10.gov.uk/output/Page15102.asp, accessed 21 March 2008.

67. Nigel Morris, 'Brown publishes first national security strategy', *The Independent Online*, 20 March 2008, http://www.independent.co.uk/news/uk/politics/brown-publishes-first-national-security-strategy-798385.html, accessed 22 March 2008.

68. 'The national security strategy of the United Kingdom: update 2009—security for the next generation', *Cm.7,590*, (London: The Stationery Office, 2009), http://www.cabinetoffice.gov.uk/media/216734/nss2009v2.pdf, accessed 9 November 2009.

69. See Andrew Dorman, 'Western Europe and Military Intervention', in *Military Intervention: From Gunboat Diplomacy to Humanitarian Intervention*, ed Andrew M Dorman and Thomas G Otte, (Aldershot: Dartmouth Publishing Ltd, 1995), p. 114.

70. 'Strategic defence review', *Cm.3,999*, (London: The Stationery Office, 1998), p.24, http://www.mod.uk/issues/sdr/index.htm, accessed 6 February 2009.

71. 'Final communique of the Defence Planning Committee and Nuclear Planning Group', Brussels, 27 May 1992, http://www.nato.int/docu/comm/49–95/c920527a.htm, accessed 9 February 2009.

72. See Paul Cornish and Andrew Dorman, 'Blair's wars and Brown's budgets: From strategic defence review to strategic decay in less than a decade', *International Affairs*, vol. 85, no. 2, March 2009, pp. 247–61.

73. See Tom King, *House of Commons Parliamentary Debates*, Statement on Defence (Options for Change), 25 July 1990, session 1989–90, vol. 195, cols. 468–71, www.publications.parliament.uk/pa/98990/cmhansard/1990–05–25/Debate-1.html, ac-

cessed 9 November 2008; 'Front line first: the defence costs study', (London: HMSO, 1994).

74. Ministry of Defence, 'Defending our future: Statement on the defence estimates, 1993', *Cm.2,270,* (London: HMSO, 1993), p.7.

75. 'Strategic Defence Review', *Cm.3,999,* (London: The Stationery Office, 1998), p.24, http://www.mod.uk/issues/sdr/index.htm.

76. See http://www.iwar.org.uk/rma/resources/uk-mod/nec.htm, accessed 8 November 2008.

77. 'Delivering security in a changing world: the Defence White Paper', *Cm.6,041–I,* (London: TSO, 2003), http://www.mod.uk/DefenceInternet/AboutDefence/CorporatePublications/PolicyStrategy/DeliveringSecurityInAChangingWorldDefenceWhitePaper2003.htm; 'Delivering security in a Changing World: Future Capabilities', *Cm.6,269,* (London: TSO, 2004), http://www.mod.uk/DefenceInternet/AboutDefence/CorporatePublications/PolicyStrategy/DeliveringSecurityInAChangingWorldFutureCapabilitiescm6269.htm, both accessed 8 November 2008.

78. 'EU battlegroups', EU Council Secretariat Factsheet, E BG01, 2005, http://consilium.europa.eu/uedocs/cmsUpload/BattlegroupsNov05factsheet.pdf., accessed 8 November 2008.

79. Bob Ainsworth, *House of Commons Parliamentary Debates,* 'Defence strategic planning', Ministerial statement 7 July 2009, col. 39WS, http://www.publications.parliament.uk/pa/cm200809/cmhansrd/cm090707/wmstext/90707m0001.htm#09070745000010, accessed 9 November 2009.

80. For a current list of UK service deaths in both campaigns, see MOD website at www.mod.uk, accessed 9 February 2009.

Chapter 5

1. Adrian Treacher, *French Interventionism: Europe's Last Global Player?,* (Aldershot: Ashgate, 2003), p. 31.

2. John Gaffney, 'Highly emotional states: French-US relations and the Iraq war', *European Security,* vol. 13, no. 3, part 1, Autumn 2004, p. 267.

3. Adrian Treacher, *French Interventionism: Europe's Last Global Player?,* (Aldershot: Ashgate, 2003), chapter 2.

4. Philip H. Gordon, *A Certain Idea of France: French Security Policy and the Gaullist Legacy,* (Princeton: Princeton University Press, 1993), p. 6.

5. General Charles de Gaulle, speech at Montreal, 24 July 1967.

6. Adrian Treacher, *French Interventionism: Europe's Last Global Player?,* (Aldershot: Ashgate, 2003), p. 59.

7. Pierre Lellouche, 'Guidelines for a European Defence Concept', in J Alford & K Hunt (eds), *Europe in the Western Alliance,* (London: MacMillan, 1998).

8. Adrian Treacher, *French Interventionism: Europe's Last Global Player?,* (Aldershot: Ashgate, 2003), p. 38.

9. Shaun Gregory, *French Defence Policy into the Twenty-first Century*, (Basingstoke: MacMillan, 2000), p. 8.

10. Patrick McCarthy, 'Condemned to partnership: The Franco-German relationship 1944–1983', in *France-Germany, 1983–1993: The Struggle to Cooperate*, (New York: St Martin's Press, 1993), p. 2.

11. Julius W. Friend, *Seven Years in France: François Mitterrand and the Unintended Revolution 1981–1988*, (Boulder, CO: Westview Press, 1989), p. 199.

12. Adrian Treacher, *French Interventionism: Europe's Last Global Player?*, ibid. (Aldershot: Ashgate, 2003), p. 34.

13. Adrian Treacher, *French Interventionism: Europe's Last Global Player?*, (Aldershot: Ashgate, 2003), p. 38.

14. Adrian Treacher, *French Interventionism: Europe's Last Global Player?*, (Aldershot: Ashgate, 2003), p. 88.

15. Jolyon Howorth, 'Britain, France and the European Defence Initiative', *Survival*, vol. 42, no. 2, Summer 2000, pp. 33–55, p. 37.

16. John Gaffney, 'Highly emotional states: French-US relations and the Iraq war', *European Security*, vol. 13, no. 3, part 1, Autumn 2004, p. 269.

17. Charles de Gaulle, quoted in Alain Duhamel, 'Le monarque républicain', *Le Point*, 22 April 1995.

18. Adrian Treacher, *French Interventionism: Europe's Last Global Player?*, (Aldershot: Ashgate, 2003), p. 15.

19. François Mitterrand, in a speech to the National Assembly, 3 December 1981.

20. For a more in-depth analysis of the domestic political structures and their contribution to French foreign and security policymaking see Adrian Treacher, *French Interventionism: Europe's Last Global Player?*, (Aldershot: Ashgate, 2003), pp. 14–19.

21. Barbara Balaj, 'France and the Gulf War', *Mediterranean Quarterly*, vol. 4, no. 3, Summer 1993, p. 110.

22. Pierre Hassner, quoted in Anand Menon, 'Continuing politics by other means: defence policy under the French Fifth Republic', *West European Politics*, vol. 17, no. 4, October 1994, p. 77.

23. For a broader investigation of the factors promoting the absence of domestic challenges to the *grandes lignes* see Adrian Treacher, *French Interventionism: Europe's Last Global Player?*, (Aldershot: Ashgate, 2003), pp. 19–21.

24. John Gaffney, 'Highly emotional states: French-US relations and the Iraq war', *European Security*, vol.13, no.3, part 1, Autumn 2004, p. 266.

25. Adrian Treacher, *French Interventionism: Europe's Last Global Player?*, (Aldershot: Ashgate, 2003), p. 103.

26. Lawrence Freedman, *The Evolution of Nuclear Strategy*, (Basingstoke: MacMillan/IISS, 1989), p. 313.

27. Philip H. Gordon, 'Charles de Gaulle and the nuclear revolution', *Security Studies*, vol. 5, no. 1, Autumn 1995, p. 147.

28. Shaun Gregory, *French Defence Policy into the Twenty-First Century*, (Basingstoke: MacMillan, 2000), p. 11.

29. Adrian Treacher, *French Interventionism: Europe's Last Global Player?*, (Aldershot: Ashgate, 2003), p. 104.

30. Shaun Gregory, *French Defence Policy into the Twenty-First Century*, (Basingstoke: MacMillan, 2000), p. 107.

31. 'France's changing view of the world', *The Economist*, 10 February 1996, p. 29.

32. Jean Guisnel, '"L'exception militaire" française', in *L'Etat de la France 1994–5*, (Paris: Editions de la Découverte, 1994), p. 588.

33. Diego A. Ruiz-Palmer, *French Strategic Options in the 1990s, Adelphi Paper 260*, (Brasseys/IISS, Summer 1991), p. 40.

34. Adrian Treacher, 'A Case of Reinvention: France and Military Intervention in the 1990s', *International Peacekeeping*, vol. 7, no. 2, p. 26.

35. Adrian Treacher, *French Interventionism: Europe's Last Global Player?*, (Aldershot: Ashgate, 2003), p. 64.

36. Alistair Cole, *French Politics and Society*, (Hemel Hempstead: Prentice Hall, 1998).

37. Jonathan Eyal, 'France freezes as Europe melts', *The Independent*, 3 December 1994.

38. J. Becker, 'Asserting EU cohesion: Common foreign and security policy and the relaunch of Europe', *European Security*, vol. 7, no. 4, 1998, p. 23.

39. J. Petras and M. Morley, 'Contesting hegemons: US-French relations in the "New World Order"', *Review of International Studies*, vol. 26, no. 1, 2000, p. 55.

40. Jacques Baumel, 'La France et l'OTAN', *Relations Internationales et Stratégiques*, no. 7, 1992.

41. John Gaffney, 'Highly emotional states: French-US relations and the Iraq war', *European Security*, vol.13, no.3, part 1, Autumn 2004, p. 266.

42. Shaun Gregory, *French Defence Policy into the Twenty-First Century*, (Basingstoke: MacMillan, 2000, p. 69.

43. Jean Qautremeyer, Editorial, *Libération*, 17 January 1996.

44. Adrian Treacher, 'Europe as a power multiplier for French security policy: Strategic consistency, tactical adaptation', *European Security*, vol. 10, no. 1, 2001, p. 36.

45. Jolyon Howorth, 'Britain, France and the European Defence Initiative', *Survival*, vol. 42, no. 2, Summer 2000, pp. 33–55, p. 36.

46. R. Graham, 'Defence pledge on European capability', *The Financial Times*, 31 May 1999.

47. Jolyon Howorth, 'Britain, France and the European Defence Initiative', *Survival*, vol. 42, no. 2, summer 2000, pp. 33–55, p. 33.

48. Madeleine K. Albright, 'The right balance will secure NATO's future', *Financial Times*, 7 December 1998.

49. Tom Lansford, 'Whither Lafayette? French military policy and the American campaign in Afghanistan', *European Security*, vol. 11, no. 3, 2002, p. 126.

50. Tom Lansford, 'Whither Lafayette? French military policy and the American campaign in Afghanistan', *European Security*, vol. 11, no. 3, 2002, pp. 133–4.

51. John Vinocur, 'Europe's leading nations use Afghan conflict to enhance world role', *International Herald Tribune*, 12 October 2001.

52. Tom Lansford, 'Whither Lafayette? French military policy and the American campaign in Afghanistan', *European Security*, vol. 11, no. 3, 2002, p. 134.

53. Tom Lansford, 'Whither Lafayette? French military policy and the American campaign in Afghanistan', *European Security*, vol. 11, no. 3, 2002, pp. 136–7.

54. Jacques Chirac, television interview to TF1 and France 2, 10 March 2003.

55. François Heisbourg, quoted in 'Europe, the US and Iraq: Where do the main European powers stand on the question of war?', *EuropeanSecurity.net*, January 2003.

56. Jacques Chirac, television interview to TF1 and France 2, 10 March 2003.

57. Thierry de Montbrial, 'Au-delà de l'affrontement', *Le Monde*, 20 March 2003.

58. Dominique de Villepin, interview given to *Newsnight*, 14 March 2003.

59. Elizabeth Pond, *Friendly Fire: the Near-Death of the Transatlantic Alliance*, (Pittsburgh: Brookings/EUSA, 2004), pp. 66–8.

60. John Gaffney, 'Highly emotional states: French-US relations and the Iraq war', *European Security*, vol. 13, no. 3, part 1, Autumn 2004, pp. 250–1.

61. John Gaffney, 'Highly emotional states: French-US relations and the Iraq war', *European Security*, vol. 13, no. 3, part 1, Autumn 2004, p. 247.

62. *The Economist*, 22 February 2003.

63. Dennis MacShane, 'Britain must not walk away from the new Europe', *The Observer*, 13 April 2003.

64. Dominique de Villepin, interview given to *Newsnight*, 14 March 2003.

65. Frédéric Bozo, 'Conseil de sécurité dans la doute', *Le Figaro*, 28 February 2003.

66. Jacques Chirac, press conference, Brussels, 21 March 2003.

67. Dominique de Villepin, speech at the International Institute for Strategic Studies, London, 27 March 2003.

68. Elizabeth Pond, *Friendly Fire: The Near-Death of the Transatlantic Alliance*, (Pittsburgh, PA: Brookings/EUSA), 2004, p. 40.

69. F. Keane, 'Hold fire on setting up this European military force: "This new force could undermine the drive for a more human rights friendly world"', *The Independent*, 9 December 2000.

70. Anand Menon, 'Why proposals for an autonomous European defence are a costly mistake', *Cicero Foundation Conference*, 15 December 2000.

71. 'Coalitions from Kabul to Baghdad', *EuropeSecurity.net*, February 2003.

72. Guillaume Parmentier, 'A fresh bridge is needed across the Atlantic', *The Financial Times*, 26 March 2003.

73. Mark Webber, Terry Terriff, Jolyon Howorth and Stuart Croft, 'The common European Security and Defence Policy and the "third country" issue', *European Security*, vol. 11, no. 2, 2002, p. 83.

74. Alain Joxe, 'La guerre de l'Irak freinée pour incohérence', *Le Débat Stratégique*, no. 66, 2003.

75. Leo Michel, 'Euro-Atlantic security relations and US-French cooperation', *Avenir de la Rélation Franco-Américaine*, Groupe Stratégique Franco-Américain,

Projet John Hopkins University—Fondation Robert Schuman, January 2009, p.5. Accessed at www.robert-schuman.eu.

76. Leo Michel, 'Euro-Atlantic security relations and US-French cooperation', in *Avenir de la Rélation Franco-Américaine*, Groupe Stratégique Franco-Américain, Projet John Hopkins University—Fondation Robert Schuman, January 2009, p. 14. Accessed at www.robert-schuman.eu.

77. Bruno Tertrais, 'Les défis stratégiques, 2009–2012', *Avenir de la Rélation Franco-Américaine*, Groupe Stratégique Franco-Américain, Projet John Hopkins University—Fondation Robert Schuman, January 2009, p. 21. Accessed at www.robert-schuman.eu.

78. Frédéric Bozo, 'France and NATO under Sarkozy: end of the French exception?', *Fondation pour l'Innovation Politique Working Paper*, March 2008, p. 4. Bozo stresses on p. 6 that 2004 saw some 100 French officers inserted into NATO's integrated commands in Mons and Norfolk.

Chapter 6

1. The views expressed in this chapter are strictly those of the author and do not reflect the views of any governmental affiliation or institution. Thanks are due to the US Naval Academy Research Council for its support of the research and the Roosevelt Study Center, Middelburg, Netherlands, for support during the writing phase.

2. For an interesting discussion of Angela Merkel and her background, see Jacqueline Boysen, *Angela Merkel: Eine deutsch-deutsche Biographie* (Angela Merkel: A German-German biography), Muenchen: Ullstein, 2001.

3. The Elf Corporation scandal and associated improprieties have led to convictions in France, but former Chancellor Helmut Kohl has not to date been charged—and probably will not be, at this point.

4. In the field, a number of theories have been advanced. John Duffield points to German security policy of continuity and moderation, which at the same time advances non-military means to achieve security. Somewhat the same argument about continuity in military integration, but growth in non-defense operations, is made by Rainer Baumann. See his "German Security Policy within NATO," in *German Foreign Policy since Unification: Theories and Case Studies*, ed. Volker Rittberger, Manchester: Manchester University Press, 2001, p. 179; and John Duffield, *World Power Forsaken*, Stanford: Stanford University Press, 1998, pp. 3–4.

5. See Steve Szabo, *The Diplomacy of German Unification*, New York, St. Martin's Press, 1992.

6. Unification occurred under Article 23 of the German Basic Law, under which the German Democratic Republic (East Germany) joined the Federal Republic of Germany (West Germany).

7. For an interesting discussion of the changes in the 1990s after the fall of the Wall, see Wolf-Dieter Eberwein and Karl Kaiser, *Germany's New Foreign Policy: Decision-Making in an Interdependent World*, Muenchen: Oldenbourg Verlag, 1998.

8. Dieter Dettke, "The Domestic and Foreign Policy Challenges of the German Grand Coalition," unpublished paper, Spring 2006, p. 11.

9. *Basic Law*, art. 24, para. 2.

10. Dieter Dettke, *Germany Says 'No': The Iraq War and the Future of German Foreign and Security Policy,* Baltimore: Woodrow Wilson Center for Scholars Press/Johns Hopkins University Press, 2009. This excluded Yugoslavia previous to 1994. The case was brought to the Constitutional Court by the SPD/FDP on the basis of two resolutions dealing with the use of German AWACS over Bosnia-Herzegovina (1992) and a Bundeswehr transport battalion in the UN operation in Somalia (1992). See Dettke above for a discussion of this constitutional decision.

11. Hanns Maull conceptualized the term 'civilian power paradigm' in his writings. See his various publications in the Bibliography.

12. Compare Hanns Maull, "Germany and Japan: The New Civilian Powers," *Foreign Affairs,* 69:5, 1990, pp. 91–106; and "Germany and the Use of Force: Still a 'Civilian Power'? *Survival* 42:2, Summer 2000, pp. 56–80.

13. The Parliamentary Participation Act of March 24, 2005, outlined the procedure by which the Bundestag (parliament) could mandate a mission. The mandate is for 12 months, although a mission may be withdrawn early. It may be renewed without a renewal vote only if the "content of the mission has not changed." The motion on a mission must include the following: "operational mission, area of operation, duration, costs, legal bases, maximum number of soldiers required, as well as their skills. Parliament may then approve or reject the German Government's motion by a simple majority. It cannot make any changes to the motion." Regular reports must be made on the mission during the 12-month periods. Http://www.bundesregierung.de/content / EN/Artikel/Auslandseinsaetze-der-bundeswehr/ (legal bases for Bundeswehr missions abroad). Note that missions to extricate people from dangerous situations may be reported after the fact, and humanitarian missions do not require a parliamentary vote.

14. See Hanns Maull,. "Zivilmacht Bundesrepublik Deutschland—Vierzehn Thesen fuer eine neue deutsche Aussenpolitik," *Europa Archiv,* 43, 1992, pp. 269–78. Also Sebastian Harnisch and Hanns W. Maull, *Germany as a Civilian Power? The Foreign Policy of the Berlin Republic,* Manchester: Manchester University Press, 2001.

15. See articles by H-P Schwarz, J. Rau, B. Geremek, D. Vernet, and H. Koehler, in "Germany's Role in Europe," *Internationale Politik,* transatlantic ed., 1/2000.

16. The first German 'out of area' operation actually was in 1992 in Bosnia, enforcing the embargo with a destroyer and three reconnaissance planes. While the Germans participated in the AWACS operations to enforce the no-fly zone, in July 1994 the Bundestag consented to the German contribution of personnel to the AWACS, but no Bundeswehr soldiers and no combat aircraft took part. An excellent historical account of the initial German military activity out of area appears in Rainer Baumann, "German Security Policy within NATO," in *German Foreign Policy since Unification,* ed. Volker Rittberger, Issues in German Politics, Manchester: Manchester University Press, 2001, pp. 170–171. Note that Germany has participated in EUFOR since 2004 in Bosnia.

17. While the concept has not enjoyed full support within the EU, it stands now at approximately 15 battlegroups committed to six-month periods. For an in-depth discussion of the issues raised for German forces, see Christian Moelling, *EU-Battlegroups: Stand und Probleme der Umsetzung in Deutschland und fuer die EU*, Diskussionspapier, Berlin: Stiftung Wissenschaft und Politik, 2007.

18. The Bundeswehr also sent 780 soldiers to the Democratic Republic of Congo to assure the first parliamentary elections from July through November 2006; for Operation Artemis, 100 soldiers assisted a Uganda transport.

19. Hugh Williamson, "Self-confident and ambitious," *Financial Times*, December 8, 2004, p. 4.

20. Poland and the Baltic states expressed skepticism about these efforts with the Russians and blocked real progress because of their concerns about the direction of Russian policies. Discussions continue.

21. Constanza Stelzenmueller, "Germany's Russia Dilemma," *Foreign Affairs*, March/April 2009, p. 91.

22. Ibid., p. 94.

23. John Thornhill. "The Old Danger that Threatens New Model Europe," *Financial Times*, December 27/28, 2008, p. 7. Thornhill further cites Chancellor Merkel's nickname, "Frau Nein," as she pursues German interests.

24. The friendship that has developed may have sobered the chancellor during her first G-8 summit in 2006 with the protective back rub she received from the US president.

25. See J. Fischer and R. Herzog, "Transatlantic Partnership," *Internationale Politik*, Transatlantic edition, 1/2000.

26. See G. Mattox's chapter on INF debate and other transatlantic issues in *The Strategic Triangle: France, Germany, and the United States in the Shaping of the New Europe*, ed. Helga Haftendorf, Georges-Henri Soutou, Stephen F. Szabo, and Samuel Wells, Jr., Washington, DC, Woodrow Wilson Center and Johns Hopkins University Press, 2007.

27. See Tom Dyson, *The Politics of German Defense and Security: Policy Leadership and Military Reform in the Post-Cold War Era*, New York: Berghahn Books, 2007, for a divergence in approach between the Foreign Ministry, in favor of greater Europeanization, versus the Defense Ministry, in favor of the traditional Atlanticism.

28. The split between the votes for her (35%) and the incumbent opposition leader Schroeder (34%) makes her governance particularly difficult, despite the growth in her popularity since the 2005 election.

29. Dettke, "The Domestic and Foreign Policy Challenges of the German Grand Coalition," unpublished paper, Spring 2006, p. 13.

30. In contrast, Chancellor Kohl seldom spoke to American audiences without mentioning the Marshall Plan and, in particular, the US care packages to his family.

31. Christian Schmidt, "Challenges of the 21st Century: The Atlantic Alliance and the New Security Environment," paper given at a conference between the American

Council on Germany and the German Council on Foreign Relations, January 12–13, 2006, Washington, DC, p. 8.

32. For a more general discussion of the EU and the United States in the broader Middle East, see Atlantic Council, ed., "Partners in Frustration: Europe, the United States and the Broader Middle East," September 2004.

33. However, the parliamentary votes have been anything but unanimous. In early 2001, the vote to send troops to Macedonia was rejected by 28 out of 294 Social Democrats and 7 out of 47 Greens. "NATO Yes, Macedonia Maybe," *Economist*, August 25, 2001, p. 43. Under the Constitutional Court ruling, the parliament must continually approve the deployment of forces. At present there are three separate missions, and each approval must be updated regularly although there has been an effort to lengthen the requirement.

34. See German government/English/German Military website, http://www.bundesregierung.de/content/EN/Artikel/Auslandseinsaetsze-der-bundeswehr.

35. Before Kosovo declared independence, German Ambassador Wolfgang Ischinger led the Contact Group effort for a settlement.

36. See Walter Posch, ed., "Iranian Challenges," *Chaillot Papers*, no. 89, May 2006.

37. Bertrand Benoit, "Schroeder Warns US on Iranian Military Action," *Financial Times*, August 15, 2005, p. 5. Benoit went on to report this as the first foray into foreign policy in a campaign 'dominated by the economy.' Shortly thereafter, of course, Iraq became another foreign policy theme for the election campaign.

38. Ivo Daalder and James Goldgeier, "Global NATO," *Foreign Affairs*, September/October 2006, pp. 105–113.

39. Maren Tomforde, "Motivation and Self-Image among German Peacekeepers," *International Peacekeeping*, 12:4, Winter 2005, p. 578.

40. Anne-Marie Le Gloannec, "Germany's Power and the Weakening of States in a Globalised World: Deconstructing a Paradox," *German Politics*, 10:1, April 2001, 117–134.

41. "Chancellor Merkel: Germany Will Take on Responsibility in the Middle East," *The Week in Germany*, August 25, p. 3.

42. For an in-depth discussion, see Agnieszka Nowak, "Civilian Crisis Management: the EU Way," *Chaillot Paper*, no. 90, June 2006.

43. See discussion of TNW in Catherine M. Kelleher and Scott L. Warren, "Getting to Zero Starts Here: Tactical Nuclear Weapons," *Arms Control Today*, 39:8, October 2009, pp. 6–12.

44. See chapter 4 , titled "Defence Spending Trends," in *European Military Capabilities*, IISS, 2008, p. 93. In fact, IISS reports that from 2000 to 2006, Germany froze its defense spending, during which time it fell from 1.5 to 1.3% GDP.

45. See especially chapter 3, titled "National Defence Reforms and Ambitions," in *European Military Capabilities*, IISS, 2008, pp. 46–48.

46. Wolfgang Munchau, "Schroeder's legacy Will Haunt Merkel," *Financial Times*, November 21, 2005, p. 15.

47. Baumann, "German Security Policy within NATO," p. 179.

Chapter 7

1. The analysis, opinions and conclusions expressed or implied in this article are those of the author and do not necessarily represent the views of the JSCSC, the UK MOD or any other government agency.

2. The Pew Global Attitudes Project, www.pewglobal.org/reports/pdf/262.pdf, 17 September 2008, p. 33.

3. For an analysis of Turkish public opinion towards the US, see Nasah Uslu, Metin Toprak, Ibrahim Dalmis and Ertan Aydin, 'Turkish public opinion toward the United States in the context of the Iraq question', *Middle East Review of International Affairs (MERIA)*, vol. 9, no. 3, September 2005, pp. 75–107, www.meria.ac.il/journal/2005/issue3/jv9no3a5.html accessed 31 March 2009. See also Omer Taspinar, 'The anatomy of anti-Americanism in Turkey', *Insight Turkey*, vol. 7, no. 2, April–June 2005), pp. 83–98.

4. Emrullah Uslu, '*Ulusalcilik:* The neo-nationalist resurgence in Turkey', *Turkish Studies,* vol. 9, no. 1, March 2008.

5. David L Arnett, 'The heart of the matter: The importance of emotion in Turkish-American relations', *Turkish Policy Quarterly*, vol. 5, no. 4, Winter 2006, pp. 31–40.

6. Mark R Parris, 'Common values and common interests? The Bush legacy in US-Turkish relations', *Insight Turkey*,Vol.10, No.4, 2008, p.5.

7. A term coined by Ian O Lesser, 'Turkey in the EU: A new US relationship', *Insight Turkey*, vol. 6, no. 4, October–November 2004, p. 36.

8. For accounts of the events leading up to the Turkish vote to refuse US troop entry into Turkey, and some of the bitterness that ensued, see Barak A Salmoni, 'Strategic partners or estranged allies: Turkey, the United States and Operation Iraqi Freedom', *Strategic Insights*, vol. 2, no. 7, July 2003, www.ccc.nps.navy/mil/si/july03/middleeast.asp accessed 31 March 2009 ; Bill Park, 'Strategic location, political dislocation: Turkey, the United States, and Northern Iraq', *MERIA*, vol. 7, no. 2, June 2003, pp. 11–23; Michael Rubin, 'A comedy of errors: American-Turkish diplomacy and the Iraq war', *Turkish Policy Quarterly*, vol. 4, no. 1, Spring 2005, pp. 69–79; and William Hale, *Turkey, the US and Iraq*, London: SAQI, 2007, pp. 94–116.

9. See www.state.gov/r/pa/prs/ps/2006/68574.htm.

10. Frank J Gaffney, Jr, 'Islamofascist coup?', *Washington Times,* March 14, 2006. Gaffney is president of the Center for Security Policy. For examples of neoconservative distrust of the AKP, see also Michael Rubin, 'Green money, Islamist politics in Turkey', *The Middle East Quarterly*, vol. 12, no. 1, Winter 2005, www.meforum.org/article/684 accessed 31 March 2009; and Robert L Pollock, 'The sick man of Europe—again', *Wall Street Journal*, 16 February, 2005.

11. A point made in a number of interviews conducted by the author with officials from the US and Turkish government in Washington DC, November–December 2005.

12. For an early analysis of Turkey's US-sanctioned cross-border military action, see Gareth Jenkins, 'A military analysis of Turkey's incursion into northern Iraq', *Terrorism Monitor*, vol. 6, no. 5, 7 March 2008, http://www.jamestown.org accessed 31 March 2009.

13. See 'Military-opposition row boils over' and 'Row over military withdrawal reveals deep mistrust', both in *Today's Zaman*, 6 March 2008.

14. Available in Turkish at www.usak.org.tr. For an English language commentary, see 'EU's Turkey critics losing popularity', *Today's Zaman*, 15 August 2009.

15. The texts of Obama's speeches to the Turkish National Assembly on 6 April 2009 and at Cairo University on 4 April 2009 are available at www.whitehouse.gov/the-press-office.

16. For early analyses of Obama's foreign policy challenges and performance with respect to Turkey, see Bill Park, 'Obama, Turkey and the Middle East: Troubles ahead?' *Turkish Policy Quarterly*, vol. 7, no. 4, Winter 2008/9, pp. 17–24; F Stephen Larrabee, 'Obama's foreign policy: Opportunities and challenges', pp. 1–11; and Omer Taspiner, 'Obama's Turkey policy: Bringing credibility to 'strategic partnership'', pp. 13–21, both in *Insight Turkey*, vol. 11, no. 1, 2009.

17. Hale, *Turkey, the US and Iraq*, p. 179.

18. See Fusun Turkmen, 'Turkish-American relations: A challenging transition', *Turkish Studies*, vol. 10, no. 1, March 2009, pp. 109–129; Aylin Guney, 'An anatomy of the transformation of the US-Turkish alliance: From 'Cold War' to 'war on Iraq'', *Turkish Studies*, vol. 6, no. 3, September 2005, pp. 341–359. See also Marios L Evriviades, 'Turkey's role in United States strategy during and after the Cold War', *Mediterranean Quarterly*, vol. 9, no. 2, Spring 1998, pp. 30–51; and Bruce R. Kuniholm, 'Turkey and the West since World War II', in Vojtech Mastny and R Craig Nation (eds), *Turkey between East and West: New Challenges for A Rising Regional Power*, Boulder, CO: Westview Press, 1996, pp. 45–69.

19. Morton Abramowitz, 'Foreword', in Graham E. Fuller and Ian O Lesser (eds), *Turkey's New Geopolitics; From the Balkans to Western China*, Boulder, CO: Westview Press/RAND, 1993, p. xii.

20. For the concept of Turkey as a bridge, see Ian O Lesser, 'Bridge or Barrier? Turkey and the West After the Cold War', in Fuller and Lesser (eds), *Turkey's New Geopolitics*, pp. 99–140.

21. Paul Kubicek, 'Turkey's inclusion in the Atlantic Community: Looking back, looking forward', *Turkish Studies*, vol. 9, no. 1, March 2008, pp. 25–27.

22. Arnett, 'The heart of the matter', p. 36.

23. Philip Robins, 'The opium crisis and the Iraq War: Historical parallels in Turkey-US relations', *Mediterranean Politics*, vol. 12, no. 1, March 2007, pp. 17–38.

24. For an analysis of Turkish-US tensions surrounding the terms of US access to Incirlik and other military facilities on Turkish territory, see Selin M Bolme, 'The Politics of Incirlik Air Base', *Insight Turkey*, vol. 9 , no. 3, 2007, pp. 82–91.

25. See Ian O Lesser, 'Turkey, the US and the delusion of geopolitics', *Survival*, vol. 48, no. 3, Autumn 2006, pp. 83–95.

26. See Maliha Benli Altunisik, 'Turkish-American security relations; The Middle East dimension', in Mustafa Aydin and Cagri Erhan (eds), *Turkish-American Relations; Past, Present and Future*, London and New York: Routledge, 2004, pp. 154–156; and William Hale, 'Turkey, the Middle East, and the Gulf crisis', *International Affairs*,

vol. 68, no. 4, October 1992, pp. 679–692, for the extent to which Turkish policy at this time was Ozal's.

27. For an account of Turkey's problems with Operation Safe Haven/Northern Watch, see Altunisik, 'Turkish-American security relations', pp. 157–163.For an account of the apparent contradictions in Turkish policy towards the KRG, see Philip Robins, *Suits and Uniforms; Turkish Foreign Policy since the Cold War*, London: Hurst and Co, 2003, pp. 312–342. For an in-depth study of Turkish policy towards northern Iraq, and the possible implications for the US-Turkish relationship, see Bill Park, *Turkey's Policy towards Northern Iraq: Problems and Prospects, Adelphi Paper*, no. 374, New York and London: Routledge/International Institute for Strategic Studies (IISS), 2005; Asa Lundgren, *The Unwelcome Neighbour: Turkey's Kurdish Policy*, London: I. B. Tauris, 2007; and Michael Gunter, 'The consequences of a failed Iraqi state: An independent Kurdish state in northern Iraq?', *Journal of South Asian and Middle Eastern Studies*, vol. 27, no. 3, 2004, pp. 1–11.

28. For further consideration of this, see Sabri Sayari, 'Turkey's foreign policy in the post-Cold War era: The challenges of multi-regionalism', pp. 169–182; and Ian O Lesser, 'Turkey in a changing security environment', pp. 183–198, both in *Columbia University Journal of International Affairs*, vol. 54, no. 1, Fall 2000; Shireen Hunter, 'Bridge or frontier? Turkey's post-Cold War geopolitical posture', *International Spectator*, vol. 34, no. 1, Jan–March 1998, pp. 63–78. See also Michael S. Radu (ed), *Dangerous Neighborhood: Contemporary Issues in Turkish Foreign Policy*, Somerset, NJ: Transaction Press, 2002; and Tariq Ismael and Mustafa Aydin, *Turkey's Foreign Policy in the 20th Century*, Aldershot: Ashgate, 2003.

29. For a consideration of this, see Nur Bilge Criss and Serdar Guner, 'Geopolitical configuration: The Russia-Turkey-Iran triangle', *Security Dialogue*, vol. 30, no. 3, Sept 1999, pp. 365–376; David Menshari (ed), *Middle Central Asia Meets the East*, London: Frank Cass, 1998; Hooman Peimani, *Regional Security and the Future of Central Asia: The Competition of Iran, Turkey and Russia*, London: Praeger, 1998; Alvin Z Rubinstein and Oleg M Smolansky (eds), *Regional Power Rivalries in the New Eurasia: Russia, Turkey and Iran*, London and New York: M. E. Sharpe, 1995.

30. For Turkey's role in the nexus between regional issues and energy cooperation, see Laurent Ruseckas, 'Turkey and Eurasia: Opportunities and risks in the Caspian Pipeline derby', *Columbia University Journal of International Affairs*, vol. 54, no. 1, Fall 2000, pp. 217–236; and Gareth Winrow, 'Pivotal state or energy supplicant? Domestic structure, external actors, and Turkish policy in the Caucasus', *Middle East Journal*, vol. 57, no. 1, Winter 2003, pp. 76–92.

31. Lt. Gen. Ethem Erdagi, 'The ISAF mission and Turkey's role in rebuilding the Afghan state', *PolicyWatch*, no. 1052, Washington Institute for Near East Policy,18 November 2005, www.washingtoninstitute.org/templateC05.php?CID=2403.

32. A point made both by Nigar Goksel, 'From the desk of the editor', p. 9; and Mark Parris, 'Allergic partners: can US-Turkish relations be saved?', p. 54, both from *Turkish Political Quarterly*, vol. 4, no. 1, Spring 2005.

33. For a flavour of this comment, see F. Stephen Larrabee, 'Turkey rediscovers the Middle East', *Foreign Affairs*, Vol.86, No.4, July-August 2007, pp.103–114.

34. For example, Soner Cagaptay, 'Turkey at the crossroads: preserving Ankara's western orientation', *Washington Institute for Near East Policy*, 2005.

35. 'PM says Turkey to pursue active foreign policy', *Turkish Daily News*, 5 January 2005.

36. See his 'Turkey's foreign policy vision: An assessment of 2007', *Insight Turkey*, vol. 10, no. 1, 2008, pp. 77–96. For assessments of his ideas, see Joshua W. Walker, "Strategic Depth' and Turkish foreign policy', *Insight Turkey*, vol. 9, no. 3, 2007, pp. 32–47; and Bulent Aras, 'The Davutoglu era in Turkish foreign policy', *Insight Turkey*, vol. 11, no. 3, Summer 2009, pp. 127–142.

37. In answer to a question that this author posed to him at the Royal United Services Institute, London, 10 June 2008.

38. Meliha Benli Altunsik, 'The possibilities and limits of Turkey's soft power in the Middle East', *Insight Turkey*, vol. 10, no. 2, 2008, pp. 41–54; William Hale, 'Turkey and the Middle East in the 'new era'', *Insight Turkey*, vol. 11, no. 3, Summer 2009, pp. 143–159.

39. 'Israel, Syria launch peace talks through Turkey', *Turkish Daily News*, 22 May 2008.

40. The Economic Policy Research Foundation of Turkey (TEPAV) website is a good source of information on this project. See www.tepav.org.tr.

41. 'Turkey raises profile in long-neglected Mideast', *Turkish Daily News*, 28 May 2008.

42. 'Iran asks help, PM to deliver message', *Hurriyet*, 26 February 2009.

43. Bulent Aras, 'Turkey and the GCC: An emerging relationship', *Middle East Policy*, vol. 12, no. 4, Winter 2005, pp. 89–97; Robert Olsen, 'Turkey's relations with the Gulf Cooperation Council from 2003 to 2007: New paradigms?', *Mediterranean Quarterly*, vol. 19, no. 3, Summer 2008, pp. 68–87.

44. See Bulent Aras and Rabia Karakaya Polat, 'From conflict to cooperation: Desecuritization of Turkey's relations with Syria and Iran', *Security Dialogue*, vol. 39, no. 5, October 2008, pp. 495–515.

45. Meliha Benli Altunisik and Ozlem Tur, 'From distant neighbours to partners? Changing Syrian-Turkish relations', *Security Dialogue*, vol. 37, no. 2, 2006, pp. 229–248.

46. Interview, Washington DC, December 2005.

47. O. Winter, 'Regional attempts to form strategic regional bloc: Syria, Turkey and Iran', memri@memri.org, 6 January 2009.

48. Nimrod Raphaeli, 'The growing economic relations between Iran and Turkey', *Inquiry and Analysis Series, MEMRI*, no. 414, 6 January 2008.

49. 'Turkey, Iran agree on active cooperation against terrorism', *The New Anatolian*, 27 February 2006.

50. See F. Stephen Larrabee, 'Obama's foreign policy: opportunities and challenges', pp. 1–11; and Omer Taspinar, 'Obama's Turkey policy: Bringing credibility to

'strategic partnership", pp. 13–21, both in *Insight Turkey*, vol. 11, no. 1, 2009, for a consideration of these prospects.

51. Fiona Hill and Omer Taspinar, 'Turkey and Russia: Axis of the excluded?' *Survival*, vol. 48, no. 1, Spring 2006, p. 90.

52. 'Black Sea force divides Turkey, US', *Turkish Daily News*, 3 March 2006.

53. For an account of the implications of the crisis for Russo-Turkish relations, see Igor Torbakov, 'The Georgia crisis and Russo-Turkish relations', The Jamestown Foundation, 2008, www.jamestown.org/uploads/media/Torbakov_Russia_Turkey.pdf accessed 31 March 2009.

54. An expression employed by a senior Turkish diplomat in discussions with the author, Washington, DC, December 2005.

55. For more information on Turkey's role in this initiative, see Ali Balci and Nebi Mis, 'Turkey's role in the Alliance of Civilizations: A new perspective in Turkish foreign policy?' *Turkish Studies*, vol. 9, no. 3, September 2008, pp. 387–406; Ramazan Kilinc, 'Turkey and the Alliance of Civilizations: Norm adoption as a survival strategy', *Insight Turkey*, vol. 11, no. 3, Summer 2009, pp. 57–75.

56. See, for example, comments made by the undersecretary of state for Political Affairs, R. Nicholas Burns, at the Washington Institute for Near East Policy, 'The US-Turkish relationship beyond Iraq: Common values, common agenda', 18 July 2005, www.washingtoninstitute.org accessed 31 March 2009. For a broader commentary on the Bush administration's Middle East initiative, see Philip H. Gordon, 'Bush's Middle East vision', *Survival*, vol. 45, no. 1, Spring 2003, pp. 155–165.

57. For a recent expression of this, see 'Gul backs US-led Middle East initiative, says it complies with Turkey's vision', *Turkish Daily News*, 6 March 2006.

58. See www.mfa.gov.tr/grupa/ai/islamicconference.1.htm, accessed 31 March 2009.

59. See www.mfa.gov.tr/ai/Gul12December2003.htm, accessed 31 March 2009.

60. Abdullah Gul, 'Turkey's role in a changing Middle East environment', *Mediterranean Quarterly*, vol. 15, no. 1, Winter 2004, p. 7.

61. A point made by Goksel, 'From the desk of the editor', p. 7. See also Mohammed Noureddine, 'Arab-Turkish cooperation in the new era', *Insight Turkey*, vol. 11, no. 1, 2009, pp. 43–51.

62. Paul Kubicek, 'The European Union and grass roots democratization in Turkey', *Turkish Studies*, vol. 6, no. 3, September 2005, pp. 361–377; see also Sefa Simsek, 'The transformation of civil society in Turkey; From quantity to quality', *Turkish Studies*, vol. 5, no. 3, Autumn 2004, pp. 46–74.

63. For a generally favourable analysis of the AKP and its record in office, see R. Quinn Mecham, 'From the ashes of virtue, a promise of light: The transformation of political Islam in Turkey', *Third World Quarterly*, vol. 25, no. 2, 2004, pp. 339–358.

64. See Bill Park, 'Turkey's deep state: Ergenekon and the threat to democratization in the republic', *The RUSI Journal*, vol. 153, no. 5, October 2008, pp. 55–59; and Gareth Jenkins, 'Turkey's latest crisis', *Survival*, vol. 50, no. 5, October –November 2008, pp. 5–12.

65. This is a theme of Malik Mufti, 'Daring and caution in Turkish foreign policy', *The Middle East Journal*, vol. 52, no. 1, Winter 1998, pp. 32–50.

66. For analyses of the domestic political role of the Turkish military, see Metin Heper and Aylin Guney, 'The military and the consolidation of democracy: The recent Turkish experience', *Armed Forces and Society*, vol. 26, no. 4, Summer 2000, pp. 635–657; Gareth Jenkins, 'Context and circumstance: The Turkish military and politics', *Adelphi Paper*, no. 337, London: IISS, 2001; Nilufer Narli, 'Civil-military relations in Turkey', *Turkish Studies*, vol. 1, no. 1, Spring 2000, pp. 107–127: Tanel Demirel, 'Civil-military relations in Turkey: Two patterns of civilian behaviour towards the military', *Turkish Studies*, vol. 4, no. 3, Autumn 2003, pp. 1–25; Tanel Demirel, 'Lessons of military regimes: The Turkish case in comparative perspective', *Armed Forces and Society*, vol. 31, no. 2, Winter 2005, pp. 245–271.

67. George Sellers Harris, 'Turkish-American relations since the Truman Doctrine', in Aydin and Erhan (eds), *Turkish-American Relations*, p. 86.

68. See a report published on 14 November 2005 by the Center for European Security Studies (CESS), The Netherlands, *Turkish-civil-military relations and the EU: Preparation for continuing convergence*, www.cess.org, accessed 31 March 2009; An abridged version is offered by the report's author, David Greenwood, in *Insight Turkey*, vol. 7, no. 4, October–December 2005, pp. 126–131.

69. Ersel Aydinli, Nihat Ali Ozcan, and Dogan Akyaz, 'The Turkish military's march towards Europe', *Foreign Affairs*, vol. 85, no. 1, January–February 2006, pp. 77–90.

70. For analysis of AKP-military relations, see Metin Heper, 'The Justice and Development Party government and the military in Turkey', *Turkish Studies*, vol. 6, no. 2, June 2005, pp. 215–231. See also Zeki Sarigil, 'Europeanization as institutional change: The case of the Turkish military', *Mediterranean Politics*, vol. 12, no. 1, March 2007, pp. 39–57; Metin Heper, 'The Justice and Development Party government and the military in Turkey', *Turkish Studies*, vol. 6, no. 2, June 2005, pp. 215–231; Gareth Jenkins, 'Continuity and change: Prospects for civil-military relations in Turkey', *International Relations*, vol. 8, no. 2, March 2007, pp. 339–335.

71. His 24 April 2009 statement can be found at www.thewhitehouse.gov/the-press-office.

72. See Alexander Iskandaryan, 'Armenian-Turkish rapprochement: timing matters', *Insight Turkey*, vol. 11, no. 3, Summer 2009, pp. 37–44.

73. Arnett, 'The heart of the matter'.

74. For a consideration of the impact of Iraq on Turkish-US relations, see William Hale, *Turkey, the US and Iraq*.

75. See comments to the Washington Institute for Near East Policy by Undersecretary of the Turkish Foreign Ministry Ali Tuygan, 'Turkish-US relations: The past, present and future', 14 April 2005, www.washingtoninstitute.org, accessed 31 March 2009.

76. 'Turkey frets over untimely US pullout', *Today's Zaman*, 18 November 2008.

77. See, for example, 'Turkey and Iraq to conduct three-phase plan against PKK—report', *Hurriyet Daily News*, 15 December 2008.

78. There has been extensive coverage of and debate about this initiative in the Turkish press. For a sample from the *Hurriyet Daily News*, see 'Political storm around Kurdish issue hits Turkey', 11 August 2009; and 'Differing views influence AKP road map', 14 August 2009. See also Joshua W. Walker, 'Kurdish issue in Turkey; A historic win-win opportunity for Washington', *Today's Zaman*, 26 August 2009.

79. For a comprehensive survey of the Kirkuk issue, see the International Crisis Group, *Iraq and the Kurds: Resolving the Kirkuk Crisis*, Middle East Report, no. 64, Brussels, 19 April 2007, www.crisisgroup.org, accessed 31 March 2009.

80. 'U.N. hopes for 'grand deal' to resolve Iraq's Kirkuk', *International Herald Tribune*, 20 August 2008. The failure to agree on the future of Kirkuk has also held up the passage of an Iraqi electoral law. See 'Iraq's parliament must pass elections law for this year', *Kurdnet,* http://www.ekurd.net/mismas/articles/misc2008/8/kirkukkurdistan444.htm, 31 August 2008.

81. O Faruk Logoglu, 'The state of US-Turkey relations: A Turkish perspective', in *Colloquium Report: The Evolution of US-Turkish Relations in a Transatlantic Context,* Frances G. Burwell (ed), April 2008, pp. 29–42, at www.strategicstudiesinstitute.army.mil.

Chapter 8

1. Transcript of President Woodrow Wilson's '14 Points' speech (1918). http://www.ourdocuments.gov/doc.php?flash=true&doc=62&page=transcript.

2. Marcin Zaborowski. 2004. *From America's protégé to constructive European. Polish security policy in the twenty-first century.* European Union Institute for Security Studies, EU-ISS Occasional Paper No. 56. December 2004.

3. Speech given by Bronislaw Geremek during a Stefan Batory Foundation Conference. 2005. 'New geopolitics of Central and Eastern Europe. Between European Union and United States'. http://www.batory.org.pl/doc/geopolityka.pdf.

4. Speech given by Bronislaw Geremek on the occasion of signing the protocols to the North Atlantic Treaty on the accession of Poland, Czech Republic and Hungary, 16 December 1997. http://www.nato.int/docu/speech/1997/s971216i.htm.

5. The topic will be returned to later the chapter.

6. Ministry of National Defence of the Republic of Poland. www.mon.gov.pl.

7. Survey held by CBOS (Public Opinion Research Center). 2009. *Dziesi?? lat w NATO* (Ten years in NATO). http://www.cbos.pl/SPISKOM.POL/2009/K_038_09.PDF.

8. Dariusz Milczarek. 2006. *Mi?dzy Waszyngtonem a Bruksel?—mo?liwe kierunki rozwoju polskiej polityki zagranicznej i bezpiecze?stwa* (Between Washington and Brussels—possible development of Polish foreign and security policy). Warsaw: Studia Europejskie, 2/2006.

9. The USAID official website: http://www.usaid.gov/pl/program.htm.

10. Report by Office of the Committee of European Integration. 2009. *5 years of Poland in the European Union*. Warsaw. http://5lat.ukie.gov.pl/en/raporty.

11. Report by Office of the Committee of European Integration. *5 years of Poland in the European Union*.

12. Report by Office of the Committee of European Integration. *5 years of Poland in the European Union*.

13. 'New geopolitics of Central and Eastern Europe. Between European Union and United States'. Speech by Timothy Garton Ash at a Stefan Batory Foundation Conference. 2005. http://www.batory.org.pl/doc/geopolityka.pdf.

14. Dariusz Milczarek. 2006. *Mi?dzy Waszyngtonem a Bruksel?- mo?liwe kierunki rozwoju polskiej polityki zagranicznej i bezpiecze?stwa* (Between Washington and Brussels—possible development of Polish foreign and security policy).

15. Report by Office of the Committee of European Integration. 2009. *5 years of Poland in the European Union*.

16. Information received from the Ministry of National Defence of the Republic of Poland, 26 August 2009.

17. Olaf Osica. 2002. 'In search of a new role: Poland in Euro-Atlantic relations'. *Defence Studies*, 2:2, 21–39.

18. David H. Dunn. 2002. 'Poland: America's new model ally'. *Defence Studies*, 2:2, 63–86.

19. Joint press conference of President George W. Bush and the president of the Republic of Poland, Aleksander Kwasniewski, 11 October 2001. www.prezydent.pl.

20. United States Diplomatic Mission to Poland. http://poland.usembassy.gov/poland/f16.html.

21. Marcin Zaborowski. 2004. *From America's protégé to constructive European. Polish security policy in the twenty-first century*.

22. Ministry of National Defence of the Republic of Poland web page dedicated to the mission in Iraq: http://www.pkwirak.wp.mil.pl/pl/index.html.

23. *Extraordinary European Council on Iraq.* http://ec.europa.eu/comm/external_relations/iraq/intro/ec170203.htm.

24. *Wall Street Journal.* 30 January 2003.

25. Dorota Eggert. 2005. *Transatlantycka wspólnota bezpiecze?stwa* (The transatlantic security community). Warsaw. Zurawia Papers 5.

26. 'Chirac lashes out at 'new Europe'', cnn.com. 18 February 2003. http://edition.cnn.com/2003/WORLD/europe/02/18/sprj.irq.chirac/.

27. John Springford. *'Old' and 'new' Europeans united: public attitudes towards the Iraq war and US foreign policy,* Centre for European Reform Background Brief. http://www.cer.org.uk/pdf/back_brief_springford_dec03.pdf.

28. David H. Dunn. 2003. 'Poland: America's new model ally'. In Marcin Zaborowski and David H. Dunn (eds.), *Poland—A new power in transatlantic security*. London: Frank Cass.

29. Marcin Zaborowski. *From America's protégé to constructive European. Polish security policy in the twenty-first century*.

30. Centre for International Relations. 2004. *Przysz?o?? CFSP/ESDP a stosunki transatlantyckie. Punkt widzenia Polski i Francji* (The future of CFSP/ESDP and transatlantic relations. The Polish and French perspective).

31. *Najpierw pomoc dla armii, wizy zobaczymy* (First aid for the army, visa, we will see). *Gazeta Wyborcza* 28 January 2004.

32. Marcin Zaborowski. *From America's protégé to constructive European. Polish security policy in the twenty-first century.*

33. The Polish Institute of International Affairs. 2008. *Rocznik Polskiej Polityki Zagranicznej* (The Polish foreign policy yearbook). Warsaw, pp. 81–82.

34. TV interview of Minister of National Defence of the Republic of Poland in military base in Lubliniec by Bogdan Klich. 21/08/2009.

35. Maria Wagrowska. *Wraz z tarcz?—nowe dylematy w polityce bezpiecze?stwa* (With the shield—new dilemmas in security policy). In: Foundation of International Studies. 2008. *Rocznik Strategiczny 2007/08* (Strategic yearbook 2007/08). Warsaw: Scholar.

36. *Gazeta Wyborcza*, 3–4 March 2007.

37. CBOS (Public Opinion Research Center). 2009. *Opinia publiczna o tarczy antyrakietowej* (Public opinion on the missile defence shield). March 2009. http://cbos.pl/PL/publikacje/raporty_2009.php.

38. *Declaration on strategic cooperation between the United States of America and the Republic of Poland.* 2008. 20 August 2008. http://www.msz.gov.pl/Declaration,on ,strategic,cooperation,between,the,United,States,of,America,and,the,Republic,of,Pol and,20785.html.

39. Radio interview of the minister of national defence of the Republic of Poland by Bogdan Klich. 21/08/2009.

http://www.polskieradio.pl/jedynka/sygnalydnia/artykul19886.html.

40. Roman Ku?niar and Wess Mitchell. In *Gazeta Wyborcza*. 18.09.2009.

41. *Gazeta Wyborcza*. 18.09.2009.

42. *Gazeta Wyborcza*. 18.09.2009.

43. Polish Minister of Foreign Affairs Radoslaw Sikorski. *Relacje transatlantyckie—szanse i wyzwania* (Transatlantic relations—chances and challenges). Warsaw, 19 January 2009. Speech given at Euro-Atlantic Association.

44. Report by Office of the Committee of European Integration. 2009. *5 years of Poland in the European Union.*

45. PAUCI website. http://www.pauci.org/en/about/history.

46. This chapter is based on my 2009 article 'Security cultures—the EU and Polish way'. Paper for the 2009 EU ISS summer school in Cambridge (European security cultures and national traditions). www.iss.europa.eu.

47. Kerry Longhurst and Marcin Zaborowski. 2007. *The new Atlanticist. Poland's foreign and security policy priorities.* The Royal Institute of International Affairs—Chatham House.

48. Wojciech Roszkowski. 2005. *The shadow of Yalta—a report.* Warsaw: Warsaw Rising Museum.

49. Kerry Longhurst and Marcin Zaborowski. *The New Atlanticist.*

50. Olaf Osica. *Polska wobec operacji NATO i polityki bezpieczenstwa i obronnej UE* (Poland towards the NATO operation and the EU's security and defence policy). In: Krzysztof Malinowski. 2003. *Kultura bezpiecze?stwa narodowego w Polsce i Niemczech,* pp. 132–133.

51. This phrase is commonly associated with times when Polish soldiers, exiled from a partitioned Poland, fought in various independence movements all over the world.

52. Comment by Olaf Osica, Research Fellow at Natolin European Centre.

53. *National security strategy of the republic of Poland.* 2007. http://www.bbn.gov. pl/.

54. CBOS (Public Opinion Research Center). *The attitude of Poles to other nations.* December 2008. http://cbos.pl/SPISKOM.POL/2008/K_193_08.PDF.

55. *An open letter to the Obama administration from Central and Eastern Europe.* July 2009.

Chapter 9

1. 'World Bank cuts 2009 global growth forecast, says world economy will shrink by 2.9 percent', June 22, 2009, http://blog.taragana.com/n/world-bank-cuts-2009–global-growth-forecast-says-world-economy-to-shrink-by-29–percent-88597/, accessed 25//07/09.

2. Peter Spiegel, 'Biden says weakened Russia will bend to the U.S.', *Wall Street Journal,* July 25, 2009, http://online.wsj.com/article/SB124848246032580581.html.

3. The analogy is made in Odd Arne Westad, *The Global Cold War: Third World Interventions and the Making of Our Times* (Cambridge: Cambridge University Press 2005), particularly chapters one and two.

4. Ghulam Dastagir Wardak (comp.), *The Voroshilov Papers: Materials from the Soviet General Staff Academy.* Vol. 1. *Issues of Soviet Military Strategy* (Washington, DC: National Defence University Press, 1989), p. 58.

5. David Glantz, *The Military Strategy of the Soviet Union: A History* (Oxford: Frank Cass, 1992), pp. 214–266.

6. I have tracked these shifts in a recent co-authored chapter. See Alex Marshall & J. Simon Rofe, 'An aborted special relationship: US-Russian relations in the post Cold War world: 1989–2007', in J. Dumbrell & A. Schaefer (eds.), *Allies & Clients: America's Special Relationships* (London: Routledge, 2009).

7. Ivan Safranchuk, 'Travelling in different boats', http://eng.globalaffairs.ru/ region-rfp/numbers/25/1241.html.

8. 'Chavez, Medvedev tour Russian warships in Venezuela', http://www.reuters. com/article/worldNews/idUSTRE4AQ6WF20081127?feedType=RSS&feedName=wor ldNews.

9. 'Remember Lenin's lessons, Chavez tells Russians', *Miami Herald,* June 28, 2007,

http://www.flacso.org/hemisferio/al-eeuu/boletines/02/76/pol_08.pdf; 'Mozhno ska-zat' chto my uzhe vernulis'", http://www.kreml.org/other/198390704.

10. Stephen Sestanovich, 'What has Moscow done?' *Foreign Affairs,* November/ December 2008, http://www.foreignaffairs.org/20081001faessay87602/stephen-sesta-novich/what-has-moscow-done.html.

11. Albert B. Evans, Jr., 'Putin's legacy and Russia's identity,' *Europe-Asia Studies,* vol. 60, no. 6 (August 2008), p. 902, http://www.informaworld.com/smpp/titleconten t=t713414944db=alltab=issueslistbranches=60—v60.

12. Two publications by Francis Fukuyama usefully bookend this arc of intellec-tual development: *The End of History and the Last Man* (London: Penguin Books, 1992) and the desperate search for viable practical tools in the wake of the debacle in Iraq embodied in *State Building. Governance and World Order in the 21st Century* (London: Profile Books Ltd., 2005).

13. Adi Ignatius, 'A tsar is born', http://www.time.com/time/specials/2007/per-sonoftheyear/article/1,28804,1690753_1690757_1690766,00.html consulted 12/12/08.

14. Edward Lucas, *The New Cold War: How the Kremlin Menaces Both Russia and the West* (London: Bloomsbury, 2008).

15. http://www.russiatoday.com/medvedev/news/33842.

16. 'Russia returns to Afghanistan, on request', July 1, 2008, http://www.sanfea-ture.com/articledetail.php?aid=1012 , consulted 05/02/09.

17. The 2000 and 2008 concepts are available online at http://www.ln.mid.ru/Bl. nsf/0/1EC8DC08180306614325699C003B5FF0?OpenDocument, consulted 12/1/09; and http://www.kremlin.ru/eng/text/docs/2008/07/204750.shtml, consulted 12/1/09.

18. This practice is defended in some quarters as a First Amendment right: http:// blogs.usatoday.com/oped/2007/09/in-defense-of-l.html consulted 12/12/08.

19. Stephen Kotkin, 'Myth of the new cold war', *Prospect,* April 2008, p. 38.

20. Robert Kagan, 'New Europe, old Russia', *Washington Post,* February 6, 2008, http://www.washingtonpost.com/wp-dyn/content/article/2008/02/05/ AR2008020502879.html consulted 01/01/09.

21. Robert Kagan, *Of Paradise and Power: American and Europe in the New World Order* (New York: Alfred A Knopf, 2003).

22. 'Russia's military reform enters "crucial stage"', 26/12/2008, http://news.xin-huanet.com/english/2008–12/26/content_10559938.htm, consulted 02/01/09.

23. http://warfare.ru/?catid=239&linkid=2279, consulted 02/01/09; Nebojsa Bjela-kovic, 'Russian military procurement: Putin's impact on decision-making and bud-geting', *Journal of Slavic Military Studies,* vol. 21, no. 3 (July 2008), p. 528. Bjelakovic's piece emphasises the challenges of fulfilling this procurement plan on time and on budget.

24. On this, see Bertil Nygren, *The Rebuilding of Greater Russia: Putin's Foreign Policy Towards the CIS Countries* (London: Routledge, 2008).

25. On an earlier lost opportunity, see Frederic Bozo, 'The failure of a grand de-sign: Mitterand's European confederation, 1989–1991', *Contemporary European His-tory,* vol. 17, no. 3 (2008), pp. 391–412. On revived thinking in this direction, see John

Palmer, 'Beyond EU enlargement—creating a united European Commonwealth', June 2008, Sussex European Institute Working Paper, http://www.sussex.ac.uk/sei/documents/working_paper_1041.pdf.

26. One work that argues for the failure of 'multiculturalism' and the ongoing persistence of a specifically Western form of values-based identity is David Gress, *From Plato to NATO: The Idea of the West and Its Opponents* (New York: Free Press, 1998).

27. Dmitri Trenin, 'Russia leaves the West', *Foreign Affairs,* July/August 2006, http://www.foreignaffairs.org/20060701faessay85407-p20/dmitri-trenin/russia-leaves-the-west.html, consulted 12/1/09.

28. *The National Security Strategy of the United Kingdom: Security in an Interdependent World* (Cabinet Office, March 2008), pp. 6–8.

29. On which, see, for example, Nikolas K. Gvosdev, 'Russia: "European but not Western?"' *Orbis,* Winter 2007, pp. 29–140; Dmitri Trenin, 'Russia leaves the West', *Foreign Affairs,* vol. 85, no. 4 (July/August 2006), pp. 87–96.

30. Albert B. Evans, Jr., 'Putin's legacy and Russia's identity', pp. 899–912.

31. Gvosdev, 'Russia: "European but not Western?"', p. 134.

32. Richard Rose & Neil Munro, 'Do Russians see their future in Europe or the CIS?' *Europe-Asia Studies,* vol. 60, no. 1 (January 2008), pp. 49–66.

33. http://en.rian.ru/russia/20080808/115900078.html.

34. John Gray, *Enlightenment's Wake: Politics and Culture at the Close of the Modern Age* (London & New York: Routledge Classics, 2007), p. 191.

35. For an abbreviated version, see *Nezavisimaia Gazeta,* April 29, 1993.

36. http://www.fas.org/nuke/guide/russia/doctrine/econcept.htm, consulted 01/01/09.

37. Neil Buckley, 'Russia plans grand projects to become a top-five economy.' *The Financial Times,* November 14, 2007.

38. http://www.kremlin.ru/eng/text/docs/2008/07/204750.shtml, consulted 01/01/09.

39. http://www.kremlin.ru/eng/text/docs/2008/07/204750.shtml, consulted 01/01/09.

40. For just some of this criticism and analysis, see Michael Fredholm, 'Gazprom in Crisis,' *Conflict Studies Research Centre,* 06/48 (October 2006);Yegor Gaidar, *Collapse of an Empire: Lessons for Modern Russia* (Washington, DC: Brookings Institution Press, 2007); Peter Rutland, 'Putin's economic record: is the oil boom sustainable?' *Europe-Asia Studies,* vol. 60, no. 6 (August 2008), pp. 1051–1072, John Edwards & Jack Kemp (chairs), 'Russia's wrong direction: what the United States can and should do', Council on Foreign Relations Independent Task Force Report No. 57, 2006. http://www.cfr.org/content/publications/attachments/Russia_TaskForce.pdf. On Georgia's culpability for the 2008 crisis, see 'The West begins to doubt Georgian leader', *Der Spiegel,* 09/15/2008 http://www.spiegel.de/international/world/0,1518,578273,00.html consulted 29/12/08.

41. David Oakley, 'Fitch cuts Russia's credit rating', *The Financial Times,* February

4, 2009; John Thornhill, 'A Russia united by anti-westernism', *The Financial Times,* February 4, 2009.

42. Peter Spiegel, 'Biden says weakened Russia will bend to the U.S.', *Wall Street Journal* July 25, 2009, http://online.wsj.com/article/SB124848246032580581.html; and 'U.S. Vice President Biden hits nerve in Russia', http://news.yahoo.com/s/ap/20090727/ap_on_re_eu/eu_russia_us consulted 29/7/09.

43. For two alternative viewpoints, see Rana Foroohar, 'Russia enters its lost decade', *Newsweek,* July 13, 2009, http://blog.newsweek.com/blogs/wealthofnations/archive/2009/07/13/russia-enters-its-lost-decade.aspx; and Christopher Weafer, 'Why EU-Russia frictions look set to an end', *Europe's World,* Summer 2009, http://www.europesworld.org/NewEnglish/Home/Article/tabid/191/ArticleType/articleview/ArticleID/21412/Default.aspx.

44. http://businessneweurope.eu/story1414/RUSSIA_2009_Paused_before_a_rally, consulted 12/1/09; 'Financial first aid in Russia', *The Economist,* October 31, 2008, http://www.economist.com/displayStory.cfm?story_id=12537922, consulted 15/1/09.

45. For a useful discussion of Russia's proposals for a new European security treaty, see Andrey S. Makarychev, 'Russia and its "new security architecture" in Europe: a critical examination of the concept,' CEPS Working Documents, 5 February 2009, available online at: http://www.ceps.be/node/1612.

46. Cornelius Ochmann, 'EU eastern partnership: fine, but what about Russia?' *Spotlight Europe,* vol. 6 (2009), pp. 1–8.

47. Isabelle Facon, 'The West and post-Putin Russia: does Russia "leave the West"?' *Note de la FRS,* no. 10 (2008), p. 7.

48. Karl Meyer, *The Dust of Empire: The Race for Supremacy in the Asian Heartland* (London: Abacus, 2004), p. 203.

Chapter 10

1. The analysis, opinions and conclusions expressed or implied in this chapter are those of the author and do not necessarily represent the views of the Joint Services Command and Staff College, the UK Ministry of Defence or any other government agency.

2. For details see Askold Krushelnycky, 'Interview with Borys Tarasyuk, Yushchenko's foreign policy advisor', Radio Free Europe, Radio Liberty, Dec 30, 2004, http://www/rferl.org/articleprintview/1056636.html, accessed Jan 10, 2009.

3. *The White Book 2005, Defence Policy of Ukraine, Kyiv, Ministry of Defence of Ukraine 2006* (Kiev: Zapovit Publishing House, 2006).

4. 'Enhancing NATO-Ukraine cooperation: Short-term actions', *NATO Online,* Apr 21, 2005, http://www.nato.int/cps/en/natolive/official_texts_21741.htm, accessed Mar 30, 2009.

5. Paul D'Anieri, *Understanding Ukrainian Politics* (London: M E Sharpe, 2007), p. 126.

6. For details of the parties and a breakdown of the election results see Steven

Woehrel, 'Ukraine: Current issues and US policy', *CRS Report for Congress* (Congressional Research Service, Library of Congress), June 7, 2006.

7. 'Ukraine-EU towards a new phase of cooperation', *National Security & Defence* (Razumkov Centre, Kiev), no. 5 (89), 2007.

8. 'Ukraine: Yanukovych assures EU that all is well', *RFE/RL*, Sept 21, 2006, www.rferl.org/content/article/1071535.html.

9. 'European Parliament calls Ukrainian politicians to follow agreements', May 31, 2007, forua.wordpress.com/2007/05/31/european-parliament-calls-ukrainian-politicians-to-follow-agreements; see also Elitsa Vucheva, 'EU wants 'political stability' in Ukraine before closer ties', Jan 29, 2008. Also see EU-Ukraine Parliamentary Cooperation Committee, Adrian Severin and Borys Tarasyuk (cochairmen), 'Final statement and recommendations pursuant to Article 90 of the partnership and cooperation agreement', 10th meeting, February 26–27, 2008, Brussels,www.europarl.europa.eu/meetdocs/2004_2009/documents/dv/737/737511/737511en.pdf.

10. 'Ukraine-EU towards a new phase of cooperation', pp. 6–7.

11. 'Merkel says Ukraine not ready for EU', *RFE/RL*, 2006, www.huliq.com/12907/merkel-says-ukraine-not-ready-for-eu.

12. 'German chancellor puts the breaks on Ukraine's EU hopes', *Deutsche Welle*, July 21, 2008, www.dw-world.de/dw/article/0,2144,3498788,00.html.

13. Peter Finn, 'Ukraine's Yanukovych halts NATO entry talks', *Washington Post*, Sept 15, 2006.

14. 'Ya is in charge', *Zerkalo Nedeli on the Web*, no. 36 (615), pp. 23–29, Sept 2006, http://www.mirror-weeklyl.com/ie/print/54604/, accessed Sept 26, 2006.

15. 'Ukrainian opposition party supports deeper cooperation with NATO' (in Russian), Interfax-Ukraine news agency, Kiev, June 1, 2006, as reported in *BBC Monitoring Online*.

16. See '240 days of the government activity in the new format', *National Security & Defence* (Ukrainian Centre for Economic & Political Studies, Razumkov Centre), no. 3 (87), 2007.

17. 'Yushchenko allies dwindling as foreign minister resigns', *RFE/RL*.

18. '240 days of the government activity in the new format', p. 5.

19. For details of the results see Taras Kuzio, 'Trends and opinion polls reveal shifting voter preferences in Ukraine', *Eurasia Daily Monitor*, vol. 4, no. 171.

20. For details see Taras Kuzio, 'Presidential party is weakest link in Orange Coalition', *Eurasia Daily Monitor*, vol. 4, no. 206, Nov 6, 2007.

21. Christina Freeland, 'Kiev's time has come, says Yushchenko', *The Financial Times*, Jan 25, 2008.

22. For details see Taras Kuzio, 'The future of the Orange Coalition will be decided in May', *Eurasia Daily Monitor*, vol. 5, no. 78, Apr 24, 2008, http://www.jamestown.org/single/?no_cache=1&tx_ttnews%Btt_news%5D=33577, accessed Jan 12, 2009.

23. Jason Bush, 'Ukraine gets an IMF bailout', *Economics*, Oct 27, 2008; also see

'Into the breach: The IMF helps eastern Europe's two most vulnerable economies. Will it stop the rot?', *The Economist,* Oct 27, 2008.

24. 'Bucharest summit declaration', issued by the heads of state and government participating at the meeting of the North Atlantic Council in Bucharest on April 3, 2008, *Press Release* (2008) 049 (see point 23 for details), http://www.nato.int/dcou/pr/2008/p08–049e.html, accessed Jan 21, 2009.

25. Pavel Koruban, 'Is Yushchenko's Ukraine ready for a NATO MAP?', *Eurasia Daily Monitor,* vol. 5, no. 188, Oct 1, 2008, http://www.jamestown.org/single/?nocache=1&tx_ttnews%Bswrods%5D=8fd5893, accessed Jan 12, 2009.

26. Ibid.

27. 'Poll reveals changing Ukrainian public attitudes to NATO', Den, Kiev, Dec 18, 2007, as reported in *BBC Monitoring Online.*

28. 'Ukraine's place in NATO: A survey of expert opinion', Centre for US-Ukrainian Relations, Kiev, June 2006.

29. For a discussion of this see Deborah Sanders, 'US naval diplomacy in the Black Sea', *Naval War College Review,* Summer 2007, vol. 60, no. 3, pp. 61–73.

30. 'Ukrainian ministry says no plans for NATO base near Crimean town' (in Russian), Interfax-Ukraine news agency, Kiev, May 31, 2006, as reported in *BBC Monitoring Online.*

31. 'Ukrainian president's envoy sues council over 'NATO-free area' in Crimea' (in Russian), Interfax-Ukraine news agency, Kiev, June 19, 2006, as reported in *BBC Monitoring Online.*

32. 'Ukraine's Crimea declared NATO-free' (in Russian), Interfax-Ukraine news agency, Kiev, June 6, 2006, as reported in *BBC Monitoring Online.*

33. 'Ukraine's latest move towards NATO', *Jane's Intelligence Digest,* Feb 15 2008.

34. '72% of Ukrainians are inclined to separatism', Dec 19, 2008, Razumkov Centre Ukraine, http://74.125.77.102/translate-c?hl=en&langpair=uk%7Cen&u=http://www.uceps.org, accessed Jan 12, 2009.

35. 'Sea Breeze 2006: the campaign to promote NATO is being lost', International Centre for Policy Studies, June 9, 2006, http://ww.icps.kiev.ua/eng/comment.html?id=189, accessed Sept 19, 2006.

36. 'Foreign Minister says number of NATO bid supporters rising in Ukraine', Inter-TV, Kiev, Feb 15, 2008, as reported in *BBC Monitoring Online.*

37. Pavel Korbudan, 'Is Yushchenko's Ukraine ready for a NATO MAP?', *Eurasia Daily Monitor,* vol. 5, no. 188, Oct 1, 2008.

38. 'Necessity of referendum on Ukraine joining NATO proved in the court', Regnum News Agency, Oct 22, 2008, http://www.regnum.ru/english/1072893.html?forprint, accessed Jan 14, 2009.

39. Poll detail quoted in 'Ukraine-EU towards a new phase of cooperation', p. 3.

40. 'Public opinion in Ukraine', findings from an IFES (International Foundation for Electoral Systems) survey funded by USAID; see slides 28 and 29 for details. http://www.ifes.org/files/UkrainePresentation.pdf.

41. Cabinet of Ministers of Ukraine, 'Conception of the national target program for informing society about European integration issue of Ukraine for 2008–2011', resolution, July 25, 2007, www.kmu.gov.ua/control/en/publish/printable_article?art_id=121658497.

42. The budget for 2007 was 5 million UAH—which is less than 1 million pounds. In 2003 the Polish government spent 50mn UAH on its Public Awareness programme. For details see 'Public participation is the key to successful European integration', *ICPS Newsletter* (publication of the International Centre for Policy Studies, Kiev), vol. 113, no. 25, June 2001, www.icps.com.ua/doc/nl_eng_20010625_0113.pdf.

43. 'Communication from the commission to the European Parliament and the Council Eastern Partnership', {SEC(2008) 2974} COM(2008) 823 final, Dec 3, 2008, http://ec.europa.eu/external_relations/eastern/docs/com08_823_en.pdf, accessed Mar 30, 2009.

44. Brian Whitmore, 'Analysis: Who 'won' the NATO summit?', Radio Free Europe, Radio Liberty, Apr 5, 2008, http:www.rferl.org/featuresarticleprint/2008/04/8 0de7039–0e0a–41el–90a0–aa579al, accessed Apr 24, 2008.

45. Vladimir Socor, 'Putin warns Ukraine against seeking NATO membership', *Eurasia Daily Monitor,* vol. 5, no. 29, Feb 14, 2008.

46. Taras Kuzio, 'Russian intelligence seeks to destabilize Crimea', *Eurasia Daily Monitor,* vol. 5, no. 188, Oct 1, 2008, http://www/jamestown.org/single/?no_cache=1&tx_ttnews%5Bswords%5D=8fd5893, accessed Jan 12, 2009.

47. 'Bush-Putin row grows as pact pushes east', *The Guardian*, Apr 2, 2008.

48. Steven Erlanger, 'Putin criticizes NATO but has praise for Bush', *International Herald Tribune*, Apr 4, 2008.

49. David Morgan, 'US urges Ukraine NATO membership, action unlikely', Reuters, Nov 11, 2008.

50. For details see 'NATO-Ukraine Annual Target Plan for the year 2008 in the framework of NATO-Ukraine Action Plan', executive summary.

51. 'Inauguration of the Secretariat of the Organization for Democracy and Economic Development—GUAM', Feb 26, 2009, http://www.guam.org.ua/en/node/630, accessed Mar 30, 2009.

52. Berdal Aral, 'The Black Sea economic co-operation after ten years: What went wrong?', *Alternatives: Turkish Journal of International Affairs*, vol. 1, no. 4, Winter 2002.

53. 'Statement by H.E. Mr Anatoliy Zlenko, Minister of Foreign Affairs of Ukraine at the First Meeting of the BSEC Council of Ministers', Oct 30, 2001, http://www.mfa.gov.ua/mfa/en/publications/print/3301.htm, accessed Jan 20, 2009.

54. 'Speaker Voldymyr Lytvyn states Black Sea economic cooperation', Ukrainian Radio, June 8, 2005, http://www.nrcu/gov.ua/index.php?id=148&listid=15187, accessed Jan 20 2009.

55. See 'Message of H.E. Viktor Yushchenko, President of the Ukraine', *Bulletin*, no. 24, PABSEC, Istanbul, Nov 2005, p. 5.

56. Grigory Perepelytsia,' The policy of Ukraine towards the BSEC and the Black Sea region', www.harvard-bssp.org/files/2007/presentation/presentations/Perepelitsa_final.doc,

57. 'Black Sea countries pledge deeper co-operation', *Southeast European Times*, June 26, 2007, http://www.setimes.com/cocoon/setimes/xhtml/en_GB/features/setimes/features/2007, accessed Jan 27, 2009.

58. Gareth Jenkins, 'Is the end of the BSEC in sight?', *Eurasia Daily Monitor*, vol. 5, no. 76, Apr 22, 2008.

59. For details see Deborah Sanders, 'Ukraine after the orange revolution: Can it complete military transformation and join the US led war on terrorism', *Strategic Studies Institute* (US Army War College), Oct 2006.

60. For a discussion of Ukraine's military reforms up to 2004 see Deborah Sanders, 'Defending Ukraine: Reform, crisis and challenge of the future,' *World Defence Systems* (CDS), vol. 8, no. 1, pp. 70–72.

61. For discussion of Ukraine's military transformation see Deborah Sanders, 'Ukraine's military reform: Building a paradigm army', *Journal of Slavic Military Studies*, 21, 2008, pp. 599–614.

62. Peacekeeping, Ministry of Defence of Ukraine website, accessed Jan 24, 2009.

63. 'Tenth rotation of Ukrainian peacekeepers starts in Kosovo', Mar 4, 2008, 14:14, Ukrinform www.kmu.gov.ua/control/publish/article?art_id=123512509.

64. Brooks Tigner, 'Ukraine outlines contribution to ESDP co-operation', *Jane's Defence Weekly*, Nov 6, 2008.

65. 'Ukraine's participation in NATO response force discussed in Kiev', UNIAN News Agency, Kiev, Feb 15, 2008, as reported in *BBC Monitoring Online*.

66. Vladimir Kravchenko, 'Leonid Kuchma's Iraq legacy', *Zerkalo Nedeli on the Web*, no. 1 (529), Jan 15–21, 2005.

67. Ibid.

68. 'Ukraine should spend 2 percent of GDP on defence—minister' (in Russian), Interfax-Ukraine news agency, Kiev, Feb 23, 2006, as reported in *BBC Online Monitoring*.

69. 'Ukraine needs over 8bn dollars to launch professional army', Interfax-Ukraine news agency, Kiev, Nov 29, 2007, as reported in *BBC Monitoring Online*.

70. 'Ukrainian MP-elect details plan to switch to contract service army in 2008', Kommersant-Ukrainian Kiev, Oct 17, 2007, as reported in *BBC Monitoring Online*.

71. Jiri Kominek, 'Country briefing: Ukraine moving west' *Jane's Defence Weekly*, Feb 1, 2006.

72. 'Hrytsenko calls up to prevent army of degradation', *ForUm*, 16:10, Feb 5, 2007, http://en.for-ua.com/news_print.php?news=8115 accessed Feb 14, 2007.

73. 'Transition to professional army to cost 7bn hryvnyas—Ukraine president', 5 Kanal TV, Kiev, Nov 10, 2007, as reported in *BBC Monitoring Online*.

74. Ibid.

75. Grzegorz Holdanowicz, 'Poland and Ukraine plan joint peace operations brigade with Lithuania', *Jane's Defence Weekly*, Nov 21, 2008.

76. 'Currency collapse in Ukraine', *The Economist Intelligence Unit*, Dec 1, 2008.

77. Bureau of European and Eurasian Affairs, Europe and Eurasia, 'US government assistance to and cooperative activities with Eurasia', Jan 2007, http://www.state.gov/p/eur/rls/rpt/92794.htm, accessed Jan 21, 2009.

78. Deputy Assistant Secretary of State Judy Garber, 'Transatlantic perspectives on Black Sea region: U.S. seeks to promote cooperation among countries in the region U.S. Department of State', keynote address at the Woodrow Wilson Center conference titled Trans-Atlantic Perspectives on the Wider Black Sea Region, Washington, DC, June 10, 2008.

79. Ian O Lesser, 'Global trends, regional consequences: Wider strategic influences on the Black Sea', Xenophon Paper, no. 4, International Centre for Black Sea Studies, Nov 2007.

80. Ronald Hatto and Odette Tomescu, 'The EU and the wider Black Sea region: Challenges and policy options', Garnet Policy Brief, no. 5, Jan 2008.

81. Ariel Cohen and Conway Irwin, 'U.S. strategy in the Black Sea region', The Heritage Foundation, executive summary backgrounder, no. 1990, Dec 13, 2006.

82. Ibid.

83. Irakli Menagarishvili, director of the Strategic Research Centre, Georgia, presentation at the Strengthening Black Sea Maritime Security international conference, in Sofia, Nov 1–3, 2005.

84. 'Ukraine as a heroin route', *Jane's Intelligence Digest*, May 11, 2007.

85. 'The list: The world's top immigrant smuggling routes', http://www.foreignpolicy.com/story/cms.php?id+3890&print=1, accessed June 2007.

86. 'Vice president's remarks at the Vilnius conference,' May 4, 2006, from the White House website, http://www.whitehouse.gov.

87. 'US risks Russia row over Ukraine', Sept 7, 2008, CNN.com/Europe.

88. Merle D Kellerhals Jr, 'United States, Ukraine sign security charter', Dec 19, 2008, www.america.gov/st/peacesec-english/2008/December/20081219155712dmslahrel lek5.079287e-02.html, accessed Apr 7, 2009.

89. For details, see David Gollust, 'US, Ukraine, sign partnership charter', US State Department, Dec 19, 2008, www.voanews.com/english/archive/2008–12/2008–12–19–voa56.cfm?moddate=2008–12–19, accessed Apr 2, 2009.

Chapter 11

1. The analysis, opinions and conclusions expressed or implied in this chapter are

those of the author and do not necessarily represent the views of the JSCSC, the UK MOD or any other government agency.

2. Both Azerbaijan and Armenia have been far less vocal about their desire to integrate with Western security structures such as the EU and NATO than neighbouring Georgia. Nevertheless, continuing integration with NATO is a key strategic goal of Azerbaijan's foreign policy, and the government has welcomed the Euro-Atlantic alliance's growing interest in the South Caucasus. Armenia is Russia's closest ally in the region, and Yerevan has sought a close relationship with Moscow to counterbalance what it perceives to be its vulnerable position between two countries that are antagonistic towards it: a militarily powerful Turkey and increasingly strong Azerbaijan.

3. For example, the EU flag is displayed alongside the Georgian flag in all official buildings in Georgia.

4. Former US president George W. Bush described Georgia as 'a beacon of liberty for this region [the Caucasus] and the world' during his visit to Tbilisi in May 2005. See Giorgi Sepashvili, "Beacon of liberty' vows to solve conflicts peacefully', *Civil Georgia*, 10 May 2005, at http://www.civil.ge/eng/article.php?id=9845, accessed 31 March 2009.

5. *Izvestiya*, 31.3.08, www.izvestiya.ru, accessed 31 March 2009.

6. Russian Minister of Foreign Affairs Sergei Lavrov, 'Commentary on the speech of British Foreign Secretary David Miliband in Kyiv on August 27 2008', www.mid.ru/brp_4.nsf/e78a48070f128a7b43256999005bcbb3/9eef4de1d8fddd4bc32574b4001e8521?OpenDocument, accessed 31 March 2009.

7. 'Statement of General Bantz J Craddock, USA Commander, United Stages European Command before the House Armed Services Committee', 13 March 2008, p. 7.

8. Speech by Lord Robertson, delivered at the French University, Yerevan, Armenia, on 15 May 2003, www.NATO.int/docu/speech/2003/s030515a.htm, accessed 31 March 2009. The EU has recently appointed its first special representative for the region in a sign of continuing, if somewhat tentative, EU engagement with the three countries.

9. *Report with a Proposal for a European Parliament Recommendation to the Council on EU Policy Towards the South Caucasus* (2003/2225(INI)), European Parliament, Committee on Foreign Affairs, Human Rights, Common Security and Defence Policy, Rapporteur: Per Gahrton, 2 February 2004, A5–0052/2004, p. 7.

10. There were violent clashes in Tbilisi in April 1989, when demonstrators protesting against Abkhazian demands for secession were killed by Soviet troops. For further details about the instability of this period see Christoph Zürcher, 'Georgia's time of troubles, 1989–1993', in Bruno Coppieters & Robert Legvold (eds), *Statehood and Security: Georgia after the Rose Revolution* (Cambridge, Mass: MIT Press, 2005).

11. Shevardnadze was Soviet foreign minister during the *perestroika* era and is widely credited as being one of the principal architects of the end of the Cold War. He become Georgian president in 1992, elected unopposed after the removal of Zviad Gamsakhurdia, the country's first post-communist leader. His experience on the international stage bolstered Georgia's transition and helped it to garner support.

12. Under Saakashvili, the role of the president has been strengthened further, at the expense of the legislature and judiciary. For further details see 'Saakashvili opponents in Georgia say president is using anti-democratic methods to advance', *Eurasia Insight*, 3.01.04, www.eurasianet.org/departments/insight/articles/eav030104.shtml, accessed 31 March 2009.

13. Parliamentary and presidential elections triggered popular protests against alleged vote-rigging in favour of the Shevardnadze regime at the expense of Saakashvili. Shevardnadze was forced to resign.

14. Shevardnadze appointed him to the position of justice minister in 2000, a post he resigned from a year later over the government's unwillingness to tackle corruption. Saakashvili subsequently formed a new political party, the United National Movement, which pledged to tackle corruption, and went on to lead the Tbilisi City Council. He stood against Shevardnadze in the November 2003 elections (which culminated in the Rose Revolution), and his manifesto, entitled 'Georgia without Shevardnadze', reflected the manifesto he had successfully campaigned under several years earlier for the chair of Tbilisi City Council, 'Tbilisi without Shevardnadze'.

15. For example, the former foreign minister, Eka Tkeshelashvili (sacked in December 2008), is 31, David Bakradze, the speaker, is 36.

16. A plebiscite on NATO membership held in early 2008 showed 77 per cent in favour of seeking membership. Daniel Fried believes that there is a 'strong national consensus' for Georgia's western and Euro-Atlantic direction, even amongst opposition groups. *US-Georgian Relations*, Daniel Fried, assistant secretary of state for European and Eurasian Affairs, at press conference following meeting with Georgian President Saakashvili, Tbilisi, 18 October 2006, www.state.gov/p/eur/rls/rm/75098.htm, accessed 31 March 2009.

17. There were claims that Moscow was behind civil unrest in 2007 in an attempt to topple the Saakashvili government. A series of anti-government demonstrations, triggered by the arrest of the former defence minister Irakli Okruashvili, culminated in violence on 7 November 2007 when the police broke up the protests and a state of emergency was imposed.

18. The dispute was over the planned revision of the electoral code and the composition of electoral commissions. Baker arrived in July with a blueprint to reduce the chances of electoral fraud. His 'special mission' confirmed the importance that the previous US administration attached to cooperation with Georgia.

19. 'Foreign operations appropriated assistance: Georgia', fact sheet, Bureau of European and Eurasian Affairs, www.state.gov/p/eur/rls/fs/108293.htm, accessed 31 March 2009.

20. Noting that no two democracies have ever fought a war against each other, former US president Bill Clinton argued that support for democratisation would be an antidote to both international war and civil conflict. Clinton's 1994 State of the Union address, *New York Times*, 26.1.94, A17, quoted in Jack Snyder, *From Voting to Violence: Democratisation and Nationalist Conflict* (New York: W W Norton & Company, 2000), p. 15.

21. Acknowledging that 'almost nowhere else has American and European assistance been as welcomed, and advice as well implemented,' Daniel Fried, assistant secretary for European and Eurasian Affairs, noted that Georgia still has 'a long way to go in building the institutions' of a 'modern, European democracy', Daniel Fried, Assistant Secretary for European and Eurasian Affairs, 'Developing Europe's east', remarks at conference, Tbilisi, 1 November 2007, www.state.gov/p/eur/rls/rm/94553.htm, accessed 31 March 2009.

22. David Darchiashvili, *Security Sector Reform in Georgia: 2004–2007* (Tbilisi: Caucasus Institute for Peace, Democracy and Development, 2008), p. 17.

23. *National Security Concept of Georgia*, approved by parliament in 2005, Ministry of Foreign Affairs, www.mfa.gov.ge/index.php?sec_id=24&lang_id=ENG, p. 1, accessed 31 March 2009.

24. Sabine Freizer, 'The pillars of Georgia's political transition' *Open Democracy*, 12.02.2004, www.opendemocracy.net/democracy-caucasus/article_1732.jsp, accessed 31 March 2009. There is some debate within Georgia regarding this Western orientation. Ghia Nodia argues that Georgia's choice of a Western liberal democratic model of governance is largely identity-driven and that what it is actually seeking is access to 'Western modernisation'. In his view, Georgia's experience with 'Westernness' is minimal: 'Never in its history has Georgia been in close contact with the West'. Ghia Nodia, 'Georgia: Dimensions of Insecurity' in Coppieters & Legvold, *Statehood and Security*, p. 69.

25. Daniel Fried, Assistant Secretary for European and Eurasian Affairs, 'Developing Europe's east', remarks at conference, Tbilisi, 1 November 2007, www.state.gov/p/eur/rls/rm/94553.htm, accessed 31 March 2009. Fried went on to clarify his view that, whilst Georgia may be in Europe, it was the 'rougher end of Europe'.

26. The US was a keen advocate of Turkey's membership in NATO during the 1950s, whilst Western European allies remained less convinced that the country would contribute to security in the Euro-Atlantic area.

27. 'Statement by Georgia President Eduard Shevardnadze at the EAPC Summit, 22 November 2002, Prague, www.nato.int, accessed 31 March 2009.

28. Communications Office of the President of Georgia, 'Declaration on development of strategic cooperation between Georgia and Ukraine', 25 March 2005at www.president.gov.ge/?l=E&m=0&sm=10&st=10&id=27 accessed 31 March 2009.

29. *Strategic Defence Review*, Final Report, 2007 (Tbilisi: Ministry of Defence of Georgia, 2007), p. 67.

30. The document summarised the requirements for military capabilities, identified major capability shortfalls and recommended force structure options for the short-, medium- and long-term, with an eight -ear planning horizon, up to 2015.

31. *Strategic Defence Review*, p. 67.

32. For example, James Sherr argues that 'command arrangements for the Sustainment and Stability Operations Programme [SSOP] were inappropriate for a conflict zone'. James Sherr, *Culpabilities and Consequences*, September 2008, REP BN08/01 (London: Chatham House), p. 3.

33. *National Security Concept of Georgia*, pp. 2–4.

34. The South Caucasus is a principal route for narcotics from Central Asia to Europe.

35. *Imedi TV*, Tbilisi, 16:02GMT, 9 September 2005, *BBC Monitoring Online*.

36. 'Russia targets Borjomi in trade war with Georgia', *Civil Georgia*, 5.5.06, www.civil.ge, accessed 31 March 2009.

37. In November 2001 Putin said that its southern neighbour was home to 'international terrorist camps', *Agence France Presse*, 30.11.01, Moscow. His allegations were apparently corroborated at the beginning of 2002, when several mercenaries from Saudi Arabia and Jordan were arrested in Georgia and accused of trying to establish 'an illegal guerrilla group in the Pankisi Gorge'. The arrested men allegedly had links with Khattab. *Agence France Presse*, 9.2.02, Tbilisi.

38. According to the Russian special services in mid-2002, over 2,000 armed men, including Ruslan Gelayev and fighters from Shamil Basayev's group, were concentrated in the gorge. *Izvestiya*, 26.8.02, p. 1. For an in-depth historical and ethnographic survey of the gorge, see Shorena Kurtsikidze and Vakhtang Chikovani, 'Georgia's Pankisi Gorge: An ethnographic survey', Berkeley Program in Soviet and Post-Soviet Studies Working Paper Series, (Berkeley: University of California Press, 2002).

39. Anna Matveeva, 'Russia and USA increase their influence in Georgia', *Jane's Intelligence Review*, May 2003, pp. 42–45.

40. Elizabeth Jones, Assistant Secretary of State for European and Eurasian Affairs, 'US engagement in Central Asia and the Caucasus: Staying our course along the Silk Road', remarks made at Central Asia: Its Geopolitical Significance and Future Impact Conference, hosted by Title VI Undergraduate International Studies and Foreign Language Programme Directors, University of Montana, Missoula, Montana, 10 April 2003, www.state.gov/p/eur/rls/rm/2003/19606pf.htm, accessed 31 March 2009. See also 'Frequently asked questions about US policy in Central Asia', fact sheet, Bureau of European and Eurasian Affairs, US Department of State, Washington DC, 27 November 2002, www.state.gov/p/eur/rls/fs/15562pf.htm, accessed 31 March 2009.

41. See Rob Parsons, 'All eyes on Georgia's future', 16 August 2003, http://news.bbc.co.uk/1/hi/world/europe/3157063.stm, accessed 31 March 2009.

42. Elizabeth Jones, Assistant Secretary of State for European and Eurasian Affairs, 'Remarks after meeting with President Saakashvili', Georgian State Chancellery, Tbilisi, 30 July 2004, www.state.gov/p/eur/rls/rm/34974.htm, accessed 31 March 2009. US support is not limited to Georgia—it also provides military aid to both Armenia and Azerbaijan. Armenia has been America's traditional ally in the Caucasus region, and in the wake of 11 September 2001 offered the use of its airspace, intelligence-sharing and other confidential support. See *The Caucasus and Caspian Region: Understanding US Interests and Policy*, hearing before the Subcommittee on Europe of the Committee on International Relations, House of Representatives, 107th Congress, First Session, 10 October 2001 (Washington, DC: US Government Printing Office, 2001), p. 5.

43. 'Georgia train and equip program', fact sheet, US European Command Public

Affairs, www.eucom.mil/directorates/ecpa/operations/gtep/englishproducts/Fact_
Sheet.htm, accessed 31 March 2009. Training was initially conducted by US Army Special Forces assigned to Special Operations Command Europe, although in December
2002 this responsibility was assumed by US Marines, under the operational control
of US Marine Forces Europe. The total number of US personnel present in Georgia,
including support staff and technicians, has been minimal, never exceeding 150.

44. 'Training for Iraq boosts security in the Caucasus', 30 June 2005, US European
Command Public Affairs, www.eucom.mil/english/FullStory.asp?art=595, accessed 31
March 2009.

45. 'Marine-led task force trains Republic of Georgia soldiers', 27 March 2006, US
European Command Public Affairs, www.eucom.mil/english/FullStory.asp?art=892,
accessed 31 March 2009.

46. 'US assistance to Georgia—fiscal year 2006', fact sheet, Bureau of European
and Eurasian Affairs, US Department of State, Washington DC, 12 May 2006, at www.
state.gov/p/eur/rls/fs/66198.htm, accessed 31 March 2009.

47. 'Statement of General Bantz J Craddock, USA Commander, United Stages European Command before the House Armed Services Committee', 13 March 2008, p. 7.

48. This trepidation was underlined by an article published in May 2003 in the
Russian daily *Nezavisimaya Gazeta*, which alleged that the Pentagon had drafted
plans for a military operation against Iran according to which US forces would use
the territories of Georgia and Azerbaijan as 'springboards'. See *Nezavisimaya Gazeta*,
29.5.03, pp. 1–5. The report was vociferously denied by all the parties concerned, with
the US ambassador to Georgia even suggesting that the report was possibly a 'joke'.
BBC Monitoring Select Central Asia and Transcaucasus, 29 May 2003, p. 4.

49. 'US-Russia relations in the aftermath of the Georgia crisis', Daniel Fried, Assistant Secretary of State for European and Eurasian Affairs, testimony before the
House Committee on Foreign Affairs, Washington DC, 9 September 2008, www.state.
gov/p/eur/rls/rm/109363.htm, p. 5, accessed 31 March 2009.

50. *United States-Georgia Charter on Strategic Partnership*, signed in Washington
DC on 9 January 2009, www.mfa.gov.ge, accessed 31 March 2009.

51. *Agence France Presse*, 15.12.02, Tblisi.

52. *National Security Concept of Georgia*, approved by parliament in 2005, Ministry of Foreign Affairs, www.mfa.gov.ge/index.php?sec_id=24&lang_id=ENG, accessed 31 March 2009.

53. *Bucharest Summit Declaration*, issued by the heads of state and government
participating in the meeting of the North Atlantic Council in Bucharest on 3 April
2008, www.summitbucharest.ro/en/doc_201.html, accessed 31 March 2009.

54. In May 2008, 400 Russian Ministry of Defence Railway troops moved into Abkhazia without Georgian permission. At the same time, a battalion of nearly 500 soldiers of the mechanized brigade based in Maikop was redeployed to Abkhazia. 'Polish think-tank sees possible "local war" in Georgia's rebel region in autumn', Text of
report in English by Warsaw Eastern Studies Centre. 4 June, *BBC Monitoring Online*,
4.6.08, BBC Mon EU1 EuroPol FS1 FsuPol 060608 nn/osc.

55. Extraordinary European Council, *Presidency Conclusions*, Brussels, 1 September 2008, 12594/08, pp. 2 and 5.

56. 'We are committed to long-term engagement in the countries of Central Asia and the Caucasus—through both diplomacy and assistance. Counterterrorism will remain a prominent and integrated element of our assistance. We plan to put more resources into counter-narcotics and law enforcement cooperation across the region, where porous borders and weak law enforcement have created significant opportunities for terrorists and those trafficking in illicit weapons and drugs . . . The United States is wholly committed to intensive engagement and dialogue with each of the nations of this pivotal region of the world.' Remarks by Elizabeth Jones, Assistant Secretary of State for European and Eurasian Affairs, at Central Asia: Its Geopolitical Significance and Future Impact Conference.

Conclusions

1. Wallace J Thies, *Why NATO Endures*, (Cambridge: Cambridge University Press, 2009).

2. Francis Fukuyama, 'The end of history?', *The National Interest*, Summer 1989; Francis Fukuyama, *The End of History and the Last Man*, (New York: Free Press, 1992).

3. Stuart McAnulla, 'Structure and Agency', in *Theories and Methods in Political Science*, edited by Favid Marsh and Gerry Stoker, 2nd ed., (Basingstoke: Palgrave Macmillan, 2002), pp. 271–94.

4. Craig McLean & Alan Patterson, 'A precautionary approach to foreign policy? A preliminary analysis of Tony Blair's speeches on Iraq', *British Journal of Politics and International Relations*, vol. 8, no. 3, August 2006, pp. 351–67; Alex Danchev, 'Tony Blair's Vietnam: The Iraq War and the 'special relationship' in historical perspective', *Review of International Studies*, vol. 33, no. 2, April 2007, pp. 189–203.

5. Alex Danchev, 'How strong are shared values in the Transatlantic relationship?', *British Journal of Politics and International Relations*, vol. 7, no. 3, 2005, pp. 429–36; Mark Smith, 'Balancing 'instinctive Atlanticism'', *Contemporary Security Policy*, vol. 26, no. 3, 2005, pp. 447–69; Warren Kimball, 'Dangerously contagious? The Anglo-American special relationship', *British Journal of Politics and International Relations*, vol. 7, no. 3, 2005, pp. 437–41.

6. Robert Kagan, *Of Paradise and Power: American and Europe in the New World Order*, (New York: Alfred A Knopf, 2003), pp. 1–2; see also H Daalder, 'Are the United States and Europe heading for divorce?', *International Affairs*, vol. 77, no. 3, July 2001, pp. 553–67.

7. Thomas E Ricks, *The Gamble: General Petraeus and the Untold Story of the American Surge in Iraq, 2006–8*, (London: Allen Lane, 2009); see also Peter R Mansoor, *Baghdad at Sunrise: A Brigade Commander's War in Iraq*, (New Haven: Yale University Press, 2008); Thomas E Ricks, *Fiasco: The American Military Adventure in Iraq*, (London: Allen Lane, 2006).

8. See Stephen Roskill, *Churchill and the Admirals*, (London: Pen and Sword Classics Ltd, 1977).

9. Michael Evans, 'US wants more NATO troops for new surge', *The Times*, 11 November 2009, p. 1.

10. Tony Blair, 'Our nation's future – defence', speech delivered on HMS *Albion*, 12 January 2007, http://www.number10.gov.uk/Page10735, accessed 12 January 2009.

Selected Bibliography

Alford, J., and Hunt, K., eds. *Europe in the western alliance*. London: Macmillan, 1998.

Allin, Dana H.; Andreani, Gilles; Errerea, Philippe; and Samore, Gary. "Repairing the damage: Possibilities and limits of transatlantic consensus." *Adelphi Paper* no. 389. Oxford: Routledge, 2007.

Altunsik, Meliha Benli. "The Possibilities and Limits of Turkey's Soft Power in the Middle East." *Insight Turkey* vol. 10, no. 2 (2008): 41–54.

Altunisik, Meliha Benli, and Tur, Ozlem. "From distant neighbours to partners? Changing Syrian-Turkish relations." *Security Dialogue* vol. 37, no. 2 (2006): 229–248.

Anderson, Jeffrey, Ikenberry, G. John, and Risse, Thomas *The end of the west? Crisis and change in the Atlantic order*. Ithaca, NY: Cornell University Press, 2008.

Aral, Berdal. "The Black sea economic co-operation after ten years: What went wrong?" *Alternatives, Turkish Journal of International Affairs* vol. 1, no. 4 (Winter 2002): 73–88.

Aras, Bulent. "The Davutoglu era in Turkish foreign policy." *Insight Turkey* vol. 11, no. 3 (Summer 2009): 127–142.

Aras, Bulent. "Turkey and the GCC: An emerging relationship." *Middle East Policy* vol. 12, no. 4 (Winter 2005): 89–97.

Aras, Bulent, and Polat, Rabia Karakaya. "From conflict to cooperation: Desecuritization of Turkey's relations with Syria and Iran." *Security Dialogue* vol. 39, no. 5 (Oct. 2008): 495–515.

Arnett, David L. "The Heart of the matter: The importance of emotion in Turkish-American relations." *Turkish Policy Quarterly* vol. 5, no. 4 (Winter 2006): 31–40.

Asmus, Ronald D., and Pollack, Kenneth M. "The new transatlantic project." *Policy Review* no. 115 (Oct.–Nov. 2002).

Aydin, Mustafa, and Erhan, Cagri, eds. *Turkish-American relations: Past, present and future* (London and New York: Routledge, 2004).

Aydinli, Ersel; Ozcan, Nihat Ali; and Akyaz, Dogan. "The Turkish military's march towards Europe." *Foreign Affairs* vol. 85, no. 1 (Jan.–Feb. 2006): 77–90.

Aylwin-Foster, Nigel. "Changing the army for counterinsurgency operations." *Military Review* (Nov.–Dec. 2005): 2–15.

Bailes, Alyson K. "The EU and a 'better world': What role for the European security and defence policy?" *International Affairs* vol. 84, no. 1 (Jan. 2008): 115–130.

Balaj, Barbara. "France and the Gulf War." *Mediterranean Quarterly* vol. 4, no. 3 (Summer 1993): 96–116.

Balci, Ali, and Mis, Nebi. "Turkey's role in the alliance of civilizations: A new perspective in Turkish foreign policy?" *Turkish Studies* vol. 9, no. 3 (Sept. 2008): 387–406.

Baldwin, David A., ed. *Neorealism and Neoliberalism.* New York: Columbia University Press, 1993.

Bartlett, C. J. *Defence and diplomacy: Britain and the Great Powers, 1815–1914.* Manchester: Manchester University Press, 1993.

Baumel, Jacques. "La France et l'OTAN." *Relations Internationales et Stratégiques* no. 7 (1992).

Baylis, John. *Anglo-American defence relations, 1939–84.* 2d ed. London: Macmillan Press Ltd., 1984.

Baylis, John. "British Nuclear Doctrine: the 'Moscow Criteria' and the Polaris Improvement Programme." *Contemporary British History* vol. 19, no. 1 (Spring 2005): 53–65.

Baylis, John, ed. *Britain's Defence Policy in a Changing World.* London: Croom Helm Ltd., 1977.

Becker, J. "Asserting EU cohesion: Common foreign and security policy and the relaunch of Europe." *European Security* vol. 7, no. 4 (1998): 12–32.

Bjelakovic, Nebojsa. "Russian military procurement: Putin's impact on decision-making and budgeting." *The Journal of Slavic Military Studies* vol. 21, no. 3 (July 2008): 527–542.

Blackwill, Robert. *The future of transatlantic relations.* New York: Council for Foreign Relations Press, 1999.

Blinken, Anthony J. "The false crisis over the Atlantic." *Foreign Affairs* vol. 80, no. 3 (May–June 2001): 35–48.

Bluth, Christoph. *Britain, Germany and western nuclear strategy.* Oxford: Oxford University Press, 1995.

Bolme, Selin M. "The Politics of Incirlik air base." *Insight Turkey* vol. 9, no. 3 (2007): 82–91.

Bozo, Frédéric. "'The Failure of a grand design: Mitterand's European confederation, 1989–1991." *Contemporary European History* vol. 17, no. 3 (2008): 391–412.

Bozo, Frédéric. "France and NATO under Sarkozy: End of the French exception?" Fondation pour l'Innovation Politique Working Paper, Mar. 2008.

Brown, Chris. *Understanding international relations*. 2d ed. Basingstoke: Palgrave, 2001.

Brzezinski, Zbigniew. "An agenda for NATO." *Foreign Affairs* vol. 88, no. 5 (Sept.–Oct. 2009): 2–20.

Bull, Hedley. *The anarchical society: A study of order in world politics*. New York: Columbia University Press, 1977.

Byrd, Peter, ed. *British defence policy: Thatcher and beyond*. Hemel Hempstead: Philip Allen, 1991.

Cagaptay, Soner. *Turkey at the crossroads: Preserving Ankara's western orientation*. Washington, DC: Washington Institute for Near East Policy, 2005.

Campbell, Alastair. *The Blair years: Extracts from the Alastair Campbell diaries*. London: Random House Group Ltd., 2007.

Chin, Warren. "Why did it all go wrong? Reassessing British counterinsurgency in Iraq." *Strategic Studies Quarterly* vol. 2, no. 4 (Winter 2008): 119–137.

Cole, Alistair. *French politics and society*. Hemel Hempstead: Prentice Hall, 1998.

Coppieters, Bruno, and Legvold, Robert. *Statehood and security: Georgia after the Rose Revolution*. Cambridge, MA: MIT Press, 2005.

Cornish, Paul. *British military planning for the defence of Germany, 1945–50*. Basingstoke: Macmillan Press Ltd., 1996.

Cornish, Paul. "The US and counterinsurgency." *International Affairs* vol. 85, no. 1 (Jan. 2009): 61–79.

Cornish, Paul, and Dorman, Andrew. "Blair's wars and Brown's budgets: From strategic defence review to strategic delay in less than a decade." *International Affairs* vol. 85, no. 2 (Mar. 2009): 247–261.

Cornish, Paul, and Edwards, Geoffrey. "Beyond the EU/NATO dichotomy: The beginnings of a European strategic culture." *International Affairs* vol. 77, no. 3 (July 2001): 587–603.

Cox, Michael. "Martians and Venutians in the new world order." *International Affairs* vol. 79, no. 3 (2003).

Criss, Nur Bilge, and Guner, Serdar. "Geopolitical configuration: The Russia-Turkey-Iran triangle." *Security Dialogue* vol. 30, no. 3 (Sept. 1999): 365–376.

Croft, Stuart, ed. *British security policy: The Thatcher years and the end of the cold war*. London: Harper Collins Academic, 1991.

Daalder, Ivo H. "Are the United States and Europe heading for divorce?" *International Affairs* vol. 77, no. 3 (July 2001): 553–567.

Daalder, Ivo H. *Crescent of crisis: U.S.-European strategy for the greater Middle East*. Washington, DC: Brookings Institution Press, 2006.

Daalder, Ivo H. "The end of Atlanticism." *Survival* vol. 45, no. 2 (June 2003) 147–166.

Daalder, Ivo H. *Europe: Rebalancing the U.S.-European relationship*. Washington, DC: Brookings Institution, 1999.

Dalata-Kreutzkamp, Petra. "Energy security and climate change." *International Journal* vol. 63, no. 3 (Summer 2008): 275–290.

Danchev, Alex. "How strong are shared values in the transatlantic relationship?" *British Journal of Politics and International Relations* vol. 7, no. 3 (2005): 429–436.

Danchev, Alex. *On specialness: Essays in Anglo-American relations.* London: Macmillan Press Ltd., 1988.

Danchev, Alex. "Tony Blair's Vietnam: The Iraq War and the 'special relationship' in historical perspective" *Review of International Studies* vol. 33, no. 2 (Apr. 2007): 189–203.

D'Anieri, Paul. *Understanding Ukrainian politics.* London: M. E. Sharpe, 2007.

Darchiashvili, David. *Security sector reform in Georgia: 2004–2007.* Tbilisi: Caucasus Institute for Peace, Democracy and Development, 2008.

Demirel, Tanel. "Civil-military relations in Turkey: Two patterns of civilian behaviour towards the military." *Turkish Studies* vol. 4, no. 3 (Autumn 2003): 1–25.

Demirel, Tanel. "Lessons of military regimes: The Turkish case in comparative perspective." *Armed Forces and Society* vol. 31, no. 2 (Winter 2005): 245–271.

Deudney, Daniel, and Ikenberry, John. "The logic of the west." *World Policy Journal* vol. 10, no. 4 (Winter 1993): 17–25.

Deutsch, Karl W., et al. *Political community and North Atlantic area: International organization in the light of historical experience.* Princeton, NJ: Princeton University Press, 1968.

Dickie, John. *"Special" no more: Anglo-American relations: Rhetoric and reality.* London: Weidenfeld & Nicolson, 1994.

Dimbleby, David, and Reynolds, David. *An Ocean Apart.* London: BBC Books, 1988.

Dockrill, Michael. *British defence policy since 1945.* Oxford: Basil Blackwell Ltd, 1988.

Dorman, Andrew; Kaufman, Joyce P.; and Stone, Craig. "Australia, Britain, Canada, the USA and the ABCA relationship." In *Handbook of Defence Politics,* ed. Isaiah Wilson III and James J. F. Forest, 227–240. London: Routledge, 2008.

Dorman, Andrew. *Defence under Thatcher.* Basingstoke: Palgrave Macmillan, 2002.

Dorman, Andrew, and Treacher, Adrian. *European security: An introduction to security issues in post-Cold War Europe.* Aldershot: Dartmouth Publishing Co. Ltd., 1995.

Dorn, Walter, and Varey, Michael. "Fatally flawed: The rise and demise of the 'three block war' concept." *International Journal* vol. 63, no. 4 (Autumn 2008): 977–978.

Dorota, Eggert. "Transatlantycka wspólnota bezpiecze?stwa" (The transatlantic security community). *Zurawia Papers,* no. 5. Warsaw, 2005.

Duffield, John. "NATO's functions after the Cold War." *Political Science Quarterly* vol. 109, no. 5 (Winter 1994–95): 763–787.

Dumbrell, John. *A special relationship: Anglo-American relations from the Cold War to Iraq.* Basingstoke: Palgrave Macmillan, 2006.

Dumbrell, John. "The US-UK special relationship: Taking the 21st century temperature." *British Journal of Politics and International Relations* vol. 11, no. 1 (Feb. 2009): 64–78.

Dunn, David H. "European security and defence policy in the American policy debate: Counterbalancing America or rebalancing NATO." *Defence Studies* vol. 1, no. 1 (Spring 2001): 146–155.

Dunn, David H. "Poland: America's new model ally." *Defence Studies* vol. 2, no. 2 (2002): 63–86.

Dunne, Tim. "'When the shooting starts': Atlanticism in British security strategy." *International Affairs* vol. 80, no. 5 (Oct. 2004): 893–909.

Edwards, John, and Kemp, Jack. "Russia's wrong direction: What the United States can and should do." *Council on Foreign Relations*, Independent Task Force Report no. 57. 2006. http://www.cfr.org/content/publications/attachments/Russia_Task-Force.pdf.

Elles, James. "Towards a new transatlantic relationship." *European Business Journal* vol. 5, no. 3: 34–41.

Erdagi, Ethem. "The ISAF mission and Turkey's role in rebuilding the Afghan state." *PolicyWatch*, no. 1052. The Washington Institute for Near East Policy, 18 Nov. 2005.

Evangelista, Matthew. *Partners or rivals?: European-American relations after Iraq.* Milan: Vita e Pensiero, 2005.

Evans, Albert B., Jr. "Putin's legacy and Russia's identity." *Europe-Asia Studies* vol. 60, no. 6 (Aug. 2008): 899–912.

Evriviades, Marios L. 'Turkey's role in United States strategy during and after the Cold War." *Mediterranean Quarterly* vol. 9, no. 2 (Spring 1998): 30–51.

Fitz-Gerald, Ann M. "A UK national security strategy: Institutional and cultural challenges." *Defence Studies* vol. 8, no. 1 (Mar. 2008): 4–25.

Fredholm, Michael. "Gazprom in crisis." *Conflict Studies Research Centre* vol. 6, no. 48 (Oct. 2006).

Freedman, Lawrence. *The evolution of nuclear strategy.* Basingstoke: Macmillan/IISS, 1989.

Freedman, Lawrence. *The official history of the Falklands campaign.* 2 vols. London: Routledge, 2005.

Friend, Julius W. *Seven years in France: François Mitterrand and the unintended revolution, 1981–1988.* Boulder, CO: Westview Press, 1989.

Fukuyama, Francis. "The end of history?" *The National Interest* (Summer 1989).

Fukuyama, Francis. *The end of history and the last man.* New York: Free Press, 1992.

Fukuyama, Francis. *State building: Governance and world order in the 21st century.* London: Profile Books Ltd., 2005.

Fuller, Graham E., and Lesser, Ian O., eds. *Turkey's new geopolitics; From the Balkans to western China.* Boulder, CO: Westview Press/RAND, 1993.

Gaffney, John. "Highly emotional states: French-US relations and the Iraq war." *European Security* vol. 13, no. 3 (Autumn 2004): 247–272.

Gaidar, Yegor. *Collapse of an empire: Lessons for modern Russia.* Washington, DC: Brookings Institute Press, 2007.

Gallis, Paul. "NATO in Afghanistan: A test of the transatlantic alliance." Congressional Research Service report for Congress, 6 May 2008, order core RL 33627.

Gamble, Andrew. *Between Europe and America: The future of British politics.* Basingstoke: Palgrave Macmillan, 2006.

Ganzle, S., and Retzlaff, S. "So, the European Union is 50 . . . " *International Journal* vol. 63, no. 3 (Summer 2008).

Gardner, Hall. *NATO and the European Union: New world, new Europe, new threats.* Burlington, VT: Ashgate Publishing, 2004.

Glantz, David M. *The military strategy of the Soviet Union: A history.* Oxford: Frank Cass & Co., Ltd., 1992.

Goldgeier, James. *Not whether but when: The U.S. decision to enlarge NATO.* Washington, DC: Brookings Institution Press, 1999.

Gordon, Philip H. "Bridging the Atlantic Divide." *Foreign Affairs* vol. 82, no. 1 (Jan.–Feb. 2003): 70–83.

Gordon, Philip H. "Bush's Middle East vision." *Survival* vol. 45, no. 1 (Spring 2003): 155–165.

Gordon, Philip H. *A certain idea of France: French security policy and the Gaullist legacy.* Princeton, NJ: Princeton University Press, 1993.

Gordon, Philip H. "Charles de Gaulle and the nuclear revolution." *Security Studies* vol. 5, no. 1 (Autumn 1995): 118–148.

Gordon, Philip H. "The end of the Bush revolution." *Foreign Affairs* vol. 85, no. 4, (July–Aug. 2006): 75–86.

Gordon, Philip, and Shapiro, Jeremy. *Allies at war: America, Europe, and the crisis over Iraq.* New York: McGraw-Hill, 2004.

Gowa, Joanne. *Allies, adversaries, and international trade.* Princeton, NJ: Princeton University Press, 1993.

Gray, John. *Enlightenment's wake: Politics and culture at the close of the modern age.* London and New York: Routledge Classics, 2007.

Gregory, Shaun. *French defence policy into the twenty-first century.* Basingstoke: Macmillan, 2000.

Gress, David. *From Plato to NATO. The idea of the west and its opponents.* New York: Free Press, 1998.

Grieco, Joseph. "Anarchy and the limits of cooperation: A realist critique of the newest liberal institutionalism." *International Organization* vol. 42, no. 3: 485–507.

Grieco, Joseph. *Cooperation among nations: Europe, American and non-tariff barriers to trade.* Ithaca, NY: Cornell University Press, 1990.

Gul, Abdullah. "Turkey's role in a changing Middle East environment." *Mediterranean Quarterly* vol. 15, no. 1 (Winter 2004): 1–7.

Guney, Aylin. "An anatomy of the transformation of the US-Turkish alliance: From 'Cold War' to 'war on Iraq.'" *Turkish Studies* vol. 6, no. 3 (Sept. 2005): 341–359.

Gunter, Michael. "The consequences of a failed Iraqi state: An independent Kurdish state in northern Iraq?" *Journal of South Asian and Middle Eastern Studies* vol. 27, no.3 (2004): 1–11.

Gvosdev, Nikolas K. "Russia: 'European but not western?'" *Orbis* vol. 51, no. 1 (Winter 2007): 129–140.

Hale, William. "Turkey and the Middle East in the 'new era.'" *Insight Turkey* vol. 11, no. 3 (Summer 2009): 143–159.

Hale, William. "Turkey, the Middle East, and the Gulf crisis." *International Affairs* vol. 68, no. 4 (Oct. 1992): 679–692.

Hale, William. *Turkey, the US and Iraq.* London: SAQI Books, 2007.

Hamilton, Daniel, and Sheldon, Daniel. *Conflict and cooperation in transatlantic relations.* Baltimore, MD: Johns Hopkins University Press, 2004.

Heisbourg, Francois. "Europe's strategic ambitions: The limits of ambiguity." *Survival* vol. 42, no. 2 (2000): 5–15.

Hendrickson, Ryan C. "The Miscalculation of NATO's Death." *Parameters* vol. 37, no. 1 (Spring 2007): 98–115.

Heper, Metin. The Justice and Development party government and the military in Turkey." *Turkish Studies* vol. 6, no. 2 (June 2005): 215–231.

Heper, Metin, and Guney, Aylin. "The military and the consolidation of democracy: The recent Turkish experience." *Armed Forces and Society* vol. 26, no. 4 (Summer 2000): 635–657.

Hill, Fiona, and Taspinar, Omer. "Turkey and Russia: Axis of the excluded?" *Survival* vol. 48, no. 1 (Spring 2006): 81–92.

Hopf, Ted. "The promise of constructivism in international relations theory." *International Security* vol. 23, no. 1 (Summer 1998): 170–200.

Howard, Michael. *The continental commitment: The dilemma of British defence policy in the era of two world wars.* London: Temple Smith, 1972.

Howorth, Jolyon. "Britain, France and the European Defence Initiative." *Survival* vol. 42, no. 2 (2000): 33–55.

Howorth, Jolyon. "France, Britain and the Euro-Atlantic crisis." *Survival* vol. 45, no. 4 (2003): 173–192.

Hunter, Shireen. "Bridge or frontier? Turkey's post-Cold War geopolitical posture." *International Spectator* vol. 34, no. 1 (Jan.–Mar. 1998): 63–78.

Huysmans, Jeff. "Shape-shifting NATO: Humanitarian action and the Kosovo refugee crisis." *Review of International Studies* vol. 28, no. 3 (July 2002): 599–618.

Ilgen, Thomas. *Hard power, soft power, and the future of transatlantic relations.* Burlington, VT: Ashgate, 2006.

Isernia, Pierangelo, and Everts, Philip P. 'European Public Opinion on Security Issues,' *European Security* vol. 15, no.4 (Dec. 2006): 451–469.

Iskandaryan, Alexander. "Armenian-Turkish rapprochement: Timing matters." *Insight Turkey* vol. 11, no. 3 (Summer 2009): 37–44.

Ismael, Tariq, and Aydin, Mustafa. *Turkey's foreign policy in the 20th century.* Aldershot: Ashgate, 2003.

Jackson, William. *Britain's defence dilemma: An inside view.* London: B. T. Batsford Ltd., 1990.

Jenkins, Gareth. "Context and circumstance: The Turkish military and politics." *Adelphi Paper,* no. 337. London: International Institute for Strategic Studies, 2001.

Jenkins, Gareth. "Continuity and change: Prospects for civil-military relations in Turkey." *International Relations* vol. 8, no. 2 (Mar. 2007): 339–355.

Jenkins, Gareth. "Turkey's latest crisis." *Survival* vol. 50, no. 5 (Oct.–Nov. 2008): 5–12.

Jockel, Joseph T. *Canada and international peacekeeping.* Toronto: Canadian Institute of Strategic Studies, 1994.

Kagan, Robert. "One year after: A grand strategy for the west?" *Survival* vol. 44, no. 4 (Winter 2002–03): 135–156.

Kagan, Robert *Of paradise and power: American and Europe in the new world order.* New York: Alfred A. Knopf, 2003.

Kampfner, John. *Blair's wars.* London: Free Press, 2003.

Katzenstein, Peter J., ed. *The culture of national security: Norms and identity in world politics.* New York: Columbia University Press, 1996.

Kaufman, Joyce P. *NATO and the former Yugoslavia: Crisis, conflict and the Atlantic alliance.* Lanham, MD: Rowman & Littlefield Publishers, Inc., 2002.

Kennedy, Paul. *Rise and fall of the great powers: Economic change and military conflict from 1500 to 2000.* London: Fontana Books, 1989.

Keohane, Robert *After hegemony: Cooperation and discord in the world political economy.* Princeton, NJ: Princeton University Press, 1984.

Keohane, Robert, and Martin, Lisa. "The promise of institutionalist theory." *International Security* vol. 20, no. 1 (Summer 1995): 39–51.

Keohane, Robert, and Nye, Joseph. *Power and Interdependence.* 3rd ed. New York: Longman, 2001.

Kilinc, Ramazan. "Turkey and the alliance of civilizations: Norm adoption as a survival strategy." *Insight Turkey* vol. 11, no. 3 (Summer 2009): 57–75.

Kimball, Warren. "Dangerously contagious? The Anglo-American Special Relationship." *British Journal of Politics and International Relations* vol. 7, no. 3 (2005): 437–441.

King, Anthony. 'The future of the European security and defence policy." *Contemporary Security Policy* vol. 26, no. 1 (2005): 44–61.

Kotkin, Stephen. "Myth of the new cold war." *Prospect* (Apr. 2008): 38.

Krahmann, Elke. "Regulating private military companies: What role for the EU?" *Contemporary Security Policy* vol. 26, no. 1 (2005): 103–125.

Krasner, Stephen D., ed. *International regimes.* Ithaca, NY: Cornell University Press, 1983.

Kubicek, Paul. "The European Union and grass roots democratization in Turkey." *Turkish Studies* vol. 6, no. 3, (Sept. 2005): 361–377.

Kubicek, Paul. "Turkey's inclusion in the Atlantic community: Looking back, looking forward." *Turkish Studies* vol. 9, no. 1 (Mar. 2008): 25–27.

Kummel, G., and Prufert, A., eds. *Military sociology.* Baden-Baden: Nomos Verlagsgesellschaft, 2000.

Kupchan, Charles. "In defence of European defence: An American perspective." *Survival* vol. 42, no. 2 (2000): 16–32.

Kupchan, Charles. *The end of the American era: U.S. foreign policy and the geopolitics of the twenty-first century.* New York: Knopf, 2002.

Kupchan, Charles. "Rethinking Europe." *The National Interest* no. 56 (Summer 1999): 73–79.

Lansford, Tom. "Whither Lafayette? French military policy and the American campaign in Afghanistan." *European Security* vol. 11, no. 3 (2002): 126–145.

Lapid, Yosef, and Kratochwil, Friedrich V., eds. *The return of culture and identity in IR theory.* Boulder, CO: Lynne Rienner, 1996.

Larrabee, F. Stephen. "Obama's foreign policy: Opportunities and challenges." *Insight Turkey* vol. 11, no. 1 (2009): 1–11.

Larrabee, F. Stephen. "Turkey rediscovers the Middle East." *Foreign Affairs* vol. 86, no. 4, (July–Aug. 2007): 103–114.

Layne, Christopher. "America as European hegemon." *The National Interest* vol. 13, no. 2 (Summer 2003): 17–30.

Leech, John. *Whole and free: NATO, EU enlargement and transatlantic relations.* London: Federal Trust for Education and Research, 2002.

Lesser, Ian O. "Turkey in a changing security environment." *Columbia University Journal of International Affairs* vol. 54, no. 1 (Fall 2000): 183–198.

Lesser, Ian O. "Turkey, the US and the delusion of geopolitics." *Survival* vol. 48, no. 3 (Autumn 2006): 83–95.

Liddell Hart, Basil. *The British way in warfare.* London: Penguin, 1942.

Lindberg, Tod. "We: A community in agreement on fundamentals." *Policy Review* no. 128 (Dec. 2004–Jan. 2005): 3–19.

Lindberg, Tod, ed. *Beyond paradise and power: Europe, America, and the future of a troubled partnership.* New York: Routledge, 2005.

Little, Richard. *The balance of power in international relations: Metaphors, myths and models.* Cambridge: Cambridge University Press, 2007.

Longhurst, Kerry, and Zaborowski, Marcin. *The new atlanticist: Poland's foreign and security policy priorities.* London: Royal Institute of International Affairs, 2007.

Lucas, Edward. *The new cold war: How the Kremlin menaces both Russia and the West.* London: Bloomsbury, 2008.

Lundgren, Asa. *The unwelcome neighbour: Turkey's Kurdish policy.* London: I. B. Tauris, 2007.

Luttwak, Edward N. "Toward post-heroic warfare." *Foreign Affairs* vol. 74, no. 3 (May–June 1995): 109–122.

Mandelbaum, Michael. *The dawn of peace in Europe.* New York: Twentieth Century Fund Press, 1996.

Mansoor, Peter R. *Baghdad at sunrise: A brigade commander's war in Iraq.* New Haven, CT: Yale University Press, 2008.

Mastny, Vojtech, and Nation, R. Craig, eds. *Turkey between east and west: New challenges for a rising regional power.* Boulder, CO: Westview Press, 1996.

McCalla, Robert. "NATO's persistence after the cold war." *International Organization* vol. 50, no. 3 (Summer 1996): 445–475.

McIntosh, Malcolm. *Managing Britain's defence.* London: Macmillan Academic & Professional Ltd., 1990.

McLean, Craig, and Patterson, Alan. "A precautionary approach to foreign policy? A preliminary analysis of Tony Blair's speeches on Iraq." *British Journal of Politics and International Relations* vol. 8, no. 3 (Aug. 2006): 351–367.

Mead, Walter Russell. *God and gold: Britain, America and the making of the modern world*. London: Atlantic Books, 2007.

Mearsheimer, John. "Back to the future: Instability in Europe after the cold war." *International Security* vol. 15, no. 1 (Summer 1990): 5–56.

Mearsheimer, John. "The false promise of international institutions" *International Security* vol. 19, no. 3 (Winter 1994–95): 5–58.

Mearsheimer, John. "The future of the American pacifier." *Foreign Affairs* vol. 80, no. 5 Sept.–Oct. 2001): 46–61.

Mearsheimer, John. *The tragedy of great power politics*. New York: Norton, 2001.

Mecham, R. Quinn. "From the ashes of virtue, a promise of light: The transformation of political Islam in Turkey." *Third World Quarterly* vol. 25, no. 2 (2004): 339–358.

Menon, Anand. "Continuing politics by other means: Defence policy under the French Fifth Republic." *West European Politics* vol. 17, no. 4 (Oct. 1994): 74–96.

Menshari, David, ed. *Middle Central Asia meets the east*. London: Frank Cass, 1998.

Meyer, Christopher. *DC confidential*. London: Weidenfeld & Nicolson, 2005.

Michta, Andrew A. "Transatlantic Troubles." *The National Interest* (Nov.–Dec. 2006): 62–67.

Milczarek, Dariusz. *Mi?dzy Waszyngtonem a Bruksel?- mo?liwe kierunki rozwoju polskiej polityki zagranicznej i bezpiecze?stwa* (Between Washington and Brussels—possible development of Polish foreign and security policy). Studia Europejskie, 2006.

Mildner, Stormy-Annika. "Junior partner Canada." *International Journal* vol. 63, no. 3 (Summer 2008): 30–39.

Moens, Alexander. "Afghanistan and the revolution in Canadian foreign policy." *International Journal* vol. 63, no. 3 (Summer 2008).

Moore, Rebecca. *NATO's new mission: Projecting stability in a post-cold war world*. Westport, CT: Praeger Security International, 2007.

Moore, Richard. "British nuclear warhead design 1958–66: How much American help? *Defence Studies* vol. 4, no. 2 (Summer 2004): 207–228.

Morgenthau, Hans J. *Politics among nations: The struggle for power and peace*. New York: Alfred A Knopf, 1953.

Mufti, Malik. "Daring and caution in Turkish foreign policy." *The Middle East Journal* vol. 52, no. 1 (Winter 1998): 32–50.

Narli, Nilufer. "Civil-military relations in Turkey." *Turkish Studies* vol. 1, no. 1 (Spring 2000): 107–127.

Noetzel, Timo, and Schreer, Benjamin. "Does a multi-tier NATO matter?" *International Affairs* vol. 85, no. 2 (2009): 211–226.

Noureddine, Mohammed. "Arab-Turkish cooperation in the new era." *Insight Turkey* vol. 11, no. 1 (2009): 43–51.

Nye, Joseph S. *The paradox of American power: Why the world's only superpower can't go it alone*. New York: Oxford University Press, 2002.

Nye, Joseph S. *Soft power: The means to success in world politics.* New York: Public Affairs, 2004.

Nygren, Bertil. *The rebuilding of greater Russia: Putin's foreign policy towards the CIS countries.* London: Routledge, 2008.

Olsen, Robert. "Turkey's relations with the Gulf Cooperation Council from 2003 to 2007: New paradigms?" *Mediterranean Quarterly* vol. 19, no. 3 (Summer 2008): 68–87.

Onuf, Nicholas. *World of our making: Rules and rule in social theory and international relations.* Columbia: University of South Carolina Press, 1989.

Osica, Olaf. "In search of a new role: Poland in Euro-Atlantic relations." *Defence Studies* vol. 2, no. 2 (2002): 21–39.

Ovendale, Ritchie. *Anglo-American relations in the twentieth century.* Basingstoke: Macmillan Press Ltd., 1998.

Park, William. *Defending the west: A history of NATO.* Brighton: Wheatsheaf Books Ltd., 1986.

Park, William. "Obama, Turkey and the Middle East: troubles ahead?" *Turkish Policy Quarterly* vol. 7, no. 4 (Winter 2008–2009): 17–24.

Park, William. "Strategic location, political dislocation: Turkey, the United States, and northern Iraq." *MERIA* vol. 7, no. 2 (June 2003): 11–23.

Park, William. "Turkey's deep state: Ergenekon and the threat to democratization in the republic." *The RUSI Journal* vol. 153, no. 5 (Oct. 2008): 55–59.

Park, William. "Turkey's policy towards northern Iraq: Problems and prospects." *Adelphi Paper,* no. 374. New York and London: Routledge/International Institute for Strategic Studies, 2005.

Parris, Mark R. "Common values and common interests? The Bush legacy in US-Turkish relations." *Insight Turkey* vol. 10, no. 4 (2008): 5–14.

Parsi, Vittorio Emanuele. *The inevitable alliance: Europe and the United States beyond Iraq.* New York: Palgrave Macmillan, 2006.

Peimani, Hooman. *Regional security and the future of Central Asia: The competition of Iran, Turkey and Russia.* London: Praeger, 1998.

Petras, J., and Morley, M. "Contesting hegemons: US-French relations in the 'New World Order.'" *Review of International Studies* vol. 26, no. 1 (2000): 49–67.

Pond, Elizabeth. *Friendly fire: The near-death of the transatlantic alliance.* Washington, DC: Brookings Institution Press/European Union Studies Association, 2004.

Poulter, Jeremy. "NATO as a security organization: Implications for the future role and survival of the alliance." *RUSI Journal* vol. 151, no. 3 (2006): 58–62.

Rabinow, Paul, and Sullivan, William M., eds. *Interpretative social science: A second look.* Berkeley: University of California Press, 1987.

Radu, Michael S., ed. *Dangerous neighborhood: Contemporary issues in Turkish foreign policy.* Somerset, NJ: Transaction Press, 2002.

Raphaeli, Nimrod. "The growing economic relations between Iran and Turkey." *Inquiry and Analysis Series, MEMRI* no. 414 (Jan. 2008).

Reynolds, Christopher. "Military capability development in the ESDP: Towards effective governance?" *Contemporary Security Policy* vol. 28, no. 2 (2007): 357–383.

Rice, Condoleezza. "Promoting the national interest." *Foreign Affairs* vol. 79, no. 1, (Jan.–Feb. 2000): 45–78.

Ricks, Thomas E. *Fiasco: The American military adventure in Iraq.* London: Allen Lane, 2006.

Ricks, Thomas E. *The gamble: General Petraeus and the untold story of the American surge in Iraq, 2006–8.* London: Allen Lane, 2009.

Roberts, Andrew. *A history of the English-speaking peoples since 1900.* London: Phoenix Paperback, 2007.

Robins, Philip. "The Opium crisis and the Iraq war: Historical parallels in Turkey-US relations." *Mediterranean Politics* vol. 12, no. 1 (Mar. 2007): 17–38.

Robins, Philip. *Suits and uniforms; Turkish foreign policy since the cold war.* London: Hurst & Co., 2003.

Rose, Richard, and Munro, Neil. "Do Russians see their future in Europe or the CIS?" *Europe-Asia Studies* vol. 60, no. 1 (Jan. 2008): 49–66.

Roskill, Stephen. *Churchill and the admirals.* London: Pen and Sword Classics Ltd., 1977.

Rubin, Michael. "A comedy of errors: American-Turkish diplomacy and the Iraq war." *Turkish Policy Quarterly* vol. 4, no. 1 (Spring 2005): 69–79.

Rubinstein, Alvin Z., and Smolansky, Oleg M., eds. *Regional power rivalries in the new Eurasia: Russia, Turkey and Iran.* London and New York: M. E. Sharpe, 1995.

Rudd, David. "Canada and the post-Atlantic world." *Strategic Datalink no. 127.* Toronto: Canadian International Council, Apr. 2005.

Ruiz-Palmer, Diego A. "French strategic options in the 1990s." *Adelphi Paper,* no. 260. London: Brasseys/IISS, Summer 1991.

Ruseckas, Laurent. "Turkey and Eurasia: Opportunities and risks in the Caspian pipeline derby." *Columbia University Journal of International Affairs* vol. 54, no. 1 (Fall 2000): 217–236.

Rutland, Peter. "Putin's economic record: Is the oil boom sustainable?" *Europe-Asia* vol. 60, no. 6 (Aug. 2008): 1051–1072.

Salmoni, Barak A. "Strategic partners or estranged allies: Turkey, the United States and Operation Iraqi Freedom." *Strategic Insights* vol. 2, no. 7 (July 2003).

Sanders, Deborah. "Defending Ukraine: Reform, crisis and challenge of the future." *World Defence Systems* vol. 8, no. 1: 70–72.

Sanders, Deborah. "Ukraine's military reform: Building a paradigm army." *Journal of Slavic Military Studies* vol. 21, no. 4 (Oct. 2008): 599–614.

Sanders, Deborah. "US naval diplomacy in the Black Sea." *Naval War College Review* vol. 60, no. 3 (Summer 2007): 61–73.

Sarigil, Zeki. "Europeanization as institutional change: The case of the Turkish military." *Mediterranean Politics* vol. 12, no. 1 (Mar. 2007): 39–57.

Scheffer, Jaap de Hoop. "New trans-Atlantic unity." *NATO's Nations and Partners for Peace* (2004): 20–24.

Schmidt, Gustav, ed. *A history of NATO: The first fifty years*. 3 vol. Basingstoke: Palgrave, 2001.

Schwartz, David N. *NATO's nuclear dilemmas*. Washington, DC: Brookings Institution, 1983.

Seldon, Anthony. *Major: A political life*. London: Weidenfeld & Nicolson, 1997.

Sestanovich, Stephen. "What has Moscow done?" *Foreign Affairs* vol. 87, no. 6 (Nov.–Dec. 2008): 12–29.

Sheehan, Michael. *The balance of power: History and theory*. London: Routledge, 1996.

Sigal, Leon V. *Nuclear forces in Europe: Enduring dilemmas, present prospects*. Washington, DC: Brookings Institution, 1984.

Simpson, John. *The independent nuclear state: The United States, Britain and the military atom*. 2d ed. London: Macmillan Press Ltd., 1986.

Simsek, Sefa. "The transformation of civil society in Turkey: From quantity to quality." *Turkish Studies* vol. 5, no. 3 (Autumn 2004): 46–74.

Smith, Lance. "Is the transatlantic relationship still important?" *Vital Speeches of the Day* vol. 73, no. 6 (June 2007): 249–252.

Smith, Mark. "Balancing 'instinctive Atlanticism.'" *Contemporary Security Policy* vol. 26, no. 3 (2005): 447–469.

Snyder, Jack. *From voting to violence: Democratisation and nationalist conflict*. New York: W. W. Norton & Co., 2000.

Steinberg, James B. "An elective partnership: Salvaging transatlantic relations." *Survival* vol. 45, no. 2 (June 2003): 113–146.

Taspinar, Omer. "The anatomy of anti-Americanism in Turkey." *Insight Turkey* vol. 7, no. 2 (Apr.–June 2005): 83–98.

Thies, Wallace J. *Why NATO endures*. New York: Cambridge University Press, 2009.

Treacher, Adrian. "A case of reinvention: France and military intervention in the 1990s." *International Peacekeeping* vol. 7, no. 2 (Summer 2000): 23–40.

Treacher, Adrian. "Europe as a power multiplier for French security policy: Strategic consistency, tactical adaptation." *European Security* vol. 10, no. 1 (2001): 22–44.

Treacher, Adrian. *French interventionism: Europe's last global player?* Aldershot: Ashgate, 2003.

Trenin, Dmitri. "Russia leaves the west." *Foreign Affairs* vol. 85, no. 4 (July–Aug. 2006): 87–96.

Turkmen, Fusun. "Turkish-American relations: A challenging transition." *Turkish Studies* vol. 10, no. 1 (Mar. 2009): 109–129.

Uslu, Nasah; Toprak, Metin; Dalmis, Ibrahim; and Aydin, Ertan. "Turkish public opinion toward the United States in the context of the Iraq question." *Middle East Review of International Affairs (MERIA)* vol. 9, no. 3 (Sept. 2005): 75–107.

Walker, Joshua W. "'Strategic depth' and Turkish foreign policy." *Insight Turkey* vol. 9, no. 3 (2007): 32–47.

Wallace, William. "Broken bridges." *The World Today* vol. 60, no. 12 (Dec. 2004): 13–16.

Wallace, William, and Phillips, Christopher. "Reassessing the special relationship." *International Affairs* vol. 85, no. 2 (Mar. 2009): 263–284.

Walt, Stephen. *The origins of alliances.* Ithaca, NY: Cornell University Press, 1987.

Waltz, Kenneth. *Theory of international politics.* Reading, MA: Addison-Wesley, 1979.

Webber, Mark; Croft, Stuart; Howorth, Jolyon; Terriff, Terry; and Krahmann, Elke. "The governance of European security." *Review of International Studies* vol. 30, no. 1 (Jan. 2004): 3–26.

Webber, Mark; Terriff, Terry; Howorth, Jolyon; and Croft, Stuart. "The common European security and defence policy and the 'third country' issue." *European Security* vol. 11, no. 2 (2002): 75–100.

Weidenfeld, Werner. *From alliance to coalitions: The future of transatlantic relations.* Gütersloh: Bertelsmann, 2004.

Wendt, Alexander. "Anarchy is what states make of it: The social construction of power politics" *International Organization* vol. 46, no. 2 (Spring 2002): 391–425.

Westad, Odd Arne. *The global cold war: Third world interventions and the making of our times.* Cambridge: Cambridge University Press, 2005.

Wheatcroft, Geoffrey. *Yo, Blair!* London: Politico's Publishing, 2007.

Wheeler, Nicholas J. *Saving strangers.* Oxford: Oxford University Press, 2000.

Williams, Geoffrey Lee. *NATO and the transatlantic alliance in the 21st century.* Basingstoke: Palgrave Macmillan, 2001.

Winrow, Gareth. "Pivotal state or energy suppliant? Domestic structure, external actors, and Turkish policy in the Caucasus." *Middle East Journal* vol. 57, no. 1 (Winter 2003): 76–92.

Wojciech, Roszkowski. *The shadow of Yalta—A report.* Warsaw: Warsaw Rising Museum, 2005.

Zaborowski, Marcin. "From America's protégé to constructive European: Polish security policy in the twenty-first century." *EU-ISS Occasional Paper* no. 56. Paris: Institute for Security Studies, 2004.

Zaborowski, Marcin, and Dunn, David H., eds. *Poland—A new power in transatlantic security.* London: Frank Cass Publishers, 2005.

Index

ABCA, 79

Abkhazia, 207, 214, 220

Acheson, Dean, 78, 87, 94

Afghanistan, 2, 6, 13, 33, 34, 36, 40, 42, 45, 47, 48, 49, 50, 51, 52, 53, 56, 57, 58, 65, 66, 67, 69, 72, 74, 78, 79, 85, 86, 89, 90, 92, 93, 94, 108, 111, 117, 118, 119, 123, 125, 128, 129, 130, 131, 132, 133, 134, 161, 170, 179, 179, 182, 205, 222, 225, 232, 233, 236, 237; Afghan Transitional Authority, 66; Elections in, 50, 56; War in 2, 5, 6, 50, 56, 57, 58, 65–68, 79, 81, 85, 86, 88, 92, 93, 94, 107, 108, 111, 118, 119, 123, 125, 128, 129, 134, 225, 232, 237. *See also* International Security Assistance Force

Africa, 91, 126, 186

Albania, 36, 142, 203

Albright, Madeleine, 107

Algeria, 96,185

Allied Command Transformation (ACT), 42

Allied Rapid Reaction Corps, 91

Al-Qaeda, 48, 65, 69, 124, 128, 236

American Relief Association, 175

Anglo-French, 93

Annan, Kofi, 66

Arctic, 34, 38, 46, 52

Armenia, 166, 179, 183, 199, 202, 203

Armenian Genocide, 151

Assad, Bashar, 146

Asia, 21, 25

Asmus, Ronald, 23, 24

Atlantic Charter, 2, 169

Australia, 8, 79, 84, 86, 107

Austria, 116, 168

Austro-Prussian, 103

AWACS, 62

Aylwin-Foster, Nigel, 86

Azerbaijan, 142, 143, 166, 183, 199, 202, 203, 207, 214, 217, 220, 222, 227, 229

BAE Systems, 86

Baker, James, 215

Balance of Power, 19, 31, 79, 181

Balkans, 25, 88, 92, 116, 118, 119, 127, 128, 131, 132, 134, 135, 141, 144, 204, 225. *See also* Yugoslavia

Ballistic Missile Defence, 163, 164

Baltic Sea, 121

Beaufort Sea, 45

Belarus, 121, 166, 167, 179, 199, 201, 202

Baltic states, 200
Belgium; 17, 62, 116, 124, 236
Berlin Plus Agreement, 144
Berlin Wall, 103, 115
Beslan, 186
Biden, Joe, 175, 186, 187, 209
Bin Laden, Osama, 222
Bismarck, Otto von, 95, 97, 148
Black Sea, 147, 207, 227
Black Sea Economic Cooperation, 143, 201, 202, 203
Black Sea Fleet, 199, 201
Blair, Tony, 2, 5, 65, 66, 80, 81, 88, 89, 90, 98, 105, 108, 234, 237
Bland, Douglas, 50, 51
Blinkin, Anthony, 25, 26
Bosnia-Herzegovina, 11, 119, 120, 127, 130, 204. *See also* Balkans; Yugoslavia
Brazil, 177, 179
Britain. *See* United Kingdom
Brown, Gordon, 5, 80, 81, 82, 87, 89, 93
Brzezinski, Zbigniew, 58
Bucharest Summit, 108, 121, 193, 196, 197, 228, 229
Bulgaria, 142, 148, 202, 203
Bush, George H. W., 81
Bush, George W., 4, 5, 6, 12, 13, 17, 40, 48, 57, 59, 60, 61, 62, 63, 65, 66, 67, 69, 71, 72, 73, 75, 76, 79, 81, 82, 83, 87, 107, 108, 109, 111, 116, 123, 127, 137, 138, 141, 161, 206, 207, 208, 209, 223, 231, 236; Bush Doctrine, 17

Cambodia, 118, 130
Cameron, David, 82, 89
Canada, 2, 4, 15, 27, 33–55, 57, 65, 67, 68, 76, 79, 84, 107, 139, 197, 235, 236, 237; Canada First Defense Strategy (CFDS), 38, 39, 43, 46; Canadian forces, 33, 38, 43; Comprehensive Political Guidance, 44; Domestic politics in, 34–37, 43, 45, 48–50, 52, 53; EU relations, 47, 53; International

Policy Statement (IPS), 38, 39, 43, 47; Military transformation, 33; and NATO, 37, 38, 42, 50, 51; Peacekeeping role, 41–42; Quebec, 40, 41, 49; Relations with UK, 40; Relations with US, 35, 40, 41, 42, 45, 47, 50, 53, 54, 76, 236; Strategic culture of, 37–42; "Three-D," 43; War in Afghanistan, 33, 36, 40, 43, 47, 48, 51, 67, 68, 236, 237. *See also* Stephen Harper
Caribbean, 78, 177, 183
Caspian Sea, 212, 213, 231
Caucasus, 148, 183, 211, 212, 213, 216, 220, 221, 222, 223, 227, 229, 231
Central African Republic, 161
Central Asia, 143
Central Intelligence Agency, 189
Chad, 161, 205
Chavez, Hugo, 177
Chechnya, 222, 226
Cheney, Richard, 208
China, 174, 179, 188, 189
Chinook, 35
Chirac, Jacques, 5, 95, 103, 104, 105, 107, 108, 109, 110, 112, 162
Churchill, Winston Spencer, 169, 235
Clark, General Wesley, 85
Clausewitz, Carl von, 175
Climate Change, 45
Clinton, Bill, 4, 11, 12, 81
Clinton, Hillary Rodham, 80, 82, 139
Coast Guard, 39
Cold War, 2, 3, 7, 9, 11, 16, 17, 18, 19, 21, 24, 27, 40, 42, 75, 85, 87, 88, 91, 92, 97, 99, 100, 103, 104, 113, 116, 119, 124, 129, 134, 140, 141, 142, 143, 144, 145, 152, 153, 155, 174, 175, 177, 178, 179, 181, 182, 184, 197, 216, 233, 234, 235, 236, 249n19; End of, 2, 3, 17, 18, 21, 23, 27, 42, 88, 102, 104, 113, 140, 142, 177, 182, 236; Post–Cold War period, 3, 24, 28, 90, 92, 99, 102, 103–107, 113, 116, 119, 124,

140, 142, 143, 148, 171, 174, 178, 235, 236, 246n7

Collective Security Treaty Organisation, 179, 183

Combined Task Force, 150, 234

Comintern, 175

Common European Security and Defence Policy. *See* European Security and Defense Policy

Common Foreign and Security Policy, 4, 116, 159, 163, 166, 170

Commonwealth of Independent States, 183, 184, 202

Comprehensive Approach, 44, 52

Constructivism, 18, 29, 30, 31

Contact Group, 2, 243n9

Council of Europe, 141

Crimea, 197, 198, 200

Croatia, 36

Cuba, 176; Cuban Missile Crisis, 99

Culture, 33, 41

Curzon Line, 169

Cyber Security, 52,

Cyprus, 13, 139, 141, 143, 144

Czech Republic, 57, 71, 125, 159, 160, 162, 164, 165, 172, 200

Daalder, Ivo, 24, 132

Darfur, 89, 130

Dayton Agreement, 119

Defense Capabilities Initiative, 91

De Gaulle, Charles, 10, 95, 96, 97, 99, 101, 103, 104, 182, 234

De Villepin, Dominique, 110

Democratic Republic of Congo, 104,120, 130, 204

Denmark, 79, 92, 159, 162, 236

Desert Storm. *See* Persian Gulf War

Détente, 97

Deudney, James, 25, 26

Eastern Europe, 24; Eastern Bloc, 3,11

East Timor, 88

Eden, Anthony, 80

Egypt, 185

Elles, James, 25, 26

Enhanced Radiation Warhead (ERW), 7

Erdogan, Tayyip, 138, 144–45

Estonia, 52, 159, 202

Euro, 21, 87, 159

Eurasian Economic Community, 179

Euro-Gaullism, 111

Europe, 1, 7, 10, 18, 20, 21, 22, 23, 24, 25, 26, 27, 28, 30, 31, 34, 42, 45, 47, 50, 53, 57, 58, 59, 60, 63, 64, 65, 67, 68, 70, 71, 73, 74, 75, 76, 77, 79, 83, 91, 93, 94, 95, 99, 104, 105, 106, 107, 108, 111, 113, 114, 116, 117, 119, 120, 121, 123, 125, 126, 131, 133, 134, 136, 151, 157, 163, 165, 172, 174, 183, 186, 188, 189, 190, 198, 217, 228, 234, 235, 236; Euro-American partnership, 25, 29; European-Atlantic Partnership Council, 12, 228; European Commission, 162, 194, 199, 229

Euro-Mediterranean Partnership, 4

European Community, 120

European Defense Community, 96

European Economic Community, 120. *See also* European Union

European Neighbourhood Policy, 166

European Recovery Act, 9; Marshall Plan, 96, 125

European Security and Defense Identity, 99, 105

European Security and Defense Policy (ESDP), 4, 13, 105, 106, 107, 111, 112, 125, 133, 143, 144, 159, 163, 170, 172, 173, 205, 237

European Union (EU), 4, 7, 8, 9, 11, 12, 13, 14, 21, 34, 35, 44, 45, 51, 53, 54, 57, 59, 75, 76, 91, 94, 102, 104, 105, 106, 107, 110, 111, 112, 113, 114, 115, 116, 117, 119, 120, 121, 122, 125, 126, 131, 132, 133, 135, 139, 143, 144, 144, 148, 149, 151, 155, 156, 157, 158, 159, 160, 162, 163, 166, 167, 170,

171, 172, 173, 174, 180, 182, 183, 187, 188,
189, 191, 192, 193, 194, 198, 199, 201, 203,
204, 205, 209, 211, 212, 213, 218, 221, 226,
227, 228, 229, 230, 236, 238; EU-3 132;
EU Battlegroup concept, 91, 93, 160;
EU Cohesion Fund Policy, 159; EU
Council, 159; EUFOR, 127; EUSEC,
120; Expansion of, 21, 143, 144,
149, 150, 151; Political and Security
Committee, 13; Relationship to
NATO, 8, 13–14, 144; Statement
on Arctic Security, 45. *See also*
European Community

Falklands Conflict, 11, 88
Fifth Republic, 96, 99, 102, 103, 106
Finland, 116, 171
First World War. *See* World War I
Fischer, Joschka, 127
Force de Frappe, 101, 102
Foreign direct investment (FDI), 25
Four Power Agreement, 115
Fourth Republic, 96
France, 7, 10, 11, 15, 17, 29, 60, 62, 64, 67,
76, 95–112, 113, 115, 117, 120, 121, 122,
124, 133, 162, 168, 197, 200, 228, 230, 233,
238; and EU, 102, 105, 106, 107, 110,
111, 122; Franco-American relations,
62, 76, 95, 96, 97, 101, 104, 106, 107–10,
110, 111; Franco-German relations,
29, 62, 95, 96, 97–98, 103, 104, 109, 115,
120, 121–22, 124, 133; Invasion of Iraq,
29, 62, 95, 98, 108, 109, 110, 111; and
NATO, 95, 102, 104, 105, 106, 110, 111,
112, 233, 238; Nuclear weapons, 10, 97,
101, 103; Relations with UK, 80, 104,
106, 107; Strategic culture of, 100–103;
War in Afghanistan, 107, 108. *See
also* De Gaulle, Charles; Mitterand,
François; Chirac, Jacques; Sarkozy,
Nicholas
Freedman, Lawrence, 101
Fukuyama, Francis, 232

G-7, 26, 27, 33,
G-8, 35, 114, 115, 148, 179
G-20, 25, 26, 74, 82, 87, 115, 179, 237
Gaffney, John, 96, 99, 109
Gallis, Paul, 67, 68
Gates, Robert, 67, 70
Gaza, 145
Gaullism. *See* deGaulle
GCHQ, 84,
Georgia, 3, 12, 14, 15, 36, 121, 130, 142, 147,
161, 166, 172, 176, 181, 183, 185, 186, 188,
197, 199, 200, 201, 202, 203, 204, 207,
209, 210, 211, 213, 214, 215, 216, 217, 218,
219, 220, 221, 222, 223, 224, 225, 226,
227, 228, 229, 230, 235, 238; and EU,
211, 218, 226, 227–30, 238; National
Military Strategy, 219, 225, 227;
National Security Concept, 216, 218;
NATO membership, 147, 148, 181,
185, 197, 201, 211, 212, 215, 216, 218, 224,
225, 226, 227–30, 238; Relations with
Russia, 215, 220–23, 224, 225, 226, 228,
230; Relations with Ukraine, 217, 218;
Relations with US, 211, 214, 216, 217,
223–26, 230, 231; Strategic Defense
Review, 218; War with Russia, 52, 147,
148, 174, 176, 183, 186, 197, 199, 200, 208,
209, 210, 218, 221, 230, 235
Germany, 4, 15, 17, 21, 29, 59, 60, 61, 62,
64, 65, 67, 78, 95, 96, 97, 98, 102, 103,
109, 113–36, 160, 165, 167, 168, 169, 171,
189, 197, 200, 228, 232, 236; and EU,
114, 115, 117, 120, 121, 122, 126, 131, 135;
Invasion of Iraq, 29, 62, 118, 120,
124, 125, 127, 129; and NATO, 115, 117,
118, 119, 122, 125, 127, 131, 132, 134, 136;
Relations with France, 95, 96, 97–98,
103, 104, 109, 115, 120, 121–122, 124, 133;
Relations with Russia, 115, 116, 121,
134, 189; Relations with UK, 115, 120;
Relations with US, 59, 62, 114, 115, 116,
122, 123, 124, 125, 126, 127, 128, 131, 132,
133, 134, 135, 136; Troop deployments,

116, 118, 119, 120, 127, 129, 131, 132, 133, 134, 271n16; Unification of, 103, 115, 117, 118, 133; War in Afghanistan, 117, 118, 119, 123, 125, 128, 129, 132, 133, 134. *See also* Merkel, Angela; Kohl, Helmut; Schmidt, Helmut; Schroeder, Gerhard

Glasgow, 75

Gorbachev, Mikhail, 174, 175, 182, 213

Gordon, Philip H., 58, 72, 97, 101

Gore, Al, 81

Great Britain. *See* United Kingdom

Greece, 9, 75, 120, 141, 144, 189, 197, 203

GUAM, 201, 202; GUUAM, 202

Guantanamo, 73, 84, 124

Gul, Abdullah, 138, 145,148, 149

Gulf Cooperation Council, 146

Gulf War 1990–1991. *See* Persian Gulf War

Haiti, 40

Hariri, Rafik, 146

Harper, Stephen, 35, 39, 48; Harper government, 41

Heath, Edward, 80

Helsinki Final ct, 177

Helsinki Headline Goals 91

Hitler, Adolf, 78, 155

Hobbes, 1, 23, 181, 189, 234

Hoon Geoff, 91

Hopf, Ted, 29, 30

Horn of Africa, 129, 130, 134

Human Rights, 28, 29

Human Security, 15, 76

Hungary, 160, 162

Hussein, Saddam, 61, 62, 108, 109, 119, 163

Ikenberry, John, 25, 26

Implementation Force, 119, 143

India, 179, 185

Indo-China, 96

International Atomic Energy Agency, 132

International Criminal Court, 22, 34, 139

International Institute of Strategic Studies, 50

International Monetary Fund, 25, 27, 143

International relations theory, 6,

International Security Assistance Force (ISAF), 34, 40, 41, 43, 48, 52, 66, 67, 117, 128, 13 134, 143, 161, 205, 213

International Traffic in Arms Regulation, 86, 87

Iran, 57, 63, 71, 73, 125, 131, 132, 132, 136, 137, 139, 142, 146, 147, 164, 185, 212

Iraq, 7, 29, 56, 57, 58, 61, 62, 64, 65, 67, 68, 69, 72, 73, 75, 78, 82, 88, 90, 92, 94, 98, 102, 108, 110, 111, 117, 120, 123, 124, 125, 127, 129, 130, 135, 136, 137, 139, 142, 144, 146, 151, 161, 162, 163, 205, 232, 234, 236, 237; Iraq War (2003), 7, 17, 18, 28, 62, 81, 85, 86, 88, 89, 93, 95, 98, 108, 109, 110, 111,120, 124, 125, 129, 137, 139, 146, 162, 205, 225, 231, 234, 237

Israel, 7, 129, 131, 133, 136, 139, 145, 147, 223, 232

Italy, 17, 64, 67, 197, 228

Jackson, Lieutenant-General Mike, 85

Japan, 61, 118, 202

Joint Strike Fighter, 86

Jospin, Lionel, 107, 108

Kagan, Robert, 1, 5, 20, 22, 23, 30, 180, 181, 188, 189, 234

Kandahar, 34, 48

Kant, Immanuel, 1, 234

Kazakhstan, 179, 201

Kennedy, John F., 99

Kenya, 89

Kohl, Helmut, 114, 123, 133

Korea, 33, 69

Kosovo, 12, 28, 88, 106, 107, 108, 111, 119, 120, 127, 130, 131, 133, 161, 200, 204, 237; War in, 12, 28, 40, 85, 88, 92, 107, 108, 110, 111, 116, 128, 129, 134, 176

Kupchan, Charles, 20, 22, 26

Kurds, 142, 152, 236
Kuwait, 61, 102, 129, 130, 134, 205
Kyoto Protocol, 28, 123, 139
Kyrgyzstan, 176, 179, 223

Latin America, 78, 97
Latvia, 159, 202
League of Nations, 96
Lebanon, 129, 130, 133, 146, 161
Lellouche, Pierre, 97, 109
Lenin, Vladimir, 175
Liberal Internationalism, 37
Liberia, 204
Libya, 11, 177, 185
Lisbon Treaty, 120
Lithuania, 159, 160, 168
Lomonosov Ridge, 46
London, 75, 89
London Summit (2009), 25
Luttwak, Edward, 1
Luxembourg, 62

Maastricht Treaty, 106, 116
Macdeonia, 120, 127, 130, 135
Madrid, 75
Major, John, 81, 88
Manhattan Project, 84
Marshall Plan. *See* European Recovery
    Act
McCain, John, 60, 83, 177
McChrystal, General Stanley, 56, 67
McMahon Act, 84
Mearsheimer, John, 2, 17, 18, 19, 20, 21,
    22, 235
Medvedev, Dmitri, 176, 177, 179, 183, 187
Merkel, Angela, 4, 5, 114, 118, 121, 122, 123,
    124, 125, 127, 132, 133, 134, 134, 135, 136,
    194, 201, 232
MI5, 84
MI6, 84
Middle East, 62, 67, 93, 125, 131, 139, 140,
    141, 142, 144, 145, 147, 148, 149, 165, 174,
    230
Migration, 24

Military Transformation, 33
Mitterand, François, 100, 103
Moldova, 166, 167, 199, 201, 202, 203, 207
Montreux Convention, 148
Multilateral Force, 10
Multilateralism, 37, 39, 50, 55, 142

Nagorno-Karabakh, 183, 207
Napoleon, 95
Napoleon III, 95
Nassau Agreement, 84
National Defense Strategy, 70, 71;
    National Security Strategy, 70, 71
Neo-liberalism, 17, 18, 24, 25, 26, 27, 28,
    29, 30, 31
Neo-realism, 17, 18–24, 27, 28, 30, 31, 233,
    247n10
Netherlands, 64, 68, 79, 92, 128, 159, 236,
    237
New Strategic Concept, 91
New Zealand, 8, 79, 84, 92
Nicaragua, 177
North Africa, 93
North American Aerospace Defense
    (NORAD), 47
North American Free Trade Agreement
    (NAFTA), 35, 236
North Atlantic Council, 12, 13, 61
North Atlantic Treaty, 3, 10, 97; Article
    2, 3, 10, 11, 36; Article 4, 62; Article
    5, 2, 3, 10, 12, 37, 48, 52, 58, 61, 62, 63,
    107, 119, 126, 157, 162, 173, 218. *See also*
    Washington Treaty
North Atlantic Treaty Organization
    (NATO), 2, 3, 4, 5, 10, 14, 15, 19, 20, 21,
    22, 23, 24, 25, 26, 27, 28, 31, 33, 34, 35,
    37, 38, 40, 42, 43, 44, 47, 48, 49, 50, 51,
    52, 53, 54, 56, 57, 58, 59, 61, 62, 63, 64,
    65, 66, 68, 70, 71, 74, 76, 79, 85, 91, 92,
    95, 96, 97, 99, 102, 104, 105, 106, 107, 108,
    110, 112, 115, 116, 117, 118, 119, 121, 123, 126,
    127, 128, 131, 133, 134, 135, 136, 140, 141,
    143, 144, 147, 148, 155, 156, 157, 158, 159,
    160, 161, 163, 165, 166, 167, 170, 171, 172,

173, 174, 176, 180, 181, 182, 184, 185, 186, 188, 189, 191, 192, 193, 194, 195, 196, 197, 198, 199, 200, 201, 204, 208, 209, 211, 212, 213, 215, 216, 217, 218, 219, 224, 225, 226, 227, 228, 229, 230, 231, 232, 233, 234, 236, 237, 238; Comprehensive Political Guidance, 43; Defense Planning Committee, 62; Enlargement (expansion) of, 1, 3, 4, 11–13, 36, 161, 181, 184, 185, 197, 200, 209, 245n22; History of 9/11, 79, 87; Membership Action Plan, 121, 193, 195, 196, 200, 228; NATO-Georgia Commission, 229; Relationship to EU, 13–14, 236; Strains in, 2, 4, 10, 12, 62, 63, 197, 21, 228, 236; Strategic Concept, 51, 54, 91, 184; Summit (2009), 33; War in Afghanistan, 2, 34, 65–68, 85, 88, 93, 181, 237. See also International Security Assistance Force (ISAF)

North Korea, 73,
Northern Ireland, 83, 86, 236
Northern Watch, 142
Nye, Joseph, 25,

Obama, Barack, 2, 6, 34, 47, 50, 51, 53, 56, 57, 58, 59, 60, 62, 63, 67, 68, 71, 73, 74, 76, 77, 80, 82, 87, 94, 112, 113, 124, 125, 128, 135, 139, 146, 147, 151, 154, 165, 172, 171, 173, 187, 209, 237
Operation Active Endeavour, 147, 204
Operation Concordia, 127
Operation Desert Fox, 88
Operation Desert Storm. See Persian Gulf War
Operation Enduring Freedom, 85, 107, 108, 129
Operation Iraqi Freedom, 212, 225
Orange Revolution, 191, 192, 199, 203, 207
Organization for Democracy and Economic Development, 202
Organization for Security and Cooperation in Europe, 115, 170, 188, 202, 211

Organization of Islamic Conference, 148
Oretga, Daniel, 177
Ottawa Treaty, 28

Pakistan, 69, 129, 137, 185
Palestine Liberation Organization, 122
Palestinian Authority, 145
Palin, Sarah, 83
Partiya Karkari Kurdistan, 138, 146
Partnership for Peace, 228
Persian Gulf, 142
Persian Gulf War (1991), 3, 62, 85, 88, 92, 100, 102, 105, 118, 126, 133
Petersburg Tasks, 111
Petraeus, General David, 86, 235
Pew Global Attitudes Project, 60, 63–65, 70, 74, 77, 137
Philippines, 224
Plymouth Rock, 78
Poland, 11, 15, 57, 64, 71, 121, 125, 155–173, 199, 202, 205, 236; and EU, 155, 156, 157, 158–60, 162, 163, 166, 170, 171, 172; Iraq War, 162, 163, 170; and NATO 155, 156–58, 159, 160, 163, 166, 170, 171, 172; Relations with Germany, 155, 168, 169, 171; Relations with Russia, 155, 156, 158, 159, 164, 167, 168, 169, 171, 172; Relations with Ukraine, 166, 167; Relations with US, 155–73; War with Afghanistan, 170. See also Solidarity Movement
Pollack, Kenneth, 23, 24
Pompidou, Georges, 99
Portillo, Michael, 79, 81
Portugal, 75, 162
Powell, Colin, 215
Prague Capabilities Commitment, 36
Prague Summit, 217
Prussia, 95, 97, 168
Putin, Vladimir, 177, 178, 179, 180, 183, 185, 199

Quadrennial Defense Review, 69, 70

Rasmussen, Anders, 71
Reagan, Ronald, 16, 72, 156
Realist, 6, 19, 247n10
Ribbentrop-Molotov Pact, 157
Rice, Condoleezza, 60, 61, 72, 75, 81, 137, 208
Riga Summit, 43, 67
Robertson, Lord George, 62, 213
Rogue States, 24
Roosevelt, Franklin Delano, 169
Romania, 64, 142, 148, 202, 203
Rome Statute, 28
Rome Treaty, 120
Rose Revolution, 211, 214, 215, 229
Rumsfeld, Donald, 1, 69, 70, 237
Russia, 8, 15, 36, 44, 46, 51, 57, 71, 78, 102, 115, 116, 121, 122, 134, 142, 147, 148, 158, 164, 165, 166, 167, 168, 169, 171, 172, 174–90, 192, 197, 198, 199, 200, 201, 202, 203, 209, 210, 212, 215, 216, 218, 220, 221, 222, 223, 224, 226, 228, 230, 235, 236; and EU, 180, 181, 182, 183, 188, 189, 201; Foreign Policy Concept, 174, 180, 182, 183, 184, 185, 187; Relations with Germany, 115, 116, 121, 134, 189; Relations with Georgia, 215, 220–23, 225, 226, 228, 230; Relations with NATO, 176, 182, 184, 185, 186, 188, 189; Relations with Poland, 155, 156, 158, 159, 164, 167, 168; Relations with Turkey, 141, 147; Relations with Ukraine, 176, 185, 186, 191, 196, 200, 201, 201, 228, 236; Relations with US, 57, 147, 174, 175, 176, 177, 182, 187, 188, 212, 224; Strategic culture of, 179–85; War with Afghanistan, 176; War with Georgia, 52, 147, 174, 176, 183, 186, 188, 197, 199, 200, 208, 209, 218, 221, 230, 235. See also Gorbachev, Mikhail; Medvedev, Dmitiri; Putin, Vladimir; South Ossetia
Russia-EU Cooperation partnership Agreement, 121

Russia-NATO Council, 188
Rwanda, 130

Saakashvili, Mikhel, 211, 214, 215, 217, 219, 220, 221, 225, 229, 231, 293n12
Sarkozy, Nicholas, 4, 5, 112, 121, 230, 233
Saudi Arabia, 45, 137, 185
Scheffer, Jaap de Hoop, 51
Schmidt, Helmut, 7, 10, 123
Schroeder, Gerhard, 5, 114, 121, 123, 124, 127, 128, 130, 131, 134
Scotland, 83
Second World War. See World War II
September 11 (9/11), 3, 4, 12, 15, 18, 19, 23, 24, 46, 47, 48, 61, 62, 66, 69, 75, 89, 92, 107, 110, 113, 123, 144, 148, 176, 207, 223, 237
Serbia, 110, 203
Shanghi Cooperation Organization, 179
Shevardnadze, Eduard, 214, 215, 216, 217, 224, 292n11, 293n12
Sierra Leone, 88, 92
Slovakia, 160
Solidarity Movement, 156, 170
Somalia, 85, 143,
South Ossetia, 121, 186, 202, 207, 214, 220, 221, 226, 227
Soviet Union, 7, 8, 15, 16, 19, 21, 24, 28, 61, 78, 79, 87, 92, 101, 140, 141, 142, 156, 143, 155, 163, 168, 175, 176, 177, 180, 184, 186, 190, 200, 207, 213, 214, 230; Collapse of, 18, 21, 25, 116, 176, 214; Former Soviet Union countries (FSU), 11. See also Russia
Special Relationship, 79, 81, 83, 84, 87
Spain, 65, 162, 197
St Malo Declaration, 106
Stabilization, 43
Stalin, Joseph, 169
Status of Forces Agreement, 56, 165
Strategic Airlift Interim Solution, 36
Strategic Concept, 51, 54
Strategic Culture, 37, 38, 39, 54, 100, 168, 179

Strategic Defense Initiative, 7

Sub-Saharan Africa, 104

Sudan, 130, 204

Suez Crisis, 7, 10, 16, 72, 80, 96, 110

Sweden, 105, 116, 159, 161, 166, 171

Syria, 145, 146, 147, 161, 185

Taliban, 48, 49, 66, 68, 86, 128

Tajikistan, 179, 223

Terrorism, 23, 66

Thatcher, Margaret, 80, 88

Thor-Jupiter, 10

Transnistria, 202

"Transatlantic Trends," 63–65

Trident, 85

Truman, Harry, 9; Truman Doctrine, 9

Turkey, 13, 15, 62, 63, 64, 77, 137–54, 185, 203, 212, 217, 234; Cold War relations, 140–41; Domestic context, 149–51; EU membership, 122, 139, 143, 144, 149, 150, 151; Kurds, 125, 152, 236; and NATO, 140, 141, 148; Relations with Israel, 143, 145; Relations with Russia, 140, 141, 142, 147, 148; Relations with Syria, 145, 146; Relations with US, 137, 138, 139, 140, 141, 142, 143, 146, 147, 149, 150, 151, 152, 153, 154; War with Iraq, 146, 152. See also Erdogan, Tayyip; Gul, Abdullah; Karkari, Partiya; Kurdistan

Tymoshenko, Yulia, 192, 193, 194, 195, 196, 200

Ukraine, 3, 12, 14, 15, 35, 44, 121, 142, 148, 166, 167, 176, 181, 186, 188, 191–210, 212, 228, 229, 232, 233, 235, 238; and EU 167, 191, 192, 193, 194, 198, 199, 201, 203, 204, 218, 238; Domestic politics, 192–201; NATO membership, 148, 167, 181, 185, 191, 192, 193, 194, 196, 197, 198, 199, 200, 201, 204, 20, 209, 212, 218, 228, 229, 233, 238; Relations with Georgia, 217; Relations with Poland, 166, 167;

Relations with Russia, 176, 186, 191, 196, 199, 200, 201, 202, 208, 228, 236; Relations with US, 191, 197, 206–9 Ukraine-EU Cooperation Council, 193. See also Viktor Yushchenko; Viktor Yanukovych; Yulia Tymoshenko

UKUSA Agreement, 84

United Kingdom 4, 7, 9, 10, 11, 15, 17, 24, 35, 40, 60, 64, 65, 67, 68, 78–94, 98, 102, 105, 107, 109, 113, 115, 120, 122, 125, 131, 134, 141, 159, 162, 168, 182, 197, 233, 234, 236; Anglo-American relationship, 79, 80, 81, 82, 83, 84, 85, 86, 87, 88, 89, 91–92, 94; Domestic politics, 80–87; and EU 79, 91, 94; Falklands War, 11; National Security Strategy, 89, 90, 182; NATO, 91, 92; Nuclear weapons, 10; Relations with Canada, 40, 79,; Relations with France, 80, 93, 104, 107; Strategic culture of, 87–89; War in Afghanistan, 67, 68, 79, 81, 85, 86, 88, 92, 93, 94, 233, 234; War in Iraq, 81, 82, 85, 86, 88, 92, 93, 94, 234. See also Blair, Tony; Brown, Gordon; Cameron, David

United Nations, 12, 15, 33, 37, 38, 40, 41, 46, 51, 62, 66, 88, 98, 103, 104, 105, 108, 110, 111, 117, 119, 120, 129, 130, 131, 132, 133, 135, 139, 143, 152, 160, 161, 170, 181, 184, 204; Charter, 37; Peacekeeping, 46, 90, 117, 145; Security Council, 40, 62, 66, 90, 98, 104, 108, 109, 110, 117, 129, 130, 131, 135, 179, 184; UNPROFOR, 143

United States, 1, 4, 5, 7, 9, 10, 11, 12, 15, 16, 18, 19, 20, 21, 22, 23, 25, 26, 27, 29, 30, 31, 34, 35, 41, 42, 45, 47, 48, 49, 50, 51, 54, 55, 56–77, 78, 79, 80, 82, 83, 84, 85, 86, 87, 88, 92, 93, 94, 95, 96, 98, 99, 101, 102, 104, 105, 111, 112, 114, 115, 116, 117, 119, 120, 121, 122, 123, 124, 125, 126, 127, 128, 130, 131, 132, 134, 135, 137, 138, 139,

140, 141, 142, 143, 144, 145, 145, 146, 147,
148, 149, 150, 151, 152, 153, 154, 155, 156,
157, 158, 159, 160, 161, 162, 163, 164, 165,
166, 167, 170, 171, 172, 173, 174, 175, 176,
177, 180, 181, 183, 187, 188, 190, 191, 192,
197, 200, 202, 205, 206, 207, 208, 209,
210, 211, 212, 214, 215, 216, 217, 219, 222,
223, 224, 225, 226, 227, 228, 229, 230,
231, 234, 235, 236, 237; and EU ,59, 75,
106, 159; Invasion of Iraq (2003), 12,
17, 57, 58, 63, 64, 65, 67, 69, 70, 72, 75,
108, 109, 125, 139; Libya, bombing of,
11; and NATO, 65–68, 70, 71, 74, 87;
Nuclear arsenal, 10; Nuclear missile
shield, 57, 71; Relations with Canada,
35, 40, 41, 42, 48, 51, 53, 54, 57, 65, 76,
107, 236; Relations with France, 59,
62, 95, 96, 97, 101, 104, 106, 107–10, 111;
Relations with Georgia, 211, 214, 216,
217, 223–26, 230, 231; Relations with
Germany, 59, 60, 62, 65, 115, 116, 122,
123, 124, 125, 126, 127, 128, 131, 132, 133,
134, 135, 136; Relations with Poland,
155–73; Relations with Russia, 57,
71, 147, 174, 175, 177, 182, 187, 188, 212,
224; Relations with Turkey, 137, 138,
139, 140, 141, 142, 143, 146, 147, 149,
150, 151, 152, 153, 154; Relations with
UK, 62, 65, 79, 80, 83, 84, 85, 86, 87,
88, 89, 91–92, 94, 107, 111; Relations
with Ukraine, 191, 197, 206–9;
September 11 (9/11), 60–63, 69, 75,
207; USAID, 158, 198; US-Georgia
Charter on Strategic Partnership,
226, 231; Vietnam War, 11, 16, 234;
War of Independence, 155; War with
Afghanistan, 56, 57, 58, 65–68, 69, 70.
See also Bush, George W.; Obama,
Barack
Unmanned Aerial Vehicle, 35
US-Ukraine Charter on Strategic
Partnership, 191
USSR. *See* Soviet Union

Uzbekistan, 179

Venezuela, 176, 177
Vietnam, 11, 16, 177, 234
Voice of America, 155

Wales, 83
Walesa, Lech, 171
Walt, Stephen, 18, 20, 21, 22, 23,
War on Terror, 79, 108, 128, 144, 148, 162,
223, 224, 225, 231
Warsaw Pact. *See* Warsaw Treaty
Organization
Warsaw Treaty Organization, 1, 2, 15, 37,
164, 176, 234
Warsaw Uprising, 168
Washington, George, 155
Washington Treaty, 37, 48, 51, 184, 218
Weapons of Mass Destruction, 23, 61, 66,
108, 109, 146, 162, 207
Weimar Group, 160
Western European Union (WEU), 96,
105, 119
Wilson, Woodrow, 155
World Trade Organization (WTO), 27,
166
World War I, 9, 96, 97
World War II, 9, 37, 40, 58, 61, 96, 97, 98,
115, 116, 120, 122, 124, 125, 126, 155, 163,
168, 185

Yalta Conference, 155, 157, 169
Yanukovych, Viktor, 191, 193, 194, 195, 201
Yeltsin, Boris, 179, 180
Yugoslavia, 2, 92, 104, 105, 130; Wars in
11–13, 91, 116, 118
Yushchenko, Viktor, 191, 192, 193, 194, 195,
196, 199, 203, 204, 206, 209, 232
Vysegrad Group, 160

Zaire. *See* Democratic republic of Congo
Zimbabwe, 89